Issues
&.Ethics
in
the Helping
Professions
2nd Edition

Issues & Ethics in the Helping Professions

2nd Edition

Gerald Corey

California State University, Fullerton
Diplomate in Counseling Psychology,
*   American Board of Professional Psychology*

Marianne Schneider Corey

Private Practice

Patrick Callanan

Private Practice

Brooks/Cole Publishing Company
Monterey, California

Brooks/Cole Publishing Company
A Division of Wadsworth, Inc.

Printed in the United States of America

10   9   8   7   6   5

Library of Congress Cataloging in Publication Data

Corey, Gerald F.
  Issues and ethics in the helping professions.

  2nd ed. of: Professional and ethical issues in counseling and psychotherapy. © 1979.

  Bibliography: p.
  Includes index.
    1. Psychotherapy ethics.   2. Counseling ethics.
  3. Psychotherapy—Practice.   4. Counseling—Practice.
  I. Corey, Marianne Schneider, [date]   .
  II. Callanan, Patrick.   III. Title. [DNLM:
  1. Counseling.   2. Ethics, Professional.
  3. Professional-patient relations.   4. Psychotherapy.
  WM 62 C797p]
  RC455.2.E8C66   1983   174'.2   83-10119
  ISBN 0-534-02819-5

Sponsoring Editor: Claire Verduin
Production Editor: Fiorella Ljunggren
Manuscript Editor: William Waller
Permissions Editor: Carline Haga
Interior and Cover Design: Victoria Van Deventer
Photos pp. vi and vii: Jim Pinckney
Typesetting: Graphic Typesetting Service, Los Angeles, California
Printing and Binding: R. R. Donnelley & Sons Co., Crawfordsville, Indiana

*To the significant people in our lives;
to our friends and colleagues*

Gerald Corey, Professor and Coordinator of the Human Services Program at California State University at Fullerton and a licensed psychologist, received his doctorate in counseling from the University of Southern California. He is a Diplomate in Counseling Psychology, American Board of Professional Psychology; is registered as a National Health Service Provider in Psychology; and is a Fellow of the American Psychological Association (Counseling Psychology). Jerry's special interests are in teaching undergraduate courses in theories of counseling and practicum in group leadership. He has taught courses and conducted workshops in England and Germany as a visiting adjunct professor at George Peabody College of Vanderbilt University's European branch. With his colleagues (Marianne Schneider Corey, Patrick Callanan, and J. Michael Russell), he conducts regular in-service training and supervision workshops for counselors, mental-health professionals, and group workers and offers personal-growth workshops.

Jerry is a member of the American Association for Counseling and Development, the American Group Psychotherapy Association, the Association for Specialists in Group Work, the Western Psychological Association, the National Association of Human Services Educators, the American Orthopsychiatric Association, and the Western Association for Counselor Education and Supervision.

The recent books he has authored or co-authored (all published by Brooks/Cole Publishing Company) include:

- *Theory and Practice of Counseling and Psychotherapy, 2nd Edition*
- *Manual for Theory and Practice of Counseling and Psychotherapy, 2nd Edition*
- *Case Approach to Counseling and Psychotherapy*
- *Theory and Practice of Group Counseling*
- *Manual for Theory and Practice of Group Counseling*
- *I Never Knew I Had a Choice, 2nd Edition*
- *Groups: Process and Practice, 2nd Edition*
- *Casebook of Ethical Guidelines for Group Leaders*
- *Group Techniques*

Marianne Schneider Corey is a licensed marriage and family therapist in private practice in Idyllwild, California. She has been actively involved in leading groups for different types of populations as well as providing training and supervision workshops for group leaders and mental-health practitioners. She currently conducts a training and supervision group with graduate students in the Marriage and Family Therapy Program at Loma Linda University and counsels adolescents, couples, families, and adults in private practice. With her husband, Jerry, Marianne has conducted training workshops and personal-growth groups in Germany and Mexico, as well as in the United States. She also co-leads week-long residential workshops in Idyllwild.

Marianne and Jerry were the co-chairpersons of the Professional Standards and Ethics Committee of the Association for Specialists in Group Work in 1981–1982. Marianne is a Clinical Member of the American Association for Marriage and Family Therapy and holds membership in the California Association of Marriage and Family Therapists, the American Association for Counseling and Development, the Association for Specialists in Group Work, the Western Psychological Association, and the Western Association for Counselor Education and Supervision.

Marianne has co-authored several articles that have been published in the *Journal for Specialists in Group Work*, as well as the following books (published by Brooks/ Cole Publishing Company):

- *I Never Knew I Had a Choice, 2nd Edition*
- *Groups: Process and Practice, 2nd Edition*
- *Casebook of Ethical Guidelines for Group Leaders*
- *Group Techniques*

Patrick Callanan is a licensed marriage and family therapist in private practice in both Santa Ana-Tustin and San Juan Capistrano, California. He graduated with a bachelor's degree in human services from California State University at Fullerton and then received his master's degree in clinical psychology from United States International University. In his private practice he works with couples, families, and mental-health practitioners in workshops and training groups in various states. With Marianne and Jerry, he has conducted regular training workshops for the treatment staff at a state mental hospital. Patrick also offers his time each year to provide training workshops for group leaders at California State University at Fullerton and to co-lead week-long residential growth groups in Idyllwild, also with Marianne and Jerry. He is a member of the California Association of Marriage and Family Therapists, the Western Psychological Association, the Association for Specialists in Group Work, and the American Association for Counseling and Development.

Patrick has co-authored several articles that have been published in the *Journal for Specialists in Group Work*, as well as the following books (published by Brooks/ Cole Publishing Company):

- *Casebook of Ethical Guidelines for Group Leaders*
- *Group Techniques*

Preface

Issues and Ethics in the Helping Professions is written primarily for undergraduates and beginning graduate students in the helping professions. It is suitable for courses in any field involving human-services delivery, from counseling psychology to social work. It can be used as a core textbook in courses such as practicum, internship, field work, and ethical and professional issues, or as a supplementary text in courses teaching skills and theory. Since the issues we discuss are likely to be encountered throughout one's professional career, we have tried to use language and concepts that will be meaningful both to students who are doing their field work and to professionals who are interested in sharpening their skills through continuing-education seminars or in-service workshops.

Throughout this book we attempt to engage the reader in a struggle with the professional and ethical issues that most affect the actual practice of counseling and therapy—a struggle that we hope will span the reader's professional career. To this end we raise such questions as these: What is the influence of the character and personality of the therapist on the outcomes of therapy? How do the therapist's theoretical assumptions affect the course of therapy? Do the therapist's values have a place in therapy? What are the rights and responsibilities of clients and therapists? What are the unique problems associated with group work?

In raising these and many other questions, our goal is not merely to provide a body of information but to teach students a process of raising and thinking about the basic issues they will face as practitioners. On many issues we present a number of viewpoints to stimulate discussion and reflection. We also present our own views when it seems appropriate to do so, because we believe that our readers will be better able to formulate their own positions if we are open with ours.

We don't mean to suggest that professionals are free to formulate any "ethics" they choose. In the text, we do cite the ethical codes of various professional organizations, which offer some guidance for professional practice. However, these guidelines leave many questions unanswered. We believe that students and professionals alike ultimately must struggle with many issues of responsible practice, including the questions of how accepted ethical standards apply in the specific cases they encounter.

We have tried to make this book a personal one that will involve our readers in an active and meaningful way. To this end we have provided our readers with many opportunities to respond to our discussions and to draw upon their experiences in field work, volunteer work, or professional practice. Each chapter begins with a self-inventory designed to help readers focus on the key topics to be discussed in the chapter. Within the chapters, we frequently ask readers to think about how the issues apply to them and to write brief responses on the blanks provided. Open-ended cases and situations are presented to stimulate thought and assist readers in formulating their own positions. Finally, the activities, exercises, and ideas for thought and discussion contain many suggestions for expanding on the material and applying it in concrete ways, both inside and outside of class.

This book is thus a combination of textbook, student manual, and instructor's resource manual. Instructors will find an abundance of material and suggested activities, surely more than can be covered in a single course. We decided to retain the many questions, exercises, issues, and cases so that instructors and students can select the material that is most relevant to the teaching style of the instructor, the nature of the course, and the level and interests of the students. We would like to emphasize once again that this book is intended to stimulate an ongoing process of serious reflection on ethical and professional issues. In this sense, it is designed to raise many more questions than it will neatly answer.

This second edition of *Issues and Ethics in the Helping Professions* has been extensively revised. Topics have been added, and the coverage is far more comprehensive than that of the first edition. Some of the additions and expanded areas are:

- inclusion of the codes of ethics of the major mental-health professions in the Appendix, with excerpts in each chapter
- a focus on ethical issues special to marriage and family therapy
- increased attention to legal issues and legal liability in counseling and psychotherapy
- a focus on ethical issues related to cross-cultural counseling
- inclusion of specialty guidelines for counseling and therapy with women
- greater focus on informed consent and the rights of clients
- coverage of the ethical issues in psychotherapeutic research
- material on unethical practice and malpractice
- a focus on ethical considerations in the supervision process
- a focus on professional issues special to the fields of marriage and family counseling, social work, psychiatry, clinical and counseling psychology, and other allied mental-health professions
- increased attention to the controversy over professional licensing

A note on terminology: We frequently refer to terms such as *mental-health professional, practitioner, counselor, therapist,* and *psychotherapist* and also *the helping professions, psychotherapy,* and *counseling.* We use these as generally interchangeable terms, but we have also tried to reflect the differing nomenclature of the various professions that we cover.

We thank the following people who looked at the first edition of the book and offered valuable suggestions for improvement: James Bray of Texas Woman's University, Harold B. Engen of the University of Iowa, Wilma Greenfield of Florida Atlantic University, Diane Henschel of California State University, Dominguez Hills, Jean LaCour of California State University, Los Angeles, Norene Matsushima and Jorja Manos-Prover of California State University at Fullerton, and Linda Webb-

Woodard of North Texas State University. We are also greatful to the reviewers who examined the completed manuscript for this edition and gave us support and good ideas. They are Lawrence M. Brammer of the University of Washington, Gordon M. Hart of Temple University, Allen E. Ivey of the University of Massachusetts, Amherst, Beverly B. Palmer of California State University, Dominguez Hills, and Alexander J. Tymchuk of the University of California, Los Angeles. Linda Callanan provided many useful suggestions for the revision, devoted countless hours to proofreading the manuscript at various stages of its development, and prepared the index. Thank you, Linda. We also appreciate the helpful comments and suggestions by our students, especially Jan Davison, Joanna Doland, Susan Gattis, Chuck Geddes, Andrea Mark, and Bob Tait. Finally, we want to express our appreciation to those people at Brooks/Cole who have contributed their talents to making this a better book, especially Fiorella Ljunggren and Claire Verduin, and to Bill Waller for his excellent editing job.

Gerald Corey
Marianne Schneider Corey
Patrick Callanan

Contents

C   H   A   P   T   E   R   F   O   U   R

Theoretical Issues in Counseling and Psychotherapy   97

C   H   A   P   T   E   R   F   I   V   E

Ethical Issues I: Therapist Responsibilities, Therapist Competence, and Confidentiality   145

C   H   A   P   T   E   R   S   I   X

Ethical Issues II: The Client/Therapist Relationship   190

C H A P T E R   S E V E N

Ethical and Professional Issues Special to Group Work   235

C H A P T E R   E I G H T

The Counselor in the Community and in the System   274

References and Reading List   309

A P P E N D I X

Professional Codes of Ethics   321

Index   373

Issues
& Ethics
in
the Helping
Professions
2nd Edition

C H A P T E R   O N E

Introduction

How this book came into being

For a number of years the three of us have worked together as a team co-leading therapy and personal-growth groups. During this time, we have watched one another grow and change personally and professionally. Although we have developed our own therapeutic styles and sometimes challenge one another's ideas, we do share a common philosophy in the way we view people and the nature of helping relationships.

Over the years we have worked independently in our own counseling practices as well as with one another. All three of us have had to confront many professional and ethical issues that do not have clear-cut solutions. Exchanging our ideas has helped each of us formulate, revise, and clarify our positions on these issues. Our interactions with students and fellow professionals have shown us that others wrestle with similar questions. It has become clear to us that students in the counseling field should confront the issues that will be a large part of their professional experience and would benefit by giving serious thought to their positions on these issues before they begin practicing.

Some of the issues we are referring to involve the fact that counselors, no less than clients, are *people*; they have their own personalities, private lives, strengths, and personal struggles. In Chapter 2, for instance, we point out that it's impossible to separate the kind of person a counselor is from the kind of help the counselor will be able to provide. Whether a counselor is willing and able to form honest and caring relationships with his or her clients is one particularly significant issue. To take another example, in Chapters 2 and 8 we talk about the problem of counselor "burn-out." How can we, as people who have our own limits of energy and emotional resources and who have our own lives to think of, stay alive as therapists, both to our own feelings and to those of our clients?

Other issues involve the nature of the therapeutic process and the helping relationship. What theoretical stance should we choose, and how important is it to have a clear theoretical approach to counseling? What role do our personal values play in the counseling relationship? What ethical responsibilities and privileges do clients and counselors have? What special ethical and professional problems are involved in group counseling? What is the counselor's role in the community and in the institutional structure within which he or she must work?

In considering these questions, we found very few books that were devoted exclusively to a treatment of professional and ethical issues in counseling and psychotherapy. We therefore decided to write such a book, one that would be meaningful to experienced practitioners as well as to students about to embark on their professional careers. Many of the issues that are relevant to beginning professionals surface again and again and take on different meanings at the various stages of one's professional development.

Just as we have found no easy answers to most of the issues that have confronted us in our professional practice, we have attempted to write a book that does not fall into the trap of dispensing prescriptions or providing simple solutions to complex issues. Our main purpose is to provide you with the basis for discovering your own guidelines within the broad limits of professional codes of ethics and divergent theoretical positions. We raise what we consider to be central issues, present a range of diverse views on these issues, discuss our own position, and provide you with many opportunities to refine your own thinking and to become actively involved in developing your own position.

In making the statement that you are the one who will ultimately discover your own guidelines for responsible practice, we are not endorsing a position of absolute freedom. We're not implying that students are free to choose any set of ethics merely on the basis that it "feels right." The various human-services professions have developed codes of ethics that are binding upon the members of professional organizations. Any professional should, of course, know the ethical code of his or her specialty and should be aware of the consequences of practicing in ways that are not sanctioned by the appropriate professional organization. Even within the broad guidelines of ethical codes, responsible practice implies that professionals base their practice on informed, sound, and responsible judgment. To us, this implies that professionals should consult with colleagues, keep themselves current in their specialties through reading and periodic continuing-education activities, and be willing to engage in an honest and ongoing process of self-examination. Codes of ethics provide general standards, but these guidelines are not sufficiently explicit to deal with every situation. Often it is difficult to interpret them in practice, and there are differences of opinion concerning their application in specific cases. Consequently, counselors retain a significant degree of freedom and will meet many situations that demand the exercise of sound judgment. They will face issues in which there are no obvious answers, and they will have to struggle with themselves in an honest way to decide how they should act in order to further the best interests of their clients.

It is worth emphasizing that the issues dealt with in the text need to be periodically reexamined throughout your professional life. Even if you thoughtfully resolve some of these issues at the initial stage of your professional development, there is no guarantee that everything will be worked out once and for all. They may take on new dimensions as you gain more experience, and questions that are of relatively minor importance at one time may become major concerns at another time as you progress in your profession. In addition, it may not be possible or even desirable to have solutions for all the professional concerns you will encounter. Many students burden themselves with the expectation that they should resolve all possible issues before they are ready to begin practicing, but we see the definition and refinement of the issues we raise as being an evolutionary process that requires a continually open and self-critical attitude.

Trends in the teaching of ethics and ethical decision making

In the evolution of the mental-health profession, our special interest is the development of an ethical and professional attitude toward practice. We endorse the practice of teaching students the process of ethical decision making from the very beginning of their training programs. Teaching ways of grappling with ethical and professional issues can be especially meaningful in seminars held in conjunction with practicum, internship, and field-work experiences.

Tymchuk and his associates (1979) surveyed ethics training in clinical psychology programs approved by the American Psychological Association (APA). They emphasized that new approaches to psychological treatment had created an increasing need for guidelines to help psychologists make ethical decisions. Although virtually all of the respondents in the survey expressed a need for ethical training, only 67% of the programs offered formal courses in ethics. According to Tymchuk and his colleagues, the essential problem is not how ethical issues are ultimately resolved but whether psychologists are prepared to reason these issues through in a careful manner. They suggested that ethics training might be one way of solving the problem. In a more recent study by Tymchuk and his associates (1982), the respondents expressed a desire to learn about new legal decisions, the ethical implications of new treatment approaches, and current directions in the area of individual rights. Although practitioners have the APA's *Ethical Principles of Psychologists* (1981a) as a guide, the problem seems to be in applying these principles to a variety of difficult situations. When psychologists cannot find a specific standard, they must then draw from their own value systems, using the spirit of the APA standards as a guide.

In their 1982 study, Tymchuk and his associates found that clinical supervision had been a mode of ethics training for 69% of the psychologists; discussion with colleagues was indicated by 65% of the sample. More structured ways of learning about ethical issues were reported less frequently: case conferences were mentioned by 48% of the respondents, course work and seminars by 37%, professional conferences by 21%, and workshops by 5%. The researchers also found that, although virtually all of the psychologists who responded to the study indicated familiarity with the earlier edition of *Ethical Standards of Psychologists*, published in 1977, 58% believed that they were not well enough informed about ethical issues. Many of the respondents thought that decision-making guidelines needed further attention by the profession. Also, 89% felt that training in ethics should be required of all psychology graduate students. Similarly, *Criteria for Accreditation of Doctoral Training Programs and Internships in Professional Psychology* (APA, Council of Representatives, 1979) mandates instruction in "scientific and professional ethics and standards for all students in every doctoral program in professional psychology" (p. 6).

Tymchuk and his associates (1982) pointed out some of the ways of training psychologists in ethical awareness: formal course work, the use of hypothetical situations and case materials, supervised discussions, instruction in professional codes and legal issues, clarification of values that have an impact on the psychologists' lifestyles and on the way they are likely to counsel others, and the use of a comprehensive decision-making protocol. More helpful than specific rules that define behavior as "right" and "wrong," they wrote, are broader and more basic decision-making standards.

The point of these studies is that greater attention to the content and process of professional education in ethics is needed as a basic component in the development of psychologists, social workers, and counselors.

Some suggestions for using this book

If you're like many students, you've probably found some textbooks difficult to relate to in a personally meaningful way, because you found them dry and abstract. Perhaps you have frequently found yourself reading passively just to acquire information, without being challenged to make a real synthesis of the ideas in the text with your own ideas and experiences or to formulate your own positions. Because we believe that this passive relationship of the reader to the material in the textbook is unfortunate, we've tried to write a book that will involve you in a personal and active way. This book deals with the central professional and ethical issues that you are likely to encounter in your work with clients, and we have made every effort to make it a practical book without making it a source of ready-made answers. Our aim has been to provide a context within which you can actively formulate your own positions.

In writing this book, we frequently imagined ourselves in conversations with our students, and we hope you will find it informal, personal, and designed to elicit your reactions to what we discuss. Whenever it seems appropriate, we state our own thinking and discuss how we came to the positions we hold. We think it's important to openly state our biases, views, convictions, and attitudes so that you can critically evaluate our stance rather than assume the validity of our views without a process of serious reflection. On many issues, we present a diverse range of viewpoints so that you'll have material to use in formulating your own thoughts. Our hope is that you will give constant attention to ways of integrating your own thoughts and experiences with the issues we explore, so that you will not only absorb information but also deepen your understanding.

The format of this book is therefore different from that of most traditional textbooks. This is intended to be a personal manual that can be useful to you at various stages in your professional development. There are many questions and exercises interspersed in the text that we hope will stimulate you to become an active reader and learner. If you take the time to do these exercises and complete the surveys and inventories, the book will become both a challenge to reflect personally on the issues and a record of your reactions to them.

You should know that we have intentionally provided an abundance of exercises in each chapter, more than can be expected to be integrated in one semester or in one course. We invite you to look over the questions and other exercises to decide which of them have the most meaning for you. At a later reading of the book, you may want to consider questions or activities that you omitted on your initial reading.

We'd like to make several other specific suggestions for getting the most from this book and your course. Many of these ideas come from students who have been in our classes. In general, you'll get from the experience of this book and course whatever you're willing to invest of yourself, so it's important to clarify your goals and to think about ways of becoming actively involved. The following suggestions may help you to become more active as a learner.

1. *Preparation.* You can best prepare yourself to become active in your class by spending time outside of class reading and thinking about the questions we pose. Completing the exercises and responding to the questions and open-ended cases will help you focus on where you stand on some controversial issues.

2. *Dealing with your expectations.* Often students have unrealistic expectations of themselves. Even though they have had very little counseling experience, they may think that they should have all the right answers worked out once and for all before they begin to work with people, or they may feel that they lack appropriate experiences. If you haven't had much experience in counseling clients, you can begin to become involved in the issues we discuss by thinking about situations in which friends have sought you out when they were in need of help. You can also reflect on the times when you were experiencing conflicts and needed someone to help you gain clarity. In this way, you may be able to relate the material to events in your own life even if your counseling experience is limited.

3. *Self-assessment.* At the end of this chapter there is a multiple-choice survey designed to help you discover your attitudes concerning most of the issues we deal with in this book. We encourage you to take this inventory before you read the book to see where you stand on these issues at this time. You may want to take the inventory in more than one sitting so that you can give careful thought to each question. We also encourage you to take the inventory again after you complete the book. You can then compare your responses to see what changes have occurred in your attitudes as a result of the course and your reading of the book.

4. *Pre-chapter self-inventories.* Each chapter begins with a self-inventory designed to stimulate your thinking about the issues that will be explored in the chapter. You might want to bring your responses to class and compare your views with those of fellow students. You may also find it useful to retake the inventory after you finish reading the chapter to see whether your views have changed.

5. *Examples, cases, and questions.* Many examples in this book are drawn from actual counseling practice in various settings with different types of clients. We frequently ask you to consider how you might have worked with a given client or what you might have done in a particular counseling situation. We hope you'll take the time to think about these questions and briefly respond to them in the spaces provided.

6. *End-of-chapter exercises and activities.* Each chapter ends with exercises and activities intended to help you integrate and apply what you've learned in the chapter. They include suggestions for things to do both in class and on your own, as well as ideas for thought and discussion that you can consider alone in a personal way or use for small-group discussions in class. The purpose of these aids is to make the issues come alive and to help you apply your ideas to practical situations. We think the time you devote to these end-of-the-chapter activities can be most useful in helping you achieve a practical grasp of the material treated in the text.

7. *The journal idea.* Many students have found it very valuable to keep a journal for the duration of the course in which they can do some more extensive writing about their positions on the issues discussed in class. A spiral notebook is ideal for keeping a record of some of your thoughts and experiences. Some students have found it most valuable to read their journals a year or two later, because in this way they achieve a sense of how their thinking has evolved as they have gained more experience.

8. *The tape-recorder idea.* Some of our students use a tape recorder as an alternative to writing a journal. After a number of sessions with several clients, they think aloud about the concerns and issues that have come up. For instance, they may ask themselves: "Am I doing most of the talking in our sessions?" "Am I really listening to what my clients are saying?" "How can I know whether my clients are getting anything from our sessions?" By talking into a tape recorder (and dating your conversations), you may achieve some clarity and be able to focus on the issues that tend to be ongoing. Then, by listening to the recordings you've made over a period of time, you might find that new issues have replaced earlier ones or that you're facing again at a later period in your development some of the struggles or questions you faced when you began counseling.

9. *Selected outside reading.* At the end of the book you'll find a reading list of additional sources you might want to consult. By developing the habit of doing some reading on issues that have meaning to you, you can gain new insights that you can integrate with your own frame of reference.

Most of all, we encourage you to use this book in any way that assists you to become involved in the issues. We hope that you'll feel free to focus selectively on the questions and activities that have the most meaning for you at this time and that you'll remain open to new issues as they assume importance for you.

Some suggestions for getting the most out of your professional education

In the preceding section we urged you to become an active learner as you use this book. Now we'd like to broaden this idea to include your entire program of training or professional preparation. Even though it may not be in your power to alter your program substantially, you can do more than simply meet an external set of requirements; you can choose to play an active role in making your education meaningful for yourself. To do so, you need to give some thought to the kind of education *you* need and want.

Although the nature of counselor-education programs is a vital professional issue, the scope of this book does not permit us to discuss it here. Inste   we'll offer suggestions for getting the most out of whatever program you happen to be in.

Some trends in the mental-health profession

You are probably already involved with the mental-health profession in some way or are planning to become involved. At this time in your career you may be asking yourself how much graduate work you will need, as well as what you hope to make your specialty. As you read this book, you will be introduced to the ethical codes of the professions of social work, counseling, psychology, and marriage and family therapy. We hope that you will begin to study various graduate programs that will best suit your personality, your professional interests, and your career goals. You might consider the findings of Anderson, Parenté, and Gordon (1981), who surveyed the opinions of mental-health providers in order to predict trends in the field. They summarized data collected from psychologists, psychiatrists, mental-health administrators, counselors, psychiatric nurses, and psychiatric social workers. What follows are some of their results:

1. Most providers believed that the need for mental-health professionals with master's degrees would continue for the following decade.

2. Most predicted that graduate program accreditation would become necessary before 1985. They also thought that program quality would increase as training institutions became accredited and as programs became highly specialized.

3. They predicted mandatory certification for mental-health specialists before 1989. They forecast that by the mid-1980s both certification and a doctorate would be required for private practice and that by the 1990s graduate training at the master's level would become highly specialized. They predicted that by the 1990s certification procedures would change, in that examinations for competency would be more common.

4. The respondents did not expect the mental-health specialties to decline in popularity; they did not expect that psychiatry would fade away; and they did not expect revolutionary new counseling techniques or chemotherapy to replace current treatment approaches.

After reflecting on these predictions, think of how they are likely to affect you, assuming that they are accurate. As a class activity, you might discuss with other students how this view of the future of the mental-health profession is likely to affect your career plans. What changes in your plans might you want to make in light of this forecast?

This might also be a good place to think about and discuss your long-term goals. What do you hope to achieve personally and professionally in ten years? Are you mainly interested in research, clinical practice, community work, administration of human services, or teaching and training? Then ask yourself what you must do to attain your professional goals.

Self-screening and ongoing self-appraisal

People preparing for professional careers in counseling-related fields ordinarily undergo various types of screening, selection, and evaluation. Depending on the kind and level of program, greater or lesser weight may be given to such factors as grades, course work completed, personality tests, personal interviews, and the like. Even if these measures were perfectly appropriate and efficient, however, they could not take the place of your own self-screening and self-appraisal. Assuming that you meet some standard of suitability for a mental-health career, you must still decide, on an ongoing basis, whether your interests, wants, and abilities make this the right career for *you*.

Of course, this kind of self-evaluation would be important in any career choice, but it is particularly essential if you're considering a career in which you will have a direct, intimate impact on the lives of others. As we discuss in the next chapter, the personal needs and motivations of counselors can significantly influence the therapeutic relationship, and a high degree of self-awareness on the part of counselors is therefore indispensable. Yet many people are attracted to a career in the helping professions for reasons they haven't thought through. Consequently, we urge you to ask yourself such questions as these:

- What were some of my reasons for entering or considering a counseling program?
- What appeals to me about this kind of work?
- What led me to choose or consider a particular program rather than some other one?
- What abilities and traits do I have that I think would help me to be a good counselor?

One way to focus on the question of your suitability for a counseling career is to look at the screening and evaluation procedures used by your program or institution. If you're in an advanced program, why were you selected? What do the screening procedures imply about the abilities and traits considered important in the kind of work you're contemplating? If *you* were in charge of screening or evaluating students, what changes would you make in these procedures? What importance would you attach to such factors as grade-point average, academic preparation, personality tests, and personal screening by faculty or peers? What motivations would you look for in students? How would you evaluate the progress of students in your program? Returning to these questions from time to time in the course of your training might help you to determine the qualities you think are important in a good counselor and the extent to which you feel this career and the particular program you're involved in are right for you.

Your self-appraisal shouldn't stop with your initial choice of a counseling career. At each step in your professional preparation, you can ask yourself how much you're satisfied with your progress and what kinds of development you still feel you need. Indeed, such self-appraisal will be important to you throughout your professional career.

Taking responsibility for your own education

It's easy to criticize a program as boring or irrelevant and to find fault with the courses, the requirements, or the instructors. If at times you feel dissatisfied with your education, however, it would perhaps be more honest—and certainly more profitable— to look at yourself and at what *you* can do to make your professional preparation more meaningful. How much of yourself are you investing in your courses? Is your academic preparation merely something to tolerate, or is it an opportunity to learn new material and apply it to your own needs? Are you willing to take the personal risk of talking with your instructors and giving your own ideas? In short, if you see deficiencies in your education and training, what are you doing to fill in the gaps?

To take responsibility for your education, you need to have a grasp of your own needs and wants. You might begin by asking yourself such questions as these:

- Which courses in my program do I value most? Why?
- Which courses are least meaningful to me? Why?

- What kind of practical experience should I have? What kind of training and supervision would I like to receive?
- What personal, experiential opportunities would I like to have as a part of my preparation? What life experiences would it be valuable to have before I begin working?
- What value do I place on experiencing my own therapy, both individual and group, as a part of my program?

One very important way of taking responsibility for your education is to work on obtaining the practical experience that will be most helpful to you in your future work. In writing on "directions for tomorrow," Brooks (1977a) asserted that students could no longer be expected to emerge from "traditional" training programs with the confidence and competence demanded by the new roles of the mental-health professional. In Brooks's view, these roles will require greater emphasis on interdisciplinary training, the development of consulting skills, and the encouragement of professionals to be agents for change in the community. Extensive practicum placements will be especially important—ones "that get trainees out of the university and into the community, where they are closer to the human needs and issues of the majority of the population" (p. 366).

Observations of practicing professionals and supervised work with clients are invaluable parts of your training. We agree with Wrenn (1973) that students should have contact with clients as soon as possible and continue to have practical experience for the duration of the program. This procedure, Wrenn maintained, enables students to get a realistic idea of what counseling is like and to relate their learning to "flesh-and-blood realities." In Wrenn's words, "Early and parallel contact with human realities must be introduced if candidates are not to turn into cognitive skeletons as counselors" (p. 276).

We encourage you, therefore, to explore the opportunities you have for early practical experience. In addition, we'd like to offer some suggestions for choosing practicum placements.

First, consider obtaining your field work in a variety of settings, with various types of clients. Although you may feel most comfortable in working with adolescents, for instance, you might consider broadening your experience to include working with young adults, the middle-aged, and the elderly. There is also much to be learned about the problems and procedures encountered in different types of agencies. Over a period of several semesters you might work at a community clinic, a state hospital, a school, and a mental-health center.

Second, take into consideration several different types of professional work to test your area of interest and help you decide on your area of specialization. For example, at different times you might counsel individuals, work with families, and co-lead a group.

Third, try to arrange for adequate on-the-job supervision, including individual meetings with your supervisor as you need them. In addition, if there is no provision for regular meetings of the student counselors, you might get together with fellow students on a weekly basis to discuss your experiences and receive feedback on different ways of working with your clients. An ongoing training and supervision group can give you the opportunity to discuss the issues you're struggling with, to share insights, and to learn about your own dynamics in your relationships with clients.

In this chapter, we've encouraged you to become active in your education and training. We'd also like to suggest that you try to keep an open mind about the issues you encounter during this time and throughout your professional career. An important part of this openness is a willingness to focus on yourself as a person and as a professional, as well as on the questions that are more obviously related to your clients. We hope this book will assist you in developing this openness to self-examination and growth as a person and as a counselor.

Self-assessment: An inventory of your attitudes and beliefs about professional and ethical issues in the helping professions

Directions: The purpose of this inventory is to survey your thoughts on various professional and ethical issues in the field of counseling and psychotherapy. Most of the items relate directly to topics that are explored in detail later in the book. The inventory is designed to introduce you to these issues and to stimulate your thought and interest. You may want to complete the inventory in more than one sitting, so that you can give each question your full concentration.

This is *not* a traditional multiple-choice test in which you must select the "one right answer." Rather, it is a survey of your basic beliefs, attitudes, and values on specific topics related to the practice of therapy. For each question, write in the letter of the response that most clearly reflects your viewpoint at this time. In many cases the answers are not mutually exclusive, and you may choose more than one response if you wish. In addition, a blank line is included for each item. You might want to use this line to provide another response more suited to your thinking or to qualify a chosen response.

Notice that there are two spaces before each item. Use the spaces on the left for your answers at the beginning of the course. At the end of the course, you can retake this inventory using the spaces on the right and covering your initial answers so that you won't be influenced by how you originally responded. Then you can see how your attitudes have changed as a result of your experience in this course.

You may want to bring the completed inventory to your beginning class session so that you can compare your views with those of others in the class. Such a comparison might stimulate some debate and help get the class involved in the topics to be discussed. In choosing the issues you want to discuss in class, you might go back over the inventory and circle the numbers of those items that you felt most strongly about as you were responding. You may find it instructive to ask others how they responded to these items in particular.

—— —— 1. The personal characteristics of counselors are
   a. not really that relevant to the counseling process.
   b. the most important variable in determining the quality of the counseling process.
   c. shaped and molded by those who teach counselors.

    d. not as important as the skills and knowledge the counselors possess.

    e. _____

___ ___ 2. Which of the following is the most important personal characteristic of a good counselor?
   a. willingness to serve as a model for clients
   b. courage
   c. openness and honesty
   d. a sense of being "centered" as a person

    e. _____

___ ___ 3. Concerning self-disclosure on the part of counselors to their clients, I believe that
   a. it is essential if a relationship is to be established.
   b. it is inappropriate and merely burdens the client.
   c. it should rarely be done and only when the therapist feels like sharing.
   d. it is useful for counselors to reveal how they feel toward their clients in the context of the therapy sessions.

    e. _____

___ ___ 4. A client/therapist relationship characterized by warmth, acceptance, caring, nonjudgmentalness, empathy, and respect is
   a. a necessary and sufficient condition of positive change in clients.
   b. a necessary but not sufficient condition of positive change in clients.
   c. neither a necessary nor a sufficient condition of positive change in clients.

    d. _____

___ ___ 5. Of the following factors, which is the most important in determining whether counseling will be effective?
   a. the kind of person the counselor is
   b. the skills and techniques the counselor uses
   c. the motivation of the client to change
   d. the theoretical orientation of the therapist

    e. _____

___ ___ 6. Of the following, which is the most important attribute of an effective therapist?
   a. knowledge of the theory of counseling and behavior
   b. skill in using techniques appropriately
   c. genuineness and openness
   d. ability to specify a treatment plan and evaluate the results

    e. _____

___ ___ 7. I believe that, for those who wish to become therapists, personal psychotherapy
   a. should be required by law.
   b. is not an important factor in developing the capacity to work with others.
   c. should be encouraged but not required.
   d. is needed only when the therapist has *real* problems.

   e. _____

___ ___ 8. I believe that, in order to help a client, a therapist
   a. must like the client personally.
   b. must be free of any personal conflicts in the area in which the client is working.
   c. needs to have experienced the very same problem as the client.
   d. needs to have experienced feelings similar to those being experienced by the client.

   e. _____

___ ___ 9. In regard to the client/therapist relationship, I think that
   a. the therapist should remain objective and anonymous.
   b. the therapist should be a friend to the client.
   c. a personal relationship, but not friendship, is essential.
   d. a personal and warm relationship is not essential.

   e. _____

___ ___ 10. I should be completely open, honest, and transparent with my clients
   a. when I like and value them.
   b. when I have negative feelings toward them.
   c. rarely, if ever, so that I will avoid negatively influencing the client/therapist relationship.
   d. only when it intuitively feels like the right thing to do.

   e. _____

___ ___ 11. I expect that I will experience professional "burn-out" if
   a. I get involved in too many exciting and demanding projects.
   b. I must do things in my work that aren't personally meaningful.
   c. my personal life is characterized by conflict and struggle.
   d. my clients complain a lot and fail to change for the better.

   e. _____

___ ___ 12. I think that professional burn-out
   a. can be avoided if I'm involved in personal therapy while working as a professional.
   b. is inevitable and that I must learn to live with it.
   c. can be lessened if I find ways to replenish and nourish myself.

    d. may or may not occur, depending on the type of client I work with.

    e. _____

___ ___ 13. If I were an intern and were convinced that my supervisor was encouraging trainees to participate in unethical behavior in an agency setting, I would

    a. first discuss the matter with the supervisor.

    b. report the supervisor to the director of the agency.

    c. ignore the situation for fear of negative consequences.

    d. report the situation to the ethics committee of the state professional association.

    e. _____

___ ___ 14. Of the following, my greatest fear when I think about beginning professional counseling is

    a. that I'll make mistakes.

    b. that my clients won't change fast enough.

    c. that I'll identify too much with my clients' problems.

    d. that I won't know enough or be skillful enough in using techniques.

    e. _____

___ ___ 15. If I had strong feelings, positive or negative, toward a client, I think that I would most likely

    a. discuss my feelings with my client.

    b. keep them to myself and hope they would eventually disappear.

    c. discuss my feelings with a supervisor or colleague.

    d. accept my feelings as natural unless they began to interfere with the counseling relationship.

    e. _____

___ ___ 16. I won't feel ready to counsel others until

    a. my own life is free of problems.

    b. I've experienced counseling as a client.

    c. I feel very confident and know that I'll be effective.

    d. I've become a self-aware person and developed the ability to continually reexamine my own life and relationships.

    e. _____

___ ___ 17. If a client evidenced strong feelings of attraction or dislike for me, I think that I would

    a. help the client work through these feelings and understand them.

    b. enjoy these feelings if they were positive.

    c. refer my client to another counselor.

    d. direct the sessions into less emotional areas.

    e. _____

___ ___ 18. Of the following motivations, the one that best expresses my reason for wanting to be a professional helper is
   a. my desire to help people find their answers within themselves.
   b. my hope of changing the world in some way.
   c. my need to straighten other people out.
   d. the prestige and status that I associate with being a professional helper.

   e. _____

___ ___ 19. When I consider being involved in the helping professions, I value most
   a. the money I expect to earn.
   b. the security I imagine I will have in the job.
   c. the knowledge that I will be intimately involved with people who are searching for a better life.
   d. the personal growth I expect to experience through my work.

   e. _____

___ ___ 20. I see counseling as
   a. a process of reeducation for the client.
   b. a process whereby clients are taught new and more appropriate values to live by.
   c. a process that enables clients to make decisions regarding their own lives.
   d. a process of giving advice and setting goals for clients.

   e. _____

___ ___ 21. With respect to value judgments in counseling, therapists should
   a. feel free to make value judgments about their clients' behavior.
   b. actively teach their own values when they think that clients need a different set of values.
   c. remain neutral and keep their values out of the therapeutic process.
   d. encourage clients to question their own values and decide upon the quality of their own behavior.

   e. _____

___ ___ 22. Counselors should
   a. teach desirable behavior and values by modeling them for clients.
   b. encourage clients to look within themselves to discover values that are meaningful to them.
   c. reinforce the dominant values of society.
   d. very delicately, if at all, challenge clients' value systems.

   e. _____

___ ___ 23. In terms of appreciating and understanding the value systems of clients who are culturally different from me,

a. I see it as my responsibility to learn about their values and not impose mine on them.
b. I would encourage them to accept the values of the dominant culture for survival purposes.
c. I would attempt to modify my counseling procedures to fit their cultural values.
d. I think it is imperative that I learn about the specific cultural values my clients hold.

e. _____

_____ _____ 24. If a client came to me with a problem and I could see that I would not be objective because of my values, I would
a. accept the client because of the challenge to become more tolerant of diversity.
b. tell the client at the outset about my fears concerning our conflicting values.
c. refer the client to someone else.
d. attempt to influence the client to adopt my way of thinking.

e. _____

_____ _____ 25. I believe that the real reason for professional licensing and certification is
a. to provide information to the public about mental-health services.
b. to protect the public by setting minimum levels of competence for psychological services.
c. to upgrade the helping professions by assuring that the highest standards of excellence are promoted.
d. to protect the self-serving interests of various helping professions and to reduce competition.

e. _____

_____ _____ 26. I would tend to refer a client to another therapist
a. if I had a strong dislike for the client.
b. if I didn't have much experience working with the kind of problem the client presented.
c. if I saw my own needs and problems getting in the way of helping the client.
d. if the client seemed to distrust me.

e. _____

_____ _____ 27. My ethical position regarding the role of values in therapy is that, as a therapist, I should
a. never impose my values on a client.
b. expose my values, without imposing them on the client.
c. teach my clients what I consider to be proper values.

d. keep my values out of the counseling relationship.

e. _____

____ ____ 28. The main criterion to determine whether I'm competent to practice counseling is
a. whether I have a state license to do counseling.
b. whether I've had training, supervision, and experience in the areas I am practicing in.
c. whether my clients feel they are being helped.
d. whether I feel confident and secure in what I'm doing.

e. _____

____ ____ 29. Of the following, I consider the most unethical form of therapist behavior to be
a. promoting dependence in the client.
b. becoming sexually involved with clients.
c. breaking confidentiality without a good reason to do so.
d. accepting a client who has a problem that goes beyond the therapist's competence.

e. _____

____ ____ 30. Regarding the issue of counseling friends, I think that
a. it is seldom wise to accept a friend as a client.
b. it should be done rarely and only if it is clear that the friendship will not interfere with the therapeutic relationship.
c. friendship and therapy should not be mixed.
d. it should be done only if it seems appropriate to both the client and the counselor.

e. _____

____ ____ 31. Regarding confidentiality, I believe that
a. it is ethical to break confidence when there is reason to believe that the client may do serious harm to himself or herself.
b. it is ethical to break confidence when there is reason to believe that the client will do harm to someone else.
c. it is ethical to break confidence when the parents of a client ask for certain information.
d. it is ethical to inform authorities when a client is breaking the law.

e. _____

____ ____ 32. Therapists should terminate therapy with a client when
a. the client decides to do so and not before.
b. they judge that it is time to terminate.
c. it is clear that the client is not benefiting from the therapy.
d. the client reaches an impasse.

e. _____

___ ___ 33. A sexual relationship between a client and therapist is
   a. ethical if the client initiates it.
   b. ethical if the therapist decides it is in the best interests of the client.
   c. ethical only when client and therapist discuss the issue and agree to the relationship.
   d. never ethical.

   e. _____

___ ___ 34. Concerning the issue of physically touching a client, I think that touching
   a. is unwise, because it could be misinterpreted by the client.
   b. should be done only when the therapist genuinely feels like doing it.
   c. is an important part of the therapeutic process.
   d. is ethical when the client requests it.

   e. _____

___ ___ 35. A clinical supervisor has initiated sexual relationships with former trainees (students). He maintains that, because he no longer has any professional responsibility to them, this practice is acceptable. In my view, this behavior is
   a. clearly unethical, because he is using his position to initiate contacts with former students.
   b. not unethical, because the professional relationship has ended.
   c. not unethical but is unwise and inappropriate.
   d. somewhat unethical, because the supervisory relationship is similar to the therapeutic relationship.

   e. _____

___ ___ 36. Regarding the place of theory in counseling, I think that therapists should
   a. ignore it, since it has no practical application.
   b. select *one* theory and work within its framework.
   c. borrow something from most of the theories of therapy.
   d. select a theory on the basis of the client's personality and presenting problem.

   e. _____

___ ___ 37. In the practice of marital and family therapy, I think that
   a. the therapist's primary responsibility is to the welfare of the family as a unit.
   b. the therapist should focus primarily on the needs of individual members of the family.
   c. the therapist should attend to the family's needs and try to hold the amount of sacrifice by any one member to a minimum.
   d. the therapist has an ethical obligation to state his or her bias and approach at the outset.

   e. _____

_____ _____ 38. The most important function of a therapist is
a. to encourage a client to face reality.
b. to interpret the meaning of a client's symptoms.
c. to simply be with clients, so that they will have the courage to look at aspects of their lives they might not otherwise be able to look at.
d. to give specific instructions concerning what the clients should do outside the therapy sessions.

e. _____

_____ _____ 39. Regarding the issue of who should select the goals of counseling, I believe that
a. it is primarily the therapist's responsibility to select goals.
b. it is primarily the client's responsibility to select goals.
c. the responsibility for selecting goals should be shared equally by the client and therapist.
d. the question of who selects the goals depends on what kind of client is being seen.

e. _____

_____ _____ 40. Concerning the role of diagnosis in counseling, I believe that
a. diagnosis is essential for the planning of a treatment program.
b. diagnosis is counterproductive for therapy, since it is based on an external view of the client.
c. diagnosis is dangerous in that it tends to label people, who then are limited by the label.
d. whether to use diagnosis depends on one's theoretical orientation and the kind of counseling one does.

e. _____

_____ _____ 41. Concerning the place of testing in counseling, I think that
a. tests generally interfere with the counseling process.
b. tests can be valuable tools if they are used as adjuncts to counseling, particularly when a client requests them.
c. tests are essential for people who are seriously disturbed.
d. tests can be either used or abused in counseling.

e. _____

_____ _____ 42. Regarding the issue of psychological risks associated with participation in group therapy, my position is that
a. clients should be informed at the outset of possible risks.
b. these risks should be minimized by careful screening.
c. this issue is exaggerated, since there are no real risks.
d. careful supervision will offset some of these risks.

e. _____

___ ___ 43. Concerning the counselor's responsibility to the community, I believe that
   a. the counselor should educate the community concerning the nature of psychological services.
   b. the counselor should attempt to change patterns that need changing.
   c. community involvement falls outside of the proper scope of counseling.
   d. counselors should become involved in helping clients use the resources available in the community.

   e. _____

___ ___ 44. On the issue of advertising and announcing psychological services, I believe that the professional counselor should
   a. teach the public how to be wise consumers.
   b. allow clients to discover for themselves what services are available.
   c. provide guidelines for consumers so that they will learn how to evaluate psychological services.
   d. help members of the community overcome their fears about asking for professional assistance.

   e. _____

___ ___ 45. As an intern, if I thought my supervision was inadequate, I would
   a. talk to my supervisor about it.
   b. continue to work without complaining.
   c. seek supervision elsewhere.
   d. feel let down by the agency I worked for.

   e. _____

___ ___ 46. My view of supervision is that it is
   a. something that I could use on a permanent basis.
   b. a threat to my status as a professional.
   c. valuable to have when I reach an impasse with a client.
   d. a way for me to learn about myself and to get insights into how I work with clients.

   e. _____

___ ___ 47. When it comes to working within institutions, I believe that
   a. I must learn how to survive with dignity within a system.
   b. I must learn how to subvert the system so that I can do what I deeply believe in.
   c. the institution will stifle most of my enthusiasm and block any real change.
   d. I can't blame the institution if I'm unable to succeed in my programs.

   e. _____

___ ___ 48. If my philosophy were in conflict with that of the institution I worked for, I would
   a. seriously consider whether I could ethically remain in that position.
   b. attempt to change the policies of the institution.
   c. agree to whatever was expected of me in that system.
   d. quietly do what I wanted to do, even if I had to be devious about it.

   e. _____

___ ___ 49. In working with clients from different ethnic groups, I think it is most important to
   a. be aware of the sociopolitical forces that have affected these clients.
   b. understand how language can act as a barrier to effective cross-cultural counseling.
   c. refer these clients to some professional who shares their ethnic and cultural background.
   d. help these clients modify their views so that they will be accepted and not have to suffer rejection.

   e. _____

___ ___ 50. To be effective in counseling clients from a different culture, I think that a counselor must
   a. possess specific knowledge about the particular group he or she is counseling.
   b. be able to accurately "read" nonverbal messages.
   c. have had direct contact with this group.
   d. treat these clients no differently from clients from his or her own cultural background.

   e. _____

Suggested readings

Brammer, L., & Shostrom, E. *Therapeutic psychology: Fundamentals of counseling and psychotherapy* (4th ed.). Englewood Cliffs, N.J.: Prentice-Hall, 1982. This survey textbook deals with a number of professional issues, including diagnosis and testing in counseling, advice, the role of values in counseling, trends in professional practice, barriers to the counseling relationship, and counseling with couples and families. It is a comprehensive text that contains a good discussion of issues of current interest.

Goldenberg, H. *Contemporary clinical psychology* (2nd ed.). Monterey, Calif.: Brooks/Cole, 1983. This up-to-date and well-written book contains several excellent chapters that are relevant for professional issues in psychotherapy. Chapters of special interest cover models of clinical training, diagnostic and assessment issues, contemporary approaches to therapy, and social and community interventions.

Professional Psychology. Published bimonthly, this journal contains a variety of articles dealing with professional and ethical issues in the field of clinical and counseling psychology. The journal is an excellent resource for both students and practitioners who wish to keep up to date.

Rosenbaum, M. (Ed.). *Ethics and values in psychotherapy: A guidebook.* New York: Free Press, 1982. This is a most valuable resource for further study, as it presents an in-depth discussion of many of the topics that are briefly introduced in the present book. Some chapters include ethical issues in training of therapists, ethics and the individual client, ethical problems in group therapy, ethics and sex therapy, ethical problems in the use of videotape, and ethical considerations in psychotherapeutic research.

Tymchuk, A. J., Drapkin, R., Major-Kingsley, S., Ackerman, A. B., Coffman, E. W., & Baum, M. S. Ethical decision making and psychologists' attitudes toward training in ethics. *Professional Psychology,* 1982, *13*(3), 412–421. The point of this article is that guidelines are available for making ethical decisions that protect the rights of clients in therapy. As new treatments are developed, however, these old guidelines may be inadequate. The results of a questionnaire sent to clinical psychologists suggest that there is inconsistency in ethical decision making. The authors give suggestions for improving this decision-making process.

Van Hoose, W., & Kottler, J. *Ethical and legal issues in counseling and psychotherapy.* San Francisco: Jossey-Bass, 1977. The authors deal with a variety of professional issues, such as incompetent and unethical behavior, psychotherapy and the law, legal regulations of professional psychology, ethics in group work, the marketing of therapeutic services, issues in behavior therapy, issues related to diagnosis and assessment, value problems in psychotherapy, and ethical principles in the practice of therapy. Readers will find this a useful resource for further study.

The Counselor as a Person and as a Professional

Pre-chapter self-inventory

The purpose of the pre-chapter self-inventories is to assist you in identifying and clarifying your attitudes and beliefs concerning the issues to be explored in the chapter. Keep in mind that the "right" answer is the one that best expresses your thoughts at this time. We suggest that you complete each inventory before reading the chapter; then, after reading the chapter and discussing the material in class, you can retake the inventory to see whether your positions have changed in any way.

Directions: For each statement, indicate the response that most closely identifies your beliefs and attitudes. Use the following code:

5 = I *strongly agree* with this statement.
4 = I *agree*, in most respects, with this statement.
3 = I am *undecided* in my opinion about this statement.
2 = I *disagree*, in most respects, with this statement.
1 = I *strongly disagree* with this statement.

__4__ 1. Therapists' attitudes are more important than their theoretical orientations in terms of initiating positive personality changes in clients.

__5__ 2. The personal qualities of therapists are at least as important as their knowledge and skills in effecting client change.

__3__ 3. Therapists should remain relatively anonymous and avoid disclosing much of themselves, so that they don't unduly influence their clients.

____ 4. For therapy to be successful, the relationship between client and therapist must be characterized by acceptance, trust, and personal warmth.

____ 5. Part of the counselor's task is to serve as a model for clients, because clients learn a great deal by imitating the behavior of the therapist.

____ 6. The ability of a therapist to establish a good personal relationship with a client is essential, but it is not sufficient by itself to bring about behavioral change.

_____ 7. Unless therapists have a high degree of self-awareness, there is a real danger that they will use their clients to satisfy their own needs.

_____ 8. Before therapists begin to practice, they should be free of personal problems and conflicts.

_____ 9. Counselors or therapists should be required to undergo their own therapy before they are licensed to practice.

_____ 10. Counselors who actually are satisfying personal needs through their work are behaving unethically.

_____ 11. Most professionals in the counseling field face a high risk of burn-out because of the demands of their jobs.

_____ 12. Counselors who know themselves can avoid experiencing overidentification with their clients.

_____ 13. Strong feelings about a client are a sign that the counselor needs further therapy for himself or herself.

_____ 14. Feelings of anxiety as a beginning counselor indicate unsuitability for the counseling profession.

_____ 15. A competent counselor can work with any client.

_____ 16. I expect that I'll have difficulty making demands on my clients.

_____ 17. A professional counselor will avoid both getting involved socially with clients and counseling friends.

_____ 18. A major fear I have is that I'll make mistakes and seriously hurt a client.

_____ 19. Real therapy does not occur unless a transference relationship is developed.

_____ 20. A professional counselor will not withhold anything personal about himself or herself from a client.

_____ 21. The most important personal quality of a therapist is empathy, for this is the basis for forming relationships.

_____ 22. For a counselor to be effective with a client, he or she must have experienced the same type of problems as the client.

_____ 23. For a counselor to be effective with a client, the two must have a similar "world view"; that is, they must share a common set of values, beliefs, cultural mores, and experiences in life.

_____ 24. As a counselor, I think it is important that I be willing to adapt my therapeutic style (techniques and approaches) to the cultural backgrounds of my clients.

_____ 25. Counselors who experience countertransference can be very sure that they are not personally competent to form therapeutic relationships with clients, since they obviously are primarily concerned with meeting their own needs at the expense of their clients.

Introduction

One of the most basic issues in the counseling profession concerns the significance of the counselor as a person in the therapeutic relationship. Since counselors are asking people to take an honest look at themselves and to make choices concerning how they want to change, it seems critical to us that counselors themselves be searchers who hold their own lives open to the same kind of scrutiny. Counselors should repeatedly ask themselves such questions as the following: What makes me think I have a right to counsel anyone else? What do I personally have to offer others who are struggling to find their way? Am I doing in my own life what I urge others to do?

Counselors and psychotherapists can acquire an extensive theoretical and practical knowledge and can make that knowledge available to their clients. But to every therapeutic session they also bring themselves as persons. They bring their human qualities and the life experiences that have molded them. It is our belief that professionals can be well-versed in psychological theory and can learn diagnostic and interviewing skills and still be ineffective as helpers. It seems obvious to us that, if counselors are to promote growth and change in their clients, they must be willing to promote growth in their own lives by exploring their own choices and decisions and by striving to become aware of the ways in which they can ignore their own potential for growth. This willingness to attempt to live in accordance with what they teach and thus to be positive models for their clients is what makes counselors "therapeutic persons."

Surely, counselors have more to offer their clients than themselves as persons. They have some knowledge of the dynamics of behavior and possess intervention skills that are invaluable tools for helping others. However, we believe that such knowledge and skills are most effective in the hands of counselors who apply them to themselves as well as to others.

It is difficult to talk about the "counselor as a professional" without considering the personal qualities that influence the kind of professional he or she becomes. A counselor's values, beliefs, personal attributes, life experiences, and way of living are intrinsically related to the way he or she functions as a professional. However, counselors do have a professional identity, and some issues are specifically related to their professionalism as counselors. Although some of the questions we discuss are of special concern to the beginning counselor, you'll probably find yourself struggling with most of these issues again and again throughout your professional career.

The counselor's personality and character: How important?

In this section we describe how two contrasting theoretical perspectives assess the significance of the therapist's personal characteristics and the quality of the client/therapist relationship in determining the outcomes of therapy. Although these are extreme viewpoints on this issue, most theoretical models are based on the assumption that the client/therapist relationship must be characterized by caring, trust, acceptance, understanding, and respect if therapy is to have a positive outcome. Most theorists also agree that the kind of person a therapist is crucially influences the kind of relationship that develops between the client and the therapist.

Two opposing views: Carl Rogers versus Albert Ellis

Carl Rogers.   The range of viewpoints on the importance of the therapist as a person is well represented by the opposing views of Carl Rogers and Albert Ellis. For Rogers (1961), the attitudes and feelings of the therapist are more important than techniques and theoretical orientation. He lists three personal characteristics of therapists that form the core of a positive therapeutic relationship: (1) congruence, or genuineness, (2) unconditional positive regard for the client, and (3) accurate empathic understanding. Rogers claims that communicating these attitudes to clients releases inherent growth forces and enables clients to drop facades and begin a deeper exploration of their defenses. If, by virtue of the persons they are, therapists succeed in creating an accepting and caring climate, then clients will move in these directions:

- They will experience and understand aspects of themselves that they previously repressed.
- They will become better integrated and able to function more effectively.
- They will increasingly become the persons they would like to be.
- They will become more self-directing and self-confident.
- They will move toward an internal locus of evaluation.
- They will become more accepting and understanding of others.
- They will move away from pleasing others, away from oughts and shoulds, away from lives based on the expectations of others, and away from pretenses.
- They will become more open to new experiences.

In a discussion of "empathy as an unappreciated way of being," Rogers (1980) gives the highest priority to empathy when people are hurting, confused, alienated, anxious, and doubtful of their self-worth and identity. In his words: "The gentle and sensitive companionship offered by an empathic person provides illumination and healing. In such situations deep understanding is, I believe, the most precious gift one can give to another" (pp. 160–161).

For Rogers, then, the most significant contributions of therapists to positive change in their clients are their personal attributes and the relationships these attributes enable them to establish with their clients. Within this perspective, who therapists are as persons is far more important than what they do or what techniques they use in counseling.

Albert Ellis.   At the other end of the spectrum from Rogers's view of the importance of the therapeutic relationship is the view of therapy espoused by Albert Ellis, the founder of rational-emotive therapy (RET). In *Humanistic Psychotherapy*, Ellis (1973) has this to say about the role of the client/therapist relationship in personality change:

> Actually, quite effectual therapy, leading to a basic personality change, can be done without any relationship whatever between client and therapist. It can be accomplished by correspondence, by readings, and by tape recordings and other audiovisual aids, without the client having any contact with, or knowing practically anything about, the person who is treating him [p. 140].

Ellis maintains that clients can make positive changes even when they feel lectured at and think their therapists dislike them. They can follow exercises prescribed by their therapists and maintain unpleasant relationships with them and still show evidence of behavioral change. Thus, for Ellis, personal warmth, affection, and caring are secondary; good therapy can be done without them.

Later, Ellis (1979) modified his previous position by stating that "therapists had better give clients unconditional self-acceptance, carefully listen to their complaints, and see things from the clients' frames of reference" (p. 64). These attitudes, along with therapist support and encouragement, may help clients feel better. Ellis cautions, however, that *feeling better* is not equivalent to *getting better*. According to Ellis, clients are challenged to change by a process of learning how to examine their irrational beliefs that lead to behavioral disturbances. The role of the therapist is to teach clients how to think scientifically so that they will be able to effectively annihilate self-defeating ideas now and in the future. Thus, the therapist's attitudes are important in the therapeutic relationship but may not be sufficient to produce behavioral change.

Personal characteristics of effective counselors

In the previous section, we discussed two theoretical views of the importance of the counselor as a person. Our own position is that the personal characteristics and the behavior of counselors are vitally related to the formation of significant relationships that will stimulate clients to move forward. For this reason, we see the personal attributes of the therapist as the single most important determinant of successful therapy. In this section we examine some of the characteristics that we think are important for effective counselors to have, and we ask you to think of the personal attributes *you* deem to be vital. Of course, no counselor is likely to possess all the attributes we mention; we're not contending that being a successful counselor is synonymous with being a model of perfection! We do believe, though, that counselors who are willing to continually look within themselves and struggle toward becoming more effective human beings are the ones who are most likely to make a positive difference in the lives of their clients.

The following is a list of personal traits and characteristics that we believe represent an ideal that counselors might aim for. As you read over our list, ask yourself whether you agree with each item and whether there are other traits that you think are important. Then you can use your list of significant personal characteristics as a starting point for reflection on your own struggle to become a more effective person.

1. *Good will.* Effective counselors must have a sincere interest in the welfare of others. The way they relate to others shows that they respect, trust, and value other people. Caring about others doesn't necessarily imply merely showing warmth and giving support. It may involve challenging others to look at aspects of their lives they might just as soon ignore. It may involve a refusal to tolerate dishonest behavior and a corresponding willingness to encourage others to live without their masks and shields. Caring is perhaps best shown when counselors avoid using clients to meet their own needs.

2. *The ability to be present for others.* By the ability to be emotionally present for clients, we mean the ability and willingness to be with them in their experience of pain or joy. This ability stems from the counselor's openness to his or her own struggles and feelings. This is not to say that counselors must talk with their clients about their own experiences but rather that being in contact with their own emotions enables counselors to be compassionate and empathic with their clients.

3. *A recognition and acceptance of their personal power.* Effective counselors

recognize their personal power, not in the sense that they dominate or exploit their clients but in the sense that they are in contact with their own strength and vitality. They feel confident and alive and have no need to diminish others or feel superior to them. They recognize that two people in a relationship can both be powerful, and they don't have to assume a superior role to feel competent. Indeed, one of their aims is to help clients discover their own autonomy and competence.

4. *The knowledge that they have found their own way.* Effective counselors strive to develop counseling styles that are expressions of their own personalities. They are open to learning from others and may borrow concepts and techniques from different schools of therapy, but their styles are ultimately their own.

5. *A willingness to be vulnerable and to take risks.* Ideally, counselors exemplify in their own lives the kind of courage and openness they hope to promote in their clients. Thus, they are willing to take risks, to be vulnerable at times, to trust their intuitions even when they're unsure of the outcome, to be emotionally touched by others, to draw on their own experiences in order to identify with the feelings and struggles of other people, and to disclose what they think and feel about their clients when it is appropriate to do so.

6. *Self-respect and self-appreciation.* Counselors will be most effective if they feel like "winners." In other words, they should have a strong sense of self-worth that enables them to relate to others out of their strengths rather than out of their weaknesses.

7. *A willingness to serve as models for their clients.* One of the best ways to teach others is by example. Accordingly, effective counselors don't ask their clients to do things they aren't willing to do themselves. If they genuinely value risk taking, openness, honesty, self-examination, and so on, then they will exhibit some degree of these qualities in their own lives.

8. *A willingness to risk making mistakes and to admit having made them.* Effective counselors realize that they will accomplish little if they rarely take the chance of failing. They know they will make mistakes, and they try to learn from them without burdening themselves excessively with self-recrimination.

9. *A growth orientation.* The most effective counselors remain open to the possibility of broadening their horizons instead of telling themselves they have "arrived." They question the quality of their existence, their values, and their motivations. Just as they encourage their clients to become more autonomous, they attempt to live by their own values and standards rather than by the expectations of others. They are committed to a continual search for self-awareness, and they know that an appreciation of their own limitations, strengths, fears, and vulnerabilities is essential if they are to foster this kind of self-understanding in their clients.

Now that we've listed some traits that we think are important for effective counselors to have, we'd like to give you the chance to reflect a moment on your reactions.

1. From our list of personal traits of effective counselors, select one or two that you think are most important, and state why. Also, think of people who were helpful to you. What were their characteristics?

_____

_____

_____

2. If you were working with a colleague who lacked what *you* considered to be important characteristics of an effective counselor, what would you do?

_____

_____

_____

3. At this point in your evolution as a counselor, what do you consider to be the major *personal strengths* that will be assets to you as a counselor?

_____

_____

_____

4. Now list the personal areas that you see as being potential liabilities for you as a counselor.

_____

_____

_____

Therapist self-awareness and the influence of the therapist's personality and needs

Since counselors ask clients to examine their behavior and lives in order to understand themselves more fully, it is incumbent upon them to be equally committed to awareness of their own lives. Moreover, without a high level of self-awareness, counselors will obstruct the progress of their clients. The focus of the therapy will shift from meeting the client's needs to meeting the needs of the therapist. Consequently, counselors and therapists should be aware of their own needs, areas of "unfinished business," personal conflicts, defenses, and vulnerabilities—*and* how these may intrude on their work with their clients. In this section we consider some specific areas that we think counselors need to examine.

Personal benefits

One critical question that counselors can ask themselves is "What do I personally get from doing counseling?" There are many answers to this question. Many therapists experience excitement and a deep sense of satisfaction from being with people who are struggling to achieve self-understanding, who recognize that their lives aren't the way they want them to be, and who are willing to experience pain as they seek a better life for themselves. Some counselors enjoy the feeling of being instrumental in others' changes; others appreciate the depth and honesty of the therapeutic relationship. Still other therapists value the opportunity to question their own lives as they work with their clients. Therapeutic encounters can in many ways serve as mirrors in which therapists can see their own lives reflected. As a result, therapy can become a catalyst for change in the therapist as much as in the client.

Personal needs

Therapeutic progress can be blocked when therapists use their clients, perhaps unconsciously, to fulfill their own needs. For example, out of a need to nurture others or to feel powerful, people sometimes feel that they have the answers concerning how others should live. The tendency to give advice and try to direct another's life can be especially harmful in a therapist, because it leads to excessive dependence on the part of clients and only perpetuates their tendency to look outside themselves for answers. Therapists who need to feel powerful or important may begin to think that they are indispensable to their clients or, worse still, make themselves so.

The goals of therapy can also suffer when therapists who have a strong need for approval focus on trying to win the acceptance, admiration, respect, and even awe of their clients. Some therapists may be primarily motivated by a need to receive confirmation of their value as persons and as professionals from their clients. It is within their power as therapists to control the sessions in such a way that these needs are continually reinforced. Because clients often feel a need to please their therapists, they can easily encourage therapists who crave continuous reinforcement of their sense of worth.

One of the goals of therapy, as we see it, is to teach the *process* of problem solving, not just to solve problems. When clients have learned the process, they have less and less need of their therapists. Therapists who tell clients what to do or use the sessions to buttress their own sense of self-worth diminish the autonomy of their clients and invite increased dependence in the future.

When therapists are not sufficiently aware of their own needs, they may abuse the power they have in the therapeutic situation. Some therapists and counselors gain a sense of power by assuming the role of directing others toward solutions instead of encouraging them to seek alternatives for themselves and choose among them. A solution-oriented approach to counseling may also spring from the therapist's need to feel a sense of achievement and accomplishment. Some therapists feel very ill at ease if their clients fail to make instant progress; consequently, they may either push their clients to make decisions prematurely or even make decisions for them. This tendency can be encouraged even more by clients who express gratitude for this kind of "help."

Of course, therapists *do* have their own personal needs, but these needs don't have to assume priority or get in the way of clients' growth. Most people who enter the helping professions do want to nurture others, and they do need to know that they are instrumental in helping others to change. In this sense, they need to hear from clients that they are a significant force in their lives. In order to keep these needs from interfering with the progress of their clients, therapists should be clearly aware of the danger of working primarily to be appreciated by others instead of working toward the best interests of their clients. If they are open enough to recognize this potential danger, the chances are that they will not fall into using their clients to meet their own needs.

It's hard to find fault with therapists who find excitement in their work. The rewards of practicing psychotherapy are many, but one of the most significant rewards is the joy of seeing clients move from being victims to assuming control over their lives. Therapists can achieve this reward only if they avoid abusing their influence and maintain a keen awareness of their role as facilitators of others' growth. As you consider your own needs and their influence on your work as a therapist, you might ask yourself the following questions:

1. How can you know when you're working for the client's benefit and when you're working for your own benefit?

_____

_____

_____

2. How much do you think you might depend on clients to tell you how good you are as a person or as a therapist? Are you able to appreciate yourself, or do you depend primarily on others to validate your worth and the value of your work?

_____

_____

_____

3. How can you deal with feelings of inadequacy, particularly if you seem to be getting nowhere with a client?

_____

_____

_____

Unresolved personal conflicts

We have suggested that the personal needs of a therapist can interfere with the therapeutic process, to the detriment of the client, if the therapist is unaware of their impact on his or her work. The same is true of personal problems and unresolved conflicts. This is not to say that therapists must resolve all their personal difficulties before they begin to counsel others; such a requirement would eliminate almost everybody from the field. In fact, it's possible that a counselor who rarely struggles or experiences anxiety may have real difficulty in relating to a client who feels desperate or caught in a hopeless conflict. Moreover, if therapists flee from anxiety-provoking questions in their own lives, they probably won't be able to effectively encourage clients to face such questions. The important point is that counselors can and should be *aware* of their biases, their areas of denial, and the issues they find particularly hard to deal with in their own lives.

To illustrate, suppose that you're experiencing a rough time in your life. You feel stuck with unresolved anger and frustration. Your home life is tense, and you're wrestling with some pivotal decisions about how you want to spend the rest of your life. Perhaps you're having problems with your clients or your spouse. You might be caught between fears of loneliness and a desire to be on your own, or between your fear of and need for close relationships. Can you counsel others effectively while you're struggling with your own uncertainty?

To us, the critical point isn't *whether* you happen to be struggling with personal questions but *how* you're struggling with them. Do you see your part in creating your own problems? Are you aware of your alternatives for action? Do you recognize and try to deal with your problems, or do you invest a lot of energy in denying their existence? Do you find yourself generally blaming others for your problems? Are you willing to consult with a therapist, or do you tell yourself that you can handle it, even when it becomes obvious that you're not doing so? In short, are you willing to do in your own life what you encourage your clients to do?

If you're not working on being aware of your own conflicts, then you'll be in a poor position to pay attention to the ways in which your personal life influences your work with clients, especially if some of their problem areas are also problem areas for you. For example, suppose a client is trying to deal with feelings of hopelessness and despair. How can you intensively explore these feelings if, in your own life, you're busily engaged in cheering everybody up? If hopelessness is an issue you don't want to face personally, you'll probably steer the client away from exploring it. As another example, consider a client who wants to explore her feelings about homosexuality. Can you facilitate this exploration if you haven't been open to your own feelings about homosexuality? If you feel discomfort in talking about homosexual feelings and experiences, and you don't want to have to deal with your discomfort, can you stay with your client emotionally when she brings up this topic?

Since you'll have difficulty staying with a client in an area that you're reluctant or fearful to deal with, consider what present unfinished business in your own life might affect you as a counselor. What unresolved conflicts are you aware of, and how might these conflicts influence the way you counsel others?

_____

_____

_____

_____

_____

_____

The issue of personal therapy for counselors

In the last section, we stressed the importance of counselors' self-awareness. A closely related issue is the value of personal therapy for those who wish to become counselors. There are several reasons why we think potential counselors should be encouraged to experience their own therapy.

First of all, we believe that those who expect to counsel others should know what the experience of being a client is really like. We don't assume that most potential therapists are "sick" and in need of being "cured," but then we don't make that assumption about most clients, either. Many clients are attracted to counseling because they want to <u>explore the quality of their lives and the</u> alternatives they have for a <u>richer existence.</u> Potential counselors can approach therapy in much the same way. Therapy can help us take an honest look at our motivations in becoming helpers. It can help us explore how our needs influence our actions, how we use power in our lives, what our values are, and whether we have a need to persuade others to live by them. We can look at our need to be recognized and appreciated, at painful memories and past experiences that have shaped our ways of living, and at the sources of meaning in our lives. In the process, we can experience first-hand what our clients experience in therapy.

Another reason for undergoing therapy is that all of us have <u>blind spots</u> and <u>unfinished business</u> that may interfere with our effectiveness as therapists. All of us have areas in our lives that aren't fully developed and that can keep us from being as effective as we can be, both as persons and as counselors. Personal therapy is one way of coming to grips with these and other issues.

Ideally, we'd like to see potential counselors undergo a combination of individual and group therapy, because the two types supplement each other. Individual therapy provides the opportunity to look at ourselves in some depth. Many counselors will experience a reopening of old psychic wounds as they engage in intensive work with their clients. For example, their therapeutic work may bring to the surface guilt feelings that need to be resolved. If they are in private therapy at the same time as they are doing their internship, they can productively bring such problems to their sessions.

<u>Group therapy</u>, on the other hand, can provide the opportunity to get <u>feedback</u> <u>from others on how they experience us.</u> It allows us to become increasingly aware of our personal styles and gives us a chance to experiment with new behavior in the group setting. The reactions we receive from others can help us learn about personal attributes that could be either strengths or limitations in our work as counselors.

Many training programs in counselor education recognize the value of having students involved in personal-awareness groups with their peers on an ongoing basis. A group can be set up specifically for the exploration of personal concerns, or such exploration can be made an integral part of training and supervision groups. Whatever the format, students will benefit most if they are willing to focus on themselves personally and not merely on their "cases." Unfortunately, many beginning counselors would rather focus exclusively on client dynamics. Their group learning would be more meaningful if they were open to exploring such questions as: How am I feeling about my own value as a counselor? Do I like my relationship with my client? What kinds of reactions are being evoked in me as I work with this client? In short, if counselors in training are willing to become personally invested in the therapy process, they can use their training program as a real opportunity for expanding their own awareness.

Although we have emphasized the need for personal therapy during training, we do not want to convey the idea that practicing professionals are exempt from periodic and ongoing introspection. At times, experienced practitioners can profit from a program that will challenge them to reexamine some of their beliefs and behaviors, especially as these pertain to their effectiveness in working with clients.

We hope that honest practitioners will see the value of making it a lifelong practice to engage in a variety of ways of self-examination as a means of keeping honest with themselves and others.

Common concerns of beginning counselors and therapists

Many students in counselor-training programs tend to bring up the same fears, resistances, self-doubts, concerns, and questions. They may wonder whether they have what it takes to be professional counselors, or they may seriously question the nature of their impact on the people they counsel. Moreover, students inevitably discover that there is a gap between their formal, academic learning and the actual work they do when they come face to face with clients. The discovery that they have mainly themselves to work with—that, although techniques can be helpful, they must ultimately draw on themselves as persons—can be a frightening one. You should keep in mind, however, that these kinds of concerns are rarely resolved once and for all; even as an experienced counselor, you'll probably find yourself struggling from time to time with doubts and anxieties about your adequacy or the value of your work.

The following questionnaire is drawn from statements we frequently hear in practicum and internship courses; they represent a sampling of the issues faced by those who begin to counsel others. Apply these statements to yourself, and decide to what degree you see them as your concerns. If a statement is more true than false for you, place a "T" in front of it; if it is more false than true for you, place an "F" in front of it.

_____ I'm afraid that I'll make mistakes.

_____ My clients will really suffer because of my blunders and my failure to know what to do.

_____ I have real doubts concerning my ability to help people in a crisis situation.

_____ I demand perfection of myself, and I constantly feel I should know more than I do.

_____ I would feel threatened by silences in counseling situations.

_____ It's important to me to know that my clients are making steady improvement.

_____ It would be difficult for me to deal with demanding clients.

_____ I expect to have trouble working with clients who are not motivated to change or who are required to come to me for counseling.

_____ I have trouble deciding how much of the responsibility for the direction of a counseling session is mine and how much is my client's.

_____ I think that I should be successful with all my clients.

_____ I expect to have trouble in being myself and trusting my intuition when I'm counseling.

_____ I am afraid to express feelings of anger to a client.

_____ I worry that my clients will see that I am a beginner and wonder if I am competent.

_____ I am concerned about looking and acting like a professional.

_____ Sometimes I'm concerned about how honest I should be with clients.

_____ I'm concerned about how much of my personal reactions and my private life is appropriate for me to reveal in counseling sessions.

_____ I tend to worry about whether I'm doing the proper thing.

_____ I sometimes worry that I may overidentify with my client's problems to the extent that they may become *my* problems.

_____ During a counseling session I would frequently find myself wanting to give advice.

_____ I'm afraid that I may say or do something that might greatly disturb a client.

_____ I can see myself trying to persuade clients to take certain actions.

_____ I wonder how much of my values I should reveal to clients.

_____ I'm concerned about counseling clients whose values are very different from my own.

_____ I would be concerned about whether my clients liked and approved of me and whether they would want to come back.

_____ I'm concerned about being mechanical in my counseling, as though I were following a book.

Once you've gone through these statements, you might go back over them and select the issues that represent your greatest concerns. You can then begin to challenge some of the assumptions behind these concerns. Suppose, for example, that you feel greatly afraid of making mistakes. You may be saying to yourself: "I should know more than I do, and I should have answers for my clients. If I were to get stuck and not know what to do with a given client, that would be terrible; it would completely erode my self-confidence. If I make mistakes, I might drive my clients away, and they would be far worse off than when they began counseling with me." If you burden yourself with these or similar expectations, you might begin to challenge your basic assumptions by asking yourself such questions as these:

- Why should I be all-knowing?
- Who told me that making mistakes would be fatal?
- Am I really expected to provide solutions for clients?
- Are my clients so fragile that they won't be able to survive my mistakes?

As we discuss some of the issues encountered by practicing counselors, ask yourself how you relate to these issues and whether you should begin to question some of your assumptions. You might also find it useful to write about other concerns you now have as you think about becoming a professional counselor. What issues are most pressing for you? What assumptions underlie your concerns? How valid are these assumptions?

Anxiety

Many counselors experience some anxiety about their work, particularly if they have had little or no experience as counselors. As you think of facing your first clients, you may ask yourself: What will my clients want? Will I be able to give them what they want? What will I say, and how will I say it? Will they want to come back? If they do, what will I do then?

Although raising such questions can be part of a process of self-inquiry and growth for even an experienced counselor, it's possible to become so anxiety-ridden that you cannot deal with the questions effectively. Your anxiety may feed on itself, especially if you think that it's abnormal or tell yourself that you wouldn't be experiencing so much anxiety if you were really suited for the counseling profession. It may help if you realize that a certain amount of anxiety indicates an awareness of the uncertainty that surrounds your work with clients. Although anxiety can get out of hand and freeze a counselor into inactivity, some anxiety is certainly to be expected. In fact, we become concerned when we encounter student counselors who never exhibit any kind of self-doubt or self-questioning, which we believe to be part of the evolutionary process of becoming a counselor. The experience of anxiety can lead to honest self-appraisal. We often hear students say that their peers seem so much more knowledgeable, skilled, and confident than they themselves feel. When such students have the courage to bring their feelings of inadequacy into the open, they frequently discover that they aren't alone and that those who appear the most self-confident also have doubts about their capabilities as counselors.

This is where regular meetings with your fellow students and your instructor are vitally important. There are no easy solutions to the kind of anxiety you are likely to experience; in any event, we think it's counterproductive to try to remove all anxiety. With your peers you can discuss your fears, worries, and questions, and you can gain a sense of how they deal with such feelings. You can also explore with them how much of your anxiety reflects a genuine appreciation of the uncertainties inherent in your chosen profession. This kind of exchange offers invaluable opportunities for personal and professional growth. And, since it takes courage to share your feelings, doing so may defuse some of the anxiety that is unrealistic.

Before you continue reading, pause a moment to list some of your current fears or worries concerning your professional work.

Expecting instant results

Many beginning counselors become discouraged when they don't see immediate, positive results in their clients. These counselors may be assuming that their role is to solve any and all problems their clients bring to the sessions. Accordingly, they may ask: Is my client getting better or worse? How do I know if what I'm doing during our sessions is really worth anything?

The fact is that clients generally don't make immediate gains. Indeed, it's far more common for them to report an increase in anxiety in the early stages of counseling and at various points later on. In trying to be honest with their counselors and with themselves, they are giving up many of their defenses and are likely to experience an acute sense of vulnerability. Counselors therefore need to be able to continue working without knowing the full extent to which they're having positive effects on a client. They may not know the nature of their impact until months after the conclusion of a therapeutic relationship, if then.

Dealing with difficult clients

To a beginning counselor, almost every client seems difficult, in part because any counselor wants to succeed and needs to see signs of progress in the client. Even for experienced counselors, however, there are genuinely difficult clients. Some of these clients pose particular problems that tend to come up fairly often in a counseling practice. As we describe each of these clients, allow yourself to imagine that you are their counselor. What kinds of feelings and thoughts do they evoke in you? How do you imagine you would deal with each one?

Silent clients.   The silent client is particularly troublesome for beginning counselors, who may interpret a client's silence as evidence that they aren't using the "right technique." For some counselors, a silent moment in a therapeutic session may seem to last an hour. Out of their anxiety they may employ a barrage of questions in an attempt to get the client to open up. Or they may break silences with noisy chatter because of their own discomfort and fail to pursue what the silence means.

Although silence *may* be an indication that the sessions are not very fruitful, there are some distinct values to silence, and counselors need to learn that silence can have many meanings. The client may be waiting for the therapist to initiate a direction, particularly if the therapist has developed a style of asking many questions, making suggestions, or otherwise taking major responsibility for the sessions. The client may be quietly thinking or simply allowing himself or herself to experience some feelings aroused by the session. The client may feel stuck and not know what to say next or feel bored and anxious for the session to end. Both client and therapist may be resisting moving to a deeper level of interaction. Thus, silence may or may not be counterproductive, and it's important to explore the particular meaning of silence in each instance. You might ask yourself: How do I generally respond to long silences? Am I able to communicate with another person through silence as well as through words? What would I be likely to do if a client habitually said very little?

Overly demanding clients.   Overly demanding clients are especially troublesome for counselors who feel that their function is to meet all the demands of their clients. Because they perceive themselves as helpers, they might convince themselves that they should give unselfishly, regardless of the nature of the demands made upon them. They may therefore have difficulty dealing with clients who call them at home to talk at length about ever-present crises, or who want to be seen more frequently, or who become so dependent that they need to be told what to do at every turn. Such clients may insist that, if their counselors really cared for them, they would be more "giving." Counselors can easily become entangled with such clients and not know how to extricate themselves. Out of a sense of guilt, or out of a failure to be assertive in setting realistic limits, they may allow themselves to be controlled by excessive demands.

If you've had some counseling experience, review any experiences you've had with overly demanding clients. What were some of the demands that were placed upon you? In what ways were these demands unrealistic or unreasonable? Do you find that you're able to set reasonable limits? Are you able to make demands for yourself?

In dealing with overly demanding clients, you may have to work through your own need to be needed. An extremely dependent client who continually tells you that you're indispensable is relating to you as a child to a parent. It's easy to keep this kind of client dependent on you, so that you can continue to feel needed. You might convince yourself that you're expected to be available to your clients at all times, while ignoring the benefit you obtain from being needed.

Unmotivated clients. Some clients have little investment in their counseling or little motivation to change in any significant way. Perhaps their main motivation for being in counseling is that someone else thought it would be a good idea. Again, counselors need to be alert to the dangers of allowing themselves to be perpetually drawn into games with their clients. If you find that you're doing most of the work and that you seem to care more about some clients than they care about themselves, you have good reason to believe that your own needs, not those of your clients, are being served.

We have discussed only a few examples of clients who may pose special problems for you. What other kinds of clients might be "difficult clients" for you? How do you see yourself reacting to them?

_____

_____

_____

_____

_____

_____

_____

Learning your limits

All counselors are faced with the task of learning their limits, which includes recognizing that they aren't going to succeed with every client. Even experienced therapists sometimes doubt their effectiveness with clients they just can't seem to reach. For new counselors, the inability to reach a client can be even more threatening, particularly since it's easy to believe at first that they should be able to work effectively with any client. Many beginning counselors tell themselves that they should like all the people who come to them for help or that they should be willing to work with anyone.

It takes courage as well as wisdom to admit that you can't work effectively with everyone. You might work well with children but have real problems in trying to understand adolescents. Or you might be very close to certain children but feel removed and distant from others. Some counselors find meaning in working with the elderly, whereas others become depressed and discouraged. At some point you may need to consider whether it's better to accept a client you feel you cannot relate to or to admit to the client that another counselor would be more suitable.

Ask yourself what kinds of clients you would most like to work with and what kinds of clients you would least like to work with. Then it might be useful to look honestly at some of your motivations for preferring certain clients over others. Do you want only those clients whom you feel comfortable with or who promise the greatest hope of success, or are you willing to endure some level of discomfort as you learn to work with a greater range of people? Are you able to admit to yourself and to your prospective clients that you don't *have* to succeed with everyone?

Clients I would find the easiest to work with:

_____

_____

_____

_____

Clients I would have the most trouble working with:

_____

_____

_____

_____

On demanding perfection

Many counselors burden themselves with the belief that they must be perfect—that they must always know the appropriate thing to say or do, must never make mistakes, and must always have the skill needed to deal with any kind of counseling situation. Yet the fact is that all of us, new or experienced, are going to make mistakes. We fail to do our clients justice when we think of them as being so fragile that they will fall apart if we make mistakes. By overemphasizing the importance of avoiding mistakes, we diminish our clients' role in working toward their own decisions. Furthermore, if most of our energies go into presenting the image of the polished professional, we have little energy left for actually working with the client. Perhaps this is where the client is really cheated. It's hard to conceive of a genuine therapeutic relationship growing from such a situation.

A practicum in which you're getting supervision and have an opportunity to discuss your work might be a good place to bring up the issue of perfection. Sometimes students involved in group supervision are reluctant to talk about their inadequacies for fear of what their peers or instructors will think. It can take a good deal of ego strength to be willing to share your mistakes and apprehensions. It isn't easy to say: "I'd like some time to talk about the difficulties I'm having with one of my clients. Our relationship is stirring up a lot of feelings in me at this point, and I'm not sure how to proceed." Although it does take courage to ask for others' perceptions and feedback, this is an excellent way to learn not only about how to proceed with the client but also about your own dynamics. In this connection, you might ask yourself the following questions:

1. Am I reluctant to use my practicum (group supervision) sessions to talk freely about what I'm experiencing as I work with certain clients? If so, what is holding me back?

   _____

   _____

   _____

2. If I feel insecure about making mistakes and about how I'll be perceived by my instructor and my peers, am I willing to share my insecurities with them? If not, what is holding me back?

   _____

   _____

   _____

3. What are some specific insecurities that I'd be willing to explore with fellow students and an instructor or supervisor?

   _____

   _____

   _____

Self-disclosure and being yourself

Many counselors, regardless of their years of experience, struggle with the issue of how much self-disclosure is appropriate in their counseling. It is not uncommon to be guilty of either extreme—disclosing too little or disclosing too much.

Excessive self-disclosure: Denying your professional role. Most beginning counselors (and many experienced ones) have a need to be approved of by their clients. It's easy for these counselors to engage in the sharing of intimate details so that their clients will perceive them as being human. They may talk about themselves a great deal, regardless of how appropriate their self-disclosure is for a given client, in the hope that their openness about their private lives will encourage their clients to trust them and share more of themselves.

Counselors who engage in excessive self-disclosure are often trying to avoid getting lost in a professionally aloof role. Some of these counselors would rather be seen as a friend than as a professional with specialized helping skills, and some use the client/counselor relationship to explore their own needs. The danger of this approach is that a pseudo-realness can develop out of their need to be seen as human. Trying too hard to prove their humanness, they may not only fail to be authentic but also limit their potential effectiveness. When therapists disclose detailed stories about themselves, they take the focus away from the client. Although they are supposedly sharing their problems and experiences for the benefit of their clients, more often than not such sharing serves their own needs.

Van Hoose and Kottler (1977) admit that self-disclosure by the therapist has many values, but they caution that there is a fine distinction between appropriate, timely self-disclosure and self-disclosure that serves the therapist's own needs. They contend that, whenever therapists take the focus off their clients and put it on themselves, they are in danger of abusing their clients. They put the issue bluntly:

> Whenever the therapist engages in long-winded stories or anecdotes irrelevant to the client's pressing concern, he is keeping the focus on himself and acting unethically. Each and every time that the therapist takes the focus off the client and puts it on himself he is wasting valuable time in the interview and negating the client's importance [p. 61].

Self-disclosure on the part of the counselor need not be excessive, however. Facilitative disclosure, which is hard for many of us to learn, enhances the therapeutic process. It admits the client into the therapist's private world when to do so is relevant and timely within the context of the therapeutic relationship. Appropriate disclosure can focus on the reactions of the therapist to the client in the here-and-now encounter between them. With a few words, and sometimes even nonverbally, the therapist can express feelings of identification and understanding. The focus thus remains on the client, and the self-disclosure is not a contrived technique to get the client to open up. Appropriate self-disclosure is one way of being yourself without trying to prove your humanity to the point of being inauthentic or serving your own needs at the expense of the client. At this point, take some time to reflect on the following questions and on your own criteria for determining whether your self-disclosure is facilitative. You might bring these questions up for class discussion:

- How important is it to you that your clients like you?
- How much of your outside life are you willing to make known to your clients? For what reasons would you reveal your personal life?
- How might your clients be helped or hindered when you talk about yourself?
- How do you decide whether to share your personal reactions and feelings, positive and negative, concerning the client and your relationship?
- Would you tell a client that you were finding it difficult to concentrate on him or her during a particular session if you were in turmoil over some personal matter of your own? Why or why not?

Too little self-disclosure: Hiding behind your professional role.   If some counselors go to the extreme of denying their professional role in order to be seen as friendly and human, some go to the opposite extreme. They hide themselves behind professional facades, becoming so caught up in maintaining stereotyped role expectations that they let little of themselves show in their interactions. Perhaps out of a fear of appearing unprofessional or otherwise losing the respect of their clients, they tend to keep their personal reactions out of the counseling session. Consider for a moment whether it's possible to perform your functions as a professional without being aloof and impersonal. Is it possible that the more insecure, frightened, and uncertain you are in your professional work, the more you will tend to cling to the defense afforded by a professional image?

We believe that "professional" aloofness may stem from unrealistic expectations that some counselors have concerning their role in therapy. Trying to live up to these expectations neither helps clients nor fosters your own growth. Consider the following statements, and check the ones that describe your expectations of yourself:

___ I should always know what to say and do in a counseling session, for I need to appear competent if I am to earn the trust of my clients.

___ I should always care for my clients, and I should care for all of them equally.

___ I should like and enjoy my clients; I must be all-accepting, all-understanding, and fully empathic.

___ To be an effective counselor, I must have everything "together" in my own life; any indication that I have personal problems diminishes my effectiveness.

___ I should be able to figure out what my clients want and need, even if they don't know themselves or don't reveal their wants and needs to me. Further, I should be able to provide them with solutions to their problems.

___ I must remain neutral and objective at all times and avoid having personal feelings and reactions toward my clients.

We believe that these kinds of notions concerning what it means to be a professional lead counselors to hide behind professional facades instead of being themselves in a nonmechanical and real way. By accepting these and other lofty standards, counselors end up playing roles that aren't always congruent with the way they feel. In moments of uncertainty with clients, they may act all-knowing; if they find it difficult to care about or like certain clients, they may deny their negative feelings by focusing on positive ones; if they feel disinterested or bored, they may try to force themselves to pay attention. If you find that you tend to adopt an inauthentic professional role, you might ask yourself whether you can realistically expect your clients to shed inauthentic behavior and become increasingly genuine with themselves and with you. After all, what kind of behavior are you modeling for your clients if you fail to be authentic with them?

Sidney Jourard (1971) makes a helpful distinction between hiding behind professional roles (which is undesirable) and being a person who plays many roles (which is inevitable). He points to the fact that, when we get lost in our roles, we become alienated from ourselves. For Jourard, one of the major roles of therapists is to be transparent with their clients, at least with respect to their experiences in the counseling relationship. This kind of authenticity is basic to effective psychotherapy, he argues, because it offers the possibility of a genuine encounter between therapist and client. Clients will not be fooled if therapists attempt to hide their basic feelings by resorting to expert techniques: "Patients are seldom that insensitive. Moreover, if a therapist thus hides his being, he is engaging in the same inauthentic behavior that generated symptoms in the patient, and supposedly, he is trying to undo this self-alienating process" (p. 148).

Pause a moment now to consider specific kinds of feelings that you would *not* be willing to disclose to your clients. Why would you be unwilling to make these disclosures? Think also about the kinds of feelings and experiences you can see yourself sharing with your clients.

Self-deception

Even with the best of intentions and motives, both counselors and clients can fall prey to the phenomenon of self-deception. Self-deception occurs in subtle ways and is not to be confused with conscious lying. The client and the therapist both want to see productive results come out of the therapeutic relationship, and both may convince themselves that what they are doing is worthwhile, regardless of the reality. Let's consider client self-deception first.

It's safe to assume that people who are clients by choice have an investment in experiencing positive changes. They are committing themselves financially and emotionally to a relationship in the hopes that they will experience less conflict, feel better about themselves, get along with others better, and feel more in charge of their own lives. Given these kinds of expectations and the personal investment involved, there is always the possibility that clients will overestimate what they are really getting from counseling. Some may have to feel they are benefiting in order to justify the personal sacrifices they are making to obtain counseling. In failing to be open to the reality of the situation, however, they render the counseling experience less effective.

Counselor self-deception sometimes operates in subtle ways to reinforce the self-deception of clients. Counselors, too, have an investment in seeing their clients make progress. Less experienced counselors, in particular, may find it very hard to tolerate periods in which their clients seem to make little progress or actually seem to regress. Counselors whose egos are heavily invested in a successful outcome may not want their clients to talk about their ambivalent feelings concerning the value of their counseling. Similarly, if counselors need to feel that they are solving problems and "straightening out" their clients, they are likely to be less skeptical than they should be in evaluating therapeutic outcomes. Although there is no sure-fire method of avoiding self-deception, being aware of the hazard may lessen the chance that you'll "see" nonexistent results in order to satisfy your expectations and those of your clients. As a way of exploring how self-deception can arise in counseling, consider the following questions:

- How would you feel if several of your clients complained that they weren't really getting anywhere? How would you respond?
- How would you be affected if you couldn't detect any signs of progress with a client?

Dealing with transference and countertransference

As you become involved in the practice of counseling or psychotherapy, you will inevitably have to come to grips with issues relating to transference and countertransference, even though you may not use these terms. It is beyond the scope of this book to deal with these topics in great detail, but we do encourage you to think about how you can deal with the feelings clients may direct toward you and the feelings you may have toward certain clients. We believe that counselors' handling of these feelings has a direct bearing on therapeutic outcomes.

Transference.   *Transference* refers to the unconscious process whereby clients project onto their therapists past feelings or attitudes toward significant people in their lives. The concept of transference stems from psychoanalysis, which stresses clients' unrecognized or unresolved feelings concerning past relationships, but the phenomenon is not restricted to psychoanalytic therapy.

In transference, a client's unfinished business produces a distortion in the way he or she perceives the therapist. The feelings that are experienced in transference may be positive or negative; they may include love, anger, affection, hate, dependence, ambivalence, and others. The essential point is that they are connected with the past but are now directed toward the therapist.

The therapeutic value of transference is that it allows clients to express distorted feelings without getting the response they expect. This is the crucial difference between the therapy and their past experience. If a client is treating the therapist as a stern and rejecting parent, the therapist does not respond with the expected defensive and negative feelings. Instead, the therapist accepts the client's feelings and helps the client understand them. As Brammer and Shostrom (1982) explain, "The general principle here is that counselors should not fit themselves into the client's projections, so as to satisfy the client's neurotic needs. If the counselor fulfills the client's expectations, there is the possibility they will be perpetuated by virtue of having been reinforced" (p. 219).

There are various viewpoints on the place of transference in therapy. Some therapeutic approaches view transference as the very core of the process, and others tend to ignore it as an issue. From the psychoanalytic perspective, transference is an essential part of the therapeutic process. Thus, Alexander (1956) writes, "The principal therapeutic tool is transference, in which the patient relives, in relationship to the therapist, his earlier interpersonal conflicts. Regression to the dependent attitude of infancy and childhood is a constant feature of the transference, and in the majority of cases, the central one" (p. 193). For psychoanalysts, transference allows clients to relive their past in therapy, using the therapeutic relationship to work through unresolved emotional conflicts. In this way, they can counteract the effects of early painful experiences and achieve insight into how the past interferes with their present functioning.

In contrast to the psychoanalytic view, Rollo May (1967) warns that too much emphasis on transference as a reenactment of past relationships can detract from the meaning of the client's present encounter with the therapist. Transference, May argues, can become an intellectualized notion that therapists hide behind in order to avoid the intensity of personal encounters with their clients.

For Corlis and Rabe (1969) transference is a special case of resistance. They argue that, if it does occur and is worked out, a new and different relationship develops between client and therapist. After transference feelings are explored, the client no longer treats the therapist as a "repository of past experiences" but as a separate human being that he or she is discovering anew: "The distortions of past conditioning drop away, and the interpersonal relationship begins to rest on existential grounds" (pp. 95–96).

Rogers (1951) contends that transference, in the psychoanalytic sense of the term, does not tend to develop in the client-centered therapy he espouses. As he puts it, "If the definition being used is the transfer of infantile attitudes to a present relationship in which they are inappropriate, then very little if any transference is present" (p. 200).

In writing on the place of transference in Reality Therapy, William Glasser (1965) also rejects the psychoanalytic view that the relationship between client and therapist should involve a reexperiencing of past attitudes and feelings. For Glasser, the client's relationship with the therapist is based on the here-and-now: "Psychiatric patients are not seeking to repeat unsuccessful involvements, past or present; they are looking for a satisfying human involvement through which they can fulfill their needs now" (p. 52).

Some writers argue that concepts such as transference can be used by therapists to protect and control their clients. Steinzor (1967), for example, cites the tendency of many therapists to deflect a client's criticism by formulating elaborate concepts to explain it as a manifestation of the client's irrational and unconscious aggression. In this context, he makes a point that anyone involved in the helping professions should consider: "Any approach to a patient is potentially wicked which places the person in an inferior position and constantly emphasizes his weakness and relative lack of power" (p. 138).

Even if transference is viewed as a real and significant phenomenon in therapy, it should be recognized that it is not a catch-all intended to explain every feeling that clients express toward their therapists. For example, if a client expresses anger toward you, it may be justified. If you haven't been truly present for the client, responding instead in a mechanical fashion, your client may be expressing legitimate anger and disappointment. Similarly, if a client expresses affection toward you, these feelings may be genuine; simply dismissing them as infantile fantasies can be a way of putting distance between yourself and your client. Of course, most of us would probably be less likely to interpret positive feelings as distortions aimed at us in a symbolic fashion than we would negative feelings. It is possible, then, for therapists to err in either direction—to be too quick to explain away negative feelings or too willing to accept whatever clients tell them, particularly when they are hearing how loving, wise, perceptive, or attractive they are. In order to understand the real import of clients' expressions of feelings, therapists must actively work at being open, vulnerable, and honest with themselves. Although they should be aware of the possibility of transference, they should also be aware of the danger of discounting the genuine reactions their clients have toward them.

Transference can be worked with in a therapeutic fashion, with the result of fostering the client's awareness and ability to change. It can also be a barrier to the client/therapist relationship, and if transference feelings are not dealt with skillfully, the result can be increased dependency on the client's part. Brammer and Shostrom (1982) discuss the following points related to the therapeutic value of working with transference:

• The client/therapist relationship can be improved if the client is encouraged to express distorted feelings without defensive reactions from the counselor. In everyday life, people often respond from their projections. If the therapist does not respond with countertransference feelings, however, the client is able to explore his or her projections.

• Clients are likely to develop more trust and confidence in their counselor through the sensitive and effective handling of transference in therapy.

• Transference can enable clients to become aware of the origin and meaning of certain feelings in their lives now, through the process of interpretation.

• By exploring some of their distorted reactions toward their therapist, clients are in a position to realize that all men are not like their fathers and that all women are not like their mothers. The process frees them to respond to people in new ways. They are not tied to rigid perceptions from their childhood if they are able to successfully work through transference in therapy.

We will now present a series of brief, open-ended cases in which we ask you to imagine yourself as the therapist. How do you think you would respond to each client? What are your own reactions?

Your client, Sharon, seems extremely dependent upon you for advice in making even minor decisions. It is apparent that she doesn't trust herself and often tries to figure out what you might do in her place. She asks you personal questions about your marriage, how you get along with your children, and so forth. Evidently she has elevated you to the position of one who has it "all together" and is trying to emulate you in every way. At other times Sharon tells you that, whenever she tries to make her own decisions, they turn out badly. Consequently, when faced with a decision, she vacillates and becomes filled with self-doubt. Although she claims to realize that you cannot give her "the" answer, she keeps asking you what you think about her decisions.

- Would you be inclined to give Sharon advice by telling her what you think she should do? If not, what would you say to her?
- How would you respond to Sharon's questions about your private life?
- Would you explore her past reactions to important people in her life in order to determine how she developed her dependence and lack of self-trust? Why or why not?
- How would you feel about her desire to emulate you? If many of your clients expressed this desire, do you think you might come to believe that what they said about you was true? How might this belief affect your counseling?

Gayle expresses unrealistic expectations about what you "should" be for her. She tells you that you should be more available to her, that you should give more than you're giving, that you don't care for her in the way that she would like you to, and that you should be far more accepting of her feelings.

- How would you deal with Gayle's unrealistic expectations?
- How would you convince her that her demands were unrealistic? Or would you?

Carl seems to treat you as an authority figure. He once said that you were always judging him and that he was reluctant to say very much because you would consider everything he said to be foolish. Although he has not confronted you directly since then, you sense many digs and other signs of hostility. On the surface, however, Carl seems to be trying very hard to please you by telling you what he thinks you want to hear. He seems convinced that you will react negatively and aggressively if he tells you what he really thinks.

- How would you feel toward Carl?
- How might you deal with his indirect expression of hostility?
- How might you encourage him to express his feelings and work through them?

Countertransference.   So far we have focused on transference and the feelings of clients toward their therapists, but therapists also have emotional reactions to their clients, some of which may involve their own projections. *Countertransference* occurs when a therapist's own needs become entangled in the therapeutic relationship, obstructing or destroying his or her objectivity. Countertransference can be manifested in a number of ways, some of which we will now discuss.

1. *The need for constant reinforcement and approval* can be a source of countertransference. Just as clients may develop an excessive need to please their therapists in order to feel liked and valued, so too therapists may have an inordinate need of reassurance concerning their effectiveness. Ellis (1973) contends that therapists must be willing to let go of the irrational idea that their clients must think well of them. They need to challenge and confront their clients' irrational and self-defeating thinking, and they can do so only if they are willing to risk their clients' disapproval.

- Do you feel you need to have the approval of your clients? How willing are you to confront them even at the risk of being disliked?
- If you have some counseling experience, what is your style of confronting a client? Do you tend to confront certain kinds of clients more than others? What does this tell you about you as a therapist?

2. *Seeing yourself in your clients* is another form of countertransference. This is not to say that feeling close to a client and identifying with that person's struggle is necessarily an instance of countertransference. However, one of the problems many beginning therapists have is that they identify with clients' problems to the point that they lose their objectivity. They become so lost in their clients' worlds that they are unable to separate their feelings from those of their clients. Or they may tend to see in their clients traits that they dislike in themselves.

- Have you ever found yourself so much in sympathy with others that you could no longer be of help to them? What would you do if this were to happen with a client?
- From an awareness of your own dynamics, list some personal traits clients might have that would be most likely to elicit overidentification on your part.

3. One of the common manifestations of transference or countertransference is the development of *sexual or romantic feelings* between clients and therapists. When this kind of transference occurs, therapists can exploit the vulnerable position of their clients, whether consciously or unconsciously. Seductive behavior on the part of a client can easily lead to the adoption of a seductive style by the therapist, particularly if the therapist is unaware of his or her own dynamics and motivations. On the other hand, it's natural for therapists to be attracted to some clients more than to others, and the fact that they have sexual feelings toward some clients does not have to mean that they cannot counsel these clients effectively. More important than the mere existence of such feelings is the manner in which therapists deal with them. Feelings

of attraction can be recognized and even acknowledged frankly without becoming the focus of the therapeutic relationship. The possibility that therapists' sexual feelings and needs might interfere with their work is one important reason why therapists should experience their own therapy when starting to practice and should continue to be willing to consult another professional when they encounter difficulty because of their feelings toward certain clients.

- What do you think you would do if you experienced intense sexual feelings toward a client?
- How would you know if your sexual attraction to a client was countertransference or not?

4. Countertransference can also take the form of *compulsive advice giving*. Many nonprofessionals and even some professionals equate counseling with giving advice. A tendency to give advice can easily be encouraged by clients who are prone to seek immediate answers to ease their suffering. The opportunity to give advice places therapists in a superior, all-knowing position—one that some counselors can easily come to enjoy—and it isn't difficult for therapists to delude themselves into thinking that they do have answers for their clients. They may also begin to give advice because they feel uncomfortable if they're unable to be prescriptive or because they find it difficult to be patient with their clients' struggles toward autonomous decision making.

In all these cases, the needs of the therapist are taking priority over those of the client. Even if a client has asked for advice, there is every reason to question whose needs are being served when therapists fall into advice giving.

- Do you ever find yourself giving advice? What do you think giving advice does for you?
- Are there any times when advice is warranted? If so, when?

5. *A desire to develop social relationships with clients* may stem from countertransference, especially if it is acted upon while therapy is taking place. Occasionally clients let their therapist know that they would like to develop more of a relationship than is possible in the limiting environment of the office. They may, for instance, express a desire to get to know their therapist as "a regular person." Even experienced therapists sometimes must struggle with the question of whether to blend a social relationship with a therapeutic one. When this question arises, therapists should assess whose needs would be met through such a friendship and decide whether effective therapy can coexist with a social relationship. Some questions you might ask yourself in this context are:

- If I establish social relationships with certain clients, will I be as inclined to confront them in therapy as I would be otherwise?
- Will my own needs for preserving these friendships interfere with my therapeutic activities and defeat the purpose of therapy?
- Am I sensitive to being called a "cold professional," even though I may strive to be real and straightforward in the therapeutic situation?

The following items are guidelines for helping you detect some of the possible signs of countertransference. Now reflect on the signs of countertransference listed below. Place a check in the space provided if you have found yourself with the tendency described or if you think you would be vulnerable to it.

_____ I am likely to become overly involved on an emotional level with certain types of clients.

_____ I can see myself fantasizing about some of my clients.

_____ I might find a number of ways to avoid clients who elicited negative feelings in me.

_____ I've had some clients who put me to sleep and some whom I had a very difficult time listening to.

_____ I have found that I make it a practice to begin sessions late (or cut sessions short) with some clients, and I have consistently run overtime with other clients.

_____ I worry that I may have a strong need to give lots of advice and that I will manipulate clients to think and act the way I think they should.

_____ I am concerned that I will bring the problems of certain clients home with me and that I will overidentify with some of my clients.

_____ I can easily imagine myself getting angry and upset over clients who do not appreciate me.

_____ I tend to respond very defensively to certain types of people or certain kinds of statements.

_____ There are some topics that I know I would feel extremely uncomfortable exploring with clients, and I am likely to steer them away from talking about these subjects.

_____ I am concerned that I will assume most of the responsibility if a client does not improve, and I expect that I might work harder in the counseling relationship than most of my clients.

Of course, not every item above indicates the presence of countertransference. Use this checklist as one way to think about some of the ways that your own unresolved problems might intrude in your work as a counselor. Can you think of other ways that you can increase your awareness of your own needs so that they do not get in the way of your effectiveness?

It is impossible to deal adequately here with all the possible nuances of transference and countertransference. In this section we have called attention to some of the ways in which either of these phenomena can militate against good therapeutic outcomes. Although transference can be used to help the client achieve insight, both transference and countertransference can work against the best interests of the client. Certainly, therapists must be prepared to recognize and deal with these phenomena. A high degree of self-awareness and a relative freedom from unfinished business are the therapist's best protection.

Counselor burn-out

Counselor burn-out is receiving a great deal of attention at professional conferences and conventions. Many people in the helping professions find that they grow tired and lose the energy and enthusiasm they once experienced in their work. They talk of feeling drained, empty, and fragmented by the pull of many different projects.

Since burn-out is an occupational hazard that most professional helpers face at one time or another, it is important to be prepared for it. Burn-out can rob you of the vitality you need if you are to communicate hope and provide healthy modeling for your clients.

Professional helpers need to see that what they do is worthwhile; yet the nature of their profession is such that they often don't see immediate or concrete results. This lack of reinforcement can have a debilitating effect as counselors begin to wonder whether anything they do makes a difference to anyone. The danger of burn-out is all the greater if they practice in isolation, have little interchange with fellow professionals, or fail to seek an explanation of their feelings of deadness.

To offset this hazard, many professionals find other ways to experience a sense of productivity and freshness. At a recent conference on counselor burn-out and self-renewal, professionals from the audience shared some of the ways in which they kept their sense of aliveness. Some found satisfaction in making things with their hands. Some taught special-interest courses at local colleges or offered workshops. Others found renewal in writing about their professional interests or in attending conventions and workshops where they had a chance to share ideas and experiences with colleagues. Still others reported that they needed to separate themselves completely from their work at times, perhaps by traveling to new and different places.

In a workshop on death and dying, Dr. Elisabeth Kübler-Ross indicated that she found working with dying patients to be demanding and draining. Consequently, instead of devoting herself full-time to this work, she spent part of her time giving lectures and workshops for other professionals. Sharing her specialized talents with others in the field provided her with a sense of freshness and vitality and kept her from becoming overly taxed emotionally by the demands of her specialty.

In our own consulting practice, the three of us encounter mental-health workers who claim to be suffering from burn-out. We find that, when we visit a hospital for several days at a time as consultants, we need to take precautions to prevent ourselves from becoming depressed and cynical. For one thing, the three of us decided to split the stipend and to work as a team, because we were very aware that doing this kind of work alone would have been extremely taxing. Although working as a team reduced our individual financial rewards, the benefits of mutual support and the exchange of ideas far outweighed these financial losses. Each trip to the hospital took a great deal of energy from us, so we had to find ways to retain our enthusiasm. Before each consulting job, we spent some personal time as a team in getting psychologically ready. This included talking about the details of our upcoming workshop. Equally important was the time that we spent debriefing each day and again at the end of the workshop.

Even though our consulting in the hospital was demanding, it was also exciting and challenging. We gained from this experience both personally and professionally. It was especially rewarding when we heard from some of the staff members that our workshops had been instrumental in bringing some life back to them and had encouraged them to trust themselves more fully by trying out new ideas. As we saw that we were having some impact on the attitudes of these staff members, our excitement increased, giving us the incentive to continue this type of consulting.

We will come back to the subject of burn-out in Chapter 8 when we discuss ways of staying alive personally and professionally while working in a system.

Fragmentation

Fragmentation is a problem that is closely related to burn-out. People may feel that they're doing too much in too little time and not doing justice to any of their activities. Or they may feel as if they're here, there, and everywhere but at the same time nowhere. Some of the factors that can lead to a sense of fragmentation are driving great distances to and from work or from one appointment to another; never taking a break between involvements in different activities; taking on diverse and sometimes conflicting commitments; being swamped with paper work; and attending innumerable meetings. Although we suggested earlier that a way to prevent burn-out is to introduce some diversity into your work, there is also the danger of becoming overextended—pulled in so many different directions that you lose all sense of yourself. At such times you may feel that there is little time between activities and that one experience seems to blur into the next.

Counselors who begin to feel fragmented should stop to ask themselves such questions as these: What effect is my work having on my clients and me? Am I merely doing chores that have been assigned to me and that give me little sense of accomplishment? If I'm in an administrative position, how willing am I to delegate responsibility to others? Do I need to have a finger in every pie?

Fragmentation is especially likely to be a problem in institutional settings, where many demands are made on professionals that have little to do with counseling expertise. Counselors in such settings who begin to feel fragmented might need to ask questions like the following:

- Am I so conscious of my security in the system that I never make any waves?
- Am I so convinced that I'm the only one capable of doing the work that I never delegate any of it?
- Do I take on work that is beyond my ability to do?
- Do I ever ask myself whether I'm doing what I really want to do?
- Do I ever say no?

Fragmentation is often a problem for beginning counselors, who may spread themselves thinner than they might wish in order to make a living. However, like burn-out, fragmentation is an issue that can be handled only by counselors themselves. They are their own monitors; they need to pay attention to their internal workings and decide on their own limits.

Some Suggestions for Further Reading

If you want to pursue the topic of professional burn-out, the following references are suggested: Pines and Aronson, 1981; Edelwich with Brodsky, 1980; Warnath, 1979; and Farber and Heifetz, 1982.

For those of you who want to read more about the personal and professional dimensions of the counselor, we recommend these sources: Jourard, 1968 and 1971; Rogers, 1961 and 1980; Maslow, 1968 and 1970; May, 1967; and Corey, 1983.

Chapter summary

In this chapter, we've discussed one of the most basic issues in the practice of therapy and counseling—the counselor's own personality as an instrument in therapeutic practice. We have stressed the idea that counselors might possess knowledge and technical skills and still be ineffective in significantly reaching clients. Our belief is that the life experiences, values, attitudes, and caring that counselors bring to their therapy sessions are crucial factors in the establishment of effective therapeutic relationships.

We have also discussed a broad range of issues related to the professional identity of counselors. They do not by any means represent an exhaustive list. However, by reflecting on these issues now, you may be better able to recognize and struggle with these and related questions as you grow in your chosen profession. We have tried to emphasize that you may need to review your resolutions of these issues periodically throughout your career. This kind of openness and honest self-appraisal is an essential quality of those who wish to be effective helpers.

Activities, exercises, and ideas for thought and discussion

These activities and questions are designed to help you apply your learnings to practice. Many of them can profitably be done alone in a personal way or with another person; others can be done in the classroom as discussion activities, either with the whole class or in small groups. We suggest that you select those that seem most significant to you and do some writing on these issues in your journal. Many of these questions are ones that prospective employers ask during job interviews. Practicing answering these questions can help you clarify your thinking and your positions, which in the long run could help you land a job.

1. In small groups in your class, explore the issue of why you're going into a helping profession. This is a basic issue, and one that many students have trouble putting into concrete words. What motivated you to seek this type of work? What do you think you can get for yourself? What do you see yourself as being able to do for others?

2. What personal needs do you have that may be met by counseling others? To what degree do you think that they might get in the way of your work with clients? How can you recognize and meet your needs—which are a real part of you—without having them interfere with your work with others?

3. After you've thought through the preceding question, form small groups in your class and discuss how counselors can take care of their needs without impinging on the welfare of their clients. Unfortunately, too many beginning counselors believe that it's wrong to have personal needs and try too hard to keep their needs out of counseling. Explore this issue with your fellow students.

4. What are some of the major problems you expect to be faced with as a beginning counselor? What are some of your most pressing concerns?

5. Do you experience anxiety when you think of working with clients? Do you worry about what you will say or do or whether you'll be of any help to your client? How do you deal with your anxiety?

6. Do you demand perfection from yourself? Can you risk making mistakes, or do you play it safe for fear of seeming incompetent?

7. What kind of results would you look for in working with clients? How would you determine the answers to such questions as: Is the counseling doing any good? Is my intervention helping my client make the changes he or she wants to make? How effective are my techniques?

8. Do you demand instant results? What happens to you if you don't get immediate feedback?

9. Think of the type of client you might have the most difficulty working with. Then become this client in a role-playing fantasy with one other student. Your partner attempts to counsel with you. After you've had a chance to be the client, change roles and become the counselor. Your partner then becomes the type of client you just role-played.

10. In dyads, explore the reasons you would have for experiencing a client as difficult. For instance, if you would find it hard to work with a hostile and aggressive client, explore the feelings that you imagine you'd experience in working with such a client. Have your partner give you feedback; then switch roles.

11. In subgroups, explore the issue of how willing you are to be self-disclosing to your clients. Discuss the guidelines you would use to determine the appropriateness of self-disclosure. What are some areas you would feel hesitant about sharing? How valuable do you think it is to share yourself in a personal way with your clients? What are some of your fears or resistances about making yourself known to your clients?

12. In subgroups, discuss some possible causes of professional burn-out. Then examine specific ways that you could deal with this problem. After you've explored this issue in small groups, reconvene as a class and make a list of the causes and solutions that your groups have come up with.

13. In dyads, one person assumes the role of the therapist, the other of a client whom the therapist doesn't like. Role-play a session in which the therapist informs the client of his or her feelings. Afterwards, discuss how each of you experienced the interaction. The purpose of the exercise is to give you practice in dealing with *your own* feelings when you work with clients you don't like.

14. In small groups, discuss how you might behave toward a client who evoked strong feelings in you. For example, how might you deal with a client who reminded you of your father? Your mother? A sibling? A former spouse?

15. Do you see it as a danger that you could be lulled into self-deception by believing everything that your clients see in you? For instance, if clients keep telling you that you have it "all together," might you begin to see yourself in ways that you'd like to be but actually are not?

Suggested readings

Corey, G. (in collaboration with M. S. Corey). *I never knew I had a choice* (2nd ed.). Monterey, Calif.: Brooks/Cole, 1983. Written from an existential viewpoint, this book is for those interested in the psychology of personal growth. It has applications for therapeutic practice and deals with choices pertaining to human themes such as autonomy, body image, love, sex, sex roles, intimacy, marriage and other intimate relationships, loneliness and solitude, death and loss, the search for meaning, values, and a philosophy to live by. The book contains many exercises and activities for personal reflection on choices and has numerous annotated suggestions for further reading in each of the areas explored.

Goldberg, C. *Therapeutic partnership: Ethical concerns in psychotherapy.* New York: Springer, 1977. This book presents an ethically enlightened approach to the practice of psychotherapy based on informed consent and psychological contracts. It deals with two major themes—the search for an understanding of human existence through therapeutic encounter and the collaborative endeavors of client and therapist in establishing a therapeutic partnership. It has implications for the counselor both as a person and as a professional.

Jourard, S. *The transparent self* (Rev. ed.). New York: Van Nostrand, 1971. Jourard has many provocative things to say about the role of the therapist and the importance of self-disclosure. He also deals with sex roles, education, drugs, privacy, encounter groups, and other professional issues. This personal book contains plenty of material for self-reflection, as well as perspectives on professional practice.

Pines, A., & Aronson, E. (with D. Kafry). *Burnout: From tedium to personal growth.* New York: Free Press, 1981. This book provides a fairly comprehensive and interesting treatment of this popular topic. The authors discuss the nature and causes of burn-out, its impact on the helping professional and on organizations, and ideas for what to do about this ever-present problem facing professional helpers.

Rogers, C. *A way of being.* Boston: Houghton Mifflin, 1980. In this highly readable collection of essays, Rogers presents a sample of writings dealing with his personal experiences and perspectives. He writes about new challenges to the helping professions, his philosophy of interpersonal relationships, and future trends in the counseling field. He has a way of capturing a reader's interest and challenging counselors to look at their own lives if they hope to work effectively with others.

Yalom, I. D. *Existential psychotherapy.* New York: Basic Books, 1980. In a book rich with clinical examples of clients engaged in life struggles in the therapy relationship, Yalom provides an in-depth discussion of key existential themes as they relate to the practice of psychotherapy (death, freedom, existential isolation, and meaninglessness). This is highly recommended for the counselor's personal and professional development.

Values and the Therapeutic Process

Pre-chapter self-inventory

Directions: For each statement, indicate the response that most closely identifies your beliefs and attitudes. Use the following code:

5 = I *strongly agree* with this statement.
4 = I *agree*, in most respects, with this statement.
3 = I am *undecided* in my opinion about this statement.
2 = I *disagree*, in most respects, with this statement.
1 = I *strongly disagree* with this statement.

____ 1. It is both possible and desirable for counselors to remain neutral and keep their values from influencing clients.

____ 2. Counselors should influence clients to adopt values that seem to be in the clients' best interests.

____ 3. It is appropriate for counselors to express their values, as long as they don't try to impose them on clients.

____ 4. The search for meaningful values is a central part of psychotherapy.

____ 5. Counselors should challenge clients to make value judgments regarding their own behavior.

____ 6. I can work only with clients whose value systems are similar to my own.

____ 7. Before I can effectively counsel a person, I have to decide whether our life experiences are similar enough that I'll be able to understand that person.

____ 8. The clarification of values is a major part of the counseling process.

____ 9. I could work effectively with people who had certain values that I did not respect.

____ 10. I might be inclined to subtly influence my clients to consider my values.

____ 11. I consider it my job to challenge my clients' philosophies of life.

____ 12. I have a clear idea of what I value and where I acquired my values.

____ 13. I tend to continually question my own values.

——— 14. I see myself as open and receptive to people whose values are different from mine.

——— 15. I tend to be intolerant of people who think very differently from the way I do.

——— 16. I see part of the counseling task as teaching clients a more effective way of living.

——— 17. I see my values as the lenses through which I view the world.

——— 18. If a client indicated that he or she was considering suicide, I would see it as my ethical and legal responsibility to prevent this course of action in *all* cases.

——— 19. Ultimately, I think, the choice of living or dying rests with my clients, and therefore I do not have the right to persuade them to make a different choice.

——— 20. As a counselor, it is my job to challenge sex-role stereotypes when they become obvious in counseling situations.

——— 21. I see myself as willing to examine my behavior and attitudes to determine the degree to which sex bias might influence the interventions I make with clients.

——— 22. I am in agreement with those writers who emphasize the need for special guidelines for counseling women.

——— 23. I think that I have an ethical obligation to continually ask myself what types of clients I am unable to effectively work with, and to seek referral in such cases.

——— 24. Ethnic and cultural differences must be taken into account whenever counselors work with clients of a different race or cultural background.

——— 25. Ethical practice demands that counselors become familiar with the various value systems of diverse cultural groups.

Introduction

The question of values permeates the therapeutic process. This chapter is intended to stimulate your thinking about your values and life experiences and the influence they will have on your counseling. We ask you to consider the possible impact of your values on those of your clients, the effect your clients' values will have on you, and the conflicts that may arise when you and your client have different values.

Perhaps the most fundamental question we can raise about values in the therapeutic process is whether it is possible for counselors to keep their values out of their counseling sessions. In our view, it is neither possible nor desirable for counselors to be scrupulously neutral with respect to values in the counseling relationship. Although we don't see the counselor's function as persuading clients to accept a certain value system, we do think it's crucial for counselors to be clear about their own values and how they influence their work and the directions taken by their clients. Since we believe that counselors' values do inevitably affect the therapeutic process, we also think it's important for counselors to be willing to express their values openly when they are relevant to the questions that come up in their sessions with clients.

Not everyone who practices counseling or psychotherapy would agree with this position. At one extreme, some counselors who have definite, absolute value systems believe that their job is to exert influence on clients to adopt their values. These counselors tend to direct their clients toward the attitudes and behaviors that *they* judge to be in their clients' best interests. At the other extreme are the counselors who are so anxious to avoid influencing their clients that they immobilize themselves. They keep themselves and their values hidden so that they won't contaminate their clients' choices. We'd like to comment briefly on each of these extremes.

First, we don't view counseling as a form of indoctrination; nor do we believe that the therapist's function is to teach clients the right way to live. We think it's unfortunate that some well-intentioned counselors believe that their job is to help people conform to socially acceptable standards or to straighten out their clients. It seems arrogant to suppose that counselors know what's best for others. We question the implication that counselors have greater wisdom than their clients and can prescribe ways of being happier. No doubt, teaching is a part of counseling, and clients do learn in both direct and indirect ways from the input and example of their counselors; but this is not to say that counseling is synonymous with preaching or instruction.

On the other hand, we don't favor the opposite extreme of trying so hard to be "objective" that we keep our personal reactions and values hidden from our clients. Counselors who adopt this style are unlikely to do more than mechanical, routine counseling. Clients demand a lot more involvement from their therapists than mere reflection and clarification. They often want and need to know where their therapists stand in order to test their own thinking. We think that clients deserve this kind of honest involvement on the part of their therapists.

Krasner (1967), a behavior therapist, has formulated a provocative concept of the therapist as a "reinforcement machine." He argues that, regardless of their theoretical approach, therapists are bound to influence the behavior and values of their clients. However neutral therapists may think they are, they are continually giving positive and negative reinforcement by their words and behavior, and this reinforcement, whether intended or not, does affect the direction clients take in therapy: "For the therapist not to accept this situation and to be continually unaware of influencing effects of his behavior on his patients would itself be 'unethical' " (p. 204).

Krasner's view points to a central issue in this chapter—the nature and degree of influence exerted by the therapist's values in the therapeutic relationship. The following questions may help you to begin thinking about the role of your values in your work with clients:

- Is it possible for therapists to interact honestly with their clients without making value judgments? Is it desirable for therapists to avoid making such judgments?
- Do you have a need to see your clients adopt your beliefs and values?
- Can you remain true to yourself and at the same time allow your clients the freedom to select their own values, even if they differ sharply from yours?
- How do you determine whether a conflict between your values and those of your client necessitates a referral to another professional?
- How does honestly exposing your clients to your viewpoint differ from subtly "guiding" them to accept your values?

- To what degree do you need to have life experiences that are similar to those of your clients? Is it possible that too much similarity in values and life experiences might result in therapy that is not challenging for the client?

Clarifying your own values and their effects on your work

If, as we have maintained, your values will significantly affect your work with clients, then it is incumbent upon you to clarify your values and the ways they enter the therapeutic process. For example, counselors who have "liberal" values may find themselves working with clients who have more traditional values. If these counselors privately scoff at conventional values, can they truly respect clients who don't think as they do? Or if counselors have a strong commitment to values that they rarely question, whether these values are conventional or radical, will they be inclined to promote these values at the expense of hindering their clients' free exploration of their own attitudes and beliefs? If counselors never reexamine their own values, can they expect to provide a climate in which clients can reexamine theirs?

Whatever your own values are, there may be many instances in which they present some difficulty for you in your work with clients. In this section we examine some sample cases and issues that may help you clarify what you value and how your values might influence your counseling. As you read through these brief examples, you might keep the following questions in mind:

- What is my position on this particular issue?
- Where did I develop my views?
- Are my values open to modification?
- Have I challenged my views, and am I open to being challenged by others?
- Do I insist that the world remain the same now as it was earlier in my life?
- Do I feel so deeply committed to any of my values that I'm likely to push my clients to accept them?
- How would I communicate my values to my clients without imposing those values?
- How do my own values and beliefs affect my eclectic and personalized approach to working with clients?

As you work through the rest of this chapter, we suggest that you look for areas where you'd be inclined to "push" your values rather than merely challenge your clients to discover and clarify their own values. We agree with Seymour's (1982) injunction that, if counselors sell their values to their clients, then they should be aware of what it is that they are selling. Also, consumers have a right to demand "truth in packaging" from counselors. We think that Seymour is giving good advice when he writes:

> We do become emotionally invested in our values, we do hold some of them to be unquestionably right, and we do act in counseling in accordance with what we believe. We, as counselors, must be aware of the emotional investment, admit to, and hopefully question those values that have been previously unquestioned, and then examine closely

how what we believe influences how we act as counselors. If our values are, in fact, the lenses through which we view the world, then we need to have our vision checked as a part of the selection and training process, and at regular intervals thereafter [p. 45].[1]

The right to die and the issue of suicide

How do you react to the following statement?

> The choice of suicide is ours to make. It is our life we are giving up, and our death we are arranging. The choice does not infringe on the rights of others. We do not need to explain and excuse.[2]

In the article from which this quotation is taken, Doris Portwood (1978) makes a case for the right of elderly people to choose to end their own lives if they decide that each day there is less to live for or if they are in a state of physical and psychological deterioration. Pointing out that many old people are subjected to an undignified ending to life, particularly if they have certain terminal illnesses, she argues persuasively that they have the right to end their lives before they become utterly miserable and a drain on their families.

Apply this argument to yourself. Might there come a time in your life when there is nothing for you to live for? Imagine yourself in a rest home, growing more and more senile. You are unable to read, to carry on a meaningful conversation, or to go places, and you are partially paralyzed by a series of strokes. Would you want to be kept alive at all costs, or might you want to end your life? Would you feel justified in doing so? What might stop you?

Now apply this line of thought to other situations in life. If you accept the premise that your life is yours to do with as you choose, do you believe it is permissible to commit suicide at *any* period in your life? In many ways, people who choose suicide are really saying that they want to put an end to the way they are living *now*. Suppose you felt this way even after trying various ways of making your life meaningful, including getting intensive psychotherapy. Imagine that you felt as if nothing worked, as if you always wound up in a dead-end street. Would you continue to live until natural causes took you? Would you feel justified in ending your own life if your active search had failed to bring you peace?

Perhaps thinking about conditions that might lead you to consider suicide is so unpleasant that you have never really allowed yourself to imagine such situations. However, if you give some thought to how this issue applies to you, you may feel less threatened in entering into real dialogues with individuals who are contemplating the balance sheet of their lives. If you are closed to any personal consideration of this issue, you may tend to interrupt these dialogues or cut off your clients' exploration of their feelings.

In discussing suicidal impulses of clients, Burton (1972) points out that therapists need to avoid becoming unduly frightened by the possibility that a client will commit

---

[1]From "Counselor/Therapist Values and Therapeutic Style," by W. Seymour. Reprinted from *Values, Ethics, Legalities and the Family Therapist* (Family Therapy Collections: No. 1. L. L'Abate, issue editor), edited by J. C. Hansen, by permission of Aspen Systems Corporation, ©1982. This and all other quotations from the same source are reprinted by permission.

[2]From "A Right to Suicide?" by D. Portwood, *Psychology Today*, January 1978, p. 68.

suicide. When suicide is explored in therapy, it is an indication that clients are being reached and that they need to be reached on a deeper level. The contemplation of suicide can be a way of refusing to live in old ways, and the therapist's task is to give protection and support as the client searches for new reasons to live. Burton sees this struggle with the issue of whether to live as a central dimension of psychotherapy:

> Long-term psychotherapy, if it is to be effective, must bring the client to question his life and its values. Since these are so often found wanting, suicidal impulses come as no great surprise. They have constructive as well as destructive aspects. A person who contemplates dying really wants to live—but in a different way [p. 66].

The ethical questions associated with suicide can come up in other ways as well. Consider the following example.

The case of Emily.   Emily, who is in her early 20s, is dying painfully with cancer. She expresses her wish to forgo any further treatment and to take an overdose of pills to end her suffering. Her parents cling to hope, however, and in any event they deeply believe that it is always wrong to take one's own life. If her parents were coming to you for counseling, what might you say to them? Do you feel that Emily has the right to end her life? What role should your opinion play in your counseling? How might your values affect the things you say to the family?

Now assume that Emily herself comes to you, her therapist of long standing, and says: "I am dying and I have no desire to suffer. I don't want to involve you in it, but as my therapist, I would like you to know my last wishes." She tells you of her plan to take an overdose of pills, an action she sees as more humane than continuing to endure her suffering. Consider the following questions:

- What are the legal implications involved here?
- Do you think you have the ethical and legal responsibility to prevent Emily from carrying out her intended course of action?
- If you were in full agreement with her wishes, how might this influence your intervention?
- What do you consider to be the ethical course of action?

The case of Betina.   Let's consider a different case involving the termination of one's life. An adolescent girl named Betina, who is living at a boarding school, has made light suicidal overtures. Although these attempts seem to be primarily attention-getting gestures, there have been several of them. Betina's counselor feels manipulated and has not reported these episodes to the girl's parents. During one of these attempts, however, Betina seriously hurts herself and ends up in the hospital.

- Did the counselor take the "cry for help" too lightly?
- What are the ethical and legal implications of the counselor's deciding that the client's attempts were more manipulative than serious and therefore should be ignored?
- What can a counselor do in a situation in which he or she determines that the attempts are manipulative rather than serious?
- Assume that the counselor had told Betina that she was going to inform Betina's

parents about these suicide attempts. Betina responded by saying that she would quit counseling if the counselor did so. What do you think the counselor should have done?

Discussion of issues involved in right-to-die cases.   Although the cases of Emily and Betina are different, they do raise similar issues that are worth considering. What is your position on these issues pertaining to the right to die?

- Do counselors have the responsibility and the right to forcefully protect people from the potential harm that their own decisions may bring?
- Do helpers have an ethical right to block clients who have clearly chosen death over life?
- What are the ethical and legal considerations of right-to-die decisions?
- Once a therapist determines that a significant risk exists, must some course of action be taken? What are the consequences of failing to take steps to prevent clients from ending their lives? Do factors such as the age of the client, the client's level of competence, and the special circumstances of each case make a difference?

In his paper *Adolescence and the Right to Die*, Powell (1982) discusses the issues of autonomy, competence, and paternalism as directly related to the right to die. Although Powell's article focuses on adolescents, his paper has broader implications, since the three concepts he discusses can be applied to all age levels in the right-to-die issue. *Autonomy* refers to a person's independence, self-reliance, and ability to make decisions that affect his or her life. Autonomy, in turn, is based upon a presumption of the person's *competence*. Competence is determined in part by the person's degree of ability to understand the potential consequences of his or her decisions. Thus, people experiencing trauma and extreme crisis and those who are actively hallucinating and clinging to false beliefs (or displaying other psychotic behaviors) are not viewed as competent to make certain critical decisions. In cases in which clients are found to be unable to direct their own lives or incompetent to make decisions of life and death, *paternalism* comes into the picture. This concept implies that the therapist (or some agent of the client) makes decisions and acts in the "best interests" of the client. In his discussion, Powell states that he has been unable to find a clear constitutional or legal statement of a person's right to choose death. What does appear to have a constitutional basis, however, is the right to refuse treatment, even life-saving treatment. Powell cites an adolescent girl, dying from bone cancer, whose refusal of a leg operation was supported by the courts. In this case, her own wishes were considered to be crucial.

Although there are some common denominators between Emily's case and Betina's, there are also some basic differences. In the case of suicidal clients such as Betina, therapists have ethical and legal responsibilities to take certain actions. The key questions appear to be: Is the therapist aware of the risk of the client's committing suicide? Does the therapist make adequate attempts to prevent self-destruction or to control the suicidal client? According to Schutz (1982), therapists have the responsibility to prevent suicide if they can reasonably anticipate the danger of self-destruction. Once a therapist determines that a significant risk does exist, appropriate action must be taken. Failure on the part of the therapist to do so can result in the therapist's being held liable. Schutz (1982) writes:

> Liability generally ensues in the management of the suicidal patient in two ways: (1) The therapist failed to act in a way to prevent the suicide; in specific, the causes of action are typically a *negligent diagnosis*, and concomitant failure to hospitalize, or *abandonment* by an inadequate response to an "emergency" situation. (2) A therapist's act directly contributed to the suicide [p. 67].

The second area of liability relates to the legal concept *proximate cause*, which means that the plaintiff must show that the therapist's actions were directly related to the suicide and that the suicide would not have occurred without these actions.

Once the therapist makes the assessment of foreseeable risk, what are some possible courses of action? What are some ethical and legal options to consider? How can counselors take appropriate steps to demonstrate that a reasonable attempt was made to control the suicidal client? Schutz (1982) maintains that the options are basically the same as those for the patient who may be dangerous to others, and he lists the following as possible courses of appropriate action:

- If at all possible, have the client agree that he or she will call you or a local emergency service in time of crisis.
- If the client possesses any weapons, make sure that they are in the hands of a third party.
- Consider increasing the frequency of the counseling sessions.
- Bring significant others into the patient's social network for support (with the client's knowledge and consent) in between the sessions.
- Arrange a method for the client to call you between sessions so that you can monitor his or her emotional state.
- Consider the use of medication as an adjunct to the therapy (with a psychiatrist's referral).
- Depending on the seriousness of the case, consider hospitalization as an option. First seek the patient's cooperation. If necessary, a commitment procedure may be called for as a way of protecting the client.

Other measures that we think are important to consider in preventing self-destructive behavior (suicide) include:

- In cases in which you think you are exceeding the boundaries of your competence, consult with your supervisor or colleagues, bring in a consultant, or arrange for a referral.
- Be clear and firm with the client and do not allow yourself to be manipulated by threats.
- Remember that ultimately any client is responsible for his or her actions and that there is only so much you can reasonably do to prevent self-destructive actions. Even if you take specific steps to lessen the chances of a client's committing suicide, he or she can still take this ultimate step at some time.
- Be willing to show your client that you care. This entails some specific actions and setting of limits on your part.
- Do not make yourself the only person responsible for the decisions and actions

of your client. Take your share of the professional responsibility, but do not accept *all* of the responsibility.

• Let the client know that you will be seeking consultation and discussing possible courses of action. It is a good idea to document in writing the steps you take in crisis cases, for documentation may be necessary to demonstrate that you did use sound professional judgment and acted within acceptable legal and ethical parameters.

Religion

What role does religion play in your life? Does it provide you with a source of meaning? What are your views concerning established and organized religion? Has religion been a positive, negative, or neutral force in your life? Even if religious issues are not the focus of a client's concern, religious values may enter into the sessions indirectly as the client explores moral conflicts or grapples with questions of meaning in life. Do you see yourself as being able to keep your religious values out of these sessions? How do you think they will influence the way you counsel? If you're hostile to organized religions, can you empathize with clients who feel committed to the teachings of a particular church?

Religious beliefs and practices affect many dimensions of human experience that are brought into counseling situations. How people handle guilt feelings, authority, and moral questions are just a few of these areas. The key issue here is whether you can understand your clients' religious beliefs and their meaning for your clients, even if these views differ from your own. For example, you may think that a client has accepted an unnecessarily strict and authoritarian moral code. Yet you need to be able to understand what these beliefs mean to your client, whatever your own evaluation of them for yourself might be.

Suppose you have a client, Janet, who seems to be suffering from a major conflict because her church would disapprove of the way she is living. Janet experiences a great deal of guilt over what she sees as her transgressions. If you sharply disagreed with the values she accepted from her church or thought they were unrealistic, how might your views affect your counseling? Do you think you might try to persuade Janet that her guilt is controlling her and that she would be better off freeing herself from her religious beliefs? Why or why not?

Consider the case of Susan, who is a devout Catholic. She was married for 25 years, until her husband left her. Later, she fell in love with another man and very much wanted a relationship with him. But her moral upbringing resulted in her having guilt feelings about her involvement with another man. She sees her situation as hopeless, for there is no way in her mind to resolve an impossible situation. She might live alone for the rest of her life, and that scares her. She might marry the man, but she fears that her guilt feelings would eventually ruin the relationship.

• What are your values that pertain to this case, and how do you think they would influence your interventions?
• Would you recommend that she see a priest to help her resolve her guilt feelings? Explain.

- Assume that Susan asks you what she should do, or at least what you think about her dilemma. What do you think you'd say to her?

In this final case, assume that you have a member in a group that you are leading who calls himself a "born-again Christian" and who feels that he has found peace and strength in his own life. In a sincere and caring way, he wants to pass on to other members in the group what has become very meaningful to him. Several members respond negatively, asserting that he is pushing his values on them and that he comes across in a superior way.

- As a group leader, how would you intervene?
- What reactions do you think you'd have toward a person who holds very strong religious values, and how might your reactions either inhibit or enhance your ability to work with such a person?
- If you hold the view that people with strong religious beliefs are essentially using religion as a way to remain dependent, how would this affect your ability to work with such a person?
- If your views were very similar to this person's what interventions might you make, and how might you react?

The family

Your views of family life may have a strong influence on how you counsel parents and children, marital partners, and people contemplating marriage or divorce. They may affect how you deal with family conflicts and what kinds of suggestions you make when you work with family-related matters. It's therefore important for you to be able to sort out your values with respect to family life and how they affect the interventions you decide to make.

Suppose you have a 25-year-old client, Sharon, who says: "I'm never going to get married, because I think marriage is a drag! I don't want kids, and I don't want to stay with one person forever." What is your reaction to this statement? Perhaps your values clash with Sharon's desire to be free of responsibility. If so, you might tell her that a refusal to accept any responsibility in life is a sign of immaturity and that she will have a more complete life if she has a family of her own. Or perhaps you envy her independence and wish that you didn't have to be responsible for anyone except yourself. In what ways do you think that you might work with Sharon differently, depending on what your own attitude toward family life is? If you don't feel comfortable with a commitment to marriage and a family, do you think you could be objective enough to help her explore some of the possibilities she might be overlooking? Or might your doubts be useful in your work with Sharon?

The case of a couple seeking marriage counseling. During the past few years, Frank and Judy have experienced many conflicts in their marriage. Although they have made attempts to resolve their problems by themselves, they have finally decided to seek the help of a professional marriage counselor. Even though they have been thinking about divorce with increasing frequency, they still have some hope that they can achieve a satisfactory marriage.

We will present the approaches of three different marriage counselors, each holding a different set of values pertaining to marriage and the family. As you read these responses, think about the degree to which they represent what you might say and do if you were counseling this couple.

Counselor A.   At the first session, this counselor states his belief in the preservation of marriage and the family. He feels that many couples take the easy way out by divorcing too quickly in the face of difficulty. He says that he sees most couples as having unrealistically high expectations of what constitutes a "happy marriage." The counselor lets it be known that his experience continues to teach him that divorce rarely solves any problems but instead creates new problems that are often worse. The counselor urges Frank and Judy to consider the welfare of their three dependent children. He tells the couple of his bias toward the saving of the marriage so that they can make an informed choice about initiating counseling with him.

- What are your personal reactions toward the orientation of this counselor?
- Is it ethical for him to state his bias so obviously?
- What if he were to keep his bias and values hidden from the couple and accept them into therapy. Do you see any possibility that he could work objectively with this couple? Explain.

Counselor B.   This counselor has been married three times herself. Although she believes in the institution of marriage, she is quick to point out that far too many couples stay in their marriages and suffer unnecessarily. She explores with Judy and Frank the conflicts that they bring to the sessions. The counselor's interventions are leading them in the direction of divorce as the desired course of action, especially after they express this as an option. She suggests a trial separation and states her willingness to counsel them individually, with some joint sessions. When Frank brings up his guilt and reluctance to divorce because of the welfare of the children, the counselor confronts him with the harm that is being done to them by a destructive marriage. She tells Frank that it is too much of a burden to put on the children to keep the family together at any price.

- Do you see any ethical issues in this case? Was this counselor exposing or imposing her values?
- Do you think that she should be a marriage counselor, given her bias and her background of three divorces?
- What kinds of interventions made by the counselor do you agree with? What are your areas of disagreement?

Counselor C.   This counselor believes that it is not her place to bring her values pertaining to the family into the sessions. She is fully aware of her biases regarding marriage and divorce, but she does not see it as her place to impose her values or to expose them in all cases. Her primary interest is to help Frank and Judy discover what is best for them as individuals and as a couple. She sees it as unethical to push her clients toward a definite course of action, and she lets them know that her job is to help them be honest with themselves.

- What are your reactions to this counselor's approach?
- Do you see it as possible for a counselor to keep his or her values out of the therapy process in a case such as this?

The role of values in marital and family therapy. The preceding case illustrates that the value system of the counselor determines the direction that counseling will take. The counselor who is dedicated to the mission of preserving marriage and family life is bound to function differently from the counselor who puts prime value on the welfare of an individual family member. What might be best for a given person might not necessarily be in the best interests of the entire family. It is essential, therefore, for counselors who work with couples and families to be aware of how their values influence the goals and procedures of therapy. We take the position that ethical practice challenges clients to clarify their own values and to choose a course of action that is best for them.

In his discussion of therapist values (especially as they are applied to marital and family therapy) Seymour (1982) summarizes their role as follows:

> It seems apparent that there is a lack of solid research in the area of counselor/therapist values, especially research directly related to the family therapist. The whole area of counselor/therapist values is frequently unrecognized, or, if recognized, ignored. The one clear area of agreement in the literature is that values need to be examined as an essential part of the training process for family therapists. The research that is available makes it obvious that values and value issues are closely tied to the results one may expect to achieve as a family therapist [p. 47].

Seymour adds that, although the literature supports the view that therapist values do influence therapeutic effectiveness, little is known from data-based research about what their actual effects are. An implication for the practice of family therapy, according to Seymour, is that more research is needed on the potential for matching clients and counselors on the basis of their values.

Sex roles and sex-role stereotypes

According to Hare-Mustin (1980), therapists who work with couples and families need to clarify their own values pertaining to traditional and nontraditional family arrangements and should also be open in divulging these values. She further contends that therapists should be prepared to explain to the family their views on issues such as stereotyped sex-role requirements, role functions, and the distribution of power between spouses and between parents and children. Such explanations are a good way to begin the process of counseling couples and families, for the clients can know from the outset what views and values are likely to influence the nature of the therapy.

Before counselors can be open in a discussion with clients about sex roles, it is essential that they be aware of their own conditioning. It is critical to become aware of the socialization process and the way in which sex-role stereotyping develops. Nutt (1979) has summarized some stereotyped attitudes toward women held, in Nutt's view, by many counselors:

1. Women are "kept in their place" through lessons they are taught about their role and their abilities while they are children.

2. For adults, sex-role socialization has these effects: Men are providers; they are seen as strong, economically powerful, lacking in emotion, independent, and competitive. Women are viewed as the nurturers; they are typically wives and mothers, and they are often characterized as dependent, submissive, helpless, weak, and highly emotional.

3. A particularly negative outcome of sex-role stereotyping is related to the aging process. With increasing age, men are often considered distinguished and respected. In contrast, older women are viewed as sexually undesirable, usually powerless, unattractive, and aggressive, and they are often the victims of economic discrimination.

Calling for a new direction in psychotherapy, Nutt advocates feminist therapy, which she sees as having the same goals as any humanistically oriented therapy. She contends that many women do not receive therapy that fosters growth, mainly because the sex-role bias of counselors interferes with their growth. She writes:

> It is therefore necessary that all therapists who wish to work with women truly respect women as individuals with a variety of strengths and weaknesses that are not sex role based, understand sex role bias, its origins, and their own personal beliefs and attitudes about sex roles, be willing to obtain further training to remove personal sex bias where it is discovered, and develop strategies to encourage the growth of women [p. 20].

In writing about feminist therapy, Gilbert (1980) summarizes the viewpoints of writers who question the usefulness of traditional therapeutic approaches. Such approaches focus exclusively on how people learn and maintain cultural and social values, and their aim is adjustment to societal norms. Gilbert points out that our society's ideology has encouraged women to accommodate without strain to a set of discriminatory role behaviors and sex-typed personality characteristics. She challenges many of the traditional approaches as encouraging women to adjust to the expectations of society. In its place, she recommends several research priorities in the area of feminist therapy.

In a similar vein, Nutt (1979) sees feminist therapy as encouraging a woman to examine how the culture has worked to keep her in traditional roles that may not be functional to her, as well as teaching her how to be assertive in meeting her needs. Feminist therapy also helps a woman to recognize and work through her anger over her oppression, to challenge sex-role stereotypes that restrict her range of freedom, to increase her self-confidence and feelings of personal power, to support and nurture herself, and to recognize the choices available to her. It assumes that a woman's unhappiness is frequently due to her being assigned the exclusive role of wife and mother, especially when such a role alone does not fulfill all her needs.

However, those who counsel couples and families need to appreciate the fact that sex-role stereotypes are functional, and thus die hard. As Scarato and Sigall (1979) have observed, a woman faces a dual problem: dealing with a partner who is unwilling or unprepared to share domestic tasks and letting go of roles that were a basic part of her identity and gave her value. They write:

> The woman often encounters a loss of approval from significant persons in her life who do not understand or feel threatened by her departure from the traditional role. At a time

when she most needs their support, they may withdraw it. At school or work, colleagues may question the investment of the woman who is simultaneously committed to a family [p. 26].

Along with an increasing number of other writers, Scarato and Sigall assert that counselors who work with couples and families must be aware of the history and impact of sex stereotyping as it is reflected in the socialization process in families. They emphasize that therapists need to be free of biases themselves in order to accept a woman's desire to combine a home with school or a career. According to Scarato and Sigall, effective practitioners must continually evaluate their own beliefs about appropriate family roles and responsibilities, child-rearing practices, multiple roles for women, and nontraditional vocations for women. Counselors also must have the knowledge to help women explore educational and vocational goals that they previously deemed unreachable.

Hare-Mustin (1979), in her article "Family Therapy and Sex Role Stereotypes," asserts that traditional family therapists who aim to restore family functioning by reinforcing conventional roles may be perpetuating the causes of conflict within families. She gives several specific recommendations of interventions that could lead to a change in the oppressive consequences of stereotyped sex roles. (See box.)

Recommended Principles for Family Counselors

1. *Knowledge.* Counselors doing family therapy:
   - are aware of the impact of generational problems and age expectations on family members, of the effects of power and distribution of family resources on family members, and of the impact of stereotypic role assignments on family members.
2. *Skills.* Counselors doing family therapy:
   - possess skills in contracting, assigning tasks for shifting functions of family members, establishing rules for balancing communication, and training people to be assertive;
   - are able to develop alliances across generations.
3. *Attitudes.* Counselors doing family therapy are aware of their attitudes toward family roles.

Adapted from "Family Therapy and Sex Role Stereotypes," by R. T. Hare-Mustin, *The Counseling Psychologist*, 1979, 8(1), 31–32. Reprinted by permission.

Margolin (1982) has given a number of recommendations on how to be a nonsexist family therapist and how to use the therapy process to challenge the oppressive consequences of stereotyped roles and expectations in the family. One recommendation is that family therapists examine their own behavior for unwitting comments and questions that imply that the wife and husband should perform different roles and hold a different status. For example, a therapist can show bias in subtle and nonverbal ways, such as looking at the wife when talking about rearing children or addressing the husband when talking about decisions that need to be made. Further,

Margolin recommends that counselors be aware of their personal views about sex roles so that they are less likely to impose these values on the family and will not judge the family from a predetermined perspective of the ideal way families ought to function. Margolin contends that family therapists are particularly vulnerable to the following biases: (1) assuming that remaining married would be the best choice for a woman; (2) demonstrating less interest in a woman's career than in a man's career; (3) encouraging couples to accept the belief that child rearing is solely the responsibility of the mother; (4) showing a different reaction to a wife's affair than to a husband's; and (5) giving more importance to satisfying the husband's needs than to satisfying the wife's needs. She raises two very important questions dealing with the ethics of doing therapy with couples and families:

1. How does the therapist respond when members of the family seem to agree that they want to work toward goals that (from the therapist's vantage point) are sexist in nature?
2. To what extent does the therapist accept the family's definition of sex-role identities rather than trying to challenge and eventually change these attitudes?

In light of the foregoing discussion, we present several open-ended cases for you to consider. What are your values with regard to each of these cases? How do you think your values might affect your manner of counseling in each case?

The case of the traditional couple.   Marge and Fred come to marriage counseling to work on the stress that they are experiencing in rearing their two adolescent sons. The couple directs the focus toward what their sons are doing and not doing. In the course of therapy, it develops that both have full-time jobs outside of the home. In addition, Marge has assumed another full-time job—mother and homemaker—but her husband flatly refuses to share any domestic responsibilities. Marge never questions her dual career and very much feels that this is her station in life. Neither Marge nor Fred shows much interest in exploring the possibility that they have uncritically adopted cultural stereotypes pertaining to what women and men "should" be. Instead, they tend to draw the attention during their sessions to getting advice on how to handle the problems with their sons.

- Is it ethical for the therapist to challenge Marge and Fred to look at their values and assumptions pertaining to traditional sex roles? Is the therapist pushing the view that awareness of sex-role development is important?
- Is it ethical for the therapist to focus simply on the expressed concerns of Marge and Fred, or is there a responsibility to at least challenge them to look at how they have defined themselves and their relationship through assumptions about sex roles?
- If you were counseling this couple, what might you do? What are your values, and how do you think they would influence the interventions you might make in this case?

Value issues and a case pertaining to traditional wives and mothers.   The traditional roles for American women are wife and mother. Not too long ago, women who rejected these roles were seen as maladjusted. Although many women are satisfied with such roles, counselors must be aware of the detrimental effects that many women experience because of the limitations of these roles.

Wyman and McLaughlin (1979) point out the shortcomings of the accepted models used in studying wife and mother roles, and they describe some nontraditional perspectives on the stereotypical female roles. They make the case that women who are unhappy with the traditional feminine roles are labeled neurotic. They add that research shows that women who totally accept their traditional roles also experience reduced chances of happiness. They offer some specific principles for working with traditional wives and mothers, which are presented in the accompanying box.

Recommended Principles in Counseling Traditional Wives and Mothers

1. *Knowledge.* Therapists are aware of factors that decrease a woman's power in marriage, of the results of unequal power distributions, and of satisfiers and dissatisfiers in the marriage relationship.
2. *Skills.* Counselors working with traditional wives and mothers:
   • are able to assess a particular relationship in terms of the potential for personal growth for both parties;
   • are able to help women develop a support system outside the nuclear family if desired.
3. *Attitudes.* Therapists are aware of their own attitudes and values toward marriage, family, women's careers, and sex roles.

Adapted from "Traditional Wives and Mothers," by E. Wyman and M. McLaughlin, *The Counseling Psychologist*, 1979, 8(1), 24–25. Reprinted by permission.

At this point ask yourself the degree to which you agree or disagree with the main points and recommended principles made by Wyman and McLaughlin. As you think about the following case, ask yourself how your values that relate to traditional wives and mothers might affect your relationship with a client like Molly.

The case of Molly.   Molly is 28, is married, and has returned to college to obtain a teaching credential. During the intake session, Molly tells you that she is going through a lot of turmoil and is contemplating some major changes in her life. A few years ago she and her husband began experimenting with an open marriage. He initiated taking her to several parties for swingers, and they tried group sex for a time. Molly never liked these activities, but her husband insisted that they were necessary to keep their marriage from becoming dull. Now Molly says that she doesn't want to stay in the marriage any longer and has found another man she wants to live with. She wants her husband to take custody of their three children, because she wants the freedom to pursue her own interests for a while without being responsible to anyone.

The following statements represent some possible responses that counselors might have to Molly, whether or not they actually voiced them to her. Which of these statements can you see yourself making to Molly? Which of them represent reactions you might have but would keep from her?

- "Maybe you should stay married and make the best of things, because that way you can finish school, and *then* you can decide what to do."
- "Don't you feel any responsibility to your children? After all, you did decide to bring them into this world, and giving them up seems rather impulsive and selfish."
- "I really think that what you are doing is terrific. You have a lot of courage, because many women in your place would continue to play the role of selfless mother and wife and fail to take care of themselves. I think you're entitled to make these changes, and I hope you won't let anyone pressure you to do otherwise."
- "It seems that, with all the turmoil you've been going through, it would be best not to make any big decisions right now. Instead, maybe you could persuade your husband to give up his affairs and put more into your marriage."
- "I'd hate to see you divorce without having some marriage counseling first to determine whether that's what you both want."
- "Maybe you ought to look at the prospects of living alone for a while. The idea of moving out of a relationship with your husband and right into a new relationship with another man concerns me."
- "Frankly, I don't know why you put up with your husband as long as you did. It seems like he's keeping you around for his convenience. I think you'll be able to respect yourself more when you do separate."

If Molly were your client, which of your own values might influence your counseling with her? For example, what do you think of divorce? Would you want her to use divorce only as a last resort? How much do you value keeping her family intact? What are your feelings about Molly's leaving the children with her husband?

———————————————————————————————

———————————————————————————————

———————————————————————————————

———————————————————————————————

———————————————————————————————

———————————————————————————————

The case of the woman who wants to pursue a law career.   The White family (consisting of wife, husband, four children, and the wife's parents) has been involved in family therapy for several months. During one of the sessions, Noel (the wife) expresses the desire to return to college to pursue a degree in law. This wish causes a tremendous resistance on the part of every other member of her family. The husband says that he wants her to continue to be involved in his professional life and that, although he admires her ambitions, he simply feels that it would put too much strain on the entire family. Noel's parents are shocked by their daughter's desire, viewing it as selfish, and they urge her to put the family's welfare first. The children express their desires for a full-time mother. Noel feels great pressure from all sides, yet she seems committed to following through with her professional plans. She is aware of the sacrifices that would be associated with her studies, but she is asking for everyone in the family to be willing to make adjustments so that she can accomplish some goals that are important to her. She is convinced that her plans would not be detrimental to the family's welfare. The family therapist shows an obvious bias by giving no support to Noel's aspirations and by not asking the family to consider making any basic adjustments. Although the therapist does not openly say that Noel should give up her plans, his interventions have the result of reinforcing the family's resistance.

- Do you think that this therapist is guilty of furthering sex-role stereotypes? With his interventions, is he showing his interest in the well-being of the entire family?
- Are there any ethical issues involved in this case? If so, what are they?
- Being aware of your own bias regarding sex roles, how would you work with this family?
- Assume that the therapist had an obvious bias in favor of Noel's plans and even pushed the family to learn to accept her right to an independent life. Do you see any ethical issue in this approach? Is it unavoidable for a therapist to take sides?

Special considerations for counseling women.   Most of the issues that we have discussed in this section relate to the values, attitudes, and practices of counselors with regard to sex roles. To deal with the problems of sex-biased therapy, the American Psychological Association has devoted special attention to the study of the oppression of women (including sex-role stereotyping in therapeutic practice). The APA (1978) Task Force on Sex Bias and Sex Role Stereotyping in Psychotherapeutic Practice was charged with investigating sexism in psychotherapy and recommending corrective actions. The task force developed "Guidelines for Therapy with Women" in 1978 for use in training and professional practice. These guidelines are found in the first of two accompanying boxes. More recently, the APA's Division of Counseling Psychology (1979b) developed a list of principles for competent practice with women. These principles are presented in the second box.

Guidelines for Therapy with Women

The Task Force on Sex Bias and Sex Role Stereotyping in Psychotherapeutic Practice described therapist behaviors in four categories: (1) fostering traditional sex roles, (2) bias in expectations and evaluation of women, (3) sexist use of psychoanalytic concepts, and (4) responding to women as sex objects. What follows are the 13 guidelines that the task force developed for ethical and effective therapy with women:

1. The conduct of therapy should be free of constrictions based on gender-defined roles, and the options explored between client and practitioner should be free of sex-role stereotypes.
2. Psychologists should recognize the reality, variety, and implications of sex-discriminatory practices in society and should help clients examine options in dealing with such practices.

3. The therapist should be knowledgeable about current empirical findings on sex roles, sexism, and individual differences resulting from the client's gender-defined identity.

4. The theoretical concepts employed by the therapist should be free of sex bias and sex-role stereotypes.

5. The psychologist should demonstrate acceptance of women as equal to men by using language free of derogatory labels.

6. The psychologist should avoid establishing the source of personal problems as being within the client when the problems can more properly be attributed to situational or cultural factors.

7. The psychologist and a fully informed client should agree upon such aspects of the therapy relationship as type of treatment, time factors, and fee arrangements.

8. Although the importance of the availability of accurate information to a client's family is recognized, the privilege of communication about diagnosis, prognosis, and progress ultimately resides with the client, not with the therapist.

9. If authoritarian processes are employed as a technique, the therapy should not have the effect of maintaining or reinforcing stereotypic dependency of women.

10. The client's assertive behaviors should be respected.

11. The psychologist whose female client has been subjected to violence in the form of physical abuse or rape should recognize and acknowledge that the client is the victim of a crime.

12. The psychologist should recognize and encourage exploration of a woman client's sexuality and should recognize her right to define her own sexual preferences.

13. The psychologist should not have sexual relations with a woman client or treat her as a sex object.

Adapted from "Guidelines for Therapy with Women," by the American Psychological Association, *American Psychologist*, 1978, 30, 1122–1123. Reprinted by permission.

Principles Concerning the Counseling and Therapy of Women

There has been some recent emphasis on special considerations in counseling women. The Division of Counseling Psychology (Division 17 of APA) endorsed the concept that special subgroups require specialized skills, attitudes and knowledge. At the 1978 APA convention, this division asserted that therapists should sensitize women clients to real-world limitations in light of the fact that contemporary society is not fair with regard to gender. Counseling with women should include an exploration of their reactions to these constraints.

The following principles are considered essential for the competent and responsible professional practice of counseling women. Therapists:

1. Are knowledgeable about women, particularly with regard to biological, psychological, and social issues that have impact on women in general or on particular groups of women in our society.
2. Are aware that the assumptions and precepts of theories relevant to their practice may apply differently to men and women. They are aware of those theories and models that proscribe or limit the potential of women clients, as well as those that may have particular usefulness for women clients.
3. Continue to explore issues related to women, including the special problems of female subgroups, throughout their professional careers.
4. Recognize all forms of oppression and how these interact with sexism.
5. Are knowledgeable and aware of verbal and nonverbal process variables (particularly with regard to power in the relationship) as these affect women in therapy so that counselor/client interactions are not adversely affected. The need for shared responsibility between clients and counselors is acknowledged.
6. Can employ skills that are particularly helpful to women in general and to particular subgroups of women.
7. Put no preconceived limitations on the direction or nature of potential changes or goals in counseling for women.
8. Are sensitive to circumstances in which it is more desirable for a woman client to be seen by a female or male therapist.
9. Use nonsexist language in counseling, supervision, teaching, and journal publications.
10. Do not engage in sexual activity with their women clients under any circumstances.
11. Are aware of and continually review their own values and biases and the effects of these on their women clients. Therapists understand the effects of sex-role socialization on their own development and functioning and the consequent values and attitudes they hold for themselves and others. They recognize that behaviors and roles need not be sex based.
12. Are aware of how their personal functioning may influence their effectiveness in counseling with women clients. They monitor their functioning through consultation, supervision, or therapy so that it does not adversely affect their work with women clients.
13. Support the elimination of sex bias toward institutions and individuals.

Adapted from "Principles Concerning the Counseling and Therapy of Women," by the American Psychological Association, Division of Counseling Psychology, *The Counseling Psychologist*, 1979, 8(1), 21. Copyright 1979 by the American Psychological Association. Reprinted by permission of the publisher.

Are separate guidelines for counseling with women a new form of sexism? Many of the writers we have cited contend that specialized knowledge, skills, and attitudes are needed for effectively working with women clients. We should point out that other writers are opposed to such separate principles on the ground that they are a new form of sexism. One of these writers is Spiegel (1979), who was among a group of women's advocates who attempted to institute changes in response to the growing evidence that women clients were at a marked disadvantage in counseling and therapy when compared with men. She rejects the premise that counseling women is sufficiently different from counseling men to warrant a separate set of standards of practice. According to Spiegel, separate standards merely change the form of sexism in therapy rather than alleviate it. Her position is that there is a need to reduce sexism in counseling but that this can best be accomplished within a single set of standards that applies to all practitioners:

> With regard to values, sexism follows when a double standard exists. Thus I am opposed to developing a separate set of values, no matter how optimal and generally applicable they may appear to be, if they are enforced only for those who choose to work with women clients. Since nonsexist values are the basis for all good therapy, a single set of standards should be adopted for all counselors/therapists [p. 50].

We think that Spiegel presents a case that is well worth considering. Our position is that women are one of the groups that have not been treated justly by the mental-health profession. We agree that women have many times been expected to adjust to the traditional values of society and to accept their roles with a minimum of disruption of the status quo. Thus, we are in agreement with the spirit of the principles and recommendations for counseling various subgroups of women. However, we do not agree with the view that holds that women can receive effective counseling only from other women. In general, we think it is a mistake to assume that the specialization strategy is the only effective way to proceed. We question the assumption that gay and lesbian clients can be genuinely understood and helped only by gay and lesbian counselors, that the concerns of certain ethnic or cultural groups can be addressed meaningfully only by counselors of that particular group, or that religious clients necessarily ought to seek out a counselor with the same beliefs.

What we think is essential is that counselors understand the feelings, values, life experiences, and concerns of whatever population they accept as clients. Therefore, to effectively counsel a woman contemplating an abortion, the counselor need not have faced this same issue, but he or she must have the capacity to understand the values, struggles, and feelings of the client. We think that ethical practice requires that counselors determine *with whom* and *in what circumstances* they are unable to be effective and that they then make an appropriate referral. Further, we agree with Spiegel's contention that work with subgroups may require specialized knowledge, skills, and attitudes but that what has been identified as "women's issues" should be within the province of all effective counselors. Spiegel presents the case of a hypothetical Black, Protestant, married, professional woman who is a mother of three children. Which set of qualifications would her counselor need to have? Some would argue that only a Black female counselor is appropriate to help her deal with racial and sexual issues. Some would say that her religious upbringing during childhood is critical and that the counselor must have shared the same Christian views and experiences. Some would urge her to seek a counselor with expertise in women's issues, since some of her conflicts may deal with the multiple roles of wife, mother, and professional woman. Our position is that well-trained counselors (who are aware of their values and do not impose them) should be able to work with all of her concerns.

For those of you who wish to do further reading in the area of women's issues as they pertain to the practice of therapy, we especially recommend Brodsky and Hare-Mustin (1980); Franks and Burtle (1974); and the special issue of *The Counseling Psychologist*, "Counseling Women III" (APA Division of Counseling Psychology, 1979a).

Sexuality

What are your values with respect to sexual behavior? Do they tend to be liberal or conservative? What are your attitudes toward:

- the belief that sex should be reserved for marriage only?
- sex as an expression of love and commitment?
- casual sex?
- group sex?
- extramarital sex?
- premarital sex?
- homosexuality?
- teenage sex?

An important issue is whether you can counsel people who are experiencing conflict over their sexual choices if their values differ dramatically from your own. For example, if you have very liberal views about sexual behavior, will you be able to respect the conservative views of some of your clients? If you think their moral views are giving them difficulty, would you try to persuade them to become more liberal and adopt your views? How would you view the guilt they may experience? Would you treat it as an undesirable emotion that they need to free themselves of? Or, if you have fairly strict sexual standards that you use as guidelines for your own life, would you tend to see the more permissive attitudes of some of your clients as a problem? Could you be supportive of choices that conflict with your own values?

The case of an extramarital affair. Virginia and Tom find themselves in a marital crisis when she discovers that he has been having sexual affairs with several women. These affairs have been going on for several years. Tom agrees to see a marriage counselor, and the couple comes for a counseling session. Tom says that he has no intention of giving up his life-style, because he doesn't think the affairs are interfering in his relationship with his wife. He says that he loves his wife and that he does not want to end the marriage. His involvements with the other women are sexual in nature rather than committed love relationships. Virginia says that she would like to accept her husband's affairs but that she finds it too painful to continue living with him while knowing of his activities.

Counselor A. This counselor has a definite bias in favor of Tom. She points out that the two seem to have a basically sound marriage, and she suggests that with some individual counseling Virginia can learn to accept and live with her husband's affairs.

- With her bias, is it ethical for this counselor to accept this couple for counseling? Should she suggest a referral to another professional?

- Is the counselor ignoring the wife's needs and values?
- Is there an ethical issue in siding with the husband?
- Would it be a better course of action for the counselor to keep her values and attitudes to herself so that she would be less likely to influence the couple's decisions?

Counselor B.   From the outset, this counselor makes it clear that she sees affairs as disruptive in any marriage. She maintains that they are typically started because of a deep dissatisfaction within the marriage. In her view, affairs are symptomatic of other real conflicts. The counselor suggests that, with couples therapy, Tom and Virginia can get to the basis of their problem. She further says that she will not work with them unless Tom is willing to give up his affairs, since she is convinced that counseling will not work unless he is fully committed to doing what is needed to work on his relationship with Virginia.

- Do you see this counselor as imposing her values?
- Is this approach appropriate, since the counselor is openly stating her conditions and values from the outset?
- To what degree do you agree or disagree with this counselor's thinking and approach?

Counselor C.   This counselor tells the couple at the initial session that from her experience extramarital affairs add many strains to a marriage, that many people tend to get hurt in such situations, and that affairs do pose some problems for couples seeking counseling. However, she adds that affairs sometimes actually have positive benefits for both the wife and the husband. She says that her policy is to let the husband and wife find out for themselves what is acceptable to them. She accepts Virginia and Tom as clients and asks them to consider as many options as they can to resolve their difficulties. Counselor C asks Virginia to consider the possibility of getting involved with other men.

- Do you see this counselor as neutral or biased? Explain.
- Does it seem practical and realistic to expect the couple to make the decision by coming up with some alternatives?
- Is it ethical for the counselor to suggest that Virginia consider becoming sexually involved with other men?

Issues in counseling women with sexual concerns.   Liss-Levinson (1979) asserts that women with sexual concerns have generally been ill-treated by the psychotherapy profession. She takes the position that women today face multiple conflicts as the attitudes of society toward female sexual expression change. She further contends that women are confused because they are being asked to play the roles of both the madonna and the whore. Many women experience self-doubt about their sexual attitudes, values, and behavior.

According to Liss-Levinson, despite the availability of viable treatment options many counselors find themselves unprepared to deal effectively with the sexual concerns of their women clients. On this assumption, she contends that counselors who wish to treat women with sexual concerns need more than the basic skills of a competent therapist. (See the accompanying box for her recommendations.)

Principles for Counselors of Women with Sexual Concerns

1. *Knowledge.* Therapists who work with women's sexual concerns:
   - know the definition, prevalence, myths, theories, and treatment of female sexual problems;
   - know the information about female sexuality: anatomy and physiology, sexual development, menstrual cycle, pregnancy, sexual-response cycle, effects of illness, drugs, disease, and sexual preferences;
   - know the information about sociocultural factors, women's roles (the relation of sex to power), and male sexual development;
   - know the referral network (including other therapists, bibliotherapy, consciousness-raising groups) and ethical issues.
2. *Skills.* Counselors treating women with sexual concerns:
   - are able to use techniques for treating specific sexual dysfunctions;
   - are able to use training in communication skills (for couples);
   - are at ease in using sexual terminology.
3. *Attitudes.* Therapists treating women with sexual concerns:
   - have an awareness of personality values about sexuality—particularly masturbation, lesbianism, sex roles, premarital and extramarital sex;
   - are open to a variety of sexual expressions (and realize the limitations to their openness).

Adapted from "Women with Sexual Concerns," by N. Liss-Levinson, *The Counseling Psychologist*, 1979, 8(1), 36–37. Reprinted by permission.

Ethical issues in counseling gay and lesbian clients.   We are devoting some space to the discussion of the issues in counseling lesbians and gay people because we have found that this is an area that typically evokes intense reactions on the part of our students. Some students have expressed their need to change a homosexual's orientation. Some students have commented that they could work with homosexuals as long as these clients were willing to work toward changing their sexual preferences. Thus, we think that counselors who agree to work with gay or lesbian clients have an ethical responsibility to be clear in their own thinking about where they stand with regard to major issues for gay people. Further, counselors should strive to be honest and clear about their views with clients who want to explore issues pertaining to homosexuality.

It is extremely helpful for counselors to become aware of special counseling emphases and needs of gay clients. Winkelpleck and Westfeld (1982) assert that counselors have not typically been sensitized to major issues facing gay couples. They mention the following as areas requiring special attention:

- Gay couples frequently mention discrimination and prejudice, including stereotypes, negative attitudes, discrimination in the job market, and lack of support for the choices they have made.
- Dealing with other family members is of special importance to gay couples. Although they often want to be honest with their families about their pains and joys, they may hesitate to share their lives with their parents because of the fear of hurting them or of receiving negative reactions from them.
- Gay couples frequently indicate that they need help on communication skills, such as learning to ask for what they want, creating trust, and learning how to identify and deal with basic issues in a relationship.
- Gay clients need assistance in developing a positive self-identity, especially in light of the fact that the development of self-pride in gay relationships is difficult in a society that does not accept this life-style.
- Gay couples who seek counseling need to be able to focus on relationship issues rather than concentrate exclusively on their sexual orientation or on how difficult survival can be as a gay person.

In discussing positive interventions with gay clients, Moses and Hawkins (1982) advocate that counselors move beyond merely helping gay clients cope and adjust to societal norms and instead help them develop innovative and satisfying ways to grow as gay people. According to Moses and Hawkins, helping professionals must learn to challenge their preconceptions about what is best for their clients—as well as some of their set ways of perceiving the world—if they hope to help gay clients establish a positive self-identity. Further, professionals need to support gay clients in expressing sexuality and gender identity in some ways that differ from traditional expectations. We fully agree with their position when they write: "If the counselor, gay or nongay, finds the client's goals incompatible with her or his needs or convictions, the client should be referred elsewhere" (p. 216).

Kingdon (1979) takes the position that theories and research on homosexuality have focused almost exclusively on males and that the perpetuation of myths and stereotypes has led to a lack of understanding of lesbianism. She adds that there is an increasing awareness of this special minority group and the unique set of problems it faces in establishing a positive self-image in a society with strong negative biases against it. These problems include dealing with counselors who have been subjected to society's negative attitudes toward lesbianism. Although Kingdon does not think that lesbian clients need to work exclusively with lesbian therapists, she does see it as essential that therapists be aware of their own sexual values and be free of homophobia. According to Kingdon, counselors working with lesbians need to have special knowledge, skills, and attitudes if they are to help these clients fully explore their sexual feelings, fantasies, and fears in an atmosphere that offers lesbianism as one acceptable life-style. (See the recommended principles in the accompanying box.)

In her article on counseling lesbians, Sophie (1982) provides several important recommendations to counselors. A major one is that counselors express complete acceptance of the client and all her feelings, including her feelings about being a lesbian. A few other specific recommendations are:

- giving clients assistance in exploring their feelings free from evaluation, judgment, and labeling

Principles for Counselors Working with Lesbians

1. *Knowledge.* Counselors:
   - know the definition of, prevalence of, theories about, and myths about lesbianism;
   - are familiar with community resources for lesbians—hot lines, coffee-houses, rap groups, church groups, bars, and bookstores.
2. *Skills.* Therapists who work with lesbian clients:
   - have skills to help clients explore and determine their sexuality;
   - have assessment skills to determine whether a lesbian's problem is due to internal dynamics or society's reaction;
   - have skills to help lesbian clients "come out."
3. *Attitudes.* Counselors who work with lesbians:
   - believe that society needs to change as well as the individual;
   - evaluate their own homophobia and heterosexism.

Adapted from "Lesbians," by M. Kingdon, *The Counseling Psychologist*, 1979, 8(1), 44–45. Reprinted by permission.

- helping clients avoid premature self-labeling
- challenging clients about their acceptance of sex roles and about the relation between sexual orientation and sex roles
- becoming familiar with gay resources in the community and encouraging clients to make use of them

Specifically, with reference to what qualities a counselor needs to make a significant impact on gay clients, we think that Moses and Hawkins (1982) have summarized it well:

> The counselor who is interested in working with gay clients in a manner that will benefit the client must be aware of his or her own level of homophobia, understand the differences between being gay and being nongay, be aware of the many different alternatives available for healthy relationships, and critically examine intervention approaches to eliminate assumptions of heteroeroticism and monogamous marriage as the only healthy models [p. 217].

We reaffirm our position that it is not the counselor's function to make decisions for clients. Rather, the therapy process should be characterized by open exploration of issues and alternatives. Although a counselor's values will surely affect this process, our position is that counselors should be clear enough with their values that they can find ways to make their values work for the good of the therapy process. Counselors who have hidden agendas will not succeed in challenging clients to take stock of their lives and to come to their own decisions about how they will be.

The case of a homosexual couple.   Scott calls a counselor for relationship counseling, saying that he and his partner are having communication problems. They have a number of conflicts that they both want to work out. Scott clearly states that he is involved in a homosexual marriage, yet his life-style is not an issue that he wants to explore. He indicates that they are comfortable with their sexual preferences but need help in learning how to communicate more effectively.

Counselor A. The counselor agrees to see Scott and his partner, and during the first session he suggests that they ought to examine their gay life-style. Counselor A says that he finds it hard to believe that their nontraditional life-style is not a contributing factor to their present difficulties.

- To what extent do you agree or disagree with the stance of Counselor A?
- Since Scott made it clear over the telephone that he and his partner did not want to explore the issue of being gay, was the counselor's intervention appropriate? Explain.

Counselor B. This counselor agrees to see the couple. During the initial session he realizes that he has strong negative reactions toward the homosexual couple. These reactions are so much in the foreground that they interfere with his effectively working with the couple's presenting problem. He tells the two men about his difficulties and reactions and suggests a referral. He lets them know that he had hoped he could be objective enough to work with them but that this is not the case.

- Was this counselor's behavior ethical?
- Given his negative reactions, should he have continued seeing the couple? Would this in itself have been unethical?
- What would be more damaging to the clients—referring them or continuing to see them?
- Is it ethical for Counselor B to charge this couple for the session? Explain your point of view.

Counselor C. This counselor agrees to see the two men and work with them much as he would with any heterosexual couple. The counselor adds that, if at any time the uniqueness of their relationship causes them difficulties, it would be up to them to bring this up as an issue. He lets them know that if they are comfortable with their life-style, he has no need to change it.

- What are your reactions to this counselor's approach?

In reviewing the approaches of these three counselors, think about which approach would be closest to yours. In clarifying your thinking on the issue of counseling gay and lesbian clients, reflect on the following questions:

- Therapists often find that the presenting problem that clients bring to a session is not the major problem. Does it show the therapist's values to assume that a couple's homosexuality might be the real problem? Do you see the counselor as justified in bringing up homosexuality as a therapeutic issue?
- What are the ethical implications of a heterosexually oriented therapist's working with homosexual couples?
- Is it an appropriate function of counselors to attempt to sway people toward a life-style deemed "acceptable" by the counselor? Is it the counselor's role to

make life decisions for clients, or should the counselor challenge clients to make their own decisions?

- What kinds of attitudes on the part of therapists are necessary for them to be instrumental in helping gay and lesbian people to accept their life-style orientations?
- Can a counselor who is not comfortable with his or her own sexuality possibly be effective in assisting homosexual clients to accept their identities?

Those of you who want to explore in more depth the topic of counseling homosexuals will find these sources helpful: Moses and Hawkins, 1982; Woodman and Lenna, 1980; Kingdon, 1979; Sophie, 1982; and Winkelpleck and Westfeld, 1982.

The issue of converting clients to your values and value conflicts in counseling

Even if you think it's inappropriate or unethical to impose your values on clients, you may unintentionally influence them in subtle ways to embrace your values. What you pay attention to during counseling sessions will reinforce what your clients choose to talk about. Even your nonverbal clues and body messages give them indications of when you like or dislike what they do. Since your clients may feel a need to have your approval, they may respond to these clues by acting in ways that they imagine will meet with your favor instead of developing their own inner direction. Suppose, for example, that an unhappily married man knew or surmised that you really thought he was wasting good years of his life in the marriage. This client might be influenced to obtain a divorce simply because he thought you would approve. So, even though you've made a clear decision not to push clients to believe and act in ways that agree with your own values, you still need to be sensitive to the subtle messages that can be powerful influences on their behavior.

Being clear about your own values doesn't eliminate the possibility that a conflict of values between you and your client may interfere with effective therapy. Do you see yourself as being able to work effectively with anyone who seeks counseling from you? Some counselors believe that they can work with any kind of client or with any type of problem. They may be convinced that being professional means being able to assist anyone. On the other hand, some counselors are so unsure of their abilities that they are quick to refer anyone they feel uncomfortable with to another counselor.

Somewhere between these extremes are the cases in which your values and those of your client clash to such an extent that you question your ability to function in a helping way. Obviously there are no easy ways to determine what to do when this happens. The burden must be on counselors to honestly assess whether their values are likely to interfere with the objectivity they need to be useful to their clients. To make such an assessment, counselors must be clear about their feelings concerning value-laden issues, they must be honest about their own limitations, and they must be honest with potential clients when they think value conflicts will interfere with the therapeutic relationship. At times counselors may need to tell clients that, because of their own views, they could not work effectively with them and that a referral to another professional would be in their best interests.

Consider the circumstances in which you would be inclined to refer a client to someone else because of a conflict of value systems. For each of the following, indicate the response that best fits you. Use the following code: A = I definitely could work with this type of person; B = I probably could work with this type of person; C = I probably couldn't work with this type of person; D = I definitely couldn't work with this type of person.

_____ 1. a man with fundamentalist religious beliefs

_____ 2. a woman who claims that she is seeking a way to put Christ in the center of her life and that, if she only could turn her life to Christ, she would find peace

_____ 3. a person who shows little conscience development, who is strictly interested in his or her own advancement and uses others to achieve personal aims

_____ 4. a homosexual couple hoping to work on conflicts in the relationship

_____ 5. a man who wants to leave his wife and children for the sake of sexual adventures with other women that might bring zest to his life

_____ 6. a woman who has decided to leave her husband and children in order to gain her independence, but who wants to explore her fears of doing so

_____ 7. a woman who wants an abortion but wants help in making her decision

_____ 8. a man who is disturbed because he periodically becomes violent with his wife and has beaten her severely a number of times

_____ 9. a person who chooses not to work

_____ 10. a man who lives by extremely rigid "macho" expectations of what a man should be

_____ 11. a person who lives by logic and is convinced that feelings are dangerous and should be avoided

_____ 12. a person whose physical attractiveness strikes you so strongly that you find it difficult to concentrate on what is said in the sessions

_____ 13. a man who strongly believes that the only way to bring up his children is by punishing them severely and, if necessary, by beating them

_____ 14. a person who sees very little value in therapy and doesn't believe that therapy can really help him or her make any real-life changes

_____ 15. a person who is convinced that his or her decisions are the right ones only if you approve of them or actually make them for the person

_____ 16. an interracial couple coming for premarital counseling

_____ 17. a husband and wife who seek counseling to discuss conflicts they are having with their adopted son, who is from a different culture

_____ 18. a lesbian couple wanting to adopt a child

_____ 19. a person whose way of life includes a consistent reliance on marijuana as a means of coping with stress

_____ 20. a man who has found a way of beating the system and getting more than his legal share of public assistance

_____ 21. a married couple, both of whom are having extramarital affairs that they are unwilling to give up

___ 22. a man and his wife, who is unwilling to give up her affair
___ 23. a interracial couple wanting to adopt a child and being faced with their respective parents' opposition to the adoption
___ 24. a client from another culture who has values very different from your own
___ 25. clients who have values that you strongly disapprove of or goals that you do not respect

Now go back over the list and pay particular attention to the items you marked "D." Why do you think you'd have particular difficulty in working with these types of people? What other kinds of people do you envision you'd have trouble working with because of a clash of values?

_____

_____

_____

_____

_____

_____

Case studies of possible value conflicts

In this section we present some case studies of possible value conflicts. Try to imagine yourself working with each of these clients. How do you think your values would affect your work with each one?

The case of Candy.   Candy is a 14-year-old client whom you are seeing because of family conflicts. Her parents have recently divorced, and Candy is having problems coping with the breakup. Eventually, she tells you that she is having sexual relations with her boyfriend. Moreover, she tells you that she's opposed to any birth-control devices because they seem so contrived. She assures you that she won't be one to get pregnant.

What are your feelings about Candy's having sex? If you sense that her behavior is an attempt to overcome her feelings of isolation, how might you deal with it? How would you respond to her decision not to use birth-control measures?

_____

_____

_____

_____

_____

After you've been working with Candy for a few months, she discovers that she is pregnant. Her boyfriend is also 14 and is obviously in no position to support her and a baby. Candy tells you that she has decided to have an abortion but feels anxious about following through on her decision. How would you respond?

____ I'd encourage Candy to do whatever she wants to do.

____ I'd encourage her to consider other options besides abortion, such as adoption, keeping the child as a single parent, marrying, and so on.

____ I'd reassure her about having an abortion, telling her that thousands of women make this choice.

____ I'd consult with a supervisor or a colleague about possible legal implications in this case.

____ I'd attempt to arrange for a family session, or at least a session with Candy and her parents, as a way to open up communication on this issue.

____ I'd encourage her to explore all the options and consequences of each of her choices.

____ I'd inform her parents, because I believe they have a right to be a part of this decision-making process.

____ I'd refer Candy to a family-planning center and encourage her to at least seek abortion counseling so that she could deal with her fears, guilt, and ambivalence pertaining to abortion as one option.

____ I'd pay particular attention to helping Candy clarify her value system; I'd be sensitive to her religious and moral values and the possible implications of specific choices she might make.

____ I'd refer Candy to another professional because of my opposition to abortion.

____ I'd tell Candy that I am personally opposed to (or in favor of) abortion but that I want to remain her counselor during this difficult time and will support whatever decision she makes for herself.

____ I would reprimand Candy and tell her that I knew this was going to happen.

Other: _____

Candy's case illustrates several thorny problems. What do you do if you feel that you cannot be objective because of your views on abortion? Do you refer Candy to someone else? If you do, might she feel that you are rejecting her because she has committed some horrible offense? If you're firmly opposed to abortion, could you support Candy in her decision to go ahead with it? Would you try to persuade her to have the baby because of your views on abortion?

A possible course of action would be to tell Candy about your values and how you felt they would influence your work with her. If you felt that you couldn't work effectively with her, perhaps you should ask yourself why. Why is it crucial that her decision be compatible with your values? Do you necessarily have to approve of the decisions your clients make?

Consider the possible decisions Candy might make, and ask yourself what your goals in working with her would be. What are *your* values in a case such as Candy's?

_____

_____

_____

Value issues pertaining to unwanted pregnancies. As can be seen in Candy's case, women are often unprepared or unwilling to include a child in their lives. When it comes to the subject of abortion, many women are reluctant to consider this as an option, either because of their value systems or because of their feelings of guilt, shame, and fear. Thus, an unwanted pregnancy and its termination constitutes a crisis for most women. In writing about counseling women who find themselves unexpectedly pregnant, Kahn-Edrington (1979) states that the counselor's goal is to mobilize each woman's coping skills, deal with the many complex aspects of each client's situation, and provide support and information during the time of crisis. She suggests that counseling should deal with areas such as the following: the woman's total life perspective (including her life plans, her economic and social situation, and her role expectations for her age and background); her attitudes toward the pregnancy (including her values pertaining to abortion, the fetus, and contraception); her relationship with the man, other children, and family members; the reactions of others to her being pregnant and to having a child; alternatives and possible consequences; her motivation for having the child or for having an abortion; and her fears or misconceptions regarding abortion.

Kahn-Edrington presents her views on the knowledge, skills, and attitudes needed by those who counsel pregnant women. (See the accompanying box.)

Principles for Effective Abortion Counseling

1. *Knowledge.* Counselors involved in abortion counseling:
   - are aware of the definition, prevalence, myths, procedures, risks, and sequels of abortion;
   - are aware of alternatives to problem pregnancy: abortion, adoption, marriage;
   - have information about sexuality, contraception, and community resources;
   - have knowledge of value systems of other cultures and religions.
2. *Skills.* Counselors have crisis intervention and problem solving skills.
3. *Attitudes.* In dealing with women with problem pregnancies, counselors:
   - evaluate personal attitudes toward birth and adoption;
   - believe that the client has the right and responsibility to make her own decisions regarding abortion.

Adapted from "Abortion Counseling," by M. Kahn-Edrington, *The Counseling Psychologist*, 1979, 8(1), 37–38. Reprinted by permission.

Value issues and a case pertaining to homosexuality. Earlier we discussed ethical issues pertaining to counseling gay and lesbian clients. We made the point that your values with respect to homosexuality would have an impact on the way you proceeded with cases involving homosexuality. Before you deal with the following case of Ronald, take a few minutes to assess some of your values involving homosexuality and religion. In the blank, put an "A" if you agree more than you disagree with the statement, and put a "D" if you disagree more than you agree.

____ 1. My views on religion would influence my approach in working with clients who have homosexual concerns.

____ 2. Regardless of what my values relating to homosexuality are, I think it would be important to disclose them to clients with homosexual concerns.

____ 3. Knowing my own values, I think I'd be inclined to steer my clients in a definite direction rather than encouraging them to choose their own path.

____ 4. From my viewpoint, I think that homosexuality should be discussed within the framework of religious and moral values.

____ 5. To be honest, I think that I have some fears of openly discussing the issue of homosexuality with clients.

____ 6. If a client said he saw himself as a "religious person" and also experienced guilt feelings because of a homosexual orientation, then his religious convictions should be challenged in therapy.

____ 7. I see guilt as a way of controlling people.

____ 8. If I were working with a client who had decided on a homosexual lifestyle, I'd tend to be supportive of his or her choice.

____ 9. Ethical practice in counseling with homosexual clients demands that at some point a referral be made to a therapist who is homosexual.

____ 10. Homosexuals in this society are subjected to unfair discrimination, and they are an oppressed minority.

Look over your responses above and attempt to clarify your own values pertaining to homosexuality. Do you think you can counsel objectively in this area? Would you be inclined to "push" your own values? In what ways do you think your values would influence the interventions you'd make? Consider these questions as you read the following case.

The case of Ronald.   Ronald is a 22-year-old college junior. He tells you that he wants to get into counseling with you in order to sort out conflicts that he is experiencing between his sexual feelings and his religion. Ronald sees himself as a good Christian and a believer in the Bible. He has had very little experience in dating and hasn't had any sexual relationships. Ronald is troubled because he experiences far more intense feelings toward men than he does toward women. This is what he tells you:

> I haven't yet acted on my sexual feelings for other men, because I feel that this would be morally wrong. My religious beliefs tell me that it's very wrong for me even to have sexual desires for other men, let alone *act* on these desires! If I did have homosexual experiences, I'd feel extremely guilty. But I just don't have much interest in women, and at the same time I'm intensely interested in having a close emotional and physical relationship with a man. I'm torn by what I feel I want to experience and what my religion tells me I *ought* to do. So, I was wondering whether you think you can help me, and I'd also like to know what your views are about religion and about homosexuality.

From what you know about Ronald, would you want to accept him as a client? Do you think you could help him clarify his feelings and achieve some resolution of his conflict? What kind of answer would you give Ronald concerning your view of homosexuality? What would you tell him about your religious values? How would your views either help or hinder Ronald in resolving his struggle?

Let's examine the responses that three different counselors might make to Ronald. As you read these responses, think about the degree to which they represent what you might say if you were counseling Ronald.

Counselor A: "Well, Ronald, the answer to whether I can help you really depends on several factors. First of all, you need to know that I'm a Christian counselor, and I share many of your beliefs about religion, morality, and the Bible. I think that I could be very supportive in helping you work through some of your religious doubts. I think you should know that I believe my clients will find real serenity when they make Christ the center of their lives and when they live by the example He gave us. Next, you need to know that I cannot condone homosexuality, because I do believe that it is immoral. I'm not implying that you're sinful for merely having homosexual wishes, but I think it would be morally wrong for you to act on these impulses."

Do you share any of Counselor A's views? Do you see Counselor A as *imposing* or merely *exposing* his or her beliefs? Do you think Counselor A can work effectively with Ronald? Why or why not?

_____

_____

_____

_____

_____

_____

Counselor B: "I'm not sure whether I'm the counselor for you or not. Ultimately, I think you'll need to decide whether you feel you want to work with me. Before you decide, you should know that I think that religion is a negative influence on most people. In your case, for example, you were taught to feel guilty over your impulses. I see guilt as a way of controlling people, so, if I worked with you, I'd probably challenge some of your religious values and the source of your guilt feelings. I'd have you look carefully at where you obtained your notions of right and wrong. As far as your homosexual feelings are concerned, I'd want to explore the relationship you had with your father and mother, and I'd challenge you to look at your motivations in not making more contact with women. Is it because you're afraid of them? Do you have enough experience with either sex to know whether you want to be homosexual or heterosexual?"

What do you agree or disagree with in Counselor B's thinking? Do you think this counselor will impose his or her views on Ronald? Or do you think that Counselor B's values will challenge Ronald to decide what *he* values?

_____

_____

_____

_____

_____

_____

Counselor C: "Ronald, your sexual preference really doesn't affect me one way or the other. I'd want you to decide to do what *you* think is right for you. For instance, if you decided on a homosexual life-style, I'd be supportive, and I'd want to help you work through any problems that might arise as a result of your choice. Your religious views also don't affect me one way or the other. I realize that your religion is a part of you, and we could work on how your teachings might cause you difficulty in living the way you want to. I really don't see why it's important that I tell you my personal values, because they won't be entering into our relationship that much, and I wouldn't want them to influence you. I want you to choose whatever way is right for you, and I'll support whatever that is."

Do you see Counselor C as being neutral, passive, or accepting and nonjudgmental? Do you think Counselor C can keep his or her values out of the therapeutic relationship? What do you agree or disagree with in Counselor C's approach?

_____

_____

_____

_____

_____

After thinking about the three different approaches we've considered, how do you think you would respond to Ronald? Would you have any reservations about accepting him as a client? Would you be able to accept his choice of homosexuality if that was what he wanted? Would you prefer that he not make this choice? Would you be more concerned about his religious struggles than about his choice of sexual orientation? Take a moment now to write down the essence of what you might want to say to Ronald about the direction your work with him would take.

_____

_____

_____

_____

_____

Values and interracial issues.   Your views on racial issues can have an impact on your manner of counseling in certain situations. As we encouraged you to clarify your values in other areas, we suggest that you take the following inventory and then think about what your responses tell you about how your values might operate in cases pertaining to racial concerns. In the space, write an "A" if you agree more than you disagree with the statement, and put a "D" if you disagree more than you agree.

_____ 1. I could effectively counsel a person of a different race.

_____ 2. I'd be inclined to refer a person of a different race to a counselor of that race, since the client is bound to have more trust in a therapist of the same race.

_____ 3. My approach to counseling would entail modifying my practices and techniques in working with clients who are racially and culturally different.

_____ 4. Interracial marriages in this society are almost doomed to failure because of the extra pressures on them.

_____ 5. Interracial marriages pose no greater strain on a relationship than do interfaith marriages.

_____ 6. I have certain racial (cultural) prejudices that would affect my objectivity in working with clients of a different race (culture) from mine.

Before you consider the following case, reflect on some values you hold that would influence your way of working with clients who present interracial issues.

The case of Robert.   Robert comes to a counselor with many difficulties and anxieties, one of which is his antipathy toward interracial marriage. He expresses his feelings of deep failure and says that he often entertains thoughts of suicide. This despondency is precipitated by his daughter's engagement to a man of another race. Robert has gone as far as to threaten to write her out of his will if she marries this man. What this client does not know is that the therapist herself is a partner in an interracial marriage. The therapist discloses this fact and lets the client know of her difficulties with what she perceives as his prejudices.

- How do you react to her self-disclosure? (Was it ethical for her to do so? Would it have been ethical not to do so? Explain.)
- Would a referral be in order? Why or why not?
- What are your values in this situation, and what might you do or say if you were the counselor?
- Would Robert's thoughts of suicide influence whether you made such a self-disclosure? Would it influence whether you accepted him as a client? Explain.

A few recommended readings in the general area of the role of values in counseling and psychotherapy are Hart, 1978b; Frankl, 1963; Lowe, 1969; Seymour, 1982; Hare-Mustin, 1980; and Kalish and Collier, 1981.

Differences in life experiences and philosophies of life

Many people would claim that the life experiences and value systems of counselors must be similar to those of their clients. The idea is that counselors can understand and empathize with their clients' conflicts only if they have had the same kinds of subjective experiences. Thus, an elderly person may feel that a counselor who hasn't reached this stage of life cannot hope to understand what it means to cope with loss, physical decline, loneliness, and anxiety about the future. Many people who belong to racial or ethnic minorities think it is extremely important to seek counselors of their own ethnic group, in the belief that counselors who haven't had to contend with discrimination and prejudice could not really understand how they see the world. Similarly, many women are convinced that men cannot effectively counsel women because their life experiences and biases prevent them from being able to understand women's needs. People who are committed to a homosexual life-style may seek gay therapists because they are convinced that heterosexual counselors lack the experience and understanding to work with them on their conflicts. Many drug addicts and alcoholics reveal failure after failure in their psychotherapy experiences with professionals who haven't experienced drug and alcohol problems.

The growth of self-help groups reflects the idea that people who have encountered and resolved certain difficulties possess unique resources for helping others like themselves. Thus, overweight people share their problems in Overeaters Anonymous. Alcoholics who have chosen to live one day at a time without alcohol provide support for fellow alcoholics who are trying to quit drinking. Many drug addicts who have entered Synanon have found that they cannot deceive former addicts with their games and that being confronted by people who once played the same games forces them to look at how they are living. Members of Recovery Incorporated find support in facing the world once they have left state mental hospitals.

To what degree do you share the view that you must have life experiences similar to those of your clients? Do you think you need to have the same philosophy of life that your clients have in order to work effectively with them? Do you think that you can be helpful to people whose experiences, values, and problems are different from yours by tuning in to their feelings and relating them to your own? Consider for a moment whether you could communicate effectively with:

- an elderly person
- a person with a strict religious background
- a person of a different race or ethnic group
- a physically handicapped person
- a delinquent or a criminal
- an alcoholic
- a person with a different sexual orientation
- an obese person

Our position is that counselors need not have experienced each of the struggles of their clients to be effective in working with them. When the counselor and the client are relating on a *feeling* level, cultural and age differences are transcended. It is possible for a relatively young counselor to work effectively with an elderly client in spite of the fact that the counselor has not yet experienced some of the problems of the older client. For example, the client may be experiencing feelings of loss, guilt, sadness, and hopelessness over a number of situations in life. The counselor still has the capacity to empathize with these feelings, for he or she can tie in to different experiences that resulted in some of the same feelings. Our point is that there can be a connection between the client and the counselor even though they have had different life experiences. What is essential is that the counselor must be sensitive to the differences in their backgrounds.

In his excellent book *Counseling the Culturally Different: Theory and Practice*, D. W. Sue (1981) points out that many counselors are "culturally blind" in the sense that they perceive reality exclusively through the filters of their own life experiences. He thinks that what is important is for counselors to become "culturally aware"—to be able to critically evaluate their conditioned values and assumptions and the conditioning of their clients. Sue sees it as imperative that counselors have a broad perspective of diverse cultural value systems. Those counselors who remain victims of their own cultural conditioning risk further oppressing minority clients.

If you are interested in reading further about the role of values in cross-cultural counseling, some of the following sources will be useful: Levine and Padilla, 1980; D. W. Sue, 1981; Pedersen and Marsella, 1982; Pedersen, Draguns, Lonner, and Trimble, 1981; and Atkinson, Morten, and Sue, 1979.

To facilitate your reflection on the issue of whether you need to have life experiences or value systems that are similar to those of your clients, we'll present a number of situations that you might be faced with as a counselor. In each case, assess what factors in your life would either help or hinder you in establishing a good working relationship with the client we describe.

Frances is a 60-year-old teacher who is thinking about going to law school just because it's something she has wanted to do for a long time. For 30 years she has taught government and history in community colleges, and now she wants to retire early in order to take up a new profession. Frances wonders whether she has the stamina to endure long hours of study, and she is asking herself whether leaving teaching at this stage in life would be a wise move.

- What experiences have you had that could help you understand Frances's desires and conflict?
- How do you respond to a person's beginning law school at the age of 60?
- Would you be inclined to encourage Frances to take a risk, or would you favor her staying with a secure job in her situation?
- How might your answers to the preceding questions affect the way you would counsel Frances?

Albert, a minority-group client, comes to a community mental health clinic on the recommendation of one of his friends. During the initial session you are aware that he is extremely guarded. He discloses little about himself or how he is feeling in this situation with you. Although he will answer your questions briefly, you sense that he is withholding much information from you, and you meet with a variety of stubborn resistances during the session. As a counselor, you may assume that self-disclosure and openness to feelings enhance one's life. In working with Albert, consider these questions:

- How sensitive are you to the client's sense of privacy? Have you considered that keeping one's thoughts and feelings to oneself might be a value in certain cultures? How might this be a survival mechanism in some cultures?

- Assume that you succeed in getting Albert to be more self-disclosing and expressive, not only with you but within his environment. What potential hazards can you see in terms of his reentry into his environment?
- Is it ethical to convert him to your point of view without first understanding the cultural context? Explain.
- One of your aims might be to teach Albert to be more autonomous (to become less dependent on his parents and his extended family). How might this be an expression of your value system, and how might that affect your client as he attempts to deal with his family?
- How might your intervention reflect your lack of understanding of the importance of the extended family in certain cultures?
- Some might label Albert's behavior as bordering on paranoia. How might his cautiousness be more adaptive than maladaptive?

At a community clinic, Sylvia, who is 38, tells you that she is an alcoholic. During the intake interview, she says: "I feel so much remorse, because I've tried to stop my drinking, and I haven't succeeded. I'm fine for a while, and then I begin to think that I have to be a 'perfect' wife and mother. I see all the ways in which I don't measure up, how I let my kids down, the many mistakes I've made with them, the embarrassment I've caused my husband, and then I get so down I feel compelled to take that next drink to stop my shaking and to blur my depression. I see that what I'm doing is self-destructive, but I haven't been able to stop, in spite of going to A.A."

- What experiences have you had that would help you understand what it's like for Sylvia to feel compelled to drink?
- How do you see Sylvia? As having a disease? As suffering from a lack of willpower? As an irresponsible, indulgent person?
- How does the fact that Sylvia is a woman affect your view of her problem?
- What is your reaction to Sylvia's being in A.A.? Do you see it as a desirable adjunct to therapy? Or do you see it as potentially working at cross purposes with your therapy? Explain.

The case of Jan, a man who lives mainly by reason.   Jan is a physicist, born and educated in northern Europe. He has several degrees from prestigious universities. Jan's life-style and interests center on intellectual pursuits, and he tends to show very little affect in most situations. His wife is having an affair, and he seeks your counsel, not so much on his own initiative but because of the encouragement of colleagues who think he can use some guidance. Jan talks calmly about the potential breakup of his family and indicates that he has discussed the matter with his wife. In essence, he has asked her to decide on the outcome. Jan is in your office to find a logical explanation for why the affair occurred, yet he does not display any strong emotional reactions to the situation. He gives no clues to how he is feeling about it.

- Would you consider Jan's cultural and educational background in dealing with Jan's reaction to his situation?
- Would you immediately pursue the expression of feeling? Can you see yourself saying: "Cut out the intellectualizing and tell me how you feel?" Why or why not?

Commentary.   This example is used to illustrate another type of cultural difference. Although we do not deny the value of expressing one's emotional reactions to a situation such as Jan's, we would be especially sensitive to his cultural background and his conditioning. In certain cultures, openly admitting to being affected by a situation such as this is equivalent to a loss of face or pride. Jan might never show the degree of emotionality that we deem appropriate, but that does not mean that he cannot express an emotional reaction. Our main point is that to push for the "norm" of "getting at feelings" could be counterproductive and potentially unethical. Although this example could apply to many American males as well, it is even more representative of Jan's cultural conditioning not to share his feelings.

You are the probation counselor for Mike, who has a history of being expelled from school. He has spent much of his life in and out of juvenile court. The customs of the gang he belongs to dictate how he lives. He's silent during most of your first session, but he does let you know that he doesn't really trust you, that he's only there because the court sent him, and that you can't possibly understand what his life is about.

- Have you had any life experiences that would qualify you to counsel Mike?
- What are your immediate reactions to Mike?
- Would you want to convert him to any of your values? For example, would you want to see him finish school? Stop being involved in gang fights? Take counseling seriously?
- If you haven't had the kinds of experiences growing up that he has had, could you still communicate effectively with him and understand his view of the world?

Frank is a middle-aged businessman who says that he's not seeking personal counseling but rather wants advice on how to manage his teenage daughter. According to Frank, his daughter is immature and unruly. She isn't learning self-discipline, she socializes too much and works too little, she doesn't respect her parents, and in other ways she is a disappointment and a worry to him. Frank seems to be oppressive rather than loving, and to him the full responsibility for the conflict in his family rests with his daughter. You surmise that he doesn't see any need to examine his own behavior or his role in contributing to the family's difficulties.

- How do you imagine you might relate to Frank, who seems very rigid and closed to looking at himself?
- Would your own values get in the way of understanding Frank's values?
- Do you think you might want to get him to look at his own part in the family disturbances? Would you want to challenge his values as they pertain to his daughter's behavior?
- Would you accept him as a client, even if he wanted to focus on how he could change his daughter?

You can add your own examples of clients whom you might have difficulty in counseling because of a divergence in values or life experiences. How would you deal with such clients? You could decide to refer most of them to other counselors, but you might also look at how to broaden yourself so that you could work with a wider range of personalities. If you have difficulty relating to people who think differently from the way you do, you can work on being more open to diverse viewpoints. This openness doesn't entail accepting other people's values as your own. Instead, it implies being secure enough in your own values that you aren't threatened by really listening to, and deeply understanding, people who think about life differently. It implies listening to your clients with the intent of understanding what their values are, how they arrived at them, and the meaning these values have for them and then communicating this acceptance. This kind of accepting attitude requires a willingness to let your clients be who they are without trying to convince them that they should see life the way you do. Achieving this acceptance of your clients can significantly broaden you as a person and as a professional.

Chapter summary

In this chapter we've looked at a variety of practical, value-laden counseling situations and issues. Of course, you'll encounter many other kinds of value questions in your work. Our intent has been to focus your attention on the ways in which your values and those of your clients will affect your counseling relationships.

The central theme of this chapter has been the importance of being clear about what *you* value. We've suggested that counselors cannot be neutral in the area of values and should frankly acknowledge those values that are related to questions clients are struggling with. It takes honesty and courage to recognize how your values affect the way you counsel, and it takes wisdom to determine when you cannot work with a client because of a clash of values. These questions have no ready-made or universally appropriate answers. They demand ongoing introspection and discussions with supervisors or colleagues to determine how to make the optimal use of your values.

Activities, exercises, and ideas for thought and discussion

1. Have a panel discussion on the topic "Is it possible for counselors to remain neutral with respect to their clients' values?" The panel can also discuss different ways in which counselors' values may affect the counseling process.
2. Invite several practicing counselors to talk to your class on the role of values in counseling. Each of these counselors can have a different theoretical orientation. For example, you might ask a behavior therapist and a humanistic therapist to talk to your class at the same time on the role of values.
3. For a week or so, keep a record of your principal activities. Then look over your record and, on the basis of what you do and how you use your time, list your values as reflected in your record in order of their priority. How do you think these values might influence the way you counsel others?
4. In class, do the following exercise in pairs. First, discuss areas that each of you might have trouble with in counseling situations because of a conflict of values. For example, one student might anticipate difficulty in working with clients who have fundamentalist religious beliefs. Then, choose one

of these situations to role-play, with one student playing the part of a client and the other playing the part of the counselor. The client brings up some problem that involves the troublesome value area. It is important for you and your partner to really get into the particular frame of reference being role-played and to feel the part as much as possible.

5. As a variation of the preceding exercise, you can assume the role of a client whose values you have difficulty identifying with. For instance, if you think you'd have trouble counseling a woman who wanted an abortion, become this client and bring her problem to another student, who plays the part of a counselor. This type of role-reversal exercise can help you understand people whose value systems are different from your own.

6. For this exercise, work in small groups. Discuss the kinds of life experiences you've had that you think will enable you to effectively counsel others. You might also talk about the *limitations* of your life experiences so far as they might hinder your understanding of certain clients.

7. Interview some practicing counselors about their experiences with values in the counseling process. You could ask such questions as: What are some kinds of clients that you've had difficulty working with because of your value system? How do you think your values influence the way you counsel? How are your clients affected by your values? What are some of the main value issues that clients bring into the counseling process?

8. Do this exercise in pairs. One student plays a counselor; the other plays a client. The counselor actively tries to convert the client to some value or point of view that the counselor holds. The student who assumes the role of the client can actually bring in a personal situation that involves a value issue. For instance, the client can be a college student trying to decide whether to go on to graduate school or get a job and start earning money. The job of the counselor is to try to persuade the client to do what the counselor thinks would be best for the client. This exercise can give you a feel for what it's like to persuade a person to adopt your point of view and what it's like to be subjected to persuasion. In the next round, the same two students can switch roles.

9. This exercise can also be done in pairs. Each person interviews the other on the following issue: What are some of your central values and beliefs, and how do you think they will inhibit or facilitate the work you will do as a counselor?

10. Invite speakers to class to talk about cross-cultural factors as they relate to values. Speakers representing special concerns of various ethnic groups can address the topic of certain values unique to their group and can discuss the implications of these values for counseling.

Suggested readings

Bazelon, D. L. Veils, values, and social responsibility. *American Psychologist*, 1982, 37(2), 115–121. A federal judge writes a challenging article for therapeutic practitioners. He contends that one of the serious problems therapists must confront when they deal with the public is their failure to be truly open with their audience. He suggests that therapists disclose the values that are at the basis of their professional work: "Unveil *your* values. Unveil *our* values. In combining those two tasks, you will be setting an enviable standard of social responsibility" (pp. 120–121).

Brodsky, A. M., & Hare-Mustin, R. T. (Eds.). *Women and psychotherapy: An assessment of research and practice.* New York: Guilford Press, 1980. For readers wanting a resource for further reading on this subject, this book is highly recommended. The topics covered include therapist attitudes and sex-role stereotyping, marital and family conflicts, traditional therapy approaches and their relevance for women, alternative approaches to counseling women, self-help and consciousness-raising groups, and approaches to crisis intervention. The authors provide a summary of research on these topics, along with recommendations for therapeutic practice and for research.

Counseling Women III. *The Counseling Psychologist,* 1979, 8(1). Cited many times in this chapter, this special edition on issues involved in counseling women is an important resource for those who want further information on this timely topic. Some of the articles deal with principles concerning the counseling of women, issues pertaining to specific subgroups of women, an overview and rationale for paying special attention to women's issues in therapy practice, and various reactions to guidelines for the counseling of women.

Hansen, J. C. (Ed.). *Values, ethics, legalities and the family therapist* (Family Therapy Collections: No. 1. L. L'Abate, issue editor). Rockville, Md.: Aspen, 1982. This short book contains an excellent variety of chapters for those wanting a survey of ethical and legal issues in the practice of family therapy. Some of the topics are ethical and professional conflicts in systems therapy, therapist values and therapeutic style, ethical divorce therapy, ethical conflicts in clinical decision making, issues in family law, and the regulation of marital and family therapy.

Margolin, G. Ethical and legal considerations in marital and family therapy. *American Psychologist,* 1982, 37(7), 778–801. This excellent article explores special problems in working with family members and with couples. The author contends that insufficiencies in the APA ethical principles for marriage and family therapy have not been fully appreciated. She deals with the thorny problems of therapist responsibility, confidentiality, informed consent and the right to refuse treatment, the role of therapist values in working with families, extramarital affairs, sex roles, and training and supervision. A number of provocative questions are raised for the practice of marital and family therapy.

Moses, A. E., & Hawkins, R. O. *Counseling lesbian women and gay men: A life-issues approach.* St. Louis: C. V. Mosby, 1982. The authors provide useful information that sheds light on the world views of gay people. Chapters deal with special issues in counseling gay clients, confidentiality issues, the rights of gay clients, dealing with gay parents, and positive intervention with gay clients. This book is a good place to begin for readers who want to further study the issues involved in counseling homosexuals.

Theoretical Issues in Counseling and Psychotherapy

Pre-chapter self-inventory

Directions: For each statement, indicate the response that most closely identifies your beliefs and attitudes. Use the following code:

5 = I *strongly agree* with this statement.
4 = I *agree*, in most respects, with this statement.
3 = I am *undecided* in my opinion about this statement.
2 = I *disagree*, in most respects, with this statement.
1 = I *strongly disagree* with this statement.

_____ 1. I have settled on a definite theory of counseling.
_____ 2. I would rather combine insights and techniques derived from various theoretical approaches to counseling than base my practice on a single model.
_____ 3. My view of people is basically positive.
_____ 4. What happens in counseling sessions is more my responsibility than it is my client's.
_____ 5. I would find it difficult to work for an agency if I was expected to perform functions that I didn't see as appropriate counseling functions.
_____ 6. I have the power to define my own role and professional identity as a counselor.
_____ 7. Clients should always select the goals of counseling.
_____ 8. I'd be willing to work with clients who didn't seem to have any clear goals or reasons for seeking counseling.
_____ 9. Giving advice is a legitimate part of counseling.
_____ 10. Enhancing a client's social adjustment is a legitimate goal of counseling.
_____ 11. A diagnosis is helpful, if not essential, when a client begins counseling.
_____ 12. There are more dangers than values associated with diagnosis in counseling.
_____ 13. Testing can be a very useful adjunct to counseling.

___ 14. I think the medical model of mental health can be fruitfully applied in counseling and psychotherapy.

___ 15. There is a real danger that counseling techniques can be used to keep the therapist hidden as a person.

___ 16. Skill in using a variety of techniques is one of the most important qualities of a therapist.

___ 17. Theories of counseling can limit counselors by encouraging them to pay attention only to behavior that fits their particular theory.

___ 18. Counselors should develop and modify their own theories of counseling as they practice.

___ 19. A theory should be more than an explanation of disturbed behavior; it should challenge my world view.

___ 20. Counselors can identify their theoretical preferences by paying attention to the way they actually practice.

___ 21. In my view of human nature, people are responsible both for creating and for solving their problems.

___ 22. Although I do not see people as responsible for creating their problems, I do see them as responsible for finding ways to deal effectively with these problems.

___ 23. It can be unethical for practitioners to fail to do some type of assessment and diagnosis, especially with "high-risk" (suicidal and dangerous) patients.

___ 24. It is questionable for therapists to help minority clients assimilate into the majority culture, for these clients can lose their unique cultural heritage.

___ 25. In assessment and diagnosis it is critical to take cultural factors into consideration if the therapist hopes to gather accurate data and come up with a valid perspective on a client.

Introduction

Professional counselors should be able to conceptualize *what* they do in their counseling sessions, as well as *why* they're doing it. Too often practitioners are unable to explain why they use certain counseling procedures. For example, when you meet a new client, what guidelines should you use in structuring your first interview? What do you want to accomplish at this initial session? Which of the following are you interested in knowing about your client? Why?

- the presenting problem (the reason the client is seeking counseling)
- the client's present style of coping with demands, stresses, and conflicts
- the client's early experiences as a child, particularly in relationship to parents and siblings
- the client's ego strength
- the client's history of successes and failures
- the client's developmental history
- the client's struggle with current choices
- the client's goals and agenda for counseling

- the client's current support system
- the client's motivation to change
- the client's level of reality testing

During your initial session, what are some of the interventions you might make in getting to know your client? How would you want to structure your future sessions? Consider the following questions, and briefly write your responses.

1. Would you want to begin with a detailed case history? Why or why not?

   _____

   _____

   _____

2. Do you consider diagnosis a necessary prerequisite to counseling? Why or why not?

   _____

   _____

   _____

3. Are tests important as a prerequisite to counseling? Would you decide whether to test, or would you allow your client to make this decision?

   _____

   _____

   _____

4. How much would you structure the session to obtain *current* information about your client's life? How much would you want to know about the client's past?

   _____

   _____

   _____

5. Would you do most of the talking? Why or why not?

   _____

   _____

   _____

6. Who would set the goals of the therapy? Who would be primarily responsible for what was discussed? Why?

   _____

   _____

   _____

7. Who would take the greater responsibility for *directing* the session? At the initial session, would you ask many questions? Would you encourage your client to structure the session?

_____

_____

_____

8. Would you develop contracts with your clients specifying what they can expect from you, what they want from counseling, and what they are willing to do to meet their goals? Why or why not?

_____

_____

_____

9. Would you be inclined to use directive, action-oriented techniques, such as homework assignments? Why or why not?

_____

_____

_____

10. What aspects of the client's life would you stress?

_____

_____

_____

In this chapter we focus on how your theoretical positions and biases influence your actual practice. Ideally, theory should help you make sense of what you do in your counseling sessions. Since your answers to the preceding questions depend on your view of personality and of counseling, looking at how you responded to these questions is one way to begin clarifying your theoretical approach. Another way of thinking about this issue is to imagine a client asking you to explain your view of counseling in clear and simple terms. Would you be able to tell your client *what* you most hoped to accomplish and *how* you would go about it?

You might consider how open you are to challenging your theoretical stance and how this openness or lack of it might influence the therapeutic outcome for your clients. Think about how your theoretical viewpoint influences your stand on questions such as these: What is the role and function of the counselor? What are some goals for counseling? What is the proper place of diagnosis and testing in the counseling process? What techniques are most appropriate in reaching certain goals of counseling?

Developing a counseling stance

Developing a counseling stance is more complicated than merely accepting the tenets of a given theory. We believe that the theoretical approach you use to guide you in your practice is an expression of your uniqueness as a person and an outgrowth of your life experience. Further, your counseling stance must be appropriate for the type of counseling you do and the unique needs of your clients.

We believe that a theoretical approach becomes more useful and meaningful after you've taken a critical look at the *theorist* who developed the theory, as well as its key concepts, since a theory of counseling is often an expression of the personality of the theorist. However, blindly following any single theory can lead you to ignore some of the insights that your life opens up to you. Of course, this is our bias, and many would claim that providing effective therapy depends on following a given theory.

A major consideration in developing or evaluating a theory is the degree to which that perspective helps you to understand what you're doing. Does your framework provide a broad base for working with diverse clients in different ways, or does it restrict your vision and cause you to ignore variables that don't fit the theory? We think there's a danger of forcing your clients to conform to your expectations if you are a "true believer" of one theory. For example, if you believe that a need for power is the underlying motive of most human behavior, your clients will tend to focus on aspects of their lives dealing with power and ignore other, perhaps equally important, aspects. If you stress body awareness, here-and-now awareness, recognizing games, remembering dreams, or working with past experiences, your clients are likely to focus on these issues and interpret much of their behavior in light of the constructs you use. It's important, therefore, to evaluate the dimensions you decide to pay attention to in your counseling work. The following questions can help you make this evaluation:

- Where did you acquire your theory? Did you incorporate many of your views from your instructors or training supervisors? Has one theory intrigued you to the point that it is the sole basis for your orientation?
- Do you embrace a particular theory because it is a justification of your own life-style, experiences, and values? For instance, do you adopt a theory that stresses an active, didactic role for the therapist because you see yourself as "straightening out" your clients? What does your approach stress, and why does it appeal to you?
- To what degree does your theory challenge your own previous frame of reference? Does your theory cause you to test your hypotheses, beliefs, and assumptions? Does it encourage you to think of alternatives? To what degree does your theory reinforce your present world view? Does your theory force you to extend your thinking, or does it merely support your biases?
- How do you see your own life experiences as an influence in your counseling style? In what ways have your life experiences caused you to modify your theoretical viewpoint?
- What are the ethical implications of a counselor's practicing in the absence of

a theoretical orientation? Does ethical practice demand having a rationale for the interventions you make?

The influence of your theoretical assumptions on practice

Your assumptions about the nature of counseling and the nature of people have a direct impact on your manner of practice. The goals that you think are important in therapy, the techniques and methods you employ to reach these goals, the way in which you see the division of responsibility in the client/therapist relationship, your view of your role and functions as a counselor, and your view of the place of diagnosis and testing in the therapeutic process—these are largely determined by your theoretical orientation.

Practicing counseling without an explicit theoretical rationale is somewhat like flying a plane without a map and without instruments. We do not see a theoretical orientation (or a counseling stance) as a rigid structure that prescribes the specific steps of what to do in a counseling situation. Rather, we see theory as a set of general guidelines that counselors can use to make sense of what they are doing.

In the following sections we look at some current theoretical trends in counseling and psychotherapy; we examine the basic assumptions underlying the contemporary theories; and we focus on theoretical differences over the issue of how responsible clients are for creating their own problems and for solving them. As you review the basic assumptions and key concepts of the major theoretical approaches to therapy, keep yourself open to selecting ideas of value from each approach.

Theoretical orientations of counseling and clinical psychologists

Ever since the beginning of psychotherapy with the psychoanalytic school, there have been a number of diverse theoretical approaches. The common schools of psychotherapy are treated in detail in books such as the following: Corey (1982c); Corsini (1979); Hansen, Stevic, and Warner (1977); Patterson (1980); and Prochaska (1979). Some of the schools of therapy that are discussed in the works cited above include psychoanalytic therapy, adaptations and extensions of psychoanalysis, existential therapy, person-centered therapy, Gestalt therapy, transactional analysis, behavior therapy, rational-emotive therapy, and reality therapy. The applications of these theories to group counseling are explored in these works: Corey (1981b); Gazda (1982); Hansen, Warner, and Smith (1980); and Kaplan and Sadock (1983).

Smith (1982) asked clinical and counseling psychologists what theoretical orientations they adhered to. He received 422 usable questionnaires, yielding the following results:

Psychoanalytic	10.84%
Adlerian	2.89%
Behavioral	6.75%
Reality	0.96%
Cognitive behavioral	10.36%
Person-centered	8.67%
Gestalt	1.69%

Existential	2.17%
Rational-emotive	1.69%
Transactional analysis	0.96%
Family	2.65%
Eclectic	41.20%
Other	9.16%

Discussion of the results.   The "other" category included developmental orientation, social-learning theory, career theory, and personal-effectiveness training. The findings indicated a continued decline in the popularity of psychoanalytic therapy and a trend toward the cognitive behavioral therapies.

Smith cites literature indicating a trend in the direction of "creative synthesis, masterful integration, and systematic eclecticism." Clearly, with 41% of the respondents indicating "eclectic" as their primary theoretical orientation, this sample preferred drawing concepts and techniques from various approaches rather than being restricted by a single theory. "These findings strongly suggest that the trend in psychotherapy is away from the exclusiveness of schools and toward some kind of eclectic system that transcends both the narrowness in schools and the mediocrity of traditional eclecticism" (p. 807).

The trend toward eclectic counseling.   An increasing number of writers point to the advantages of developing an eclectic approach. One of the reasons for this trend is the recognition that no single theory is comprehensive enough to account for the complexities of human behavior, especially when the range of client types and their specific problems are taken into consideration. It is important to stress that genuine eclecticism is not a haphazard borrowing of techniques from several theories. Rather, it is an approach that integrates concepts and procedures from various approaches in a thoughtful manner. Thus, eclecticism should not be an excuse for sloppy practice or a failure to think about the implications of theory for practice. Unfortunately, some practitioners who call themselves "eclectic" really have no theoretical stance at all but have simply collected a "bag of techniques" that they use in shotgun fashion in the hope that some techniques will work if others won't.

One advantage of an eclectic orientation is that theory can become an alive and open-ended framework. We agree with Ivey and Simek-Downing (1980) that theory need not be fixed but is best seen as an opening to new and greater possibilities in the future. Palmer (1980) proposes an eclectic approach to therapy that includes both the psychodynamic and the behavioral trends in psychotherapy. According to Palmer, since the client is a unity—an individual with internal and external experiences that interact—the task of the eclectic psychotherapist is to unify both the *psychodynamic* theory (which focuses on internal events such as ideas, dreams, projections, fears, and attitudes) and the *behavioral* theory (which stresses responses and coping behavior of the individual to the external environment).

The eclectic therapist can be distinguished from most therapists who adhere to a single approach by a willingness to use specific procedures from any orientation if they seem appropriate (Garfield, 1980). Garfield summarizes the challenges of the eclectic perspective:

Although the eclectic therapist would appear to have the advantage of having a broader orientation to psychotherapy and potential access to a wider variety of therapeutic techniques and procedures than his school-oriented colleagues, it must also be acknowledged that his path is less clearly illuminated. There is some personal comfort for the therapist in believing in and adhering to a given theoretical system. He can follow certain stated procedures and explain certain phenomena in terms of his theoretical system [p. 234].

The eclectic therapist does not have the specific structure and kind of support that many practitioners have who follow a particular theory. This can be a disadvantage. It can also be a challenge to the therapist to develop a creative integration that is an expression of his or her own unique personality and therapeutic style. According to Garfield, given the theoretical development in the field of psychotherapy and the current state of knowledge, it seems to be defensible and justifiable for the eclectic therapist to place confidence in empirical results and tenable hypotheses instead of adhering to a single theory. In the absence of research data, Garfield contends, therapists must rely on their clinical experiences and evaluations and evaluate their interventions as therapy proceeds. His view of the eclectic approach places responsibility on the therapist to make an adequate appraisal of the client and then to work out a plan for therapy that seems appropriate. Such a plan includes selecting procedures from a variety of approaches that are relevant to the specific problems presented by particular clients.

Basic assumptions underlying models of helping

As a way of conceptualizing the variety of theoretical orientations to therapeutic practice, we rely upon the new and unique analysis of Brickman, Rabinowitz, Karuza, Coates, Cohn, and Kidder (1982). In our opinion, their four models of helping provide a framework for analyzing some basic assumptions of the contemporary psychotherapies mentioned earlier. Their analysis is based upon a distinction between attribution of responsibility (who is to be held accountable for a present or past event) and attribution of responsibility for a solution (who is to control future events). They describe four general models: In the *moral model*, people are held responsible for both the problems in their lives and the solutions to them and are believed to need only proper motivation. In the *compensatory model*, people are seen as not responsible for their problems but as responsible for solutions, and they are believed to need power. In the *medical model*, people are seen as responsible for neither their problems nor the solutions and are believed to need treatment. In the *enlightenment model*, people are seen as responsible for their problems but as unable or unwilling to provide the solutions, and they are believed to need discipline.

Practitioners are not always aware of the assumptions they make about human behavior and how these assumptions affect their interventions. Therapists can function with more direction when they become aware of their assumptions about responsibility for problems and for solutions. Each of these four sets of assumptions is internally consistent, and to some degree each is incompatible with the other three.

The moral model

The moral model is based on the assumption that people are responsible both for creating and for solving their problems. Under this model people see themselves and are seen by others as unmotivated and as not making the effort needed for changing. If they hope to change, they must develop the motivation to do what is necessary to bring about change, for nobody but them can act in ways that will result in change. Practitioners with this orientation remind people how they are responsible for creating their life situations and how only they can utilize their resources to control their future. Several current theories of therapy are grounded on this model of human behavior—reality therapy, rational-emotive therapy, existential therapy, person-centered therapy, and Gestalt therapy.

Reality therapy.   The reality therapist functions as a teacher and a model and confronts clients in ways that help them face reality and fulfill basic needs without harming themselves or others. Therapists should challenge clients to make value judgments about their own behavior. It is therefore appropriate for therapy to be concerned with judgments of right and wrong. The heart of reality therapy is acceptance of personal responsibility, which is equated with mental health. Glasser (1965) developed this therapy from his conviction that traditional psychiatry is based largely on mistaken assumptions. Thus, practitioners of reality therapy focus on what clients are able and willing to do in the present situation to change their behavior and on the means for doing so. Clients must be willing to commit themselves to a program of change, develop a plan of action, and follow through. Therapists should not accept any excuses from clients for failure to follow through on their commitments.

Rational-emotive therapy.   According to Albert Ellis (1979), people's problems are not caused by others or by past events. Rather, their perception of life situations is what leads to feelings of worthlessness. Thus, it is the responsibility of the person to recognize and change distorted thinking that leads to behavioral problems. Some basic ideas of the rational-emotive approach include:

- People's belief systems and evaluations of situations, not the situations themselves, are the causes of emotional problems.
- People tend to incorporate these irrational beliefs from external sources and then continue to indoctrinate themselves with these beliefs.
- To overcome irrational thinking, therapists should use active methods of intervention, such as teaching, persuading, and giving homework assignments. The therapist's role is to exhort the client to work at changing. The goal of therapy is to substitute a rational belief system for an irrational one and to have the client eventually assume responsibility for solutions.

Existential therapy.   The existential view holds that human beings define themselves by their own choices. Although there are factors that restrict their choices, their self-determination is the ultimate basis of their uniqueness as individuals. Existential therapists assert that clients often lead "restricted existences," seeing few if any alternatives to limited ways of dealing with life situations and tending to feel trapped or helpless. A central task of the therapist is to confront these clients with the ways in which they are living restricted existences and to help them become aware of their own part in creating this condition. Through an authentic client/therapist relationship, clients become increasingly aware of factors in their past that they are excessively holding on to and of stifling modes of their present existence. They can therefore begin to accept responsibility for changing their future. Since the goal of therapy is to help clients become responsible for the direction of their own lives, what occurs in therapy is largely the clients' responsibility.

Person-centered therapy.   According to Carl Rogers, individuals have the capacity for self-direction. They can become aware of their own problems and of the means of resolving them if they are encouraged to explore present feelings and thoughts in the therapeutic relationship. This view contends that people are basically trustworthy and are striving toward growth and wholeness. Seeing people in this light means that the therapist focuses on the constructive side of human nature, on what is right with people, and on the assets they bring with them to therapy. Thus, therapy becomes something more than a process of diagnosis and treatment of problems. It focuses on how clients act in the world with others and how they can move forward in constructive directions. Clients can make progress without the therapist's interpretations, diagnoses, evaluations, and directions. What they do need from the therapist is warmth, acceptance, respect, empathy, positive regard, and caring. In the context of this type of relationship with a therapist, clients have the resources within themselves to solve whatever problems they are facing.

Gestalt therapy.   The Gestalt approach is based on the assumption that people must find their own way in life and accept personal responsibility if they hope to achieve maturity. The basic task of the therapist is to help clients fully experience their being in the here-and-now by becoming aware of how they prevent themselves from feeling and experiencing in the present. With this approach, clients carry out their own therapy as much as possible. They make their own interpretations, create their own direct statements, and find their own meanings. Clients are encouraged to experience directly in the present their struggles with "unfinished business" from their past. By experiencing their conflicts instead of merely talking about them, they gradually expand their own level of awareness and integrate the fragmented and unknown parts of their personality. A basic premise of Gestalt therapy is that people are responsible for their own feelings, and clients in therapy are challenged to look at ways in which they avoid this responsibility.

The compensatory model

The model in which people are not held responsible for their problems but are still held responsible for solving these problems is the compensatory model. This model holds that people have to compensate for obstacles imposed upon them by their situation with a special kind of effort and collaboration with others. Brickman and his associates (1982) write that the strength of this model is that it allows people to direct their efforts toward the future by trying to transform their environment without blaming themselves for creating their problems. Although clients are not blamed for their problems that originated in the past, they are given credit for coming up with solutions. Under this model we classify these approaches: Adlerian, behavioral, and transactional analysis.

Adlerian therapy.   According to the Adlerian approach, people are primarily social beings, shaped and motivated by social forces. People are creative, active, choice-making beings, not victims of fate. According to Adler, humans are pushed by the need to overcome inherent feelings of inferiority and are pulled by the striving for superiority. Adler stressed that all of us have such inferiority feelings, which stem largely from childhood, when we felt small and helpless. The individual attempts to overcome this sense of helplessness by compensating—that is, by developing a life-style in which success is possible. People's styles of life are formed early to compensate for a particular inferiority. These styles of life consist of people's views about themselves and the world and their distinctive behaviors and habits as they pursue their personal goals. People can shape their own futures by actively and courageously taking risks and making decisions in the face of unknown consequences. Counseling is viewed as a collaborative effort; both the client and therapist are active in this relationship, working toward mutually agreed-on goals.

Behavior therapy. Cognitive behavior therapy, which focuses on cognitive factors and thinking as they affect behavior, embodies many assumptions of the compensatory model. The role of the therapist is largely teaching clients how to recognize and alter maladaptive cognitive processes and environmental contingencies. For example, an alcoholic may stay away from places where alcohol is served, thus arranging the outside environment so that the problem will be less likely to occur. After clients become aware of ways that their cognitive structures relate to behavior, they are in a position to set their own goals, monitor their own performance, and reward themselves appropriately. Although behavior therapy assumes that people are basically shaped by learning and sociocultural conditioning, this approach does focus on the client's ability to eliminate maladaptive behavior and learn constructive behavior. Therapy focuses on overt behavior, thought processes that affect certain behaviors, specification of therapy goals, and evaluation of results. Therapy is not complete unless new behaviors are actually practiced in real-life situations.

Transactional analysis. Under transactional analysis (TA), clients learn ways to recognize early parental messages (injunctions) and early decisions they made in response to these injunctions. They learn how the messages they assimilated as children affect them now and how the life scripts they developed determine their actions. Therapists are expected to play an active role as teachers, trainers, and resource persons in therapy. At the same time, clients are expected to be equal partners in the therapeutic endeavor. For therapy to be effective, clients must carry out contracts to work on specific issues rather than simply talking about problems in order to gain insight. The goal of therapy is to liberate clients from past messages and decisions so that they can make new decisions about how they will live.

We've classified TA under the compensatory model because many TA therapists do not hold people accountable for the origin and development of their problems. Clients "scripted" during their early developmental years are viewed as living out the endings called for by this scripting *unless* there is some form of intervention. Such intervention can help these clients become aware of the injunctions they uncritically bought into and can increase their awareness of early decisions they made in reaction to these parental injunctions. TA acknowledges that people were influenced by the expectations and demands of significant others, especially since their early decisions were made at a time in life when they were highly dependent upon others. The founder of TA, Eric Berne (1970), wrote that human beings have the capacity to choose but that few people achieve the degree of awareness necessary for becoming autonomous:

> Man is born free, but one of the first things he learns is to do as he is told, and he spends the rest of his life doing that. Thus his first enslavement is to his parents. He follows their instructions forevermore, retaining only in some cases the right to choose his own methods and consoling himself with the illusion of autonomy [p. 194].

This pessimistic view of Berne (1961, 1970, 1972) is rejected by Goulding and Goulding (1978, 1979), well-known TA theorists and practitioners, on the ground that it is too deterministic. The Gouldings emphasize the role of "redecisions" in therapy, contending that early decisions are not irreversible. In their view, individuals make decisions in response to real or imagined injunctions and thereby "script" themselves. In this light, since individuals cooperated in making the early decisions that direct their lives, they can now make new decisions that are appropriate and will allow them to create new beginnings to their lives.

TA also qualifies for the compensatory model on the ground that its practitioners hold their clients responsible for solving their problems. These solutions are worked out in the context of a therapeutic contract that spells out the clients' responsibilities for taking certain actions designed to bring about the desired changes.

The medical model

The basic premise of the medical model is that people are not held responsible for either the origin of their problems or the solution to their problems. People are seen as victims of a disease and are considered to be subject to forces beyond their control. This model views people as incapacitated, and they are expected to accept that condition, which involves exempting them from responsibility. They must seek expert help in coping with their problems. The advantage of the medical model for coping is that it allows people to accept help without being blamed for their weakness (Brickman et al., 1982). The drawback of the model is that it fosters dependency and a sense of powerlessness.

Psychoanalytic therapy.   The approach to therapy that most embodies the assumptions of the medical model is psychoanalysis. This view of human nature holds that people are basically determined by unconscious motivation, irrational forces, sexual and aggressive impulses, and early-childhood experiences. Parental failures and the rigid demands of civilized society produce neurotic problems. Since the dynamics of behavior lie buried in the unconscious, one's hope for a cure is to participate in the lengthy process of analyzing inner conflicts that are rooted in the past. A basic procedure of analytic therapy is encouraging the development of the transference relationship, which is seen as essential for clients who hope to free themselves of the crippling effects of emotional trauma. Thus, analytic therapists remain relatively anonymous and encourage clients to project onto them the feelings they have had toward the significant people in their lives. Analyzing and interpreting the transference relationship leads to insight and personality change. For therapy to

be effective, clients must be willing to commit themselves to an intensive, long-term
process.

The enlightenment model

Under the enlightenment model, people are held accountable for contributing to or
causing their problems, but they are not believed to be responsible for solving them.
For example, people with addictive personalities often blame themselves for their
drinking problems, for the fact that they cannot live without drugs, or for their
obsession with eating. Because their impulses are out of control, they believe, they
need the discipline provided from some external authority or some type of therapeutic
community.

Examples of approaches based on the enlightenment model. Therapeutic
communities such as Alcoholics Anonymous, Daytop Village, Overeaters Anonymous, Weight Watchers, and other peer self-help groups are based on the assumption
that some form of structured therapeutic community is necessary to help addictive
personalities control their impulses. For example, some drug and alcohol rehabilitation programs use recovered alcoholics and drug addicts who have the goal of
rehabilitating fellow substance abusers. Many of these organizations provide a highly
structured environment that directs its members in the specifics of everyday living.
An example of an organization based on the enlightenment model is Alcoholics
Anonymous. Members must take responsibility for their past drinking problems and
the consequences of their life-style rather than continue to blame others for their
drinking patterns. They admit that they are alcoholics, that they have a disease, and
that they are powerless to control their drinking. Thus, they turn their lives over to
a higher power and to the community of fellow alcoholics who have been successful
in giving up drinking.

Mixing your models: A case study

The point we want to make at this juncture is that, even though these four models
help us understand the views of human nature held by the different theories of
counseling, they are not to be viewed in a rigid fashion. Let us add a note of confusion
to the picture by way of a case study.

*A Southeast Asian refugee adolescent has seen little except war, hunger, destruc-
tion, and chaos. He is a patient in a mental institution, for in a delusional moment
he killed his adoptive parents. He is diagnosed as a paranoid schizophrenic and is still
actively delusional.*

How can this person be treated in light of the four contrasting models just
described?

• He may need medication for his delusional state to calm him down (medical
model). In your opinion, would it be ethical to deny him medication because of your
view that he is responsible for his past and his actions (moral model)?

• The medication sedates him to the point at which you can converse with him.
At this point, which models can you draw from, and which can you not draw from?

• To what degree do you hold him responsible for his past? Given his unusual life experiences, do you see him as a victim of these circumstances? Why or why not? Is he responsible for changing his behavior, or does he need help? How would your answer affect your approach and your interventions in working with him? What would your approach tell you about rigid delineations of various models?

Commentary.   It is our point of view that your approach to a client is ultimately influenced by the client's circumstances and welfare, not by your loyalty to a particular view of human nature. There may be a time when the therapist needs to draw from several theoretical approaches. In the above-cited case, the therapist from the moral school may need help from the doctor (medical model) before any understanding or changing of behavior can begin.

Your views on the models of helping

Now that you have been introduced to four models of helping, we hope that you will clarify your own position on people's responsibility for creating their problems and for finding solutions to these problems. Examine the following questions on your own and bring your positions to class for a general discussion.

- What are the advantages and strengths of each of these four models? What are the disadvantages and weaknesses?
- Which model comes closest to your thinking? Why? What are the implications of embracing this model with respect to your counseling practice?
- Do you think it is important that you convey to your clients your basic assumptions and the model from which you function? Should clients know your views on the degree to which they are responsible for their problems and solutions? Explain your stand.
- Contrast the medical model with the moral model. What basic differences do you predict in the way practitioners would approach the therapeutic situation, depending upon which model they accepted?
- Think about how each model would influence a practitioner's answers to these questions: What techniques are most effective in therapy? What is expected of the client? What is the role of the therapist? What are the major goals of therapy? How does diagnosis fit into therapy?

The use of techniques in counseling and therapy

Your view of the use of techniques in counseling and therapy is closely related to your theoretical model. The issue of techniques includes such questions as *what* techniques, procedures, or intervention methods you would use and *when* and *why* you would use them. Some counselors are very eager to learn new techniques, treating them almost as if they were a bag of tricks. Others, out of anxiety over not knowing what to do in a given counseling situation, may try technique after technique in helter-skelter fashion. However, counselors should have sound reasons for using particular methods of intervention, and we question the benefit to the client of an overreliance on technique.

It can be very illuminating to see yourself working with a client on videotape or to listen to a session you've tape-recorded. Instead of focusing your attention on what your client said or did, you can monitor your own responses and get some general sense of how you related to your client. We suggest that you review your sessions with several clients in this way, paying attention to questions such as the following:

- Do you ask many questions? If so, are the questions mainly to get information, or are they open-ended ones designed to challenge your client? Do you raise questions merely because you don't know what else to do and hope that your questions will keep things moving?
- Do you tend to give advice and work quickly toward solutions? Or do you allow your client to explore feelings in depth instead of focusing on solutions to problems?
- How much direction do you give to the sessions? Who typically structures the sessions?
- How much support and reassurance do you give? Do you allow your clients to fully express what they're feeling before you offer support? Do your attempts to give support tend to cut them off from what they're feeling?
- Do you challenge your clients when you think they need it? Do your interventions get them to think about what they're saying on a deeper level?
- Who does most of the talking? Do you hear yourself as preaching or persuading? Are you responsive to what your client is saying?
- How often do you clarify what you hear? Do you check whether you're hearing what your client means to express?
- Do you reflect back to your clients what you hear them saying? If so, is your reflection done mechanically, or does it encourage a deeper self-exploration?
- Do you interpret much, telling your clients what you think certain behaviors mean? Or do you leave it to them to discover what their behavior means from their own perspectives?
- Do you use techniques primarily to get clients moving, or do you wait until they express some feelings and then use a technique geared to helping them experience their feelings on a more intense level?
- Do you use techniques that "feel right" for you and that you're comfortable using? Have you experienced these techniques yourself as a client?
- Are the counseling procedures you use drawn from one counseling approach? Or do you borrow techniques from various approaches and use them when they seem appropriate?
- When you use a particular technique, does it seem mechanical to you? Or do you feel that your techniques are appropriate and unforced?
- How do your clients generally respond to the techniques you use? Do they react negatively to any of your counseling methods?

Monitoring your own work in light of these questions can help you discover your counseling style, ask yourself why you're making the interventions you make, and evaluate the impact these counseling procedures have on your clients. This willingness to reflect on the effects your interventions have on clients is of the utmost importance.

We believe that the purpose of techniques is to facilitate movement in a counseling session and that your counseling techniques really cannot be separated from your personality and your relationship with your client. When counselors fall into a pattern of mechanically employing techniques, they become technicians and are not responding to the particular individuals they're counseling. You can lessen the chances of falling into a mechanical style by deliberately paying attention to the ways you tend to use techniques. Particular techniques may be better suited to some therapists' personalities and styles of counseling than to others'. At times you may try a technique that you've observed someone else using very skillfully, only to find that it fails for you. In essence, your techniques should fit your counseling style, and you should feel comfortable and real in using them.

We like Sidney Jourard's (1968) ideas on the issue of the role of techniques in psychotherapy. He views therapy as "a way of being with another person" rather than as a system of techniques. This is not to say that therapists shouldn't master techniques and have a grasp of theory; in fact, Jourard sees a willingness to learn theory and techniques as a sign of seriousness in one's work that distinguishes professional therapists from amateurs. His position is summed up well in the sentence "Effective psychotherapists, who succeed in inviting sufferers to change their previous ways of being, are not technicians, although they will have mastered their techniques" (p. 58).

If you are not seeing clients and have no access to videotapes of counseling sessions, you might find some ways to role-play and gain practice with fellow students. If you are relatively inexperienced, you may be afraid to apply certain techniques and thus may be unwilling to find ways to gain the practice you need. We encourage you to initiate some form of experiential practice so that you can get feedback from other students and your professors. Of course, ethical practice demands that you have training and supervision in techniques before you use them with clients. This is a further reason to find safe ways to practice as a part of the class activity.

The division of responsibility in therapy

Earlier in this chapter we discussed four models of human nature and the responsibility these models do or do not place on the client for change. In this section we explore the issue of responsibility for change in a different way.

Theories stressing the therapist's responsibility

A behavioral viewpoint.   Many behavior therapists emphasize the therapist's role in structuring sessions in such a way that clients experience success and don't drop out prematurely. In their view, claims by therapists that clients have insufficient motivation or ego strength to continue with the demands of therapy are rationalizations. As Goldstein (1973) puts it, "Therapy is the therapist's responsibility. It is the therapist who at the very least implicitly establishes himself as the expert, and any failure is the therapist's failure" (p. 222).

The rational-emotive viewpoint.   Ellis (1973) views psychotherapy as an educative process in which the therapist teaches the client ways of self-understanding and changing. The therapist therefore assumes a great share of the responsibility for directing the session. The rational-emotive therapist employs a rapid-fire, highly directive, persuasive methodology that emphasizes the cognitive aspects of therapy.

The psychoanalytic viewpoint. Typically, an analytically oriented therapist's work begins with evaluating the client to determine if the person is a suitable candidate for psychoanalytic therapy. The therapist assumes the role of expert in terms of diagnosis, evaluation, and treatment. After establishing a working relationship with the client, the therapist must then do a lot of listening and interpreting. It is the analyst's task to pay attention to the resistances of the client and then to make timely interpretations to accelerate the process of uncovering unconscious material. Further, it is the analytically oriented therapist's task to teach clients the meaning of the dynamics of their behavior so that they are able to achieve insight into their problems and thus gain more rational control over their lives.

Theories stressing the client's responsibility

The client-centered viewpoint. Although Rogers stresses the responsibility of the therapist to be authentic in the therapeutic relationship, he does see the client as responsible for directing the sessions. Clients should use the therapeutic relationship to explore areas that are deeply significant to them, and Rogers assumes that they have the best vantage point for deciding what these areas are. The therapist facilitates this process by creating a supportive climate in which clients eventually feel trusting enough to drop their defenses and find the resources for change within themselves.

Experiential viewpoints. Extreme claims that the full responsibility in therapy rests with the client have been expressed by the late founder of Gestalt therapy, Fritz Perls, and a leading figure in the encounter-group movement, William Schutz.

Perls (1969) assumed that most people become patients because of their unwillingness to accept responsibility for their own lives. Instead of relying on themselves, most people, he argued, look to external sources of support. Perls claimed that most people who seek therapy don't want to be cured; rather, they want to become "more adequate in their neurosis" (p. 75). Because of this belief, Perls used to begin his workshops with this declaration: "I am responsible only for myself and for nobody else. I am not taking responsibility for any of you—you are responsible for yourselves" (p. 74). He elaborated on this statement by saying: "So if you want to go crazy, commit suicide, improve, get 'turned on,' or get an experience that will change your life, that's up to you. I do my thing and you do your thing" (p. 75). Schutz (1971) expressed a similar conviction to participants at the outset of a workshop: "If you want to resist instructions or group pressure, that is up to you. If you want to bow to pressure, it's your decision. If you want to be physically injured or go crazy, that, too, is up to you. You are responsible for yourself" (pp. 160–161).

The psychosocial viewpoint. Counselors who operate from a psychosocial perspective assert that our lives are largely the result of the choices we make at each stage of life. The developmental model of Erikson (1963) describes human growth as occurring in eight stages over the life span, each of which is characterized by a specific crisis to be resolved. According to Erikson, each *crisis* represents a *turning point* in life. At these turning points people can either achieve successful resolution of their conflicts and move forward or fail to resolve the conflicts and regress. The developmental model builds upon and expands the psychoanalytic model, for Erikson holds that psychosexual and psychosocial growth occur together and that at each stage of life we face the task of defining some balance between ourselves and our social world. The psychosocial viewpoint is especially emphasized in the field of social work.

Dimensions of the therapist's responsibility

As you consider the range of viewpoints on the division of responsibility in therapy, think about your own position on this issue. What do you see as your responsibility, both to your client and to yourself? What do you expect from your client? Do you burden yourself with the total responsibility for what happens in therapy?

We've observed that many beginning counselors tend to deprive their clients of their rightful responsibility for their experience in therapy, because they anxiously take so much of this responsibility on themselves. If clients don't progress fast enough, these counselors may blame themselves for not knowing enough, not having the necessary skill and experience, or not being sensitive or caring enough. They may worry constantly about their adequacy as counselors and transmit their anxiety to their clients. *If only* they were better therapists, their clients would be changing in more positive directions! Of course, this may be true, but overly anxious counselors frequently fail to see the role their clients play in the outcomes of their own therapy, whether for better or for worse.

We believe that counselors do well to bring up the question of responsibility during their initial sessions with each client, so that clients can begin to think about their part in their own therapy. One way of clarifying the dimensions of responsibility in a therapeutic relationship is via contracts. A contract is based on a negotiation between the client and the therapist to define the therapeutic relationship. A contract encourages the client and the therapist to specify the goals of the therapy and the methods likely to be employed in obtaining these goals. Other aspects of a contract include the length and frequency of sessions, the duration of therapy, the cost and method of payment, provisions for the renegotiation of the contract, any factors limiting confidentiality, the extent of responsibility for each partner, and ways of determining the effectiveness of the therapeutic relationship.

We see therapy as a joint venture of the client and the therapist. Both have serious responsibilities for the direction of therapy, and this issue needs to be clarified during the initial stages of counseling. In our view, counselors who typically decide what to discuss and are overdirective run the risk of perpetuating their clients' dependence. We'd like to see clients encouraged from the start to assume as much responsibility as they can. Even directive therapies such as transactional analysis, behavior therapy, rational-emotive therapy, and reality therapy stress client-initiated contracts and homework assignments as ways clients can fulfill their commitment to change. These devices help to keep the focus of responsibility on the clients by challenging them to decide what *they* want from therapy and what *they* are willing to do to get what they want.

Although we have stressed the tendency of some therapists to take on too much responsibility, we do believe that therapists have responsibilities to their clients, including:

- being emotionally present for their clients
- keeping themselves enthused and energetic
- taking on only as many clients as they can handle effectively
- being willing to live up to their contracts with their clients
- being honest with clients
- refusing to accept clients whom they are not personally or professionally competent to counsel
- discussing any factors that may influence a client's decision to enter the therapeutic relationship
- discussing and structuring the various dimensions of the relationship

As you consider your responsibilities to your clients, try to be as specific as you can. For example, you might ask yourself whether counselors have a responsibility to arrange for regular breaks in their day's schedule. Although counselors differ in their capacity to cope with intensity, we wonder how ethical it is for counselors to work with clients continuously without taking enough time to center themselves. How much investment will you have in the clients you see at the end of a long and full day of work? Can you be as present for these clients as you were for those you saw earlier in the day?

Before you continue, write down what you consider to be some of your responsibilities toward your clients and some of their responsibilities to themselves.

I'm responsible for:

_____

_____

_____

_____

_____

My clients are responsible for:

_____

_____

_____

_____

_____

Roles and functions of counselors

The roles and functions of counselors depend on their theoretical perspectives, the type of counseling they do, where they work, and the kinds of people they counsel. We think that, to a large degree, counselors are responsible for defining their own roles and choosing their own functions as part of creating their professional identities. Too often counselors passively allow others to define their roles for them. Even if their positions involve job descriptions that limit their options, often they fail to exercise the freedom they *do* have in deciding on their job priorities.

When one of the authors was on an accreditation team visiting a high school, a counselor was asked: "How do you spend most of your time? Would you like to be doing things as a counselor that you aren't doing now?" The counselor replied that he worked on scheduling, dealt with truancy and tardiness problems, and spent most of his time dealing with students who were sent to him by teachers for disciplinary reasons. This was the role assigned to him by the school administrators, and he seemed to be satisfied with it. He didn't feel comfortable with personal or social counseling, career counseling, or other work that would involve dealing with students on a more intimate basis. There were other counselors in the same school, however, whose view of counseling included being receptive to exploring intimate issues with students. Even though some of these psychologically oriented counselors sometimes faced conflict with their administrators, they were active in defining their own roles by developing a rationale for how they were spending their time. Because they had given careful thought to what they wanted to do, they were able to create, in part, their own professional roles.

Of course, the type of counseling you do will determine some specific functions. The functions performed by career counselors are different from those performed by crisis-intervention counselors. The roles of counselors who work primarily with severely disturbed people in institutional settings will differ from those of counselors who specialize in personal-growth approaches for people without major problems. Functions that are appropriate in some counseling situations, then, may be inappropriate in others.

You can begin to consider now what functions would be appropriate for you to perform in the kind of position you hope to obtain. How would you deal with being required to perform functions that you thought were inappropriate or interfered with your effectiveness as a counselor? Could you work in an agency that expected you to perform such functions? If you accepted such a job, would it be worth the price you would have to pay? Look over the following list of activities, and ask yourself whether you see each one as an appropriate part of a counselor's job and as one that you can see yourself performing regularly. Rate each one, using the following code: A = I would accept this activity as part of my role; B = I'd have difficulty carrying out this function; C = I'm undecided.

_____ 1. checking up on clients to see if they are following through with behaviors they have contracted for

_____ 2. reporting on clients' progress to a board, a judge, an administrator, or some other authority

_____ 3. doing clerical work

_____ 4. helping people obtain legal or financial aid

_____ 5. administering tests

_____ 6. interpreting test results

_____ 7. providing information about job opportunities

___ 8. doing community work
___ 9. supervising students during lunch
___ 10. referring clients to community-service agencies
___ 11. working with family members of clients
___ 12. teaching grooming and personal hygiene
___ 13. driving a person to and from an appointment
___ 14. writing reports based on problems of clients
___ 15. doing research on the incidence of certain types of problems

In considering these activities, you should realize that at times clients need-services that aren't strictly counseling services. Thus, counselors may need to provide auxiliary helping services, such as teaching grooming, before they can do more direct counseling. Because basic physical and security needs must be met before attention can be devoted to higher-order needs (such as self-actualization), some counselors consider assisting clients to meet basic needs to be part of their work.

Deciding on the goals of counseling

Aimless therapy is unlikely to be effective, yet too often practitioners fail to devote enough time to thinking about the goals they have for their clients and the goals clients have for themselves. In this section we discuss possible goals of therapy, how they are determined, and who should determine them. Counselors' answers to these questions are directly related to their theoretical orientations.

In considering therapeutic goals, it is important to keep in mind the cultural determinants of therapy. The goals of therapy are specific to a particular culture's definition of psychological health. Levine and Padilla (1980) note that the goals for therapy in any culture can range from removal of symptoms to attitude change, behavior change, insight, improved relations with others, social effectiveness, personal adjustment, and preventive health. They give an example of Morita therapy, a popular treatment in Japan that involves discussion of the concepts of Zen Buddhism. This therapy directs the person toward an Eastern conception of mental health based on an inner-directed life acquired through peace and meditation.

As you read about therapeutic goals, think of how certain theoretical approaches represent a cultural bias. For example, the experiential therapies have the goal of helping people to move in the direction of becoming self-actualizing and autonomous, which is typically a goal of Western cultures. It should be noted, however, that this is not the goal valued in all cultures, especially Eastern ones.

Goals and theoretical approaches

When students think about what the central goals of therapy should be, they may feel perplexed by the broad range of goals specified by different theoretical approaches. Behaviorist theorists recommend specific, measurable goals, such as eliminating fears, learning how to be assertive in social situations, losing weight, curing disabling physical symptoms, reducing tensions and stresses, and coping more effectively with specific conflict situations. Relationship-oriented therapists stress such lofty goals as becoming full, autonomous, and free persons. For Rogers (1961) the general therapeutic goal is to become a fully functioning person; for Maslow (1968, 1970) the goal is to become a self-actualizing person; for May (1967) the goal is to accept one's freedom to create a unique existence and to understand one's "being-in-the-world." Frankl (1963) talks about the search for meaning and purpose, Bugental (1976) describes the search for authentic existence, and Jourard (1971) writes of the "transparent self." Unlike the specific, concrete goals of behaviorist therapists, these broad goals involve personal characteristics that are usually very difficult to measure.

Confronted with this theoretical diversity, you might conclude that no reconciliation is possible among the goals emphasized by different approaches. Yet some convergence of these goals is possible. Behavior therapists, for example, don't necessarily reject the general goals of the relationship-oriented therapists; rather, they insist that general goals should be translated into specific, short-term tasks that have observable results. These concrete goals can focus the counseling sessions, and they allow both the client and the therapist to make some assessment of the degree to which their objectives are being accomplished. In writing on this issue of the convergence of the behavioristic and humanistic views of goals, Wrenn (1966) notes that practicing counselors can integrate the "two psychological worlds" by using behavioristic techniques to accomplish humanistic goals.

Your goals as a counselor

What are some of the basic goals that you would use to guide your work with clients? The following list presents 20 therapeutic goals. Indicate how much you would emphasize each by using the following code: A = an extremely important goal; B = a somewhat important goal; C = a relatively unimportant goal.

_____ 1. that clients will take risks and open new doors that may result in increased awareness of themselves and others

_____ 2. that clients will critically examine their cultural conditioning and determine whether they want to embrace the values of their particular culture

_____ 3. that clients will develop increased pride and respect for the unique values that are a part of their culture

_____ 4. that clients will strive for and be able to form a personal as well as cultural identity

_____ 5. that clients will learn how to question a given society's definition of mental and psychological health to determine whether they want to strive toward an "ideal level of functioning" as set by the society

_____ 6. that clients will learn both the advantages and the disadvantages of living by the norms of the dominant culture in which they live

_____ 7. that clients will accept responsibility for internal support as opposed to depending on external support

_____ 8. that clients will acquire inner peace and tranquility

_____ 9. that clients will learn ways to reach out to social networks for support, especially with their families

_____ 10. that clients will make value judgments about their own behavior and then decide upon a plan of action for change should they determine that their behavior is not working effectively for them

_____ 11. that clients will learn certain coping skills that will help them deal effectively with present and future problems so that they will ultimately rely on themselves to solve problems rather than on the therapist

___ 12. that clients will recall past events and work through emotions that are blocking their full enjoyment of living now

___ 13. that clients will come to recognize that they have the capacities within themselves to reshape their lives by making new choices

___ 14. that clients will begin to question their values and assumptions about life and determine the degree to which these beliefs are valid for them now

___ 15. that clients will reduce or eliminate specific behavioral problems and replace their faulty learning with more effective behavior

___ 16. that clients will learn the process of using their resources for solving their own problems

___ 17. that clients will become more conscious of their options and more willing to make choices for themselves and accept the consequences

___ 18. that clients will acquire the information necessary to make better choices

___ 19. that clients will experience the range of their own personal power so that they can give up feeling and behaving like victims

___ 20. that clients will uncover the influence of the past on their present behavior

Now write what *you* consider to be the *most basic* and *significant* goal of counseling:

_____

_____

_____

Questionable goals

In addition to clarifying what you consider to be the central goals of counseling, it is also well to formulate your ideas concerning goals that are of questionable value. For example, is solving problems for a client a worthwhile goal? Is it part of your job to provide answers for clients if you believe that they lack the resources to solve their own problems? Consider how you might counsel clients who came to you seeking advice. How does giving advice contribute to goals of counseling that you consider worthwhile?

Other questionable objectives in counseling include "straightening out" clients, trying to get clients to conform to expected patterns of socially acceptable behavior, and imposing goals on clients that they haven't chosen for themselves. For example, is it the counselor's task to help clients become "well adjusted," in the sense of conforming to social norms? Jourard (1968) answers in the negative: "At his worst, the psychotherapist is but one more agent of socialization, a 'trainer' who adds his technical know-how to that of parents, educators, and propagandists, to ensure that people will conform to institutional norms" (p. 38). Rather, Jourard believes, the therapist's goal should be to help clients understand and go beyond the situations that restrict their responsible exercise of freedom. Therapists function at their best when they guide clients "toward liberation from the clutch of the past" and from the "bewitching effects of social pressure" (pp. 37–38). If therapists become agents of the status quo, they hinder their clients' efforts to become healthy, growing persons. Jourard would therefore like to see therapists function as "responsible anarchists" who are "committed to an endless search for ways to live that foster growth, well-being, idiosyncrasy, freedom, and authenticity" (p. 42).

Another questionable goal involves encouraging clients who are bicultural to downplay their unique traits so that they stand a better chance of acculturating to the values of the dominant culture. This issue of acculturation has special significance to many racial minorities, who have banded together as the Third World Movement (Asian Americans, Blacks, Chicanos, Native Americans, and others) as a way of dealing with the common oppression that they share in the dominant society. Effective counseling must take into consideration such cultural variables as ideals, customs, beliefs, mannerisms, and institutions. It is especially important that the diversity of cultures be taken into account as clients and counselors decide upon the goals that will direct the counseling sessions. Although there are many advantages to being bicultural, the striving for dual cultural membership has been most difficult for many ethnic and racial minorities. They often have difficulty forming an identity, and they may have the experience of being a "marginal" person in both cultural groups. D. W. Sue (1981) puts this matter clearly:

> Third World people are placed under strong pressures to adopt the ways of the dominant culture. Third World people's own ethnicity or cultural heritage is seen as a handicap to be overcome, something to be ashamed of and to be avoided. In essence, Third World people may be taught that to be different is to be deviant, pathological, or sick [p. 37].

Jourard's (1968) assertion that therapists function at their best when they guide clients away from the "bewitching effects of social pressure" and when they challenge people not to blindly conform to institutional norms has relevance in counseling clients who are culturally different. Thus, it should not be assumed that clients with dual cultural membership would be better off by assimilating into the dominant culture. One of the goals of cross-cultural counseling involves encouraging clients to retain their own cultural heritage and to avoid the trap of blurring their identity by becoming fully socialized in accordance with the standards of the dominant culture. We agree with Levine and Padilla (1980), who assert that "the degree to which the individual should acculturate or should remain a part of the minority group may be a major question in therapy" (p. 14). They suggest that the therapist must integrate an understanding of the dual cultural experience into the counseling situation, keeping in mind each client's individual differences. The matter is put concisely with their words: "The therapist must determine with the individual how much cultural separatism and/or acculturation to the majority group will facilitate personal growth" (p. 14).

Who determines therapeutic goals?

Most counseling approaches agree that the imposition of goals by the therapist does not lead to effective counseling and that goals should be set by the client and the therapist working together. However, some therapists believe that they know what is best for their clients and try to persuade their clients to accept certain goals. Others are convinced that the specific goals of counseling ought to be determined entirely by their clients and try to keep their own views out of their counseling.

One way to handle the issue of who sets counseling goals is to decide on the *general* goals you have for all your clients and then provide time in your sessions for exploring the *specific* reasons individual clients are in counseling. For example, as a general goal you may value developing clients' ability to decide for themselves and accept responsibility for their choices. This general goal can be applied to the concrete and specific goals of your clients, such as making a career decision, working on a school problem, understanding a relationship more fully, or learning to be more assertive. We believe that it's useful for counselors to share their general goals with their clients while stressing that the establishment of therapeutic goals will be an ongoing process that involves both the client and the counselor. Often clients have only vague notions about what it is they want from counseling. They may know only that they want to feel better or understand themselves better. Working on what specific things they want from counseling can itself be a crucial part of the therapeutic process.

Of course, the issue of who sets the goals of counseling must be seen in the light of the theory you operate from, the type of counseling you offer, the setting in which you work, and the nature of your clientele. If you work in crisis intervention, your goals are likely to be short-term and practical, and you may be very directive. If you're working with children in a school setting, you may aim at combining educational and therapeutic goals. As a counselor with institutionalized elderly people, you may stress teaching survival skills and ways of relating to others on their ward. What your goals are and how actively involved your client will be in determining them depend to a great extent on the type of counseling you provide.

Diagnosis as a professional issue

Psychodiagnosis refers to the analysis and explanation of a client's problems. It may include an explanation of the causes of the client's difficulties, an account of how these problems developed over time, a classification of any disorders, a specification of preferred treatment procedures, and an estimate of the chances for a successful resolution.

The main purpose of the diagnostic approach is to allow the therapist to plan treatments tailored to the special needs of the client. There are different kinds of diagnosis. *Medical diagnosis* is the process of examining physical symptoms, inferring causes of physical disorders or diseases, providing some kind of category that fits the pattern of a disease, and prescribing an appropriate treatment. *Psychodiagnosis* (or *psychological diagnosis*) is a general term covering the process of identifying an emotional or behavioral problem and making a statement about the current status of a client. This process also includes the identification of the possible causes of the person's emotional, psychological, and behavioral difficulties, and it entails suggesting the appropriate therapy techniques to deal effectively with the identified problem. *Differential diagnosis* is the process of distinguishing one form of disease or psychological disorder from another by determining which of two (or more) diseases or disorders with similar symptoms the person is suffering from. The third edition of the

American Psychiatric Association's (1980) *Diagnostic and Statistical Manual of Mental Disorders* (DSM III) is the standard reference for pathology.

Whether diagnosis should be part of psychotherapy is a controversial issue. Some mental-health professionals see diagnosis as an essential step in any treatment plan, but others view it as an inappropriate application of the medical model of mental health to counseling and therapy. Even though you may not yet have had to face the practical question of whether to diagnose a client, you will most likely need to come to terms with this issue at some point in your work. In this section we briefly review some of the arguments for and against the use of diagnosis in therapy and ask you to consider how valuable diagnosis is from your viewpoint.

Arguments for psychodiagnosis

Practitioners who favor the use of diagnostic procedures in therapy generally argue that such procedures enable the therapist to acquire sufficient knowledge about the client's past and present behavior to develop an appropriate plan of treatment. This approach stems from the medical model of mental health, according to which different underlying causal factors produce different types of disorders. Goldenberg (1977) cites six purposes of psychodiagnosis that are generally mentioned by those who support its use in therapy:

1. Each diagnostic label encompasses a wide range of behavioral characteristics, and this allows professionals to communicate common meanings effectively.
2. Diagnosis facilitates the selection of the most suitable form of therapy.
3. A diagnostic explanation of the causal factors involved in a client's problems can suggest measures that will alleviate the client's symptoms.
4. Diagnosis is useful in predicting the course and outcome of a person's disorder.
5. Diagnosis provides a framework for research into the effectiveness of various treatment approaches.
6. Diagnostic classifications facilitate such administrative tasks as the collection of statistical data regarding the incidence of particular disorders and the type of psychological services provided in the community.

Psychoanalytically oriented therapists favor psychodiagnosis, since this form of therapy was patterned after the medical model of mental health and stresses the understanding of past situations that have contributed to a dysfunction. Some psychological-assessment devices used in psychodiagnosis involve projective techniques that rest on psychoanalytic concepts.

For different reasons, practitioners with a behavioristic orientation also favor a diagnostic stance, inasmuch as they emphasize specific treatment programs. Although they may not follow the medical model, these practitioners value observation and other objective means of appraising both a client's specific symptoms and the factors that have led up to the client's malfunctioning. Such an appraisal, they would argue, enables them to use the techniques that are appropriate for a particular disorder and to evaluate the effectiveness of the treatment program.

Brammer and Shostrom (1982) see diagnosis as being broader than simply labeling clients with some category from DSM III. They argue in favor of diagnosis as a general descriptive statement identifying a client's style of functioning. Such information can motivate clients to change their behavior. They contend that practitioners must make some decisions, do some therapeutic planning, be alert for signs of pathology in order to avoid serious mistakes in therapy, and be in a position to make some prognoses. They propose that a therapist "simultaneously understand diagnostically and understand therapeutically" (p. 136). Although Brammer and Shostrom favor this broad type of diagnostic process, which consists of a process of developing hunches, they issue some cautions against accepting a narrow and rigid diagnostic approach.

Arguments against psychodiagnosis

Although many professionals see diagnosis as an essential component of psychotherapy, there are as many critics who view it as unnecessary or harmful. Generally, existential or relationship-oriented therapists fall into this group. Their arguments against diagnosis include the following:

1. Diagnosis is typically done by an expert observing a person's behavior and experience from an external viewpoint, without reference to what they mean to the client.
2. Diagnostic categories can rob people of their uniqueness.
3. Diagnosis can lead people to accept self-fulfilling prophecies or to despair over their conditions.
4. Diagnosis can narrow the therapist's vision by encouraging the therapist to look for behavior that fits a certain disease category.
5. The best vantage point for understanding another person is through his or her subjective world, not through a general system of classification.
6. There are many potential dangers implicit in the process of reducing human beings to diagnostic categories.

Many psychologists and some psychiatrists have objected to the use of diagnosis in therapy. Rogers (1942, 1951, 1961) has consistently maintained that diagnosis is detrimental to counseling because it tends to pull clients away from an internal and subjective way of experiencing themselves and to foster an objective and external conception *about* them. The result may be to increase tendencies toward dependence and cause clients to act as if the responsibility for changing their behavior rested with the expert and not with themselves. Of course, client-centered therapy is grounded on the belief that clients are in the best position to understand and resolve their personal difficulties. Rogers (1951) states: "When the client perceives the locus of judgment and responsibility as clearly resting in the hands of the clinician, he is, in our judgment, further from therapeutic progress than when he came in" (p. 223).

Rogers (1951) is also concerned about psychological diagnosis because of the long-range implications of the "social control of the many by the few" (p. 224). A similar concern is expressed by Szasz (1974), who has labeled the whole concept of nonorganic mental illness a "myth." According to Szasz's theory of human behavior, people are always responsible for their actions. What we call mental "diseases" aren't diseases at all, in the medical sense, but social/psychological phenomena. Szasz sees the classification of behavior as a control strategy. Like Rogers, he emphasizes the dangers of demeaning human beings by giving them psychiatric labels that miss the essence of the person.

Kempler (1973) argues that diagnostic categories provide therapists with pigeon-holes in which they can put people, with the result that they fail to meet their clients creatively. Diagnoses, Kempler maintains, "confuse the patient, if he hears them, and they can astigmatize the vision of the therapist who sees the chart before he sees the patient. And worst of all, they impair the vision of the therapist who makes them" (p. 275).

R. D. Laing (1967), a psychiatrist who has criticized traditional types of diag-nosis, expresses concern about the effects of diagnosis on those who are being classified *and* on those who are doing the categorizing. For the person being classified, diagnosis can result in a self-fulfilling prophecy whereby the person acts as he or she is expected to act. Thus, a person who knows he or she is diagnosed as a schizophrenic may take great delight in telling ward attendants "After all, I'm crazy! What can you expect from me?" In turn, hospital or ward personnel may see people only through the stereotypes associated with various diagnoses. If they expect certain behaviors from the patients, there is a good chance that the patients will adopt these behaviors and live up to the staff's expectations.

In his provocative book *The Death of Psychiatry*, Torrey (1974), also a psychi-atrist, develops the thesis that traditional psychiatry (including its emphasis on psy-chodiagnosis) is no longer functional. For Torrey, the medical model is based on a contract between a patient and society. This contract specifies that, although people may originally have been responsible for getting a disease, once the disease takes hold, they are no longer responsible (p. 79). Torrey contends that most people who are labeled "mentally ill" suffer from problems in living rather than from physical dis-abilities. Since they are not "sick," he believes that they are done an injustice when they are labeled and treated in the framework of the medical model. He expresses the crux of his argument concerning diagnosis as follows: "As a medical model approach to problems of human behavior, it produces confusions rather than solutions. If we are wise, we will allow it to die with dignity and not try to prop it up to do a job it is no longer able to do" (p. 5).

In basic accord with the position of Torrey in criticizing the medical model, Smith (1981) observes that perhaps the majority of clinical and counseling psychol-ogists identify with therapeutic orientations that eschew the mental-illness paradigm for diagnosing problems in living. Although these practitioners more often think in terms of a growth-oriented and developmental model, they are forced into assigning clients diagnostic categories and codes if they want to seek third-party payments for psychological services. He contends that, unless stringent efforts are made to oppose the ubiquitous influence of the mental-illness model reflected in DSM III, both providers and consumers of psychological services are bound to suffer.

Miller, Bergstrom, Cross, and Grube (1981) surveyed the use of the previous edition of the *Diagnostic and Statistical Manual* (DSM II) by practicing clinical and counseling psychologists. They came up with the following findings:

- Although practitioners did use DSM II in their practice for direct diagnosis, they rarely used the system indirectly for conceptualizing their cases.
- The overwhelming reason for using DSM II was that it was required by agencies and insurance companies (86.1%).

- Others reported using DSM II because it was the only classification system available (42.9%).
- Only a few of the respondents reported using the system for the reasons it was developed: to determine treatment (14.1%), to help arrive at a prognosis (11.8%), to aid in research (4.4%), to help make a differential diagnosis (22.1%), and to help conceptualize a case (22.4%).
- Only 2.8% of the respondents considered DSM II reliable and valid.

This study also asked for opinions about the revised DSM III to determine whether psychologists thought that it was an improvement over DSM II. Although the majority of psychologists who had read DSM III thought that it was better, most of them said that the later edition still needed further improvement. They recommended more information on communication between professionals, better reflection of current scientific knowledge, more consideration of psychological factors, more emphasis on clear and operational definitions, and better information on differential diagnoses. Apparently, many practicing psychologists see no choice but to use a diagnostic system developed by the medical profession, although few of them are satisfied with it. The following conclusion was reached:

> Given the findings of this survey, and the diverse theoretical positions within psychology, it may be that no matter what quality or quantity of manuals exist, each practitioner will draw upon his/her own knowledge, experience, and theoretical style to conceptualize a case and devise treatment [Miller et al., 1981, p. 390].

Dangers of the psychodiagnostic approach.   Some dangers of the diagnostic approach are described by Brammer and Shostrom (1982):

- The incompleteness or inaccuracy of data can lead to unreliable predictions.
- The practitioner can become preoccupied with the client's history and thus neglect present attitudes and behavior.
- The clinician may be tempted to rely on tests too quickly in the diagnostic process, which is likely to lead to client expectations of "answers" from these tests.
- The practitioner may become too preoccupied with signs of pathology and thus lose sight of a healthy and creative dimension of personality.
- Therapists could develop a judgmental attitude, with the responsibility being shifted too much in the direction of telling clients what they ought to do.

Another danger of the diagnostic approach is the possible failure of counselors to consider ethnic and cultural factors in certain patterns of behavior. Unless cultural variables are considered, some clients may be subjected to an erroneous diagnosis. Certain behaviors and personality styles might be labeled neurotic or deviant simply because they are not characteristic of the dominant culture. Sue (1981) gives the example of mental-health professionals' assertions that Asian Americans are the most repressed of all clients. Such statements indicate that these therapists expect all clients to be self-disclosing, emotionally expressive, and assertive. Such counselors do not recognize that the cultural upbringing of many Asian Americans places a value on restraint of strong feelings and on a reluctance to discuss personal matters with anyone outside the family. Thus, counselors who work with Blacks, Asian Americans, Mexican Americans, and American Indians may erroneously conclude that a client is repressed, inhibited, passive, and unmotivated. Sue makes the point that all of these personality characteristics are seen as undesirable by Western standards.

An argument against the traditional system of diagnosis rests on the assumption that psychological maladjustment can be assessed only within a cultural perspective. Classification of maladjustive behaviors varies by culture, and a culture's conception of causation fixes its system of classification. Levine and Padilla (1980) note that, in Western culture, maladjustment is attributed to biological and psychological factors and is categorized as organic or functional in origin. However, other cultures believe that metaphysical aspects also need to be accounted for, including witchcraft or other supernatural forces. Levine and Padilla take the position that, even though the definition of maladjustment is culturally specific, members of one culture cannot be considered more or less adjusted than members of another culture. They define maladjustment as the inability to function within a group; those who are unable to function effectively within the culture can be considered disturbed. This point of view has clear implications for some common practices of diagnosing clients by using traditional categories (DSM III) and by assuming that people who exhibit certain behavioral syndromes are necessarily within the boundaries of some diagnostic category.

Our own position on psychodiagnosis

We believe that diagnosis, broadly construed, is a legitimate part of the therapeutic process. The kind of diagnosis we have in mind is the result of a joint effort by the client and the therapist. We agree with Carkhuff and Berenson (1967) that "a meaningful diagnostic process flows out of an ongoing interactional process between therapist and client. There is no separate and distinct diagnostic process" (p. 235). Thus, both therapist and client should be involved in discovering the nature of the client's difficulty, a process that commences with the initial sessions and continues until therapy is terminated. Even practitioners who oppose conventional diagnostic procedures and terminology need to raise such questions as:

- What is going on in this client's life at this time?
- What are the client's resources for change?
- What does the client want from therapy, and how can it best be achieved?
- What should be the focus of the sessions?
- What are some factors that are contributing to the client's problems, and what can be done to alleviate them?
- What are the prospects for meaningful change?

The counselor and the client can discuss each of these questions as a part of the therapeutic process. Counselors will develop hypotheses about their clients, and they can talk about their conjectures with their clients in an ongoing way. The diagnosis performed by counselors does not have to be a matter of categorizing their clients; rather, counselors can describe behavior and think about its meaning. In this way, instead of being done mechanically and technically by an expert, diagnosis becomes a process of thinking *about* the client *with* the client.

From our perspective, diagnosis should be associated with treatment, and it should help the practitioner conceptualize a case. Ethical dilemmas are often created when diagnosis is done strictly for insurance purposes, which often entails arbitrarily assigning a client a diagnostic classification. As we have seen earlier, many practitioners use diagnosis for a variety of reasons other than thinking about the dynamics of a client and an appropriate treatment plan.

We also think that it is an ethical (and sometimes legal) obligation of therapists to screen clients for life-threatening problems such as organic disorders, schizophrenia, manic-depression, and suicidal types of depression. Students need to learn the clinical skills necessary to do this type of screening, which is a form of diagnostic thinking.

Current issues in diagnosis

Those who support the traditional forms of diagnosis agree that there are limitations to present classification systems and that some of the problems mentioned by the critics of diagnosis do exist. However, rather than abandoning diagnostic classifications altogether, they favor updating diagnostic manuals to reflect improvements in diagnosis and treatment procedures.

Another important issue regarding diagnosis is whether clients should know their diagnosis and have access to all the information concerning themselves that their therapists have. Some practitioners contend that they should decide how much information to reveal to their clients. Others believe that it is unethical to keep pertinent information from their clients. Can you think of situations in which you would not be willing to share your hunches or information about a client with that client?

There is also a practical matter pertaining to diagnosis—the fact that many insurance companies who pay for psychological services require a diagnosis on the insurance form. Presumably, clients who consult a therapist regarding problems that don't fit a standard category are not to be reimbursed for their psychotherapy. These insurance carriers take the position that psychotherapy is for treatment of specific mental or emotional disorders; consequently, if a therapist doesn't write down a specific diagnosis, the client's insurance may not cover his or her expenses.

We think that Smith (1981) hits the heart of the current controversy over the traditional diagnostic system when he addresses informed-consent procedures. He points out that, while unprecedented attention is being given to informed decisions by clients regarding treatment plans and expectations, most practitioners remain virtually silent on clients' rights to be informed regarding diagnostic classifications for the purpose of securing third-party payments. Smith contends that psychologists are compromising their integrity and sacrificing the dignity of their clients for economic gain by using the DSM system without the informed consent of the client. He makes a case for amending the APA's (1981a) *Ethical Principles of Psychologists* to spell out clearly that the use of categorizing and coding for insurance purposes must include informed-consent procedures. He argues for psychologists to make a bold gesture to declare to their clients whether they are advocates or opponents of the mental-illness model. They will have taken another commendable step when they begin to lobby with other mental-health professionals to persuade legislative bodies to enact laws to protect consumers from the wholesale abuse of diagnostic codes and classifications.

Questions on diagnosis.   What is your position on diagnosis? The following questions may help you formulate such position.

- After reviewing the arguments for and against psychodiagnosis, which position do you tend to support? Why?
- Some contend that clients have a right to know their diagnoses on the grounds of informed consent, whereas others maintain that clients should not be told their diagnoses because of the dangers of their living up to a self-fulfilling prophecy. What is your thinking on this matter?
- Smith (1981) asserts that practitioners should take a stand against classification and coding for the purpose of third-party payments unless clients know of their diagnoses and agree to provide this information to insurance companies. Do you see an ethical issue in this practice? Do you agree or disagree that therapists who do not accept the medical model, yet who provide diagnoses for reasons of third-party payments, are compromising their integrity? What options are open to them?
- What ethical and professional issues can you raise pertaining to diagnosis? In your view, what is the most critical issue?

The issue of using tests in counseling

At some point in your career you may need to decide on the place that testing will occupy in your counseling. This section focuses on when and how you would use tests in your work with clients.

As is true of diagnosis, the proper use of testing in counseling and therapy is the subject of some debate. Generally, those therapeutic approaches that emphasize an objective view of counseling are inclined to use testing procedures as tools to acquire information about clients or as resources that clients themselves can use to help them in their decision making. The client-centered and existential approaches tend to view testing in much the same way that they view diagnosis—as an external frame of reference that is of little use in counseling situations. Writing from an existential-humanistic viewpoint, Arbuckle (1975) has this to say about the place of testing in counseling:

> Thus if one sees the other person, in the traditional scientific pattern, as being what one is measured to be by outside criteria, then testing—and diagnosis—should be an integral part of the counseling process. If, on the other hand, one sees the basic reality of the human being from within, then testing and diagnosis will tend to remove the person even further from the reality of who he is [p. 261].

We think that the core of the issue is not whether you will use tests as an adjunct to counseling but rather under what circumstances, and for what purposes, you may want to use tests. There are many different types of tests that can be used for counseling purposes, including measures of aptitude, ability, achievement, intelligence, values and attitudes, vocational interests, and personality characteristics. The following questions may help you think about the circumstances in which you might want to use tests for counseling purposes.

1. What do you know about the tests you may use? It's important for counselors to be familiar with any tests they use and to have taken them themselves. They should know the purpose of each test and how well it measures what it purports to measure. You'll need to decide whether you're willing to invest the time necessary to become acquainted with the tests you might want to use. In many counseling centers, one person assumes the responsibility for administering and interpreting tests. If you or your clients want to use a test, you may want to refer them to a person who specializes in testing.

2. How much say do you think clients should have in the selection of tests? Some counselors assume the responsibility for deciding whether and when to use tests and prescribe specific tests for clients. Other counselors believe that clients should decide whether they want testing and, if so, what general type of testing they want (aptitude, interest, achievement, personality). These counselors claim that clients who are not actively involved in decisions about tests may become passive, relying too heavily on test results to determine what they should do instead of using the results to make informed decisions of their own.

3. Do you know *why* you want to use a particular test? Is it merely because a client asks for it? Is it because you don't know what to do next and hope that a test will point to a direction? Does your agency require that you administer certain tests? Your reasons for using tests will depend on the particular circumstances. If you're doing vocational counseling, your client may want to take a vocational-interest inventory, and you may agree that such a test could be useful in helping the client to pinpoint some areas of interest. In another case, a client's behavior may concern you, and you may want to administer some projective tests or other personality-assessment devices to help you determine the severity of his or her difficulty. Whatever your reasons for testing are, you should be able to state a clear rationale for any test you use.

4. If a client requires testing, do you explore the reasons for the request with the client? Some clients may think that a test will give them answers and, in effect, make decisions *for* them. Clients need to be aware that tests are only tools that can provide useful information about themselves, which they can proceed to explore in their counseling sessions. They also need to know what the tests are designed for and what they expect from the testing. Are you willing to explore the values and limitations of tests with your clients, as well as their reasons for wanting to take them?

5. How do you integrate the test results into the counseling sessions? How might you use them for counseling purposes? In general, it's best to give test *results*, not simply test *scores*. In other words, you should explore with your client the *meaning* the results have for him or her. However, just as clients need to be involved in the selection of tests, they also should be involved in the interpretation of the results. In this connection you'll need to evaluate your clients' readiness to receive and accept certain information, and you'll need to be sensitive to the ways in which they respond to the test results. Your clients may need an opportunity to express and explore discrepancies between what they think their abilities and interests are and what the test results indicate. Are you willing to allow your clients to talk about any possible disappointments? Do you use this opportunity to encourage them to ask whether some of their prior decisions were realistic?

6. Are you concerned about maintaining the confidentiality of test results? Test results may be handled in different ways, depending on the purpose and type of each test. Nevertheless, your clients need to feel that they can trust you and that test results will neither be used against them nor revealed to people who have no right to this information. The uses and confidentiality of test results are matters that you may want to discuss with your clients.

7. Are you critical in evaluating tests? Too often mistakes have been made because counselors have had blind faith in tests. If personality assessments have low reliability and validity, will giving a battery of these tests result in more accurate information? You should know the limitations of the tests you use, and you should keep in mind that a test can be useful and valid in one situation, yet inappropriate in another. Are you willing to acquire the knowledge you need to properly evaluate the tests you use?

Some ethical considerations in using tests

One of the key principles in using tests and other psychological-assessment techniques is that the counselor should make every effort to protect and promote the welfare of the client. Unfortunately, tests have been misused in many ways. They can be misused when they are given routinely to unwilling clients, when the clients receive no feedback, when tests are used for the wrong purposes, or when they are given by people who are not qualified. General guidelines are provided to psychologists in using assessment techniques:

> They guard against the misuse of assessment results. They respect the client's right to know the results, the interpretations made, and the bases for their conclusions and recommendations. Psychologists make every effort to maintain the security of tests and other assessment techniques within limits of legal mandates. They strive to ensure the appropriate use of assessment techniques by others [APA, 1981a].[1]

The American Personnel and Guidance Association[2] (1981) has developed a number of specific standards that provide guidance for the ethical use of tests in counseling. First of all, people taking a test should know what it is for, how it relates to their situation, and how the results will be used. Further, tests should not be used in isolation, without other relevant data. Each test should be presented in such a way that it can be placed in proper perspective with other relevant factors.

When it comes to the matter of interpreting test scores of minorities, it is especially important that all the factors that influence test results be given consideration. In its *Ethical Standards*, APGA (1981) warns that professionals "must recognize the effects of socioeconomic, ethnic and cultural factors on test scores." An additional guideline is provided: "The member must proceed with caution when attempting to evaluate and interpret the performance of minority group members or other persons who are not represented in the norm group on which the instrument was standardized" (APGA, 1981). Members of minority groups might react to testing with suspicion, since tests have been used to discriminate against them in schools and employment. To minimize such negative reactions, it is a good practice to explore a minority

---

[1]The codes of ethics of the major mental-health organizations can be found in the Appendix.
[2]Since July 1, 1983, American Association for Counseling and Development (AACD).

person's views and feelings about testing and to work with the client in resolving attitudes that are likely to affect the outcome of a test. Brammer and Shostrom (1982) offer sound advice on this matter:

> Clients have often been traumatized by tests made earlier in school. They may regard them with deep suspicion, skepticism, or outright hostility. As a first step, the counselor should determine the client's feelings about the threatening aspects of testing to avoid distortion of the results of the interpretation and possibly failure of the counseling itself [p. 287].

Another ethical issue pertaining to testing is competence. Sometimes mental-health workers find themselves expected to give and interpret tests as a basic function of their job. If they have not had adequate training in this area, they are in an ethical bind. In-service training and continuing-education programs are ways of gaining competence in using psychological-assessment devices. The APGA (1981) offers this guideline on the matter: "Different tests demand different levels of competence for administration, scoring, and interpretation. Members must recognize the limits of their competence and perform only those functions for which they are prepared."

Perhaps the most basic ethical guideline for using tests is to keep in mind the primary purpose for which they were designed: to provide objective and descriptive measures that can be used by clients in making better decisions. Further, a wide range of appraisal techniques, including both test and nontest data, should be used in providing clients with useful information. And it is wise to remember that tests are tools that should be used in the service of clients, not against clients. Brammer and Shostrom (1982) sum it up: "The main purpose of all testing in counseling is to provide clients with reliable and valid information about themselves so they will be able to make wise choices" (p. 295).

Ethical issues in psychotherapeutic research

In the early part of this chapter we described some of the major theoretical orientations of counseling and clinical psychologists. As can be seen, most of the questions that we have raised in this chapter have a direct relationship to one's therapeutic theory. Matters such as the use of specialized techniques, the balance of responsibility in the client/therapist relationship, the functions of the therapist, and the goals of treatment are tied to one's theory. In addition to the dozen traditional approaches to counseling and therapy listed earlier, a variety of so-called "newer therapies" or "innovative therapies" have been described by various writers. In his book *The Psychotherapy Handbook* Herink (1980) describes over 250 different therapies that he contends are in contemporary use! This lengthy list literally ranges from A to Z (from Active Analytic Psychotherapy to Zaraleya Psychoenergetic Technique). Corsini (1981), in *Handbook of Innovative Psychotherapies*, provides a concise and readable account of 64 major innovative therapeutic approaches in contemporary use. Surely one critical ethical question is: Does a given psychotherapeutic approach or technique work? To fail to at least attempt to base one's practice on the findings of research is tantamount to asking consumers to simply trust that practitioners know what they are doing.

Although the topic of ethical implications of conducting research in counseling and psychotherapy is vast, we do want to address a few selected ethical issues and encourage you to think about your responsibilities in this area. Some of the questions that we encourage you to keep open are as follows:

- In conducting research in a counseling setting, must the informed consent of participants always be given? Can you think of situations in which it might be justified *not* to obtain informed consent for the sake of a better research design?
- Is it ever ethical to use deception in psychological research? Is deception justified if the subjects are given the accurate details *after* the research study is completed?
- Can practitioners be considered ethical if they practice without conducting any research on the techniques employed or without having them empirically validated?

Before we discuss these and other research questions, look over the ethical guidelines for conducting research in therapeutic settings that are contained in the accompanying box. We also suggest that you look at the APA's (1973a) publication *Ethical Principles in the Conduct of Research with Human Participants* for detailed guidelines.

Ethical Guidelines for Psychotherapy Research

American Psychiatric Association (1981):
- "When involved in funding research, the ethical psychiatrist will advise human subjects of the funding source, retain his/her freedom to reveal data and results, and follow all appropriate and current guidelines relative to human subject protection."

American Association for Marriage and Family Therapy (undated):
- "The therapist is obligated to protect the welfare of his or her subjects. The conditions of the Human Subjects Experimentation shall prevail, as specified by the Department of Health, Education and Welfare guidelines."

National Association of Social Workers (1979):
- "The social worker engaged in research should consider carefully its possible consequences for human beings."
- "The social worker engaged in research should ascertain that the consent of participants in the research is voluntary and informed, without any implied deprivation or penalty for refusal to participate, and with due regard for participants' privacy and dignity."
- "The social worker engaged in research should protect participants from unwarranted physical or mental discomfort, distress, harm, danger, or deprivation."

American Personnel and Guidance Association (1981):
- "In planning any research activity dealing with human subjects, the member must be aware of and responsive to all pertinent ethical principles and ensure that the research problem, design, and execution are in full compliance with them."
- "In research with human subjects, researchers are responsible for the subjects' welfare throughout the experiment and they must take all reasonable precau-

tions to avoid causing injurious psychological, physical, or social effects on their subjects."

- "Participation in research must be voluntary. Involuntary participation is appropriate only when it can be demonstrated that participation will have no harmful effects on subjects and is essential to the investigation."

American Psychological Association (1981a):

- "In planning a study, the investigator has the responsibility to make a careful evaluation of its ethical acceptability. To the extent that the weighing of scientific and human values suggests a compromise of any principle, the investigator incurs a correspondingly serious obligation to seek ethical advice and to observe stringent safeguards to protect the rights of human participants."
- "The investigator informs the participants of all aspects of the research that might reasonably be expected to influence willingness to participate and explains all other aspects of the research about which the participants inquire. Failure to make full disclosure prior to obtaining informed consent requires additional safeguards to protect the welfare and dignity of the research participants."
- "The investigator respects the individual's freedom to decline to participate in or to withdraw from the research at any time."
- "The investigator protects the participants from physical and mental discomfort, harm, and danger that may arise from research procedures. If risks of such consequences exist, the investigator informs the participant of the fact."

The above ethical guidelines are selected examples. For a more complete description of ethical standards on this issue, consult the codes of professional ethics given in the Appendix and APA (1973a).

Some situations involving ethical issues

Situation pertaining to informed consent. Informed consent is defined as the participant's assent to being involved in a research study after having received an explanation and reached an understanding of the procedures and their associated risks and benefits (Stricker, 1982). Informed consent is important for a variety of reasons (Lindsey, in press): it protects people's autonomy, because it allows them to make decisions about matters that directly concern them; it guarantees that the participants will be exposed to certain risks only if they voluntarily agree to them; it decreases the possibility of an adverse public reaction to experimenting with human subjects; and it helps researchers carefully scrutinize their design for inherent risks. With these points in mind, consider the following situation to determine the ethics of the researcher's behavior.

This practitioner, Dr. Hamner, is committed to designing research procedures to evaluate the process and outcomes of her treatment programs. She is convinced that in order to obtain valid data she must keep the research participants ignorant in many respects. Thus, she thinks that it is important that the clients she sees be unaware that they are being studied and be unaware of the hypotheses under investigation. Although Dr. Hamner agrees that some ethical issues may be raised by her failing to inform her clients, she thinks that good research designs call for such procedures. She does not want to influence her clients and thus bias the results of her study, so she chooses to keep information from them. She contends that her practices are justified because there are no negative consequences or risks involved with her research. Dr. Hamner further contends that, if she is able to refine her therapeutic techniques through her research efforts with her clients, both they and future clients will be the beneficiaries.

Commentary.   Although some of Dr. Hamner's contentions have some merit, we think that the ends are not justified by the means that she employs in this case. Further, although she might be justified in withholding some of the details of her research studies (or the hypotheses under investigation), it seems unethical for her to fail to even mention to her clients that she is actually doing research with them as a part of her therapeutic approach. Since her clients are investing themselves both emotionally and financially in their therapy, it seems to us that they have the right to be informed about procedures that are likely to affect them. They further have the right to agree to refuse to be a part of her study. Her approach does not give them that right.

Some questions on informed consent.   Consider the following questions:

- What are your thoughts about Dr. Hamner's ethics and the rationale she gives for not obtaining informed consent?
- What do you think about the position that informed-consent procedures might actually serve to demystify the relationship between the experimenter and the subject and thus actually lead to better data, since the participant is more truly involved and committed?
- Assume that Dr. Hamner was interested in studying the effects of therapist reinforcement of certain client statements during sessions. Do you think that, if the clients knew she was using certain procedures and studying certain behaviors, this would bias the results?
- If the values of the research seem to be greater than the risks involved to participants, do you think that the researcher is justified in not obtaining the informed consent of the subjects?

Situation pertaining to deception.   In this case a family therapist routinely videotapes his initial session with families without their knowledge. He does so on the ground that he wants to have a basis for comparing the family's behavior at the outset with their behavior at the final session. He assumes that, if the family members knew they were being videotaped at the initial session, they wou behave in self-conscious and fearful ways. At this stage in the therapy he does not think that they could handle the fact of being taped. Yet he likes to have *them* be able to look at themselves on videotape at their final session, at which time he tells them that he taped their initial session. He also explains to them his reasons for not having informed them.

Some questions on deception.   Consider the following questions:

- Since the therapist eventually does tell this family that it was taped at the initial session, do you think that he is guilty of deception? Explain.

- What do you think of the ethics of his practice? Do you agree with him that family members would not typically be able to handle the fact that they were being taped? Do you think that it is worthwhile for him and the family to be able to compare the initial session with the final session? Do your answers have an impact on the ethics of this case?
- An APA research guideline reads: "Openness and honesty are essential characteristics of the relationship between investigator and research participant (1973a, p. 1). Do you think that this therapist's motivations for this practice justify his lack of openness and honesty?
- To what degree do you think that the practice of taping clients without their knowledge affects the trust level in the therapeutic relationship? Are the possible benefits of this practice worth the potential risks to the practitioner's reputation?

Commentary.   We think that the therapist's policy of videotaping clients without their knowledge and consent is unethical. Most of the professional codes of the national organizations explicitly state that such a practice is to be avoided. Since we contend that the therapeutic relationship is built upon good will and trust, we oppose any practices that are likely to jeopardize the trust that clients have toward the helping professionals. Deception cuts to the core of the helping professions, and it fosters distrust among the public toward the profession.

Situation pertaining to withholding of treatment.   Is it ethical to withhold treatment from a particular group so that it can be used as a control group? Consider this situation as you explore the question:

Dr. Hope works with depressive psychotics in a state mental hospital. In the interest of refining therapeutic interventions that will help depressed clients, she combines therapy and research procedures. Specifically, she employs cognitive behavioral approaches in a given ward. Her research design specifies treatment techniques for a particular group of patients, and she carefully monitors their rate of improvement as a part of the treatment program. Dr. Hope says that she believes in the value of cognitive behavioral approaches for depressive patients, yet she feels a professional and ethical obligation to empirically validate her treatment strategies. For her to know whether the treatment procedures alone are responsible for changes in the patients' behaviors, she deems it essential to have a comparable group of patients that does not receive the treatment. When Dr. Hope is challenged on the ethics of withholding treatment that she believes to be potent from a particular group of patients on the ward, she justifies her practice on the ground that she is working within the dictates of sound research procedures.

Some questions on withholding treatment.   Consider the following questions:

- Some researchers contend that they are necessarily caught in ethical dilemmas if they want to use a control group. Do you see an apparent contradiction between the demands of sound research methodology and sound ethical practice?
- Do you think Dr. Hope is ethical in withholding treatment so that she can test her therapeutic procedures? Would it be better for her to simply forget any

attempts at empirical validation of her procedures and devote her efforts to treating as many patients as she can? Is it ethical for her to use procedures that are untested?

A modification of the situation.   In this case, Dr. Hope uses *placebo controls*. That is, rather than merely denying treatment to a group or keeping them on a waiting list, she meets with a control group whose members think they are receiving therapy but actually are not receiving standard treatment. In short, the group is duped into believing that it is benefiting from therapy.

- What are the ethics of using placebos in counseling and clinical research?
- Does the placebo approach by its very nature constitute deception of patients? Can you think of any situations that justify the use of this approach?

Commentary.   Parloff (1979) writes that the definitive answer to the question of the role of the placebo in various forms of therapy has yet to be found. On this ground, we assert that using placebos borders on unethical practice. Stricker (1982) comments that it is possible in institutional settings either to withhold treatment for a control group or to employ placebos. However, to do so is grossly unethical if treatment is available. Further, he asserts that, if treatment is not available, then it is probably illegal to continue to incarcerate the untreated patient.

In his discussion of the ethical dilemma posed by the use of placebos, Lindsey (in press) makes the point that, when people enter treatment and develop a contract with an agency, they do so with the understanding that they will receive active treatment aimed to help them. If they receive placebos in place of this active treatment, he asserts, then this contract is violated. He adds that, if and when clients discover that they have received placebo treatment in place of the treatment they thought they were getting, they might well feel betrayed by the profession. He concludes that their autonomous choice is violated by using inaccurate and insufficient information.

O'Leary and Borkovec (1978) acknowledge the responsibility of practitioners to evaluate the efficacy of their treatment approaches by the best methods available. Further, many researchers advocate a design comparing treatment groups with placebo and nontreatment groups as an essential feature for adequate design. On the other hand, the ethical nature of using these procedures can be questioned. In their arguments against the use of placebo groups, O'Leary and Borkovec list the following sources of potential harm to subjects:

- Placebos are inherently deceptive. Though presented to clients as potentially effective treatments, they are by definition theoretically inert.
- Placebos may also be harmful in that they deter clients from seeking active treatment during the course of the experiment. During this time clients are duped into believing that the placebo condition will help alleviate their problems. When these clients do find out that they were in a placebo group, they are likely to feel angry at the waste of their time.
- If a placebo is an inert form of "treatment," then significant clinical improvement will not be likely to occur for most clients, and some of them may

deteriorate. A consequence is that clients are likely to become frustrated and cynical about the profession's ability to provide help.

For the reasons given above, O'Leary and Borkovec recommend that the term *placebo* be abandoned in psychotherapeutic research. As an alternative, they recommend that investigators develop procedures with some evidence of effectiveness for ameliorating particular problems and then use them as standards to evaluate new therapeutic interventions. These standard interventions might be the "best available" therapies, and clients would thus have equal confidence in them and in the experimental treatment. This alternative to using placebos would control for factors such as faith in the therapy or the therapist, increased attention to the problem, the expectations of clients, suggestion, and other nonspecific therapy factors.

In agreement with O'Leary and Borkovec's position is Lindsey (in press), who contends that deception such as withholding treatment leads society to distrust the helping professions. He writes:

> If the profession does not confront these crucial ethical considerations, it is likely, in time, that trust in psychologists will progressively be "chipped away" until their effectiveness is so diminished that they will have little left to contribute. If this happens, it will be because they have failed to respect the autonomy of those they strove to serve, and failed to act on their behalf.[3]

Situation pertaining to research with training and personal-growth groups.   In many graduate programs it is common for trainees in counseling internships to be expected to participate in personal-growth groups. Sometimes these groups are integrated with training or supervision groups in which the interns are encouraged to explore their own personal issues that arise in conjunction with their placements in the field.

This situation relates to a professor, Dr. White, who makes it a practice to conduct research on the process and outcomes of the personal-growth groups she leads for these counselor trainees. To begin with, all the students in Dr. White's graduate counseling program are required to attend the sessions of a personal-growth group for a full academic year. In addition to leading these growth groups for trainees, Dr. White also teaches theory courses and supervises students in writing master's theses and doctoral dissertations. Her primary theoretical orientation is Gestalt therapy, with emphasis on other experiential and role-playing techniques. She expects the students to come to the sessions and be willing to work on personal concerns. These personal concerns often pertain to issues that arise as a result of problems they encounter with difficult client situations in their internship. At the beginning of the group she asks students to take psychological tests that assess traits such as openness, dogmatism, degree of self-acceptance, level of self-esteem, and other dimensions of personality that she deems to be related to one's ability to counsel others. She again administers these same devices at the end of the year so that she has a comparison of specific dimensions. During the year, she asks a group of experts to observe her trainees in the group sessions at various points. This is done so that outsiders can

---

[3]From "Informed Consent and Deception in Psychotherapy Research: An Ethical Analysis," by R. T. Lindsey. *The Counseling Psychologist*, in press. Copyright 1983. Reprinted by permission.

assess the level of growth of individuals at different points as well as get a sense of the progress of the group as a whole.

As a part of informed consent, Dr. White tells the trainees what she is attempting to evaluate during the year, and she discusses fully with them the rationale for using outsiders to observe the group. She also promises the students that she will meet with them individually at any time during the semester if they want to discuss any personal issues. She also meets with them individually at the end of the group to discuss changes in scores on the psychological tests. As a way to correct for her bias in the investigation, Dr. White submits her research design to a university committee. The function of this committee is to review her design for any ethical considerations and to give her suggestions for improving her study.

Some questions on research with training groups.   Consider the following questions:

- Do you think it is ethical for a program to require student attendance at personal-growth groups? And is it ethical for the leader of such a group to also have these same students in academic classes and to evaluate and supervise them?
- What ethical considerations, if any, do you commend Dr. White for?
- What research practices, if any, would you say are ethically questionable?
- Do you think that it is ethically sound to have observers as a part of the design? The students know about these outsiders, but the observers will be a part of the process even if some students do not like the idea. Do you see pressure being exerted? If so, is it justified in this case?
- What recommendations can you make for improving Dr. White's research design as well as improving the quality of the learning experience for the students?

Impact of psychotherapy research on policymaking

Given the reality that society pays for services in the mental-health area, it would seem that society has the right and the responsibility to determine who is qualified to provide such services and to be concerned with how effective they are. With the expansion of private and public support of mental-health services, there will probably be an increase in the number of clients who seek specialized treatment (Parloff, 1979). The question of the effectiveness of various psychotherapeutic practices is being raised more frequently. According to Parloff, policymakers and administrators are putting more pressure on clinicians to demonstrate the degree to which their interventions are actually working. He also writes that clinicians are increasingly turning to researchers in hopes of finding support for what they are doing. There are three basic questions continually raised by critics of the therapy field, which we now consider.

1. Does the change brought about by psychosocial treatment exceed the change that is due to the passage of time alone? After summarizing the available research, Parloff concludes:

- A review of controlled studies shows that the psychodynamics therapies, client-centered therapy, behavior therapies, and cognitive therapies have achieved results that are better than no-treatment procedures. The conclusion offers an affirmative answer to the question of whether therapies are more effective than doing nothing.

- Smith and Glass (1977) summarized research studies and found that "the average client receiving therapy was better off than 75% of the untreated controls" (p. 754). They concluded that their survey of research findings overwhelmingly validated the benefit of psychotherapy.

2. Are the effects of therapy that can be attributed to specific interventions separate from nonspecific factors, such as suggestion or persuasion? Some critics of therapy argue that changes in clients are due primarily to a placebo (suggestion, expectations of getting better, and persuasion). On this issue, some findings are as follows:

- The literature that is available does suggest that treatment effects are usually more powerful than those found in the placebo or control group (Parloff, 1979).
- The review of therapy research summarized by Smith and Glass (1977) concluded that the placebo effect was less than half as large as the effects of the other elements in the therapeutic relationship.

3. Do therapists' levels of effectiveness have much to do with their mastery of specialized techniques and a related body of knowledge? Parloff points out that psychotherapy represents many different helping professions and that there is therefore no standardized training program. The policymaker is likely to turn to the researcher to distinguish any differences in effectiveness due to the unique training of each profession. In answer to this question, Parloff cites studies that reveal the following:

- Comparisons across professions and schools have revealed no characteristic differences in treatment effectiveness.
- There is little evidence that experts of different theoretical orientations differ in their relative treatment effectiveness.
- Some professionally trained therapists seem to achieve about the same results with comparable clients as do some minimally trained therapists.
- The therapist's level of experience appears to be related to the quality of the therapeutic relationship; evidence pertaining to its association with the outcomes of therapy is far less clear.
- In summary, in terms of therapy outcomes the role of specialized training and experience has not yet been empirically confirmed.

In his recommendations to researchers, Parloff (1979) urges increased attention to the standard forms of psychotherapy as they are practiced within community clinics and in private practice. He suggests that special emphasis be placed on evaluating the outcomes for specified client groups of both brief and long-term treatment approaches. Parloff's conclusions are that the psychotherapeutic professions can assure administrators and policymakers that therapy has shown some evidence of potency. But he does not think that research has yet been designed that can truly respond to some of the most important questions raised by policymakers and administrators. Parloff writes: "The best I can say after years of sniffing about in the morass of outcome research literature is that in my optimistic moods I am confident that there's a pony in there somewhere" (p. 303). We agree with Parloff's recommendation that therapy research not be designed along the lines of a "horse race" to determine the winning therapy.

Instead, he suggests that researchers seek to determine what kinds of therapeutic techniques and interventions produce what kinds of changes with particular types of clients.

In a similar vein, Garfield (1980) contends that the global question of the effectiveness of psychotherapy is destined to receive poor answers. His point is that psychotherapy is not a clearly defined and uniform process and that there is thus no basis for any objective answer to such a general question. We agree with Garfield's position that, if we expect to improve research designs to meaningfully assess the efficacy of therapy techniques, we must state questions more specifically: What therapeutic procedures will work best with what clients? What kinds of therapists will work best with what procedures and with what clients? We would add only that researchers should give top priority to addressing ethical considerations that are a part of this research.

A commentary on ethical dilemmas in therapy research

The purpose of this section on research has been to highlight a few of the ethical considerations involved. We hope that you will see that such ethical problems cannot be solved by enunciating simple principles that are based on absolutes of what is "right" and "wrong." As noted in the APA's (1973a) *Ethical Principles in the Conduct of Research with Human Participants*, ethical questions typically involve balancing the advantages and disadvantages of a particular research design. In considering benefits and costs, the APA writes, the contribution that research might make to human welfare must be weighed against the cost to individual research participants. "The general ethical question always is whether there is a negative effect upon the dignity and welfare of the participants that the importance of the research does not warrant" (APA, 1973a, p. 11).

According to the APA, the clearest guiding principles are that the participants must emerge from their research experience unharmed, that the risks must be minimized, and that participants must understand and consent to these risks as reasonable side effects of the research.

Balancing methodological rigor with ethical rigor. Lindsey (in press) has emphasized that ethical rigor must be given a central place in psychotherapeutic research alongside methodological rigor. Stricker (1982) asserts that the way out of the dilemma between violating a person's rights and doing research poorly or not at all is to make ethics and methodology consistent. This can be done by seeking alternatives for research procedures that violate a code of ethics. Stricker agrees with the research principle of the APA that the central issue may not be ethics (standards of rightness and wrongness of actions) but values (what a person holds to be significant). He contends that what is ethical, rather than being absolute, usually varies as a function of values.

Stricker makes a case for designing psychotherapeutic research on a model based on collegiality and informed consent—that is, a model in which research subjects are treated like colleagues rather than objects of study, are given the information they need to be aware of all the variables, and are asked to give their consent to certain research procedures.

In writing about general considerations pertaining to research with human beings, the APA (1973a) acknowledges that, given the ethical obligation of therapists to conduct the best research possible, ethical conflicts are at times unavoidable. It is not a matter of advocating ethical absolutes but of learning ways of resolving conflict.

Inventory of your position on research

As a way of concluding this discussion, we suggest that you clarify your own thinking on the matter of balancing scientific rigor with ethical rigor. If you agree more than you disagree with the following statements, place an "A" in the space; if you disagree more than you agree, place a "D" in the space. After you've finished the inventory, we suggest that you discuss some of your answers with fellow students.

    ____ 1. To use therapy techniques or interventions that lack a sufficient research base is irresponsible and unethical.

    ____ 2. Deception is sometimes a necessary evil in psychological research.

    ____ 3. The failure to obtain the informed consent of participants in research is always unethical.

    ____ 4. If a research study contains any risks to the participants, then its design should be changed, for by its very nature it is unethical.

    ____ 5. The use of placebo groups can be justified, for if these controls are not used, practitioners will have difficulty in evaluating the efficacy of the interventions they use.

    ____ 6. I think that researchers will ultimately get the best results if they are open and honest about the research design with the participants in the study.

    ____ 7. Psychotherapeutic research can be a useful guide to the policymaker and the administrator.

    ____ 8. In cases where "debriefing" of the subjects is used after deception has been a part of the study, the practice can be justified.

    ____ 9. Practitioners should use no techniques that have not been empirically shown to be of value.

    ____ 10. If we are concerned about producing sound research studies of therapy, we must be willing to tolerate some ethical violations.

If you have an interest in pursuing the topic of the ethical considerations of psychotherapy, we suggest that you look at the following sources: APA, 1973a; Garfield, 1980; Landman and Dawes, 1982; O'Leary and Borkovec, 1978; Parloff, 1979; Smith and Glass, 1977; and Smith, Glass, and Miller, 1980.

Chapter summary

To a large degree, your therapeutic techniques and procedures flow from your theoretical assumptions; in this sense, counseling theory and practice are closely related. Whether or not you have a clearly articulated theory, you tend to operate on the basis of fundamental views of people and of the therapeutic process. Consequently, in this chapter we've asked you to consider your basic assumptions, some aspects of various theories that most appeal to you, the role of techniques in counseling, the issue of responsibility, your role as a counselor, therapeutic goals, and practical issues related to the use of diagnosis and testing.

Although it's unrealistic to expect that you'll operate from a clearly defined and unified theory at the outset of your practice, we do think that you can at least raise the issues that we've focused on in this chapter. We believe that counselors who give little thought to the theoretical issues that affect their professional practice will spend a lot of time floundering. Reflecting on why you make the interventions you do will enable you to have a more meaningful impact on your clients and to develop a framework for assessing the effects of your therapeutic work.

Activities, exercises, and ideas for thought and discussion

1. Do this exercise in dyads. Describe your theoretical bias, and tell your partner in simple language how you see counseling.
2. In what ways do you think your theoretical assumptions will determine the way you counsel?
3. How do you determine for yourself the proper division of responsibility in counseling? How might you avoid assuming responsibility that you think belongs to your client? How might you ensure that you will accept your own share of responsibility?
4. Suppose you were applying for a job as a counselor, and the following question appeared on the application form: "Describe in not more than three lines how you see your role as a counselor." How would you respond to this question? In class, form small groups and discuss your responses.
5. Suppose the same application form asked "What are the *most important* goals you have for your clients?" How would you respond?
6. In class, debate the role of diagnosis in therapy. One person makes a case *for* diagnosis as a valuable part of the therapeutic process, and the other person argues *against* the use of diagnosis. Or have a class discussion on trends in diagnosis, its uses and abuses, and its purpose and value.
7. Suppose that a client came to you and asked you to administer a battery of interest, ability, and vocational tests. How would you respond? What kinds of questions would you ask the client before agreeing to arrange for the testing?
8. What is your position on the use of techniques in counseling? When do you think they are appropriate? How can you determine for yourself whether you're using techniques as gimmicks to allay your anxiety or as extensions of your personal style as a counselor?
9. If you are working in an institution (or have a field placement as an intern) where psychodiagnosis is a standard part of the institution's practices, consider this activity. First, make sure that the activity is appropriate and ethical and that the institution will permit you to have access to a patient's records. Select a patient who has been given a formal diagnosis that is known to you. If it is permitted, look over this person's charts. Then, talk with and try to get to know the patient. Later, talk with another person about whom you have no information. Simply attempt to get to know each of these

persons. After you have had a conversation with each, ask yourself these questions: Did knowing a person's diagnosis make a difference in my perceptions? Did I respond differently based on this knowledge or lack of knowledge? Did my knowledge bias my thinking? In terms of what I learned about the person, how fitting was his or her diagnosis?

10. Interview at least one practicing therapist in order to discuss how theoretical orientation affects his or her practice. Ask the practitioner the kinds of questions that were raised in this chapter. Bring the results of your interview to class.

11. Suppose that you were applying for a job in a community mental-health center and that the following question was asked of you during the interview: "Many of our clients represent a range of diverse cultural and ethnic backgrounds. To what degree do you think that you will be able to form positive therapeutic relationships with clients who are culturally different from you? How do you think that your own acculturation will influence the way you counsel ethnically and culturally diverse clients? Can you think of any factors that might get in the way of forming trusting relationships with these clients?"

12. Assume that you were asked another question: "Third World people are often put under strong pressure to give up their beliefs and ways in favor of adopting the ideals and customs of the dominant culture. What do you think your approach would be in working with clients who feel such pressure? How might you work with clients who see their own ethnicity or cultural heritage as a handicap that is to be overcome?"

13. What ethnic and cultural factors would you take into account if your job duties included making assessments and diagnostic impressions of clients during intake sessions? To what degree do you think that the traditional diagnostic system takes into account the cultural variables?

14. Assume that you were a committee member on a board to look over research designs to detect ethical problems associated with psychotherapy research. What kinds of things would you most be inclined to look for? What kinds of questions would you ask? What are some examples of ethical violations in doing research in counseling that you would point out? After you've thought through these questions, it would be a good idea to form small groups in your class to compare your perspectives.

15. Seek out some professors who are engaged in or interested in research in therapy. Ask them if they think that good research designs typically pose ethical issues. What ethical issues do they think are critical in doing such research? How do they attempt to balance methodological rigor with ethical rigor? What do they see as the ethical obligation of practitioners to subject their therapeutic approaches to empirical validation?

Suggested readings

American Psychiatric Association. *Diagnostic and statistical manual of mental disorders* (3rd ed.). Washington, D.C.: Author, 1980. DSM-III is the official system of classification of psychological disorders and is the resource to consult for identifying patterns of emotional and behavioral problems. It provides a rationale and method for classifying particular psychological disorders, gives specific criteria for these classifications, and shows the differences that separate the various disorders. A useful supplement to DSM-III is *DSM-III Casebook* (Spitzer, Skodol, Gibbon, & Williams, 1981). The cases presented correspond to the categories of the official guide and provide concrete examples of the diagnostic process.

Brickman, P., Rabinowitz, V. C., Karuza, J., Coates, D., Cohn, E., & Kidder, L. Models of helping and coping. *American Psychologist*, 1982, 37(4), 368–384. This article, discussed at some length in this chapter, provides a useful framework for clarifying the assumptions that guide one's therapeutic practice by drawing a distinction between attribution of responsibility for a problem and attribution of responsibility for a solution. Competing models of responsibility in education, psychotherapy, law, and welfare are described.

Corey, G. *Theory and practice of counseling and psychotherapy* (2nd ed.). Monterey, Calif.: Brooks/Cole, 1982. This text presents a survey of the major concepts and practices of nine contemporary therapeutic systems. A concise description of the following approaches is provided: psychoanalysis, psychoanalytic extensions and adaptations, existential therapy, person-centered therapy, Gestalt therapy, transactional analysis, behavior therapy, rational-emotive therapy, and reality therapy. Several charts help the reader compare the key concepts and techniques of the various therapeutic models. (For readers interested in the above theories translated into practice for group counselors, see *Theory and Practice of Group Counseling* [Corey, 1981].)

Smith, M. L., Glass, G. V., & Miller, T. I. *The benefits of psychotherapy*. Baltimore: Johns Hopkins University Press, 1980. One of the features of this book is a dispassionate view of outcome research in psychotherapy. The authors present an excellent survey of the assumptions, procedures, and results of published studies dealing with the effectiveness of psychotherapy and discuss the current state of knowledge about the effects of psychotherapy. This book is recommended for those who want to delve further into research issues and who want a summary and evaluation based on 475 controlled studies.

Szasz, T. *The myth of mental illness: Foundations of a theory of personal conduct* (Rev. ed.). New York: Harper & Row, 1974. Szasz challenges the medical-model concept as it is applied to psychotherapy. His thesis is that mental illness does not exist in the sense in which physical diseases do, and he questions the idea that people should be excused for their behavior on the ground that they are mentally ill and therefore not responsible for their acts.

Torrey, E. F. *The death of psychiatry*. Radnor, Pa.: Chilton, 1974. Written by a psychiatrist, this book develops the thesis that psychiatry and the medical-model approach to human problems are outdated and that a new approach is needed. The author writes in a lively style and raises thought-provoking issues.

Ethical Issues I: Therapist Responsibilities, Therapist Competence, and Confidentiality

Pre-chapter self-inventory

Directions: For each statement, indicate the response that most closely identifies your beliefs and attitudes. Use the following code:

5 = I *strongly agree* with this statement.
4 = I *agree*, in most respects, with this statement.
3 = I am *undecided* in my opinion about this statement.
2 = I *disagree*, in most respects, with this statement.
1 = I *strongly disagree* with this statement.

_____ 1. A therapeutic relationship should be maintained only as long as it is clear that the client is benefiting.

_____ 2. Much of therapy is really the "purchase of friendship."

_____ 3. Counselors are ethically bound to refer clients to other therapists when working with them is beyond their professional training or when personal factors would interfere with the therapeutic relationship.

_____ 4. Possession of a license or certificate from a state board of examiners shows that a person has therapeutic skills and is competent to practice psychotherapy.

_____ 5. There are no situations in which I would disclose what a client told me without the client's permission.

_____ 6. Clients should be informed of the limits of confidentiality prior to the initial counseling session.

_____ 7. What is ethical can sometimes conflict with what is legal.

_____ 8. Continuing education should be a requirement for renewal of a license to practice psychotherapy.

_____ 9. A therapist's only real responsibility is to the client.

_____ 10. Ultimately, every practitioner must create his or her own ethical standards.

____ 11. Absolute confidentiality is necessary if effective psychotherapy is to occur.

____ 12. Professional licensing protects the public by setting minimum standards of service.

____ 13. The present processes of licensing and certification encourage the self-serving interests of the groups in control instead of protecting the public from incompetent practice.

____ 14. Health-care professionals should be required to demonstrate continuing competency in their field as a prerequisite for renewal of their licenses.

____ 15. In order to practice ethically, therapists have the responsibility to become familiar with the laws related to their profession and to abide by these laws at all times.

____ 16. Special ethical guidelines should be developed for situations involving cross-cultural counseling.

____ 17. Counseling of clients from culturally diverse backgrounds by therapists who are not trained or competent to work with such groups should be regarded as unethical.

____ 18. If a person is already in a therapeutic relationship, it is unethical for another counselor to enter into a client/counselor relationship with that person without first receiving the approval of the first therapist.

____ 19. Because of the complex nature of their work, family therapists may face more ethical conflicts in their clinical decision making than most other therapists.

____ 20. In order to effectively change a family's dysfunctional patterns, a family therapist needs to use power and influence.

____ 21. It is a good idea for an attorney and a therapist to work as consultants in the service of a couple going through marital dissolution.

____ 22. Institutions that train counselors should select trainees on the basis of *both* their academic records and the degree to which they possess the personal characteristics of effective therapists (as determined by current research findings).

____ 23. Unless therapists keep abreast of the legal changes that affect their practice, they cannot be considered ethical practitioners.

____ 24. If I were working with a client whom I had assessed as potentially dangerous to another person, I would see it as my duty to warn the intended victim.

____ 25. It is my ethical obligation to take action once I make an assessment that one of my clients is suicidal or at a high risk of self-destructive behavior.

Introduction

Various professional organizations have established codes of ethics that provide broad guidelines for psychological practitioners. Examples of such ethical standards are presented in the Appendix. At this time we encourage you to carefully review these standards so that you can apply them to the issues we raise in the remaining chapters of this book. Some of the organizations that have formulated codes of ethics are the National Association of Social Workers (NASW), the American Psychological Association (APA), the American Personnel and Guidance Association (APGA), the American Association for Marriage and Family Therapy (AAMFT), and the National Academy of Certified Clinical Mental Health Counselors (NACCMHC).

In addition, there are specialty guidelines for various types of practitioners. Examples include the guidelines of the National Association of Social Workers (1981), for the private practice of clinical social work; the APA (1981c, 1981d, 1981e, 1981f), for clinical psychology, counseling psychology, industrial and organizational psychology, and school psychology; the American Psychiatric Association (1981); and the Association for Specialists in Group Work (1980).

Although you should be familiar with the ethical standards of your specialization, you will still be challenged to develop your own personal code of ethics to govern your practice. The general guidelines offered by most professional organizations do not make specific decisions for the practitioner, and they usually represent minimal standards of ethical conduct. Your own ethical awareness and your reflection on issues that aren't clear cut will determine how you interpret and translate general guidelines into your day-to-day choices as a professional.

In this chapter and the next, we provide an opportunity for you to reflect on the personal ethical system you will draw upon in making sound judgments. We present general ethical principles from the various professional organizations, as well as open-ended cases and examples that explore the therapist's responsibilities with regard to client welfare. We also discuss the ethical and legal aspects of therapist competence, with special attention given to professional licensing and certification. The legal and ethical dimensions of confidentiality, privileged communication, and privacy are explored at the end of this chapter.

In addition to becoming familiar with the ethical standards and guidelines of the various professions, you should examine the assets and limitations of such professional codes. There are several reasons why professional codes exist, and Van Hoose and Kottler (1977) give three of them:

• Ethical standards are designed to protect the profession from government interference. Professional codes are self-imposed as an alternative to having regulations imposed by legislative bodies.

• Ethical codes are designed to prevent internal disagreement and bickering within the profession.

• Ethical standards are designed to protect the practitioner in cases of malpractice, for therapists who conscientiously practice in accordance with accepted professional codes do have some measure of protection in case of litigation. As Talbutt (1981) indicates, in case of litigation a counselor's conduct would probably be judged in terms of behavior appropriate to other professionals with similar qualifications and duties. In the case of malpractice, the ethical standards would probably be the basis for comparison.

Although there are advantages to having an accepted set of ethical standards, there are also several limitations to these professional codes. First, there are conflicts within the standards. Second, there are legal and ethical issues not covered by the standards. Therefore, professional codes of ethics must be supplemented by other information (Talbutt, 1981). In an analysis of the APGA's standards (1981), Talbutt notes that since they are designed for a national audience, they do not reflect state laws. Thus counselors must obtain information on state laws from local and professional groups and state journals. Talbutt also addresses the problem of conflicts within the APGA's standards. An example is the conflicts faced by school counselors, who have multiple responsibilities to the client, institution, and other students. Ethical and legal issues are raised because of the conflicts among these three forces. Talbutt suggests that counselors should advise students from the outset of the limitations of the counseling relationship within the school setting. Another basic limitation of ethical codes is that they do not give guidance for every situation. Rather, they provide broad principles that call upon the practitioner to exercise professional judgment in applying them to specific situations. Stude and McKelvey (1979) put this matter nicely: "They [ethical codes] are statements of principle, which must be interpreted and applied by the individual or group to a particular context. They present a rationale for ethical behavior. Their exact interpretation, however, will depend on the situation to which they are being applied" (p. 453).

Another limitation of the ethical codes is their restricted applicability to cross-cultural issues in counseling and therapy (Pedersen & Marsella, 1982). These two authors address the questions: Are ethical guidelines for cross-cultural counseling and therapy needed? Do such guidelines already exist? Are the APA ethical guidelines adequate for cross-cultural counseling and therapy? Some of their main points are as follows:

- The ethical crisis of cross-cultural counseling results from the use of mental-health assumptions and interventions that were developed in one cultural context but implemented in a totally different one.
- Counseling of people of culturally diverse backgrounds by therapists who are not trained or competent to work with such groups should be regarded as unethical.
- The multiplicity of cultural values in our society has been neglected. Too often psychologists are culturally biased, and the services they render are more suited to the dominant culture than to the unique needs of various ethnic groups.
- Ethical guidelines are frequently insensitive to the client's cultural values. The dominant culture's values are often used to describe people in other cultures without its having been proved that the findings can be validly generalized from the dominant to the minority cultures.

According to Pedersen and Marsella, there have been numerous attempts to define ethical guidelines for cross-cultural situations, but not many of them have been successful. They see existing guidelines as not adequate in a cross-cultural context. They conclude:

A serious moral vacuum exists in the delivery of cross-cultural counseling and therapy services because the values of a dominant culture have been imposed on the culturally different consumer. Cultural differences complicate the definition of guidelines even for the conscientious and well-intentioned counselor and therapist [Pedersen & Marsella, 1982, p. 498].

In essence, their point seems to be that, even though practitioners are conscientiously following the established guidelines of the professional organization, they can still be practicing unethically.

Ethical responsibilities of therapists

Most professional organizations affirm that a therapist's *primary* responsibility is to the client. However, therapists also have responsibilities to members of the client's family, to the agency they work for, to a referring agency, to society, to the profession, and to themselves. In this section we explore some of these responsibilities and some situations in which conflicts arise.

Client welfare

One of the therapist's central responsibilities is to be genuinely concerned about the welfare of the client. This means that the needs of the client, not the therapist, assume primary importance in the therapeutic relationship. It also implies that a therapeutic relationship should be maintained only as long as the client is benefiting from counseling. The APA (1981a) states: "Psychologists terminate a clinical or consulting relationship when it is reasonably clear that the consumer is not benefiting from it. They offer to help the consumer locate alternative sources of assistance." A similar guideline is provided by the APGA (1981):

> If the member determines an inability to be of professional assistance to the client, the member must either avoid initiating the counseling relationship or immediately terminate that relationship. In either event, the member must suggest appropriate alternatives. In the event the client declines the suggested referral, the member is not obligated to continue the relationship.

These ethical principles of the APA and the APGA raise several questions we'd like you to consider:

- What criteria can you use to determine whether your client is benefiting from the therapeutic relationship?
- What do you do if your client feels he or she is benefiting from therapy but you don't see any signs of progress?
- What do you do if you're convinced that your client is coming to you to "purchase friendship," as Schofield (1964) calls it, and not really for the purpose of changing?

Put yourself, as a therapist, in each of the following two situations. Ask yourself what you would do, and why, if you were confronted with the problem described.

After five sessions with you, your client, George, asks: "Do you think that I'm making any headway toward solving my problems? Do I seem any different to you now than I did five weeks ago?" Before you give him your impressions, you ask him to answer his own questions. He replies: "Well, I'm not sure whether coming here is doing that much good or not. I suppose I expected resolutions to my problems before now, but I still feel anxious and depressed much of the time. It feels good to come here, and I usually continue thinking after our sessions about what we discussed, but I'm not coming any closer to decisions. Sometimes I feel certain this is helping me, and at other times I wonder whether I'm just fooling myself."

- What criteria can you employ to help you and your client assess the value of counseling for him?
- Does the fact that George continues to think about his session during the rest of the week show that he is most likely getting something from counseling? Why or why not?
- Does it sound as if George has unrealistic expectations about finding neat solutions and making important decisions too quickly? Is he merely impatient with the process?

Joanne has been coming regularly to counseling for some time. When you ask her what she thinks she is getting from the counseling, she answers: "This is really helping. I like to talk and have somebody listen to me. I often feel like you're the only friend I have and the only one who really cares about me. I suppose I really don't do that much outside, and I know I'm not changing that much, but I feel good when I'm here."

- If it became clear to you that Joanne wasn't willing to do much to change her life and wanted to continue counseling only because she liked having you listen to her, do you think you'd be willing to continue working with her? Why or why not? Would you say that she is benefiting from the relationship with you? If so, how?
- Is it ethical to continue the counseling if Joanne's main goal is the "purchase of friendship"? Why or why not?
- If you thought that Joanne was using her relationship with you to remain secure and dependent but that she believed that she was benefiting from the relationship, what might you do? How do you imagine you'd feel if you continued to see Joanne even though you were convinced that she wasn't changing?

Making referrals

Therapists also have a responsibility to know *when* and *how* to refer clients to appropriate resources. It is crucial for professionals to know the boundaries of their own competence and to refer clients to other professionals when working with them is beyond their professional training or when personal factors would interfere with a fruitful working relationship. For example, after counseling with a client for a few sessions, you might determine that he or she needs more intensive therapy than you're qualified to offer. Even if you have the skills to undertake long-term psychotherapy, the agency you work for may, as a matter of policy, permit only short-term counseling. Or you and a client may decide that, for whatever reason, your relationship isn't productive. The client may want to continue working with another person rather than discontinue counseling. As we discussed in Chapter 3, there may be times when the discrepancy or conflict between your values and those of a client necessitates a referral. For these and other reasons, you will need to develop a framework for evaluating *when* to refer a client, and you'll need to learn *how* to make this referral in such a manner that your client will be open to accepting your suggestion.

To make the art of referral more concrete, consider the following exchange between a client and her counselor. Helen is 45 years old and has seen a counselor at a community mental-health center for six sessions. Helen suffers from periods of deep depression and frequently talks about how hard it is to wake up to a new day. In other respects it is very difficult for her to express what she feels. Most of the time she sits silently during the session.

The counselor decides that Helen's problems warrant long-term therapy that he doesn't feel competent to provide. In addition, the center has a policy of referring clients who need long-term treatment to therapists in private practice. The counselor therefore approaches Helen with the suggestion of a referral:

Counselor: Helen, during your intake session I let you know that we're generally expected to limit the number of our sessions to six visits. Since today is our sixth session, I'd like to discuss the matter of referring you to another therapist.

Helen: Well, you said the agency *generally* limits the number of visits to six, but what about exceptions? I mean, after all, I feel like I've just started with you, and I really don't want to begin all over again with someone I don't know or trust.

Counselor: I can understand that, but you may not have to begin all over again. I could meet with the therapist you'd be continuing with to talk about what we've done these past weeks.

Helen: I still don't like the idea at all. I don't know whether I'll see another person if you won't continue with me. Why won't you let me stay with you?

Counselor: Well, there are a couple of reasons. I really think you need more intensive therapy than I feel I'm trained to offer you, and, as I've explained, I'm expected to do only short-term counseling.

Helen: Intensive therapy! Do you think I'm *that* sick?

Counselor: It's not a question of being sick, but I *am* concerned about your prolonged depressions, and we've talked before about my concerns over your suicidal fantasies. I'd just feel much better if you were to see someone who's trained to work with depression.

Helen: *You'd* feel better, but *I* sure wouldn't! The more you talk, the more I feel crazy—like you don't want to touch me with a ten-foot pole. You make me feel like I'm ready for a mental hospital.

Counselor: I wish I could make you understand that it isn't a matter of thinking you're crazy; it's a matter of being concerned about many of the things you've talked about with me. I want you to be able to work with someone who has more training and experience than I do, so that you can get the help you need.

Helen: I think you've worked with me just fine, and I don't want to be shoved around from shrink to shrink! If you won't let me come back, then I'll just forget counseling.

This exchange reflects a common problem. Even though the counselor explains why he wants to refer Helen to another therapist, she seems determined to reject the idea. She doesn't want to open herself up to anyone else right now. She clings to her feeling that she is being helped by her counselor, and she interprets the suggestion to see someone else as a sign that her counselor won't work with her because she's too sick.

What do you think of the way Helen's counselor approached his client? Can you see anything that you would have done differently? If you were Helen's counselor, would you agree to continue seeing her if she refused to be referred to someone else?

If you didn't want Helen to discontinue counseling, there would be a number of alternatives open to you. You could agree to see her for another six sessions, provided that your director or supervisor approved. You could let her know that you would feel a need for consultation and close supervision if you were to continue seeing her. Also, you could say that, although this might not be the appropriate time for a referral, you would want to work toward a referral eventually. Perhaps you could obtain Helen's consent to have another therapist sit in on one of your sessions so that you could consult with him or her. There may be a chance that Helen would eventually agree to begin therapy with this person. What other possibilities can you envision? What would be the consequences if you refused to see Helen or could not obtain approval to see her?

The National Association of Social Workers' code of ethics (1979) contains some principles that can help the practitioner clarify some of the issues involved:

- "The social worker should terminate service to clients, and professional relationships with them, when such service and relationships are no longer required or no longer serve the clients' needs or interests."
- "The social worker should withdraw services precipitously only under unusual circumstances, giving careful consideration to all factors in the situation and taking care to minimize possible adverse effects."
- "The social worker who anticipates the termination or interruption of service to clients should notify clients promptly and seek the transfer, referral, or continuation of services in relation to the clients' needs and preferences."

Responsibilities of marital and family therapists

We agree with Margolin's position (1982) that the APA's ethical guidelines (1981a) are designed for the practice of one-to-one therapy. When a therapist treats a number of family members together, difficult ethical questions are raised. Marital and family therapists function under a variety of theoretical models, and to a large extent these orientations determine their ways of practicing. At the same time, there are some common ethical and professional issues that all marital and family therapists need to examine. These include responsibility, confidentiality, patient privilege, informed consent and the right to refuse treatment, and the influence of therapist values on the practice of therapy.

Margolin argues persuasively that difficult ethical questions confronted in individual therapy become even more complicated when a number of family members are seen together in therapy. She observes that the dilemma with multiple clients is that in some instances an intervention that serves one person's best interests could burden another family member or even be countertherapeutic. For example, under the family-systems model, therapists do not focus on their responsibility to the individual but on the family as a system. Such therapists avoid becoming agents of any one family member since they believe that all family members contribute to the problems of the whole family. It should be clear that therapists are ethically expected to declare the nature of their commitments to each member of the family.

Therapist responsibilities are also a crucial issue in couple counseling or marriage counseling. This is especially true when the partners do not have a common purpose for seeking counseling. An interesting question is raised when one person wants divorce counseling and the other is coming to the sessions under the expectation of saving the marriage or improving the relationship. In such a situation, who is the primary client? How do therapists carry out their ethical responsibilities when the two persons in the relationship have differing expectations?

In addition to clinical and ethical considerations, Margolin mentions legal provisions that can define when the welfare of an individual takes precedence over that of a relationship. A clear example of a therapist's legal obligations is a case of child neglect or child abuse. The law requires family therapists to inform authorities if they suspect such abuse or become aware of physical or emotional abuse during the course of therapy. Even though reporting this situation may have possible negative consequences for the therapeutic relationships with some members of the family, the therapist's ethical and legal responsibility is to help the threatened or injured person. It becomes clear that there are some situations in which interventions to help an individual become more important than the goals of the family as a system, and clients should be informed of these situations during the initial session.

Margolin (1982) summarizes the complex responsibilities of a therapist who works with more than one client in a family as follows:

> Attempting to balance one's therapeutic responsibilities toward individual family members and toward the family as a whole involves intricate judgments. Since neither of these responsibilities cancels out the importance of the other, the family therapist cannot afford blind pursuit of either extreme, that is, always doing what is in each individual's best interest or always maintaining the stance as family advocate [p. 790].

Morrison, Layton, and Newman (1982) agree with Margolin's position that family therapists may face more ethical conflicts than most other therapists. They write that family therapists sometimes face accusations that they are the agents of the parents against the children, the children against the parents, or of one parent against the other. Again, family therapists often wrestle with the question of whose agent they are.

The responsibility to consult. At times marriage and family therapists must struggle over the issue of when they must consult with another professional. This is especially true of situations in which a person (or couple or family) is already involved in a professional relationship with a therapist and seeks the counsel of another therapist. What course of action would you take if a husband sought you out for private counseling while he and his wife were also seeing another therapist for marriage counseling? Would it be ethical to enter into a professional relationship with this man without the knowledge and consent of the other professional? What might you do or say if the husband told you that the reason for initiating contact with you was to get another opinion and perspective on his marital situation and that he did not see any point in contacting the other professional?

An open-ended case.   In this situation, a couple is seeing the same therapist for marriage counseling. The husband decides to quit the joint sessions and begins private sessions with another therapist. The wife remains in individual therapy with the original therapist. In the course of individual therapy, the husband comes to realize that he does not want to terminate the marriage after all. He persuades his wife to come with him for a joint session with *his* therapist to pursue the possibility of keeping the marriage intact.

- What are the ethical obligations of the husband's therapist? Does he have the responsibility of consulting with the wife's therapist?
- Do the two therapists need to get permission of their clients to consult with each other?
- Would it be ethical for the husband's therapist to do marital therapy with the couple, ignoring the work being done by the wife's therapist?

The family therapist as an agent of change.   Minuchin (1974) and his colleagues work with the structural aspects of the family system toward the goal of changing the system so that it will no longer support the symptom. The structural approach focuses on how the family organizes itself, on how its members communicate, and on how dysfunctional patterns develop. Since structural family therapy is an action-oriented approach that requires the therapist to take a highly active role in the therapeutic process, certain ethical issues are raised. Does this approach impose the therapist's value system upon the family? Should the primary responsibility for change within the family rest with the therapist rather than with the individual family members? According to Minuchin, the tool of structural family therapy is to modify the present, not to explore and interpret the past. To accomplish this, family therapists join that system and then use themselves to transform it. Minuchin writes that the family system is organized around certain functions of its members (such as support, nurturing, control, and socializing). The therapist's responsibility is clear: "Hence, the therapist joins the family not to educate or socialize it, but rather to repair or modify the family's own functioning so that it can better perform these tasks" (1974, p. 14).

Structural family therapy does emphasize the role and power of the therapist, and this power is seen as a major variable in bringing about therapeutic change. In Minuchin's words: "Change is seen as occurring through the process of the therapist's affiliation with the family and his restructuring of the family in a carefully planned way, so as to transform dysfunctional transactional patterns" (p. 91).

The use and misuse of power and influence in family therapy.   The therapist's use of power is a critical issue in family therapy. Although power is a vital component in any therapeutic relationship and of itself is not a negative force, there are dangers in using power to keep clients dependent. If power is misused, the clients may attribute to the therapist magical qualities to effect lasting change and bring about a "cure" to their troubles. They may thus be discouraged from looking within and tapping their own resources to bring about constructive change. O'Shea and Jessee (1982) note that a position of power and influence is seen by most marital and family therapists as particularly important in working with couples and families. They write: "The therapist's process of establishing rapport and joining with family members requires deciphering the communications and cracking the role of the family's meaning pattern. This enables the therapist to recognize, intervene, and assign new meaning to, and ultimately change, destructive interactional patterns in the family" (p. 5). They conclude that for a family therapist to be effective, he or she needs to be influential. Systems therapists gain this influence by being active and directive during the early phases of therapy.

Fieldsteel (1982) notes that the ethical issues raised by the structural approach involve recognizing the possible differences between the value systems of the therapist and the family. She pinpoints the danger of the therapist's assuming an inordinate share of the responsibility for change in family systems: "There is the danger that the role of the therapist as a more active agent for change may shift the responsibility for the direction of change from the patient to the therapist" (p. 262).[1] Fieldsteel raises the ethical issue of the therapist's encouraging clients to accept the therapist's perceptions as truth while at the same time the clients suspend their own perceptions by placing more trust in the therapist than in themselves. She also points out that some therapists assume that, by virtue of their professional expertise, they have the right to impose a new set of beliefs and values on the family. We agree with her position that family therapists should be aware of their clients' tendencies to attribute them with inordinate powers. These tendencies are often based on transference projections and the longing for a powerful and all-knowing parent to protect and direct them:

> The crucial issue is whether or not the therapist is seduced by the transference. The way in which it is used determines the nature of the therapeutic alliance. The goal of the therapeutic alliance should include the patient's understanding of both the problem and the process of therapy and the way in which the process helps in the resolution of the problem [p. 263].

As we've already noted, power and influence are factors in any therapeutic relationship, yet they assume even more importance in family therapy. Thus, family therapists have the obligation of continually examining the ways in which they can use or misuse personal power, for the misuse of power keeps families dependent.

Responsibilities of therapists in divorce or separation counseling. For those mental-health professionals involved in counseling couples who are planning on divorcing, there are legal issues that must be addressed. Divorce counseling raises some critical questions:

- What minimal skills and knowledge must a clinician possess to work effectively with divorcing or divorced clients?
- How are emotional factors and legal factors intertwined, and how must effective intervention combine psychological counseling and legal counsel?
- Should mental-health professionals and attorneys work together in the service of their clients who are in the process of marital dissolution?

[1]From "Ethical Issues in Family Therapy," by N. Fieldsteel. In M. Rosenbaum (Ed.), *Ethics and Values in Psychotherapy: A Guidebook.* Copyright 1982 by The Free Press, a division of Macmillan Publishing Company. This and all other quotations from the same source are reprinted by permission.

Kaslow and Steinberg (1982) make a case for cooperation between legal and mental-health professionals during a client's divorce. Divorce therapy and proceedings typically entail a great deal of psychic pain, conflicts over custody of children, possible battles over the division of property, and anger and hurt over the dissolution of the marriage and family. This reality provides a sound reason for two professionals (lawyer and therapist) to work with one client unit (the couple or the family). According to Kaslow and Steinberg, neither the therapist nor the attorney has a full sense of the interplay between the psychological and legal dimensions of divorce. They assert that practitioners who do not encourage such a joint effort in behalf of each divorcing client "may, by definition, be providing inadequate service" (p. 65). They make what we consider to be some excellent points pertaining to the basic responsibilities of therapists who are involved with clients who are divorcing:

- There is the possibility that failing to collaborate with an attorney in divorce matters might constitute malpractice.
- There are both ethical and legal reasons to suggest that attorneys be informed about the relevant studies on the impact of divorce on children.
- Often children become "trophies," with economic values given to them. Working together, the attorney and the therapist should seek ways of preventing the children from being subjected to such a travesty.
- At a minimum, therapists should become familiar with the appropriate state laws and major court decisions on divorce. They should acquire a basic knowledge of the legal aspects of custody, taxation, and property in divorce.
- Therapists can acquire the attitudes and information that will help them collaborate with lawyers through reading, seeking consultative arrangements with attorneys, and attending workshops.

Kaslow and Steinberg assert that "to practice in the delicate area of divorce and postdivorce therapy without familiarity with the legal regulations violates professional standards of practice and may also be construed as malpractice" (1982, p. 68).

The lawyer/therapist consultation team is also advocated by Korelitz and Schulder (1982), who describe such a joint project done at the Ackerman Institute for Family Therapy in New York. They make the point that family therapists are often ignorant of the law and thus unknowingly jeopardize the legal rights of their clients. For example, some therapists might suggest that a wife or a husband move out rather than live under the same roof with a warring spouse. In some states, however, the spouse who followed such advice might forfeit certain legal rights.

As a divorce lawyer, Steinberg (1980) has come to champion the creation of attorney/therapist teams as an effective vehicle to help minimize the stress of divorce. In an excellent article, "Toward an Interdisciplinary Commitment: A Divorce Lawyer Proposes Attorney-Therapist Marriages or, at the Least, an Affair," he develops the thesis that a divorce is less likely to seriously traumatize the dissolving family when both the legal and emotional issues of divorce are addressed. He writes: "I have come to understand that most of the marital issues brought to my law office are people problems, not legal problems. They are best resolved by attending to the client's needs rather than by referring to the legislature's statutes" (p. 259).

After an initial conference with a couple seeking a divorce, Steinberg asks the couple to seek marital counseling for at least a few sessions *before* returning to him for a second conference. Conversely, he suggests that family therapists should refer their clients considering marital dissolution to a divorce lawyer as soon as possible, for doing so can introduce a note of reality to the process. This practice spares the therapist the pressure of dealing with the legal dimensions of the wife's and husband's behavior. According to Steinberg, divorce does little to solve a situation unless the couple comes to an understanding of the basic causes of marital breakdown. We fully agree with his contention:

> Without such insight, many spouses are likely to repeat their self-defeating behavior during their next intimate relationship. They risk passing from, perhaps, abuser to abuser or from one passive spouse to another. Equally important, an awareness of their own contribution to the marital breakdown tends to reduce bitterness during the divorce process and increases the ability to resolve the legal issues through negotiation [p. 261].

Like Steinberg, Korelitz and Schulder (1982) write that lawyers and family therapists are increasingly working together and sharing their knowledge and specialized skills. They recommend that joint consultations with lawyers should be available at all facilities that offer services for clients considering divorce.

Ethical and legal aspects of therapist competence

The nature of competence: Various perspectives

This section examines what therapist competence is, how we can assess it, and what some of its ethical and legal dimensions are. The topic of competence is developed by giving attention to such questions as: What ethical standards do various mental-health professions have regarding competence? What are some ethical issues in the training of therapists? To what degree is professional licensing an accurate and valid measure of competence? What are some alternatives to professional licensing and certification? What are the ethical responsibilities of therapists to continue to upgrade their knowledge and skills?

We begin this discussion of competence with an overview of specific guidelines from various professional organizations. These guidelines are summarized in the accompanying box.

A reading of the guidelines shows that several questions are left unanswered. What are the boundaries of one's competence, and how do professionals know when they have exceeded them? How can they determine whether they should accept a client when they lack the experience or training they would like to have?

These questions become more complex when we consider the issue of what criteria to use in evaluating competence. Is completing a professional degree a necessary or sufficient condition of competence? There are many people who complete doctoral programs and yet lack the skills or knowledge needed to carry out certain therapeutic tasks. Obviously, degrees alone don't confer competence to perform any and all psychological services.

You also need to assess how far you can safely go with clients and when you

Professional Codes of Ethics and Competence

American Association for Marriage and Family Therapy (undated):
- "A therapist will not attempt to diagnose, prescribe for, treat, or advise on problems outside the recognized boundaries of the therapist's competence."

American Psychological Association (1981a):
- "Psychologists recognize the boundaries of their competence and the limitations of their techniques. They only provide services and only use techniques for which they are qualified by training and experience."

American Psychiatric Association (1981):
- "A psychiatrist who regularly practices outside his/her area of professional competence should be considered unethical. Determination of professional competence should be made by peer review boards or other appropriate bodies."

National Association of Social Workers (1979):
- "The social worker should accept responsibility or employment only on the basis of existing competence or the intention to acquire the necessary competence."
- "The social worker should not misrepresent professional qualifications, education, experience, or affiliations."

American Personnel and Guidance Association (1981):
- "With regard to the delivery of professional services, members should accept only those positions for which they are professionally qualified."

Standards for the Private Practice of Clinical Social Work (NASW, 1981):
- "The practitioner shall limit the practice to demonstrated areas of professional competence."
- "When using specialized methods of practice which range beyond those normally learned in a school of social work or a social work practice setting, the practitioner shall obtain training or professional supervision in the modalities employed."

should refer them to other specialists. Similarly, it's important to learn when to consult another professional if you haven't had extensive experience in working with a certain problem. If you were to refer all the clients you encountered difficulties with, you'd probably have few clients. Keep in mind that many beginning counselors experience a great deal of self-doubt about their general level of competence; in fact, it's not at all unusual for even experienced therapists to wonder seriously at times whether they have the personal and professional abilities needed to work with some of their clients. Thus, difficulty in working with some clients doesn't by itself imply incompetence.

One way to develop or upgrade your skills is to work with colleagues or professionals who have more experience in certain areas than you do. You can also learn new skills by going to conferences and conventions, by taking additional courses in areas you don't know well, and by participating in workshops that combine didactic work with supervised practice. The feedback you receive can give you an additional resource for evaluating your readiness to undertake certain therapeutic tasks.

Ethical issues in the training of therapists

Training is obviously a basic aspect of therapist competence. In our opinion, Grayson (1982) has pinpointed the most salient issues of training in his excellent article "Ethical Issues in the Training of Psychotherapists." His discussion is concerned with four key questions: (1) How do we select whom to train? (2) What should we teach? (3) What are the best ways of training? (4) What should be the criteria for certification? The following discussion is primarily a summary of the points with which we are most in agreement with Grayson.

How do we select whom to train?   Some questions that can be raised here are:

- Should the selection of trainees be based solely on traditional academic standards, or should it take into account the latest findings on the personal characteristics of effective therapists?
- To what degree is the candidate for training open to learning and to considering new perspectives?
- Does the candidate have problems that are likely to interfere with training and with the practice of psychotherapy?
- Whom do we select to work with which populations?

On the matter of selecting minority-group members, Grayson writes:

Do we select minority group members to work with their own minority groups, or do we select only those minority group members who are culturally similar enough to the young, white, successful middle-class group that when they graduate, they will simply join the abundant ranks of therapists serving this group? Do our training programs even attract minority group members who are enough a part of their own groups to be able to understand and to work effectively with them? And if this selection barrier is surmounted, would the training program itself prepare the minority therapist to work effectively with a variety of minority populations [p. 52]?

What should be taught?   Although Grayson does not think that all specialty training should be abolished, he does take the position that it is unethical to train practitioners in only one therapeutic orientation (without also providing unbiased introductions to other systems). Thus, there is merit in an analytically trained therapist's learning about alternative therapy systems such as behavior therapy. By the same token, a behavior therapist should be able to recognize the role of transference and countertransference in the therapeutic process. Therapists should learn when a particular approach is contraindicated, especially if it is their own specialty.

We are in complete agreement with Grayson's view that therapists should be objectively introduced to all of the major systems of therapy so that they can be in a position to decide which aspects of the available current therapies they will include in their own personal style. He writes: "I do not intend to present a case against specialization because I believe that it increases another kind of competence, but only if it does not produce tunnel vision as a side effect" (p. 55).

Grayson also notes that there is an ethical issue involved in presenting therapeutic approaches that have very limited applicability to working with certain ethnic or cultural populations. "Students of all ethnic and social backgrounds learn primarily white, middle-class theories and techniques of psychotherapy, many of which are not directly applicable to the minority populations, and may be particularly irrelevant for minority students who intend to work with these populations" (p. 55). Among his suggestions is that trainees find ways of broadening their life experiences and opening themselves to diverse cultural and social backgrounds.

Questions that Grayson raises on the issue of what to teach include:

- Is there a universal definition of mental health, or is mental health culturally defined?
- What are the implications of training therapists who will work with clients whose culture drives people to a variety of stress-related diseases? Should therapy help clients adjust to their culture? Or should therapy encourage clients to find ways of constructively changing their culture?
- Does the curriculum give central attention to the ethics of professional practice? Is it ethical to leave out training in ethics? Is it enough to hope that ethical issues will be addressed through the supervision process alone?

How can we best train?   Grayson stresses that trainees learn largely through the modeling of their professors and supervisors. There are clear implications here concerning the type of modeling that is provided to the trainees. Another ethical issue involves the requirement that trainees experience their own personal psychotherapy (or some other type of personal-growth experience). We fully agree with his assertion that training programs have an obligation to address the issue of what personality factors are likely to interfere with trainees' work with clients, as well as what traits are assets in developing effective therapeutic alliances.

What should the criteria be for certification or graduation?   A key question here is whether personality factors are part of the criteria for certification or whether meeting academic requirements is the sole criterion. According to Grayson, the training institution has an ethical responsibility to screen candidates so that the public will be protected from incompetent practitioners. He writes:

> The university or training institute carries the primary responsibility of protecting the public from incompetents or from those whose personality problems could potentially harm people. The states and the professional organizations cannot do it because they do not know the candidate personally. Licensing exams can only do broad screening. The institute which trains the student knows his assets and liabilities, and is therefore in the best position to make a responsible assessment [p. 63].

Regardless of the type of professional program one completes, it is rarely the end of the road to becoming a competent professional who is able to practice independently. For specializations such as clinical social work, clinical or counseling psychology, and marriage and family therapy, most states have established specific requirements of supervised practice beyond the receipt of a master's or doctor's degree. We now turn our attention to the issues involved in the debate over whether licensing procedures actually assess competence.

Professional licensing and certification as a sign of competence

Licenses and certification aren't necessarily any more useful as criteria of competence than degrees. We've met licensed psychiatrists, psychologists, social workers, and marriage and family counselors who don't possess the competencies specified by their licenses. Conversely, we've met some unlicensed people who are far more competent than are some licensed therapists. Licenses mainly assure the public that the licensees have completed *minimum* educational programs, have had a certain number of hours of supervised training, and have gone through some type of evaluation and screening. Licenses imply that their holders have had a certain level of professional training, but they don't assure the public that practitioners can effectively and competently *do* what their licenses permit them to do.

A further consideration is that most licenses are generic in nature; that is, they usually don't specify the types of clients or problems the licensee is competent to work with, nor do they specify the techniques that a practitioner is competent to use. A licensed psychologist may possess the expertise needed to work with adults yet lack the competencies for working with children. The same person might be qualified to do individual psychotherapy yet have neither the experience nor the skills required for family counseling or group therapy. Most licensing regulations do specify that licensees are to engage only in those therapeutic tasks for which they have adequate training, but it is up to the licensee to put this rule into practice. A license permits the professional to provide a wide range of services, and it is the professional's responsibility to determine which services he or she is actually competent to provide.

Be that as it may, a license is still one of the signs that a practitioner has attained at least a minimal level of competence. The licensing of clinical social workers, marriage and family therapists, psychologists, and counselors has become an area of intense professional interest, primarily because professionalism has come to be associated with some type of licensure. Indeed, practitioners who misrepresent themselves are subject to legal penalties in most states. Thus, one of the main advantages of certification and licensing is that entry into practice can be restricted and those denied entry who persist in the activities defined by statute can be prosecuted (Davis, 1981).

This section focuses on some of the basic assumptions of the practice of licensing, the relationship of licensing to competency, some arguments for and against licensing and certification for mental-health professionals, and alternatives to current licensing practices. Although licensing and certification differ in their purposes, they have some features in common. Both require applicants to meet specific requirements in terms of education and training; both generally rely on tests of competence to determine those applicants who have met the standards and who deserve to be granted a credential (Shimberg, 1981). Fretz and Mills (1980a) define licensure as "the statutory process by which an agency of government, usually of a state, grants permission to a person meeting predetermined qualifications to engage in a given occupation and/or use a particular title and to perform specified functions" (p. 7). Certification, instead, is "the nonstatutory process by which an agency or association grants recognition to an individual for having met certain predetermined professional qualifications. Stated succinctly, certification . . . is a 'limited license'—that is, the protection of title only" (Fretz & Mills, 1980a, p. 7).

The pros and cons of professional licensing.   According to Fretz and Mills (1980a), more has been written in the psychological literature in opposition to licensing than in favor of it, yet licensing legislation accelerated during the 1970s. Following are some of the central arguments over the values of licensing, along with some criticisms of the licensing process for health-care providers.

In their discussion of the pros and cons of licensure, Fretz and Mills write that most of the arguments in support of licensing fall under one of five major premises.

The first premise is that licensure is designed to protect the public by setting minimum standards of service. This argument contends that the consumer would be harmed by the absence of such standards, which are crucial since incompetent practitioners can cause long-term negative consequences. Phillips (1982) develops this position:

> For all that can be said about legal constraints on practice, one thing is most important: Their purpose is to promote the public's welfare by improving and maintaining the quality of training and practice, maximizing benefits-to-cost service delivery outcomes, and protecting the public from gross incompetents [p. 924].

Other writers, however, challenge the assumption that licensing does indeed protect consumer interests. According to Gross (1978), substantial evidence suggests that existing licensing practices are a rather confused array of policies that promise public protection but may actually serve to institutionalize a lack of public accountability. He argues that licensing of a profession does not guarantee quality or responsible behavior, and he cites medicine and law to support his argument. He asserts, in fact, that "research refutes the claim that licensing protects the public" (p. 1009). In a review of the status of licensure process in the United States, Cottingham (1980) concludes that there is no clear evidence that a lack of regulation would result in any danger to the public's welfare. Furthermore, he finds no evidence that licensure protects the quality of service or directly affects the competencies of health-care providers. He also maintains that, while failing to produce a valid system of assessing competence, the licensing process at the same time excludes many competent health professionals.

In summary then, despite the stated goals of licensing, "the available evidence suggests that the quality of services has not improved since licensing laws have been instituted, disciplinary actions are woefully inadequate, and the prevention of illegal practice is generally spotty and often aimed at eliminating competition, rather than incompetence" (Hogan, 1979, p. 254).

The second major argument listed by Fretz and Mills is that licensing is designed to protect the public from ignorance about mental-health services. This argument rests on the assumption that the consumer who needs psychological services typically does not know how to choose an appropriate practitioner or how to judge the quality of services received. According to Gill (1982), it is not clear that credentialing by itself provides the necessary information. Further, he asserts that certification and licensing tend to be more confusing than helpful for consumers. Most people do not know the basic differences between a licensed psychologist, a licensed social worker, a certified mental-health counselor, or a person who simply uses the general title of "counselor." Gross (1978) contends that licensing tends to mystify the therapeutic process by reducing the amount of information that is actually provided to the consumer. Fretz and Mills (1980a) write that no controlled studies have compared unlicensed practitioners and licensed practitioners in their effects on consumers.

Fretz and Mills give three other reasons for licensure, which we briefly describe. One is the assumption that licensing increases the chances that practitioners will be more competent and that their services will be better distributed. Hogan (1979) writes that, when a group becomes licensed, it gains increased status, privileges, and income. As a result, the group's services usually cost more after licensure, which means that the profession tends to be less willing to provide service to the poor and to minority groups. In agreement is Rogers (1973), who notes that psychology has tended to ignore serving the poor, the aged, and minorities. According to Cottingham (1980), there is no research evidence that licensure protects the quality of service or directly affects the specific competencies of providers.

Another reason offered by Fretz and Mills is the view that licensing upgrades the profession. This argument holds that a licensed profession will have more practitioners committed to improving the profession and maintaining the highest standards of excellence. By way of criticism of this position, Van Hoose and Kottler (1977) write that licensing tends to make training curricula and the definitions for service too rigid. Rogers (1980) contends that, as soon as criteria are set up for certification, the profession is inevitably frozen in a past image. He adds that there are as many *certified* charlatans as there are uncertified practitioners. Another drawback to licensing, from his viewpoint, is that professionalism builds up a rigid bureaucracy (pp. 243–248).

Finally, Fretz and Mills hold the view that licensing allows the profession to define for itself what it will and will not do. Accordingly, the profession is assumed to be more independent, since other professions or the courts cannot specify its functions. On the other hand, licensing has a tendency to incite challenges to a profession that makes definite claims, particularly in cases involving the right to offer certain services or to obtain payments from insurance companies. Thus, licensing both protects a profession's domain and also invites attack on it (Fretz & Mills, 1980a).

In summary, the essence of the argument for licensure revolves around the contention that the welfare of the consumer is better safeguarded with legal regulation than without it. Challengers to this assumption often maintain that licensing is designed to create and preserve a "union shop." Cottingham (1980) writes that licensure may serve to strengthen the self-protection of practitioners and create monopolistic helping professions rather than protecting the public from misrepresentation and poor services. He adds that the licensing process appears to be more a political issue than an objective and professional assessment of specific skills necessary for effective professional practice. In agreement with this point of view is Davis (1981), who cautions the profession to be aware of practices that encourage the self-serving interests of the groups in control of licensure, instead of protecting the public from incompetent practice.

Alternatives to licensing and certification.   The diversity of licensing procedures from state to state gives the public little confidence in the license as a sign of minimal competence in health-care practice. Although the ineffectiveness of professional licensing laws has led some (Gross, 1977, 1978; Hogan, 1979) to encourage deregulation, others who have written on this issue see that action as too extreme. One option to current licensing practices is a model based on competence, as proposed by Bernstein and Lecomte (1981). They contend that the nature of the regulatory process (rather than regulation itself) is what should be challenged. Their proposal includes a number of specific ways to assess competency. One is to review candidates who apply for entry-level licenses on a range of factors that have a demonstrable relationship to positive client outcomes. Further, those who earned a license would be required to continue to demonstrate competent performance at regular intervals as a condition for renewal.

As another alternative, Hogan (1979) proposes that the present licensing practices be replaced by full disclosure of background information about a practitioner. Gross (1977) also recommends that professionals inform clients about themselves and about the therapeutic process through the use of a professional-disclosure statement. As a result of the consumer movement the practice of disclosure appears to be gaining in popularity. In addition to giving potential clients information they need to make informed choices, disclosure also has several benefits for the professional (Gill, 1982): Writing a statement that clarifies one's professional identity is of value as a self-assessment experience. This process entails an honest examination of personal beliefs, values, strengths and weaknesses, and goals regarding the therapeutic relationship. In addition, through concisely stating who they are and what they do, counselors can begin to define for themselves the competencies that are integral to the profession.

Bernstein and Lecomte (1981), as a part of their competency-based alternative to current practices, call for licensed practitioners to participate in professional disclosure. They recommend that a disclosure statement be updated annually and filed with the licensing board. It would include information for clients about the psychologist's academic and professional background and about clients' improvement rates. Information would also be provided individually to clients about the proposed length of treatment and anticipated outcomes.

Gross (1977) provides a rather complete description of how professional disclosure can provide regulation that protects the consumer better than current licensing and certification laws. In addition to providing basic information, each practitioner would include a philosophy of counseling, information about his or her education and professional experiences, and a fee schedule.

Although disclosure can take many forms, it is essentially a process of informing prospective clients about the qualifications of a practitioner, the nature of the psychotherapeutic process, and the details of the services provided. This is done to provide clients with the data necessary for making intelligent decisions regarding the use of a particular practitioner's services.

Our position is that professional disclosure is an excellent practice, for both the consumer and the practitioner. Although it may be one alternative to current licensing practices, it can also be used by practitioners who have licenses. Disclosure provides some basis for an assessment of how well services are being provided. We support the view that it can no longer be taken for granted that, simply because professionals are licensed, they are making a significant difference in their clients' lives. Even if practitioners can legally practice by automatically renewing their licenses, ethical practice demands an approach that will keep them abreast of needed knowledge and skills.

Further, we applaud the trend toward expecting professionals to demonstrate that they are indeed accomplishing what they say they are doing. Accountability procedures are part of the current debate over licensure and continued competency demonstration. A few examples of the trend toward accountability in practice are the attention given to consumer rights, attempts to provide for informed consent, efforts to demystify the therapy process, descriptions of the nature of the client/therapist relationship through contracts that guide the process, and efforts to educate the public about psychotherapy and related services. Before proceeding to the next section, consider these questions:

• What are your views on alternatives to licensing? What do you think of the suggestions presented? Can you come up with some other ideas?

• Some states have proposed "sunset legislation" that in effect would do away with licensing of mental-health professionals. The assumption is that licensing procedures have become too rigid and restrictive and that bureaucratic factors have contributed to excluding many competent practitioners from legally practicing (while creating a restricted guild based on survival of those with licenses). Do you think that sunset legislation is a workable solution to the problems associated with licensure and certification? What might you want to say if you were on a committee that had the task of evaluating and modifying existing licensing regulations?

• What do you think the likely consequences would be if all professional licensing laws were eliminated? What would the results be for the various mental-health professions? What might the consequences be for the public?

An example of licensure: The regulation of marriage and family therapy in the United States.   You may find it valuable to consider the licensing requirements of a relatively recently regulated psychotherapeutic specialty in the United States. Nine states now regulate the practice of marriage and family therapy.[2] Although each state has developed a different definition of the practice of marriage and family counseling, most of the definitions cover certain essential elements, including theories of practice, evaluation and appraisal procedures, and therapeutic techniques. Here are three examples of partial descriptions:

• "Marriage and family counseling is that service performed with individuals, couples, or groups wherein interpersonal relationships between spouses or members of a family are examined for the purpose of achieving more adequate, satisfying, and productive marriage and family adjustments." (California)

• "Marriage and family counseling also includes premarital counseling, predivorce and postdivorce counseling, and family counseling. It consists of the application of principles, methods and techniques of counseling and psychotherapeutic techniques for the purpose of resolving psychological conflict, modifying perception and behavior, altering old attitudes and establishing new ones in the area of marriage and family life." (Georgia)

---

[2]These states, along with the date when each initially passed legislation, are California (1963), Michigan (1966), New Jersey (1969), Utah and Nevada (1973), Georgia (1976), Virginia (1978), North Carolina (1979), and Florida (1981) (Sporakowski, 1982; Sporakowski & Staniszewski, 1980).

- "Marriage and family counseling consists of the application of established principles of learning, motivation, perception, thinking, emotional, marital and sexual relationships and adjustments by persons trained in psychology, social work, psychiatry, or marital counseling." (Nevada)

A survey of the states regulating marriage and family counseling shows that an applicant must have a minimum of a master's degree in either social work, marriage counseling, pastoral counseling, or one of the behavioral sciences, including, but not limited to, sociology or psychology (Sporakowski, 1982; Sporakowski & Staniszewski, 1980). As far as further *academic* requirements are concerned, Virginia, for example, specifies a master's degree from an accredited institution in counseling. This program must include 60 graduate semester hours, with at least 15 semester hours in these areas: (1) dynamics of marriage and family systems, (2) human sexuality, (3) marriage and family counseling theory and techniques, and (4) supervised practicum in marriage and family counseling.

In addition to the academic qualifications, each state has established *experience* qualifications. These vary from Nevada's "one year of postgraduate experience in marriage and family counseling" to Georgia's, Michigan's, and New Jersey's five years of experience (Sporakowski & Staniszewski, 1980). Some states require that the majority of this clinical experience be earned after the receipt of a master's degree. For example, North Carolina requires at least 3,000 hours of clinical experience, of which 2,500 hours are to be obtained after receiving a degree in marital and family therapy or an allied mental-health field. California spells out in detail the manner in which 3,000 hours of *supervised* clinical experience is to be obtained, in not less than two years. It requires that applicants use psychotherapeutic techniques with clients in the following relationships: family, premarital, marital, and marital dissolution. This experience must include participation in assessment, diagnosis, prognosis, and treatment of dysfunctions in the relationships. A specified number of hours are included for categories such as direct counseling experience with children, couples, and families; supervised hours of "enrichment activities" (group counseling received, personal therapy received, attendance at workshops and conferences); face-to-face supervision sessions; and group supervision.

In addition to requiring candidates to file an application, give proof of academic credentials, supply letters of reference, and document hours of supervised practice, most states also give written or oral examinations or both. In Virginia, for example, applicants must pass the written and oral examinations for their generic license as a "professional counselor" and then must also take the specialty examinations for marriage and family counseling. Further, a work sample based on of their actual cases must be presented as a part of the examination process (Sporakowski, 1982).

We have presented this overview merely as an illustration of some of the requirements for a license in one field of counseling. We encourage you to write to the appropriate agency in your state to find out the specific requirements for licensing or certification of social workers, psychologists, marriage and family counselors, and other types of mental-health professionals. As you can see, the specific requirements for even the same category of licensure vary considerably from state to state. If you are seeking a professional license, it behooves you to keep informed of the changing requirements for the type of license you hope to obtain.

Continuing education and continuing competence demonstration

Most professional organizations support efforts to make continuing education a mandatory condition of relicensure. In the past, people could obtain licenses to practice professionally and then act as though there were no need to obtain any further education. We question how ethical it is to neglect taking substantive steps to keep current with new developments. In any event, the trend now is to encourage professionals to engage in ongoing education and training in areas related to their specializations.

Although the concept of continuing education for professionals is not new, the urgency of developing systematic ways to ensure professional development is increasing. As we mentioned earlier, there is a movement toward greater accountability of professions for the quality of services they deliver. Further, as Vitulano and Copeland (1980) note, there is a growing appreciation among psychologists that lifetime competency in one's practice is not guaranteed with the receipt of a doctoral degree or with licensure from a state board of examiners in psychology. An increasing number of states are mandating the periodic accumulation of continuing-education credits by psychologists as one method of protecting the consumers of psychological services (Vitulano & Copeland, 1980).

It should be noted that one of the weak points of mandatory continuing education is that professional organizations can require practitioners to accumulate the necessary hours, but they cannot require intellectual and emotional involvement. A practitioner's résumé can look very impressive in terms of knowledge acquired; the reality might be much less than the paper indicates.

In spite of the fact that there are some basic weaknesses in mandatory continuing education, it is clear that there is a trend toward states' adopting guidelines in that area (Vitulano & Copeland, 1980). Also, virtually every professional organization has established at least a general guideline governing the ethical responsibility of the practitioner to keep updated in knowledge and skills that are demanded for effective practice. Samples of these guidelines are given in the accompanying box.

Many professional organizations, if a state does not mandate continuing education as a condition for relicensure, have a voluntary program. For example, all clinical members of the American Association for Marriage and Family Therapy are encouraged to complete 150 hours every three years. The AAMFT regards the program, known as Continuing Education in Family Therapy (CEFT), as a part of an ongoing process of professional development, which has as its goal the maintenance of high-quality services to consumers.

Like the AAMFT, most of the other professional organizations (at both the state and national levels) have criteria to aid in determining whether a given activity qualifies for continuing-education credit. In our view, continuing education ought to be concerned with expanding a therapist's knowledge of legal education and the connection between ethical and legal issues. Surely, practitioners will meet many difficult situations that they are not fully equipped to cope with by virtue of their graduate training alone. Workshops dealing with ethics, the law, and professional issues could be of real value in providing practitioners with information and insights lacking in their formal training. We think that B. Schutz (1982) makes a good case for licensed practitioners to use some of their required continuing-education credits to keep abreast of legal changes that affect their practice. He notes that "psychotherapy's step into

---

Professional Guidelines Regarding Continuing Education

American Personnel and Guidance Association (1981):
- "Personal growth is continuous throughout the member's career and is exemplified by the development of a philosophy that explains why and how a member functions in the helping relationship."

American Psychiatric Association (1981):
- "Psychiatrists are responsible for their own continuing education and should be mindful of the fact that theirs must be a lifetime of learning."

Standards for the Private Practice of Clinical Social Work (NASW, 1981):
- "The clinical social worker in private practice shall meet the educational and practice requirements of the National Association of Social Workers, shall maintain current knowledge of scientific and professional developments, and shall obtain additional training when required for effective practice."

American Psychological Association (1981a):
- "Psychologists recognize the need for continuing education and are open to new procedures and changes in expectations and values over time."

American Association for Marriage and Family Therapy (undated):
- "Every member of the AAMFT has an obligation to continuing education and professional growth in all possible ways, including active participation in the meetings and affairs of the Association."

---

the legal limelight, no matter how unwelcome, is an irrevocable one and cannot be ignored in training psychotherapists" (p. 96).

In addition to the requirements to attend seminars, workshops, institutes, and special conferences, some professionals favor some form of *competency demonstration*, by which practitioners have to show what they know and can do. This might be accomplished by the practice of reexamination for relicensure or by some form of peer review.

In their discussion of the trends in competency demonstration, Vitulano and Copeland (1980) posit four reasons for health-care professionals to support some kind of continuing competency demonstration as a prerequisite for relicensure and recertification:

> First, the knowledge base for these professions is increasing at an astonishing rate. . . . One must continue to learn or suffer from professional obsolescence. Second, the enormous ethical responsibilities of our practice demand the highest standards. Licensure or certification solely at the beginning of one's career merely identifies a minimum standard for professional practice, not the ideal toward which one should strive. Third, lifetime education should constitute an important goal of the training and practice of the health professions. Fourth, a proactive commitment to the maintenance of competency over time would help maintain public confidence in the profession [p. 891].

In terms of models of assuring competence, Vitulano and Copeland describe three options. One is the continuing-education model, in which credits are given for participation in approved workshops, courses, seminars, and other avenues of ongoing professional training. Under this model the psychologist must accumulate a given number of credits over a period of time as a prerequisite for relicensure. A second option is the examination model, which would entail psychologists' taking periodic examinations to demonstrate expertise as a prerequisite for relicensure or recertification. A third model is the peer-review system. This approach would involve an elaborate system of comparing the practitioner's record of clinical practice with an established set of standards of care for the profession as a whole.

Peer review appears to be gaining popularity as one of the methods of assuring quality. This can be seen by the special issue of *Professional Psychology* ("Peer Review and Quality Assurance," February 1982). Peer review refers to an organized system of assessing quality of services—the analysis and judgment of professional practice by other practitioners within the profession. Regarded as a means rather than an end in itself, peer review has as its ultimate goal not only determining adequate present activity but also assuring an acceptable level of quality of future services (Stricker, Claiborn, & Bent, 1982). In their discussion of the philosophical underpinnings of peer review, Secrest and Hoffman (1982) make a case for such a system as the heart of a mature profession. They contend that professionals who are practicing without either reviewing the work of others or having their own work reviewed are "self-styled independents." They assert that the peer-review model would unite professionals by promoting responsible practice of the highest level:

> By encouraging frequent and extensive interchange of ideas, peer review would prevent the intellectual and professional isolation of most practitioners. Practitioners involved in peer review would have to both earn the trust of their peers and give it in return: Professional relationships would be open and honest. Above all, participating regularly and formally in peer review activities would give practitioners a much needed sense of belonging to a competent, effective, and responsible profession [p. 17].

Where do you stand on the issue of continuing competence demonstrations? We hope that some of these questions will clarify your views:

• What effects on individual practitioners do you think that the trend toward increased accountability is likely to have?

• Do you think it is ethical to continue practicing if one does not engage in any type of continuing education? Why or why not?

• What are some advantages and disadvantages to using continuing-education programs solely as the basis for renewing a license? Is continuing education enough? Explain.

• What are your reactions to competency examinations (oral and written) as a basis for entry-level applicants and as a basis for renewal of licenses? What kinds of exams might be useful?

• Kane (1982) has written the following about the validity of licensure examinations: "Because of the problems inherent in developing an adequate criterion, it is very unlikely that any measurement procedure can be shown to provide accurate predictions of the quality of individual professional performance" (p. 918). Do you agree or disagree with his position? If this is true of examinations used to assess the competency of candidates for their initial license, what are the implications for examinations as an assessment device for relicensure?

• Should evidence of continuing education be required (or simply strongly recommended) as a basis for recertification or relicensure? If you support mandatory continuing education, who do you think should determine the nature of this continuing education? What standards should be used in making this judgment?

• Can you think of both advantages and disadvantages to basing license renewal strictly upon peer-review procedures?

• What are some potential difficulties with the peer-review model? For instance, who would decide on the criteria for assessment?

• Assume that the peers who reviewed you had been chosen because they had a similar orientation to counseling (behavioral). Would they be assessing your competency or your fidelity to the tenets of the particular school? If the peers who reviewed your work had a different theoretical orientation from yours (psychoanalytic), how competent would they be to assess you within the framework of your practice?

Take a few moments now to reflect on the issue of continuing education as it applies to you. What are some kinds of continuing education you want for yourself? Through what means do you think you can best acquire new skills and keep current with advances in your field?

_____

_____

_____

_____

Before concluding this discussion of competence, we want to mention the danger of rarely allowing yourself to experience any self-doubt and being convinced that you can handle any therapeutic situation. There are therapists who feel this way; they tell themselves they have it made and attend conventions to show off how much they know and impress their colleagues with their competence. Sidney Jourard (1968) has warned about this delusion that one has nothing new to learn. Jourard maintains that contact at exciting workshops or with challenging colleagues can keep therapists growing. He urges professionals to find colleagues they can trust, so that they can avoid becoming "smug, pompous, fat-bottomed and convinced that they have *the word*." Such colleagues can "prod one out of such smug pomposity, and invite one back to the task" (p. 69).

With Jourard, we see the development of competence as an *ongoing process, not* a goal that counselors ever attain once and for all. This process involves a willingness to continually question whether you're doing your work as well as you might and to search for ways of becoming a more effective person and therapist.

Confidentiality, privileged communication, and privacy

Definition of terms

An important obligation of practitioners in the various mental-health specialties is to maintain the confidentiality of their relationships with their clients. This obligation is not absolute, however, and practitioners need to develop a sense of professional ethics that they can draw upon in determining when the confidentiality of the helping relationship should be broken. It also behooves them to be familiar with the legal protection afforded the privileged communication of their clients, as well as the limits of this protection.

Confidentiality, privileged communication, and privacy are related concepts, but there are important distinctions between them. Shah (1969) defines *confidentiality* as follows: "Confidentiality relates to matters of professional ethics. Confidentiality protects the client from unauthorized disclosures of any sort by the professional without informed consent of the client" (p. 57). In another article, Shah (1970a) notes that the purpose of confidentiality is to safeguard the client's rights and that there are sanctions for violations of confidentiality. Clients must be able to assume that their private communications with the professional will be kept private. Shah comments that psychologists have a moral, ethical, and professional obligation not to divulge information without the client's knowledge and authorization unless it is in the client's interest to do so (for example, in consulting with other professionals).

Siegel (1979) defines confidentiality as follows: "*Confidentiality* involves professional ethics rather than any legalism and indicates an explicit promise or contract to reveal nothing about an individual except under conditions agreed to by the source or subject" (p. 251). DeKraai and Sales (1982) write that confidentiality prohibits any disclosure of communications made to the therapist by the client in the course of treatment. They add a further dimension to confidentiality beyond its ethical aspects: "Confidentiality originated in professional ethics codes but has been incorporated in legislation and court rulings. Thus, disclosure of a client's communications may not only subject the psychologist to professional (ethical) reprimand but also to civil or criminal liability" (p. 251).

Shah (1969) defines *privileged communication* as "the legal right which exists by statute and which protects the client from having his confidences revealed publicly from the witness stand during legal proceedings without his permission" (p. 57). Siegel (1979) defines privilege (privileged communication) as "a legal term involving the right not to reveal confidential information in a legal procedure. Privilege is granted by statute, protects the client from having his/her communications revealed in a judicial setting without explicit permission, and is vested in the client by legislative authority" (p. 251). DeKraai and Sales (1982) assert that a special type of law, known as the privileged-communications law, is needed to protect communications of the client when the psychologist is on the witness stand. They state that the courts have held that confidentiality statutes are designed to protect clients from gossip but that these statutes do not create testimonial privilege.

Privileged communication, then, is a *legal* concept and refers to the right of clients not to have their privileged communications used in court without their consent. If a client waives this privilege, the professional has no grounds for withholding the information. Thus, the privilege belongs to clients and is meant for their protection, not for the protection of therapists. Some other relationships that are protected in various jurisdictions in the United States include those between attorneys and clients, marital partners, physicians and patients, psychiatrists and clients, priests and penitents, accountants and clients, and nurses and patients.

Exceptions to privilege.   Since the psychotherapist/client privilege is a legal concept, there are certain circumstances under which information *must* be provided by the therapist:

- when the therapist is acting in a court-appointed capacity—for example, to conduct a psychological examination (DeKraai & Sales, 1982)
- when the therapist makes an assessment of a foreseeable risk of suicide (Schutz, B., 1982)
- when the client initiates a lawsuit against the therapist, such as for malpractice (Denkowski & Denkowski, 1982)
- in any civil action when the client introduces mental condition as a claim or defense (Denkowski & Denkowski, 1982)
- when the client is under the age of 16 and the therapist believes that the child is the victim of a crime—for example, incest, child molestation, rape, or child abuse (Everstine, L., Everstine, D.S., Heymann, True, Frey, Johnson, & Seiden, 1980)
- when the therapist determines that the client is in need of hospitalization for a mental or psychological disorder (DeKraai & Sales, 1982; Schutz, B., 1982)
- when criminal action is involved (Everstine et al., 1980)
- when information is made an issue in a court action (Everstine et al., 1980)
- when clients reveal their intention to commit a crime or when they can be accurately assessed as "dangerous to society" or dangerous to themselves (DeKraai & Sales, 1982; Schutz, B., 1982)

As an example of an exception to privilege, we consider the client who is assessed as potentially violent and dangerous to others. In group therapy, family therapy, and couples therapy, the therapist must retain confidentiality and can demand it of clients. At this time, however, there is no privilege in court. Thus, disclosures of violent intentions in these treatment approaches may be repeated in court (Schutz, B., 1982).

From the foregoing discussion, it should be clear that privileged communication between therapist and client is *not* an absolute matter. There are exceptions to privilege, and therapists are legally bound to comply with the exceptions stated above. In his discussion of privileged communication, Siegel (1979) notes that, because it is a legal concept, there are variances in these exceptions from state to state and from federal to state courts. He writes that the issue involves the balance between the individual's right to privacy and the need of the public to know certain information.

The third related concept is *privacy*. Siegel (1979) defines privacy as "the freedom of individuals to choose for themselves the time and the circumstances under which and the extent to which their beliefs, behavior, and opinions are to be shared or withheld from others" (p. 251). In discussing some basic issues pertaining to privacy, Everstine and his colleagues (1980) raise the following questions:

- To what extent should beliefs and attitudes be protected from manipulation or scrutiny by others?
- How can it be decided who may intrude upon privacy and in what circumstances privacy must be maintained?
- Assuming that privacy has been violated, what can be done to ameliorate the situation?

• Do people have a right to waive their privacy, even when their best interests might be threatened?

Examples of some of the most pressing situations in which privacy is an issue include an employer's access to an applicant's or an employee's psychological tests, parental access to their child's school records and health records, and a third-party payer's access to information about a client's diagnosis and prognosis.

Most of the professional codes of ethics contain guidelines for safeguarding a client's right to privacy. Here are two examples:

• "The social worker should obtain informed consent of clients before taping, recording, or permitting third party observation of their activities" (NASW, 1979).
• "Information obtained in clinical or consulting relationships, or evaluative data concerning children, students, employees, and others, are discussed only for professional purposes and only with persons clearly concerned with the case. Written and oral reports present only data germane to the purposes of the evaluation and every effort is made to avoid undue invasion of privacy" (APA, 1981a).

One other area where privacy is an issue involves practitioners who also teach courses, offer workshops, write books and journal articles, and give lectures. If these practitioners use examples from their clinical practices, it is of the utmost importance that they take measures to adequately disguise their clients' identities. We think it is a good practice for them to inform their clients that they are likely to use some of their clinical experience in their writing and in giving lectures. One relevant guideline on this issue of privacy is given by the APA (1981a): "Psychologists who present personal information obtained during the course of professional work in writings, lectures, or other public forums either obtain adequate prior consent to do so or adequately disguise all identifying information."

Ethical and legal ramifications of confidentiality

The ethics of confidentiality rests on the premise that clients in counseling are involved in a deeply personal relationship and have a right to expect that what they discuss will be kept private. Surely no genuine therapy can occur unless clients trust that what they say will be kept confidential. Professionals therefore have an obligation to discuss with clients the circumstances that might affect the confidentiality of their relationship.

Shah (1970a) raises the question "Whose agent is the psychologist?" He notes that in some governmental agencies and in some institutions the psychologist is *not* primarily the client's agent. In such cases psychologists might be faced with conflicts between their obligations to the agency or institution and their obligations to their clients. For this reason, Shah maintains that any possible conflict should be clarified before a psychologist enters into a diagnostic or therapeutic relationship with a client. In short, clients should be informed about the limits of confidentiality. In agreement with Shah's position are Denkowski and Denkowski (1982), who contend that "it is imperative that counselors inform each client of the potential breaches that are likely to impinge on their relationship. Furthermore it seems ethically required that all reasonable steps be taken to restrict the legally sanctioned dissemination of confidential client information to its bare minimum" (p. 374).

The compelling justification for confidentiality is that it is necessary to encourage clients to develop the trust needed for full disclosure and for the work involved in therapy.

Siegel first took the extreme position that absolute confidentiality is necessary for effective therapeutic relationships, and he argued that psychologists should not break the confidentiality of a client under *any* circumstances. As Siegel noted, this viewpoint provoked a storm of reactions. He has apparently modified his view of absolute confidentiality to fit within the boundaries of the law: "While the absolute confidentiality notion still seems viable, it cannot be urged that anyone disobey the law. Language that would include the concept that confidential information may not be disclosed without consent, except if required by law, should be supported" Siegel, 1979, p. 255). Siegel holds that professionals should function within the law while at the same time working toward changes in the laws with which they disagree.

Other writers challenge the position that absolute confidentiality is necessary for effective treatment. Denkowski and Denkowski (1982) make the case for limited and qualified confidentiality. They contend that several developments over the past decade tend to refute the conventional wisdom that there can be no therapy without complete confidentiality. They do, however, give two reasons for the continued safeguarding of client confidentiality: (1) confidentiality is needed to protect the client's interests, especially from the social stigma that is frequently associated with participating in psychotherapy; and (2) confidentiality is grounded in ethical motives of promoting vital client rights, which are essential to the therapist's professed concern for the welfare of the client.

Since confidentiality is not absolute, it becomes necessary to determine under what circumstances it cannot be maintained. These circumstances are not clearly defined by accepted ethical standards, and each therapist must exercise his or her professional judgment. When assuring their clients that what they reveal will ordinarily be kept confidential, therapists should point out that they have obligations to others besides their clients. For instance, they are bound to act in such a way as to protect others from harm. Thus, the American Personnel and Guidance Association's (1981) ethical guidelines state: "When the client's condition indicates that there is clear and imminent danger to the client or others, the member must take reasonable personal action or inform responsible authorities."

All the other major professional organizations have also taken the position that practitioners must reveal certain information when there is clear and imminent danger to an individual or to society. Consistent with these guidelines from the professions is the following specific exception to the right of privileged communication and confidentiality, as created by the California Legislature: "There is no privilege if the psychotherapist has reasonable cause to believe that the patient is in such mental or emotional condition as to be dangerous to himself or to the person or property of another and that disclosure of the communication is necessary to prevent the threatened danger."

Summary of Ethical Codes on Confidentiality

American Psychiatric Association (1981):
- "Psychiatric records, including even the identification of a person as a patient, must be protected with extreme care. Confidentiality is essential to psychiatric treatment."
- "A psychiatrist may release confidential information only with the authorization of the patient or under proper legal compulsion."
- "Clinical and other materials used in teaching and writing must be adequately disguised in order to preserve the anonymity of the individuals involved."

National Association of Social Workers (1979):
- "The social worker should share with others confidences revealed by clients, without their consent, only for compelling professional reasons."
- "The social worker should inform clients fully about the limits of confidentiality in a given situation, the purposes for which information is obtained, and how it may be used."

Standards for the Private Practice of Clinical Social Work (NASW, 1981):
- "The clinical social worker in private practice may find it necessary to reveal confidential information disclosed by the patient to protect the patient or the community from imminent danger."
- "When the clinical social worker in private practice is ordered by the court to reveal the confidences entrusted by patients, the practitioner may comply or may ethically hold the right to dissent within the framework of the law."

American Association for Marriage and Family Therapy (undated):
- "The therapist is responsible for informing clients of the limits of confidentiality."
- "Written permission shall be granted by the clients involved before data may be divulged."
- "Information is not communicated to others without consent of the client unless there is clear and immediate danger to an individual or to society, and then only to the appropriate family members, professional workers, or public authorities."

American Psychological Association (1981a):
- "Psychologists have a primary obligation to respect the confidentiality of information obtained from persons in the course of their work as psychologists. They reveal such information to others only with the consent of the person or the person's legal representative, except in those circumstances in which not to do so would result in clear danger to the person or to others. Where appropriate, psychologists inform their clients of the legal limits of confidentiality."

Much has been written in the psychological literature about the case of *Tarasoff v. Board of Regents of the University of California*. In August 1969 Prosenjit Poddar, who was a voluntary outpatient at the student health service on the Berkeley campus of the university, informed the psychologist who was counseling him that he was planning to kill his girlfriend. The therapist later called the campus police and told them of this threat. He asked them to observe Poddar for possible hospitalization as a person who was dangerous. The campus officers did take Poddar into custody for questioning, but they later released him when he gave evidence of being "rational." The psychologist followed up his call with a formal letter requesting the assistance of the chief of the campus police. Later, the psychologist's supervisor asked that the letter be returned, ordered that the letter and the therapist's case notes be destroyed, and asked that no further action be taken in the case. It should be noted that no warning was given, either to the intended victim or to her parents.

Two months later, Poddar killed Tatiana Tarasoff. Her parents filed suit against the Board of Regents and employees of the university for failing to notify the intended victim of the threat. A lower court dismissed the suit; the parents appealed; and the California Supreme Court ruled in favor of the parents in 1976 and held that a failure to warn the intended victim was irresponsible.

The duty to warn.   In their discussion of the implications of the *Tarasoff* case, Everstine and his associates (1980) note that the crucial point of the Supreme Court decision involved the failure of the psychologist and his supervisor to provide a warning of violence to the intended victim or to her parents. In its conclusion, the court affirmed the guiding principle that was basic to its decision: "The public policy favoring protection of the confidential character of patient-psychotherapist communications must yield to the extent to which disclosure is essential to avert danger to others. The protective privilege ends where the public peril begins."

In their assessment of "*Tarasoff*: Five Years Later," Knapp and Vandecreek (1982) make the point that variations in state laws make the procedures involved in the "duty to warn" a difficult matter. In the *Tarasoff* case, the identity of the victim was known. However, therapists are often concerned about their legal responsibility when the identity of the intended victim is unknown. What are the therapist's obligations in cases of generalized statements of hostility? What is the responsibility of the therapist to predict future violence? In their recommendations to therapists, Knapp and Vandecreek (1982) write: "Psychotherapists need only follow reasonable standards in predicting violence. Psychotherapists are not liable for the failure to warn when the propensity toward violence is unknown or would be unknown by other psychotherapists using ordinary skill" (pp. 514–515).

Their point is that therapists should not become intimidated by every idle fantasy, for every impulsive threat is not evidence of imminent danger. In their opinion recent behavioral acts can best predict future violence. In addition to warning potential victims, Knapp and Vandecreek suggest, practitioners should consider other alternatives that could diffuse the danger and, at the same time, satisfy their legal duty. They recommend seeking consultation with other professionals who have expertise in dealing with potentially violent people, and also documenting the steps taken.

In commenting on the Supreme Court's decision in the *Tarasoff* case, Siegel (1979) asserts that "this was a day in court for the law and not for the mental health professions" (p. 253). He argues that, if absolute confidentiality had been the policy, the psychologist might have been able to keep Poddar in treatment, ultimately saving the life of Tarasoff. According to Siegel, the potential protection of Tarasoff was eliminated when the therapist contacted the police, but it might not have been eliminated if the psychologist had kept Poddar in treatment. However, other professionals are willing to accept the duty to warn, and it appears that for the indefinite future this will remain a legal requirement. There are certain conditions under which a therapist must exchange the professional role for the role of a citizen; therapists cannot hide behind the shield of privileged communication (Everstine et al., 1980).

In his assessment of the *Tarasoff* case Schutz (1982) points out the risk factors that led the court to determine that a duty to warn was a valid expression of due care in this case. First of all, the therapist did indeed make the prediction of violence based on the client/therapist relationship. Then this prediction came to pass, which reinforced the principle of foreseeability of risk through special knowledge. Finally, in the view of the court the unsuccessful attempt to commit Poddar was poorly handled.

Guidelines for dealing with dangerous clients. Stimulated mainly by this ruling, most college counseling centers have developed guidelines regarding the limits of confidentiality when the welfare of others is at stake. These guidelines generally specify how to deal with emotionally disturbed students, violent behavior, threats, suicidal possibilities, and other circumstances in which counselors may be legally and ethically required to break confidentiality.

The question raised by these documents is: What are the responsibilities of counselors to their clients or to others when, in the professional judgment of the counselor, there is a high degree of probability that a client will commit suicide, seriously harm another person, or destroy property? Many counselors find it difficult to predict when clients pose a serious threat to themselves or to others. Clients are encouraged to engage in open dialogue in therapeutic relationships; believing that what they say is confidential, they may express feelings or thoughts about ending their own lives or doing physical harm to others. Generally, these are expressions of feelings, and relatively few of these threats are actually carried out. Counselors should therefore *not* be expected to routinely reveal all threats, for such a policy of disclosure could seriously disrupt clients' relationships with their therapists or with the persons who are "threatened." Counselors have the obligation *not* to disclose confidential material unless such disclosures are necessary to prevent harm to clients or to others.

What is expected of counselors is that they exercise reasonable professional judgment and apply practices that are commonly accepted by professionals in their specialty. If they determine that clients pose a serious danger of violence to others, they are obliged to exercise reasonable care to protect the would-be victims. Some guidance may be obtained from the following procedures, developed for use in the counseling center at California State University, Fullerton:[3]

---

[3] Adapted from "Counselor's Duty: Emotionally Disturbed or Potentially Violent Students" and "Procedures for Handling Potentially Violent Counselees." Used by permission of California State University, Fullerton.

1. When clients make threats against others, everything that goes on in the session should be recorded and documented. Counselors may be legally expected to prove that they used "sound professional judgment."
2. Counselors should inform the director of the center in writing of any serious threat.
3. Counselors should consult with professional colleagues for other opinions and suggestions concerning how to proceed. This consultation should also be documented.
4. The police and other proper authorities should be alerted.
5. The intended victim must be notified; in the case of a minor, the parents should also be notified.
6. Counselors need to inform their clients of the possible actions they must take to protect a third party.

The last point above imposes an obligation on professionals to inform their clients that the duty to warn exists. Everstine and his colleagues (1980) comment that it is only fair to tell clients in advance that certain statements are inadmissible to therapy. They add that clients have a right to be warned of the existence of the "duty to report" in certain cases (such as suspected instances of child abuse or incest) where the therapist is legally obligated to contact the appropriate authorities.

Some guidelines for dealing with potentially violent clients are given by Roth and Meisel (1977). These guidelines are designed to retain the therapeutic relationship at the same time that the potential victim is informed:

- Therapists might consider asking clients themselves to warn the persons whom they have threatened. If this approach is likely to escalate a dangerous confrontation, however, the therapist should warn the client of this possibility.
- The therapist should attempt to get the client's consent for the therapist to warn the intended victim.
- The therapist might consider having a joint session with the client and the intended victim to disclose the threat, to examine the factors leading up to it, and to explore ways of resolving the situation.
- The therapist could have the client turn in any weapons he or she possesses.
- The therapist might consider medication as an adjunct to the therapy process.
- The therapist might consider voluntary hospitalization.

A question often raised is when the therapist should inform clients that discussions of violent impulses might lead to a breach of confidentiality. Depending upon the type of population with whom you work, you might want to consider giving some of this information (including your reasons for disclosing material) to clients in writing at the initial session. Contending that many clients are not violent and have no concerns about violence, B. Schutz (1982) says that it is best to consider bringing up reasons for breaking confidentiality in those situations when the issue arises, but not as a matter of course to all clients.

Some legal trends in confidentiality.   In their discussion of the legal status and implications of client/counselor confidentiality, Denkowski and Denkowski (1982) list several conclusions that evolved from a review of trends and developments in the area:

- There are ethical grounds for the safeguarding of confidentiality, which is a professional requirement.
- How counselors should carry out this professional obligation is increasingly being specified by law.
- The extent that confidentiality can be assured under a legal framework is not absolute.
- The therapeutic process seems to proceed adequately without the existence of absolute confidentiality.

Denkowski and Denkowski note that the overall trend seems to be a legislative inclination to bind all mental-health practitioners to confidentiality while at the same time limiting the scope of confidentiality. "Apparently the conviction has sprouted among legislators that confidentiality is necessary for therapy, but it need not be absolute to promote such treatment effectively" (p. 374). They conclude that a "major challenge that will confront counselors over the next decade will be to implement legitimately the increasingly restricted legal definition of confidentiality, while safeguarding client privacy" (p. 374).

Another trend toward legislation that weakens confidentiality involves the stringent regulations imposed upon professionals to report a variety of suspected crimes against the person. For example, California has laws regarding the duty to report instances of child abuse, child molestation, and incest. Everstine and his associates (1980) make the point that many professionals are appalled that it has been necessary to pass laws with penalties for failing to report. They conclude that therapists are being called upon to serve as "gatekeepers of the criminal justice system." This raises some questions that should be carefully considered:

- When does a therapist become an informer?
- Can therapists carry out their therapeutic functions effectively and at the same time function as "gatekeepers"?
- What are the therapist's obligations when there are suspicions of crimes but at the same time circumstances that make these suspicions doubtful? For instance, what might the therapist do when incest is reported by an angry daughter yet denied by the father? What should the therapist do if he or she has serious doubts about the validity of the daughter's assertions? Is it the place of the therapist to become a judge?
- If therapists do report a client for a crime (or a suspected crime), what are their obligations to the client? Should they attempt to continue the therapy process if at all possible?
- If your client informed you that he intended to kill his girlfriend but did not disclose her identity, what should you do? Is it incumbent on you to investigate? Are you responsible for contacting the authorities?

The more one considers some of the legal ramifications of the issues that we've raised in this section, the clearer it becomes that most matters are not neatly defined. At a convention, a lawyer presented a detailed discussion of the many fine lines that exist in the legal system as it is applied to psychotherapeutic practice. This attorney's central point was that therapists must become familiar with local and state laws that govern their specializations but that this legal knowledge alone will not be enough for them to make sound decisions. Each case is unique; there are many subtle points in the law; there are various and sometimes conflicting ways to interpret a law; and professional judgment always plays a significant role in resolving these cases.

At a conference on ethical and legal issues in counseling, a great deal of interest and anxiety was expressed about the issue of dealing with potentially violent clients. Most of the counselors expressed fears of lawsuits and were very concerned about what "exercising sound professional judgment" really means. In discussing the tone of this conference, the three of us became concerned that some counselors are primarily worried about protecting themselves and not about their clients' welfare. Although counselors will surely want to protect themselves legally, we hope that they don't allow this problem to paralyze them and render them useless. While minimizing unnecessary risks, professionals do need to realize that counseling is a risky venture. Although they should be familiar with the laws that govern privileged communications and should know what they can and cannot do legally, counselors should not become so involved in legalism that they cease being sensitive to the *ethical* implications of what they do in their practice.

Confidentiality issues in marital and family therapy

There are some special issues involved with confidentiality in marital and family therapy. Therapists hold differing views on this topic. One view is that therapists should not divulge in a family session any information given to them by individuals in earlier private sessions. In the case of marriage counseling, some practitioners are willing to see each spouse for individual sessions. Information given to them by one spouse is honored as confidential, which means that it is not brought into individual sessions with the other spouse without the explicit consent of the disclosing client. Some therapists, however, reserve the right to bring up certain issues in a joint session, even if one person brought up the issue in a private session.

Some therapists who work with entire families, in contrast, have the policy of refusing to keep information secret that was shared individually. The view here is that secrets are counterproductive for open family therapy. Therefore secrets and "hidden agendas" are seen as material that should be brought out into the open during a family session. Still another view is that therapists should inform their clients that any information given to them during private sessions will be divulged as they see fit in accordance with the greatest benefit for the couple or the family. These therapists reserve the right to use their professional judgment about whether to maintain individual confidences. In our opinion, this latter approach is the most flexible, in that it avoids putting the counselor in the awkward position of having to either divulge secrets or keep secrets at the expense of the welfare of the family. According to Margolin (1982), therapists who have not promised confidentiality have more options open and thus must carefully consider the therapeutic ramifications of their actions.

What we think is absolutely essential to ethical practice is that each marital and family therapist make his or her stand on confidentiality clear to each family member from the outset of therapy. In this way, each family member can make a decision of whether to participate in the therapy and can then decide how much to disclose to the therapist. For example, a husband might disclose less in a private session if he knew that the therapist was assuming the right to bring these disclosures out in joint sessions. Consider the following case:

A husband is involved in one-to-one therapy to resolve a number of personal conflicts, of which the state of his marriage is only one. Later, his wife comes in for some joint sessions. In their joint sessions, much time is spent on how betrayed the wife feels over having discovered that her husband had an affair in the past. She is angry and hurt but has agreed to remain in the marriage and to come to these therapy sessions as long as the husband agrees not to resume the past affair or to initiate new ones. Reluctantly, the husband agrees to her demands. The therapist does not explicitly state her views of confidentiality, yet the husband assumes that she will keep to herself what she hears in both the wife's private sessions and his private sessions. During one of the joint sessions, the therapist does state her bias that, if they are interested in working on their relationship, then maintaining or initiating an affair is counterproductive. She states that it is her strong preference that, if they both want to work on improving their marriage, they agree not to have extramarital affairs.

In a later individual session, the husband tells the therapist that he has begun a new affair. He brings this up privately with his therapist because he feels some guilt over not having lived up to the agreement. But he maintains that the affair is not negatively influencing his relationship with his wife and has helped him to tolerate many of the difficulties that he has been experiencing in his marriage. He also asks that the therapist not mention this in a joint session, for he fears that his wife will leave him if she finds out that he is involved with another woman. Think about these questions in taking your position on the ethical course of action:

- Since the therapist has not explicitly stated her view of confidentiality, is it ethical for her to bring up this matter in a joint session?
- How does the therapist handle her bias and conviction regarding affairs in light of the fact that the husband tells her that it is actually enhancing, not interfering with, the marriage?
- Does she attempt to persuade the husband to give up the affair? Does she persuade the client to bring up this matter himself in a joint session? Is the therapist colluding with the husband against the wife by not bringing up this matter?
- Do you think that she could have avoided getting herself into this dilemma? If so, how?
- Does the therapist discontinue therapy with this couple because of her strong bias? If she does suggest termination and referral to another professional, might not this be tantamount to admitting to the wife that the husband is having an affair? What might the therapist say to the wife if she is upset over the suggestion of a referral and wants to know the reasons for the therapist's desire to terminate?

Cases to consider: Confidentiality issues

To assist you in considering the practical issues involved in confidentiality we'll present two case studies, one involving drug use and the other involving a suicide threat. We'll describe the actions of the counselor in each case and ask you to evaluate the counselor's handling of the situation.

An adolescent who uses drugs.   Larry was 14 years old when he was sent to a family-guidance clinic by his parents. He was seen by a counselor who had nine years of counseling experience. At the first session, the counselor saw Larry and his parents together. She told the parents in Larry's presence that what she and Larry discussed would be confidential and that she would not feel free to disclose information acquired through the sessions without Larry's permission. The parents seemed to understand that confidentiality was necessary in order for trust to develop between their son and his counselor.

Larry was reluctant at first to come in for counseling, but eventually he began to open up. As the sessions went on, he told the counselor that he was "heavily into drugs." Larry's parents knew that he had been using drugs at one time, but he had told them that he was no longer using them. The counselor listened to anecdote after anecdote about Larry's experimentation with dangerous drugs, about how he "got loaded" at school every day, and about a few brushes with death when he was under the influence of drugs. Finally, she told the client that she did not want the responsibility of knowing he was experimenting with dangerous drugs and that she would not agree to continue the counseling relationship unless he stopped using them. At this stage, she agreed not to inform his parents, on condition that he quit using drugs, but she did tell him that she would be talking with one of her colleagues about the situation.

Larry apparently stopped using drugs for several weeks. However, one night while he was under the influence of PCP, he had a serious automobile accident. As a result of the accident, he became paralyzed for life. Larry's parents angrily asserted that they had had a legal right to be informed that he was unstable to the point of committing such an act, and they filed suit against both the counselor and the agency.

1. What is your general impression of the way Larry's counselor handled the case?
2. Do you think the counselor acted in a responsible way toward (a) herself? (b) the client? (c) the parents? (d) the agency?
3. Suppose you had been Larry's counselor and had been convinced that he was likely to hurt himself or others because of his drug use and his emotionally unstable condition. Would you have informed his parents, even though doing so would probably have ended your counseling relationship with him? Why or why not?
4. Which of the following courses of action might you have taken if you had been Larry's counselor? Check as many as you think are appropriate.
   ____ stating during the initial session the legal limits on you as a therapist
   ____ consulting with the director of the agency
   ____ referring Larry for psychological testing to determine the degree of his emotional disturbance
   ____ referring him to a psychiatrist for treatment
   ____ continuing to see him without any stipulations

____ insisting upon a session with his parents as a condition of continuing counseling

____ informing the police or other authorities

____ requesting supervision and consultation from the agency

____ documenting your decisional process with a survey of pertinent research

5. Discuss in class other specific courses of action you might have pursued.

A client who threatens suicide.   Emmanuel was a middle-aged man who complained of emptiness in life, loneliness, depression, and a lack of will to live any longer. He was in individual therapy for seven months with a clinical psychologist in private practice. Using psychodiagnostic procedures, both objective tests and projective techniques, she determined that he had serious depressive tendencies and was potentially self-destructive. Emmanuel had come to her for therapy as a final attempt to find some meaning that would show him that his life had significance. In their sessions he explored in depth the history of his failures, the isolation he felt, the meaninglessness of his life, and his bouts with feelings of worthlessness and depression. With her encouragement, he experimented with new ways of behaving in the hope that he could find reasons to go on living. Finally, after seven months of searching, he decided that he wanted to take his own life. He told his therapist that he was convinced he had been deluding himself in thinking that anything in his life would change for the better and that he felt good about finally summoning the courage to end his life. He informed her that he would not be seeing her again.

The therapist expressed her concern that Emmanuel was very capable of taking his life at this time because so far he had not been able to see any light at the end of the tunnel. She acknowledged that the decision to commit suicide was not a sudden one, for they had discussed this wish for several sessions, but she let him know that she wanted him to give therapy more of a chance. He replied that he was truly grateful to her for helping him to find his answer within himself and that at least he could end his life with dignity in his own eyes. He stated firmly that he didn't want her to attempt to obstruct his plans in any way. She asked that he postpone his decision for at least a week and return to discuss the matter more fully. He told her he wasn't certain whether he would keep this appointment, but he agreed to consider it.

The therapist did nothing further. During the following week she heard from a friend that Emmanuel had committed suicide by taking an overdose of sleeping pills.

1. What do you think of the way the therapist dealt with her client?
2. What is your view of suicide?
3. What might you have done differently if you had been Emmanuel's therapist?
4. How do you think that your viewpoint regarding suicide influenced your answer to the preceding question?
5. Which of the following courses of action might you have pursued if you had been Emmanuel's counselor?

____ committing Emmanuel to a state hospital for observation, even against his will, for a period of 48 hours

____ consulting with another professional as soon as you determined that Emmanuel was acutely depressed or as soon as he began to discuss suicide as an option

    ___ respecting his choice of suicide, even if you didn't agree with it

    ___ informing the police and reporting the seriousness of his threat

    ___ informing members of his family of his intentions, even though he didn't want you to

    ___ bargaining with him in every way possible in an effort to persuade him to keep on trying to find some meaning in life

6. Discuss in class any other steps you might have taken in this case.

Some open-ended situations involving confidentiality

The following are some brief cases that deal with ethical and legal aspects of confidentiality. What do you think you would do in each of these situations?

You're working with a young man, Kevin, whom you think is potentially violent. During his sessions with you, Kevin talks about his impulses to hurt others and himself, and he describes times when he has seriously beaten his girlfriend. He tells you that she is afraid to leave him because she thinks he'll beat her even more savagely. He later tells you that sometimes he gets so angry that he comes very close to killing her. You believe that he is very likely to seriously harm and possibly even kill the young woman. Which of the following would you do?

    ___ I would notify Kevin's girlfriend that she may be in grave danger.

    ___ I would notify the police or other authorities.

    ___ I would keep Kevin's threats to myself, because I couldn't be sure that he would act on them.

    ___ I would seek a second opinion from a colleague.

    ___ I would inform my director or supervisor.

    ___ I would refer Kevin to another therapist.

    ___ I would arrange to have Kevin hospitalized.

What else might you do?

You're counseling a client, Tony, who is on probation. Tony knows that his probation officer contacts you regularly to learn of his progress. In the course of your counseling sessions, he reveals to you that he has stolen some very expensive lab equipment from the chemistry department of the community college that he attends. He tells you that the only reason he has revealed the theft to you is that he feels he can trust you not to tell anyone else. Although Tony has no intention of returning the equipment, he assures you that he won't steal again in the future. What would you do in this situation?

    ___ I would make sure that Tony knows the limits of confidentiality during our first session.

    ___ I would persuade Tony to find a way of returning the equipment without disclosing his identity.

    ___ I would report the matter to the campus police after informing Tony of my intended action.

    ___ I would consult several colleagues or a supervisor and ask what action they would take.

___ I would let Tony know that I planned to tell the chemistry department about his action.

___ I would let Tony's probation officer know what I had found out.

___ I would continue counseling Tony only if he reported the theft to his probation officer.

What else might you do?

You're a student counselor. For your internship you're working with college students on campus. Your intern group meets with a supervisor each week to discuss your cases. One day, while you're having lunch in the campus cafeteria with three other interns, they begin to discuss their cases in detail, even mentioning names of clients. They joke about some of the clients they're seeing, while nearby are other students who may be able to overhear this conversation. What would you do if you were in this situation?

___ I would tell the other interns to stop talking about their clients where other students could overhear them, and I would say that I thought they were behaving unprofessionally.

___ I would bring the matter up in our next practicum meeting with the supervisor.

___ I wouldn't do anything, since the students who could overhear the conversation would most likely not be that interested in what was being said.

___ I wouldn't do anything, because it's natural to discuss cases and make jokes to relieve one's own tensions.

___ I would encourage them to stop talking and to continue their discussion in a private place.

What else might you do in this situation?

You're leading a counseling group on a high school campus. The members have voluntarily joined the group. In one of the sessions several of the students discuss the drug traffic on their campus, and two of them reveal that they sell marijuana and various pills to their friends. You discuss this matter with them, and they claim that there is nothing wrong with using these drugs. They argue that most of the students on campus use drugs, that no one has been harmed, and that there isn't any difference between using drugs (which they know is illegal) and relying on alcohol (which many of them see their parents doing). What would you do in this situation?

___ Since their actions are illegal, I'd report them to the police.

___ I'd do nothing, because their drug use doesn't seem to be a problem for them and I wouldn't want to jeopardize their trust in me.

___ I would report the *condition* to the school authorities, while keeping the identities of the students confidential.

___ I would let the students know that I planned to inform the school authorities of their actions and their names.

___ I wouldn't take the matter seriously, because the laws relating to drugs are unfair.

___ I would explore with the students their reasons for making this disclosure.

What else might you do in this situation?

You're counseling children in an elementary school. Barbara was referred to you by her teacher because she was becoming increasingly withdrawn. After several sessions Barbara tells you that she is afraid that her father might kill her and that he frequently beats her as a punishment. Until now she has lied about obvious bruises on her body, claiming that she fell off her bicycle and hurt herself. She shows you welts on her arms and back but tells you not to say anything to anyone because her father threatened a worse beating if she told anyone. What would you do in this situation?

____ I would respect Barbara's wishes and not tell anyone what I knew.

____ I would report the situation to the principal and the school nurse.

____ I would immediately go home with Barbara and talk to her parents.

____ I would take Barbara home with me for a time.

____ I would report the matter to the police.

____ I would ask Barbara why she was telling me about the beatings if she didn't want me to reveal them to anyone else.

____ I would tell Barbara that I had a legal obligation to make this situation known to the authorities but that I would work with her and not leave her alone in her fears.

What else might you do in this situation?

Chapter summary

This chapter has focused on the therapist's ethical responsibilities, particularly with respect to client welfare, referrals, competence, and confidentiality. One of the most important ethical responsibilities of therapists is to safeguard the confidential nature of the therapeutic relationship. However, therapists also have responsibilities to their agencies, to the profession, to the community, to the members of their clients' families, and to themselves.

Ethical dilemmas arise when there are conflicts of responsibilities—for instance, when the agency's expectations conflict with the concerns or wishes of clients, or when the obligation of confidentiality conflicts with the rights of others to be protected from harm. Members of the helping professions need to know and observe the ethical codes of their professional organizations and the standards of ethics that have been generally agreed upon by members of the profession. However, many times they are called upon to exercise judgment by applying and interpreting these guidelines to specific instances. In this chapter we've encouraged you to think about specific ethical issues and to develop a sense of professional ethics and knowledge of state laws so that your judgment will be based on more than what "feels right."

Activities, exercises, and ideas for thought and discussion

1. Invite several practicing counselors to talk to your class about ethical issues they encounter in their work. You might have a panel of practitioners who work in several different settings and with different kinds of clients. For example, you could invite a therapist in private practice, a counselor who works in a college counseling center, and a counselor who works in a community mental-health center.

2. Choose one or more of the open-ended cases presented in the chapter to role-play with a fellow student. One of you can choose a client you feel you can identify with, and the other can become the counselor. Conduct a counseling interview. Afterwards, talk about how each of you felt during the interview, and discuss alternative courses of action that could have been taken. If time permits, you can reverse roles; this will give you a chance to experience both sides of the encounter and to see a different way of dealing with the same situation.

3. In small groups, explore the topic of when and how you might make a referral. If there is time, role-play a referral, with one student playing the client and another the counselor. After a few minutes, the "client" and the other students can give the counselor feedback on how he or she handled the situation. As a variation, one student can play the role of a client who simply does not want to accept a referral. Each person in the group can have a few minutes to work with the client. When everyone has had a chance to work with the client, the client can talk about how he or she felt with each person. This role playing can lead into a discussion about ways of making referrals without alienating a client.

4. In small groups, explore what you think the criteria should be for determining whether a therapist is competent. Make up a list of specific criteria, and share it with the rest of the class. Are you able as a class to come up with some common criteria?

5. In small groups, discuss specific circumstances in which you would break confidentiality, and see whether you can agree on some general guidelines. When your class convenes for a general meeting, the results of all the small groups can be shared and discussed.

6. Review the arguments for and against professional licensing and certification. For a class debate, some students can argue the position that licensure improves the quality of health care, and others can present alternatives to present licensing regulations.

7. Work out a proposal for a continuing-education program. In small groups, the class can develop a realistic model of ensuring competency for professionals once they have been granted a license. What kind of design most appeals to you? A peer-review model? Competency examinations? Taking courses? Other ideas?

8. Assume that you are applying for a job or writing a résumé to be used by you in private practice. Write up your own professional disclosure statement in a page or two. You might consider writing the essence of your views of matters such as these: the nature and purpose of counseling; what clients might expect from the process; a division of responsibilities between your client and you; a summary of your theoretical position, including the main techniques you are likely to use; a statement of the kinds of clients and problems that you are best qualified to work with; matters that might affect your relationship with your clients (such as legal restrictions, agency policy, and limits of confidentiality); and any other topics you think could help clients decide if they wanted to consult with you. Another suggestion is to

bring your disclosure statements to class and have fellow students review what you've written. They can then interview you, and you can get some practice in talking with "prospective clients." This exercise can help you clarify your own positions and give you valuable practice for job interviews.

9. As a class project, several students can form a committee to investigate some of the major local and state laws that apply to the practice of psychotherapy. This project can entail doing some reading in the current laws pertaining to therapeutic practices in your state, and it can involve interviewing people who work in a variety of human-services agencies. You might want to ask mental-health professionals what major conflicts they have experienced between the law and their professional practice. Another suggestion is to invite some of the people you speak with to come to your class to discuss legal and ethical concerns they have faced in their practices and how they have dealt with some of these problems.

10. In a class debate, one side can take the position that absolute confidentiality is necessary to promote full client disclosure. The other side can argue for a limited confidentiality that still promotes effective therapy.

11. Discuss some ways in which you can prepare clients for issues pertaining to confidentiality. How can you teach them about the purposes of confidentiality and the legal restrictions on it? How can you do this in various situations such as school, group work, marital and family counseling, and counseling with minors?

12. What confidentiality issues do you think are particularly relevant to the practice of marriage and family therapy? In what ways might these issues in counseling couples or families be different from those in individual counseling?

13. If you are interested in eventually obtaining some type of professional license to practice counseling and psychotherapy, we suggest that you write to the state board that regulates such licenses to find out the specific requirements in education and experience. It would be a good class project to have different students report on each of the separate types of licensure in your state.

14. Look over all of the professional codes of ethics in the Appendix. What are your impressions of each of these codes? To what degree are they complete? To what degree do they provide you with the needed guidelines for ethical practice? What are the values of such codes? What limitations do you see in these ethical codes? What do the various codes of ethics have in common?

15. Assume that you were a member of a committee that was making recommendations for the professional training program in which you are now involved. What changes would you most want to make in your training program? As you see it, what are the strengths and the weaknesses of your program? After you have done this exercise, bring some of your ideas to your professors.

Suggested readings

Everstine, L., Everstine, D. S., Heymann, G. M., True, R. H., Frey, D. H., Johnson, H. G., & Seiden, R. H. Privacy and confidentiality in psychotherapy. *American Psychologist*, 1980, 35(9), 828–840. Among the topics discussed in this article are procedures for

obtaining informed consent; federal requirements for breaching, and provisions for guard-
ing. confidentiality; the vulnerability of records kept for insurance purposes; and trust as
he therapeutic relationship. The authors provide conclusions and

or.y ~~~
App. G

, D. H. *Licensing and certification of psychologists and counselors.* San
Bass, 1980. For readers who are interested in a comprehensive discussion
fessional licensure and certification, this book is a good place to start.
e to the organizations, laws, and regulations that govern professional
signed to acquaint professionals with current policies and procedures
ty of licenses. The authors summarize licensing laws for psychologists
ze pertinent court cases in which laws have been challenged, and
ons of the professional organizations that have modified licensing and
ons.

arecek, J., Kaplan, A. G., & Liss-Levinson, N. Rights of clients,
erapists. *American Psychologist*, 1979, 34(1), 3–16. The authors make
taking responsibility for incorporating ethical standards into their
ts' rights will be an integral part of the therapeutic relationship. They
situations: providing clients with information necessary to make
out therapy, using contracts as a basis for structuring the client/
responding to clients' challenges to therapists' competence, and
plaints.

alpractice for psychologists. *Professional Psychology*, 1980, 11(4),
defines malpractice and explains the statutory and judicial criteria
. He concludes that psychologists can reduce malpractice risks by
pport with clients, documenting informed consent and important
eking outside consultation when appropriate, and acting cautiously
lients.

amily therapy. Cambridge, Mass.: Harvard University Press, 1974.
structural family therapy. In a lively manner, the author discusses
es of this approach. Also provided are case examples of Minuchin's
ustrations of intervention strategies for restructuring families.

psychotherapy. San Francisco: Jossey-Bass, 1982. The author has
ractitioner's guide to risk management that should be of interest
rofessions. He provides clear definitions and discussions of such
ent, contracts, managing the therapeutic relationship, the dan-
dal patient, the effects of the malpractice crisis on therapeutic
, and legal aspects of practice. Examples and cases make this a readable book on
an important subject.

Ethical Issues II: The Client/Therapist Relationship

Pre-chapter self-inventory

Directions: For each statement, indicate the response that most closely identifies your beliefs and attitudes. Use the following code:

5 = I *strongly agree* with this statement.
4 = I *agree*, in most respects, with this statement.
3 = I am *undecided* in my opinion about this statement.
2 = I *disagree*, in most respects, with this statement.
1 = I *strongly disagree* with this statement.

_____ 1. Unethical behavior is best defined as anything that is in violation of a professional code of ethics.

_____ 2. Unethical behavior is anything that results in harm to the client.

_____ 3. Clients should be made aware of their rights at the outset of a diagnostic or therapeutic relationship.

_____ 4. Involuntary commitment is *not* a violation of the human rights of people when they are unable to be responsible for themselves or their actions.

_____ 5. Mental patients in institutions should be consulted with respect to the type of treatment they might receive.

_____ 6. Dependence on the part of the client should be avoided, since it is generally counterproductive in therapy.

_____ 7. There are ethical problems involved in treating only one member of a couple in sex therapy.

_____ 8. It is ethical and often wise to use a sex surrogate for a client who doesn't have a partner, provided that the surrogate is not the sex therapist of the client.

_____ 9. Touching, whether erotic or not, is best avoided in counseling, because it can easily be misunderstood by the client.

_____ 10. Although it may be unwise to form social relationships with clients during the time they are in counseling, there are no ethical or professional limits concerning social relationships with clients *after* the termination of counseling.

___ 11. It is ethical for family therapists to use pressure and even coercion to get a reluctant person to participate in family therapy, since the welfare of the entire family is at stake.

___ 12. It is appropriate for therapists who work with children and adolescents to serve as their advocates in certain legal situations.

___ 13. Therapists who touch clients of the opposite sex, but not those of the same sex, are guilty of a sexist practice.

___ 14. Ethical practice demands that therapists develop procedures to assure that clients are in a position to make informed choices.

___ 15. Therapists have the responsibility to become knowledgeable about community resources and alternatives to therapy, so that they can present these alternatives to their clients.

___ 16. The state should have the authority to protect the community from people whose psychological condition makes them dangerous.

___ 17. Mystification of the client/therapist relationship tends to intensify client dependence and decrease the ability of the client to assert his or her rights in therapy.

___ 18. When a child is in psychotherapy, the therapist has an ethical and legal obligation to provide the parents with information they request.

___ 19. Minors should be allowed to seek psychological assistance in matters pertaining to pregnancy and abortion counseling *without* parental consent or knowledge.

___ 20. It is unethical for therapists who work with children to fail to get their informed consent.

___ 21. If another professional were doing something I considered to be unethical, I would report him or her to the state licensing agency.

___ 22. Before entering therapy, clients should be made aware of the purposes, goals, techniques, policies, and procedures involved.

___ 23. A good therapist gets involved in the client's case without getting personally involved in the client's personality.

___ 24. Therapists have an ethical responsibility to discuss a termination date with clients during the initial session(s) and then to review this matter with clients periodically during the course of therapy.

___ 25. Clients need to know about alternatives to traditional therapy, so that they can decide whether therapy or some other helping system is most appropriate for them.

Introduction

In this chapter we discuss unethical practice relating to the client/therapist relationship. In this context we raise specific issues about the rights of clients and explore several examples of unethical or questionable practice. Although some of these issues and cases may seem clear-cut to you, in the sense that you might judge certain behavior to be clearly unethical, others may not be so clear-cut. In these cases it becomes a personal challenge to make an honest appraisal of your behavior and its impact on clients. To us, unethical behavior is behavior that reflects a lack of awareness or concern about the impact of the behavior on clients. For some counselors, it may take the form of placing their personal needs above the needs of their clients, at the expense of their clients' welfare. Since this abuse of clients is often done in a subtle way, you might think about specific ways of recognizing when and how you might be meeting your needs at the expense of your clients. We hope you will develop your own guidelines for determining when you're exploiting your clients.

Consider the following list of behaviors, and ask yourself whether you think these practices are ethical. Use the following code:

A = This is both illegal and unethical.
B = This is clearly unethical.
C = This is borderline. A decision depends on some of the other particulars in the situation.
D = This is unwise or clinically inappropriate.
E = This is ethical.

_____ 1. tape-recording a counseling session without the client's knowledge or consent

_____ 2. discussing with her parents the details revealed to you by a 15-year-old girl, without the girl's permission

_____ 3. reporting one of your clients to the authorities after you find out that he is peddling drugs on campus

_____ 4. developing a social relationship with a client

_____ 5. kissing and embracing a client

_____ 6. having sexual intercourse with a client

_____ 7. having sexual intercourse with a former client

_____ 8. consistently putting the focus on yourself in a session by talking about your present or past problems

_____ 9. encouraging your client to have more frequent sessions, mainly because you need money

_____ 10. not referring a client, even when you doubt whether you can be useful to the person, because you don't want to admit that you can't work with everyone

_____ 11. deceiving a client, under the guise of being helpful

_____ 12. accepting close friends or relatives as clients

_____ 13. imposing your values on clients by subtly steering them toward goals you think are worthwhile

_____ 14. consulting with a colleague about a specific client without that client's permission

_____ 15. agreeing to enter into a counseling relationship with a minor without first securing parental permission

_____ 16. imposing treatment upon unwilling patients who have been committed to a state institution because of antisocial actions

___ 17. failing to give patients who have been committed to a mental hospital information about their diagnosis and their condition

___ 18. deliberately fostering client dependency, with the rationale that it is essential for clients to relive early-childhood wishes and dependencies in the therapy situation before they can become autonomous

___ 19. keeping clients unaware of the process of therapy and increasing the mystery of therapy, on the ground that it gives the therapist the power and influence necessary to effect significant change

___ 20. ignoring unethical practices by a colleague out of fear that any action would create an unpleasant strain in your working situation

Now decide which of these behaviors you consider to be the most serious breaches of professional ethics. What are your reasons for considering them unethical? Are there any conditions under which you think they might be ethical?

The rights of clients

Part of ethical practice is talking with clients about their rights. Depending on the setting and the situation, this discussion can involve such questions as the possibility of involuntary hospitalization, the possibility of being forced to submit to certain types of medical and psychological treatment, matters of privacy and confidentiality, the possible outcomes and limitations of therapy, the circumstances that may affect the client's decision to enter the therapeutic relationship, and the responsibilities of the therapist toward the client.

Frequently, clients don't realize that they have any rights. Because they are vulnerable and sometimes desperate for help, they may unquestioningly accept whatever their therapist says or does. There may be an aura about the therapeutic process, and clients may have an exaggerated confidence in the therapist. It is much like the trust that many patients have in their physician. For most clients, the therapeutic situation is a new one, so they are unclear about what is expected of them, what they should expect from the therapist, and what their rights are as clients. For these reasons we think that it is the responsibility of the therapist to protect clients' rights and teach them about these rights. The ethical codes of most professional organizations require that clients be given adequate information to make informed choices about entering and continuing the client/therapist relationship. By helping clients accept their rights and responsibilities, the practitioner is encouraging them to develop a healthy sense of autonomy and personal power.

Informed consent

Perhaps the best way of protecting clients' rights is to develop procedures designed to assure that clients are in a position to make informed choices. Hare-Mustin, Marecek, Kaplan, and Liss-Levinson (1979) have suggested a model that spells out the rights of clients and the responsibilities of therapists. They suggest that, before people enter a therapeutic relationship, they should have some information about the process. Hare-Mustin and her colleagues write that there are three broad areas of information that clients must know about in order to make informed choices: (1) the procedures

---

The Rights of Clients and Informed Consent: Some Ethical Codes

American Psychological Association (1981a):
- "Psychologists fully inform consumers as to the purpose and nature of an evaluative, treatment, educational, or training procedure, and they freely acknowledge that clients, students, or participants in research have freedom of choice with regard to participation."

National Association of Social Workers (1979):
- "The social worker should provide clients with accurate information regarding the extent and nature of the services available to them."
- "The social worker should apprise clients of their risks, rights, opportunities, and obligations associated with social service to them."

Standards for the Private Practice of Clinical Social Work (NASW, 1981):
- "The private practitioner and client shall agree to a contract during the initial visit(s). Conditions of the contract shall be clear and explicit. These shall include:
  1. Agreement about fees; insurance; length, frequency, and location of sessions; appointments missed or canceled without adequate notice; vacation coverage during an absence; collateral contracts.
  2. Agreement regarding goals of treatment.
  3. Informing the client of his/her rights."

---

and goals of therapy, along with its side effects; (2) the qualifications and practices of the therapist; and (3) available sources of help besides traditional therapy. Under these broad categories, let's consider a number of aspects of therapy about which clients should be informed.

The therapeutic process.   Although it may be difficult to give clients a detailed description of what occurs in therapy, some general ideas can be explored. We support the practice of letting clients know that counseling might open up levels of awareness that could cause pain and anxiety. Clients who want ongoing counseling need to know that they may experience changes that could produce disruptions and turmoil in their lives. Some clients may choose to settle for a limited knowledge of themselves rather than risking this kind of disruption. We believe that a frank discussion of the chances for change and its personal and financial costs is an appropriate way to spend some of the initial sessions. Clients should have a knowledge of the procedures and goals of therapy. This is especially true if any unusual or experimental approaches or techniques are to be employed. The ethical standards of the American Personnel and Guidance Association (1981) state that "the member must inform the client of the purposes, goals, techniques, rules of procedure and limitations that may affect the relationship at or before the time that the counseling relationship is entered."

In his discussion of client rights and therapist responsibilities, Morton Berger (1982) writes that clients have a right to be informed of the plan of treatment and to give their consent in advance. As an essential part of the therapeutic alliance, the following are the responsibilities of the therapist, according to Berger:

- to develop a written treatment plan
- to present this plan to clients, making sure that they understand the nature of therapy and obtaining their informed consent
- to review and revise the treatment plan as appropriate in consultation with clients

Berger's "patient's bill of rights" also includes this statement:

The patient has a right to a therapist who is committed solely and completely to promoting his or her best interests and personal welfare. Associated with this is the client's right to be provided with the necessary information to enable him or her to make an informed choice regarding therapy [p. 82].

This right of the client implies that therapists should provide from the outset information concerning goals, procedures, and the therapist's theoretical orientation.

Background of the therapist. The matter of therapists' developing professional disclosure statements was covered in the previous chapter. Such a statement is an excellent way to help clients decide whether they will make use of the practitioner's services. Therapists should provide clients with a description of their training and education, any specialized skills, and the types of clients and types of problems that they are best trained to deal with. If the counseling will be done by an intern or a paraprofessional, then the clients should know this. This clear description of the practitioner's qualifications, coupled with a willingness to answer any questions clients have about the process, reduces the unrealistic expectations of clients about therapy.

Costs involved in therapy. The ethics code of the American Association for Marriage and Family Therapy (undated) specifies: "The therapist recognizes the importance of clear understandings on financial matters with clients. Arrangements for payments are settled at the beginning of a therapeutic relationship." Morton Berger (1982) lists as one of the "patient's bill of rights" the right to a reasonable financial arrangement. According to Berger, this right entails several therapist responsibilities, some of which are:

- providing information regarding all fees by the end of the initial session, including the arrangement for a payment schedule
- avoiding exploitation of clients by prolonging therapy needlessly or convincing them to undergo unnecessary diagnostic or treatment procedures
- making clients aware of insurance reimbursement, and taking whatever steps are necessary to help them collect payments from a third party
- not springing unexpected costs upon the client

Matters of finance are delicate, and if they are handled poorly, they can easily result in a strained relationship between the client and therapist. Thus, the manner in which fees are handled has much to do with the tone of the therapeutic partnership.

The length of therapy. Some therapists make it a practice to discuss with their clients an approximate length for the therapeutic process. They may make this matter a part of the written or verbal contract during the initial session(s). Other therapists maintain, on theoretical grounds, that, since the problems that brought the client into therapy are typically complex and long-standing, therapy will necessarily be long-term. These therapists may be unwilling to talk during the initial phase about the length of treatment, simply because of their conviction that individual differences among clients make such a prediction impossible.

Regardless of the therapist's theoretical orientation, we think, clients do have a right to expect that their therapy will end when they have realized the maximum benefits from it or have obtained what they were seeking when they entered it. We think that the issue of termination needs to be openly explored by the therapist and client and that the decision to terminate ultimately rests with the client. Morton Berger (1982) maintains that therapists have the responsibility to set a tentative termination date with clients and then review this date and revise it when appropriate.

Many agencies have a policy of *limiting* the number of sessions that a client can have. In this case, clients need to be informed at the outset that they cannot receive long-term therapy. They should not be informed at the next-to-last session that they will not be allowed to return. Also, clients have the right to expect a referral so that they can continue exploring whatever concerns initially brought them to therapy. In short, clients should not be abandoned by therapists. Concerning this issue of abandonment, the NASW (1979) has the following ethical guideline: "The social worker who anticipates the termination or interruption of service to clients should notify clients promptly and seek the transfer, referral, or continuation of services in relation to the clients' needs and preferences."

Consultation with colleagues.   Student counselors generally meet regularly with their supervisors and fellow students to discuss their progress and any problems they encounter in their work. It is good policy for counselors to inform their clients that they are meeting with others and may be talking with them about some of the sessions. Clients can be assured that their identities will not necessarily be disclosed, and they can be informed of the reasons for these meetings with supervisors and others. Even though it is ethical for counselors to discuss their cases with other counselors, it's wise to routinely let clients know about this possibility. Clients will then have less reason to feel that the trust they are putting in their counselors is being violated. Counselors can explain that these discussions may well focus on what *they* are doing and feeling as counselors, rather than on their clients as "cases."

The limits of confidentiality.   Any limitations on the confidentiality of the counseling relationship should be explained to clients at the outset. These limitations may be greater in some settings and agencies than in others. If clients are informed about the conditions under which confidentiality may be broken, they are in a better position to decide whether to enter counseling; if they're required to "get counseling," they can decide what personal material they will or will not disclose in their sessions.

As a part of the confidentiality issue, counselors might discuss with the client their record keeping and taking of notes. Counselors are expected to keep their counseling relationships confidential. If they do not, they open themselves up to lawsuits for malpractice. Further, the release of material deemed confidential can amount to invasion of privacy, and the client may sue for damages. On this matter, the APGA (1981) has the following guideline:

Records of the counseling relationship, including interview notes, test data, correspondence, tape recordings, and other documents, are to be considered professional information for use in counseling and they should not be considered a part of the institution or agency in which the counselor is employed unless specified by state statute or regulation. Revelation to others of counseling material must occur only upon the expressed consent of the client.

Related to the preceding APGA guideline is Morton Berger's statement that "the patient has a right to have an accurate record kept of the therapeutic process, to have access to that record, and to have copies made available to other practitioners or appropriate individuals at his or her direction" (1982, p. 87).

Tape-recording or videotaping of sessions.   Many agencies require recording of interviews for training or supervision purposes. Clients have a right to be informed about this procedure at the initial session, and it is important that they understand why the recordings are made, how they will be used, and who will have access to them. Often therapists make recordings because they can benefit from listening to them or perhaps having colleagues listen to their interactions with clients and give them feedback. Again, if this is to be done, clients should be informed and their consent obtained. Frequently, clients are very willing to give their consent if they are approached in an honest way. Clients, too, may want to listen to a taped session during the week to help them remember what went on or to evaluate what is happening in their sessions.

The freedom to be diagnosed and categorized by a therapist.   We agree with D. Smith's position (1981) that one of the basic rights of a client is the freedom to choose to be coded and classified by a psychologist or psychiatrist. He urges that the psychologist obtain the consent of clients when they are diagnosed for the purposes of insurance reimbursement. We think that an open discussion with clients about their condition, including a formal diagnosis if this is a part of the therapy procedure, is one way to demystify the client/therapist relationship. We endorse the maximum possible openness with clients about our procedures, so that they can become active and informed agents in their own therapy and not dependent upon the magical healing powers of a therapist.

Personal relationships.   Before therapists accept supervisees, students, employees, colleagues, close friends, or relatives as clients, it is essential that they discuss with these prospective clients the problems that may be associated with what is known as a "dual relationship." It should be stressed that most of the ethical codes caution against dual relationships and point to the need to avoid exploitation of clients out of the therapist's needs.

Clients have a right to expect that their therapist will be primarily concerned with their welfare. This concern implies that therapists will have some degree of "therapeutic distance," or objectivity. It also implies that therapists will be aware of their own countertransference feelings, so that they do not unnecessarily complicate the therapy process. On this matter Wolman (1982) contends that a good therapist "must not become personally involved with patients, or get caught in the murky waters of morbid counter-transference feelings" (p. 193). Seeing personal involvement as a gross violation of therapeutic ethics, Wolman offers this advice: "A good psychotherapist gets involved with the patient's case without getting involved with the patient's personality" (p. 191).

Alternatives to traditional therapy.   Clients need to know about alternative helping systems. Therefore, therapists must become knowledgeable about community resources so that they can present these alternatives to a client. The following are some examples of alternatives to psychotherapy (Hare-Mustin et al., 1979):

- *individual self-help*: use of self-help books and bibliotherapy, recreational activities, religious activities, and changes in social relationships or life-style
- *programs designed for personal effectiveness training*: parent effectiveness training, assertiveness training, and marriage encounter
- *peer self-help groups*: Parents Without Partners, Alcoholics Anonymous, Weight Watchers, consciousness-raising groups, and a variety of support groups
- *crisis intervention systems*: rape crisis centers, suicide hot-lines, shelters for battered wives, and pregnancy and abortion counseling
- *psychological and psychiatric helping systems*: day-treatment and out-patient hospital programs and partial hospitalization
- *other institutional helping systems*: legal assistance, social-welfare agencies, and medical and other health-care facilities

This information about therapy and its alternatives can be presented in writing, through an audiotape or videotape, or during an intake session. Hare-Mustin and her associates caution practitioners to present alternatives to therapy fairly. They also note that an ethical dilemma may arise when a therapist has clear convictions about what course of action is in the best interests of a given client. Although the therapist may ethically state his or her views when a client is tending toward a different course of action, the therapist who insists upon a definite approach diminishes the client's right to free choice. An open discussion of therapy and its alternatives may, of course, lead some clients to choose sources of help other than therapy. For practitioners who make a living providing therapy services, this possibility can produce anxiety. On the other hand, the practice of openly discussing therapy and its alternatives is likely to reinforce many clients' decisions to continue therapy.

Informed consent in marital and family therapy

We have been focusing on the issue of informed consent and clients' rights within the framework of individual therapy. As Margolin (1982) notes, however, informed consent and the right to refuse treatment are also a critical ethical issue in the practice of marital and family therapy. When therapists work with an entire family, there are both ethical and practical reasons for taking the time to obtain informed consent from everyone. When this is done, the message is conveyed that no one family member is the "crazy person" who is the source of all the family's problems. Margolin suggests that the therapist explore with the family the following topics at the outset: the purposes and procedures of family therapy; the role and function of the person doing the therapy; the risks involved; the benefits that can be expected, along with the price that must be paid for these benefits; the option that each family member can withdraw his or her consent and discontinue participation in therapy at any time; and some discussion of the possibility that family therapy will lead to outcomes deemed undesirable by some participants but advantageous by others in the same family.

Most family therapists consider it essential that all members of the family participate. This raises ethical questions about exerting pressure upon an individual to participate, even if that person is strongly against being involved. Although coercion of a reluctant person is generally viewed as unethical, many therapists strongly suggest to such a person that he or she give a session or two a try to determine what potential value there might be to family therapy. Some resistance can arise from the feeling that a family member will be "ganged up on" and will be the focus of the sessions. In several sessions this resistance can be lessened and perhaps even eliminated if the therapist does not allow the family to use one member as the scapegoat. Although getting the informed consent of each member of the family is ideal from an ethical point of view, actually carrying out this practice may involve difficulties. On this point, Margolin (1982) writes:

> Thus, even though clients deserve an accurate portrayal of therapy in informed consent procedures, complete objectivity and openness may not be possible. At the same time that families need factual information to make an informed decision about therapy, they also need the therapist's support, encouragement, and optimism for taking this risky step [p. 795].

Like Margolin, Haas and Alexander (1981) contend that there are ethical problems in insisting that all the family members must attend sessions. They indicate that the therapist who requires all members of a family to be a part of therapy may be colluding with the most resistant family member in keeping the more willing members from beginning or continuing therapy as a family. This position is often taken when the family therapist identifies the client as "the family" or "the system."

Protecting children's rights is typically made easier by treating the whole family, according to Haas and Alexander. They note that parents are generally considered to retain the legal authority to consent to (or prohibit) their children's treatment and to know what is occurring in this therapy. Family therapy eliminates certain problems, including the parents' "right to know," since they are a part of the therapy process. The issue of informed consent is open for discussion as a family topic, avoiding a conflict that might involve the therapist's siding with either the child or the parent. Haas and Alexander recommend that family therapists establish ground rules for dealing with matters such as family secrets or the confidences of an individual member. If these rules are made a part of the informed-consent procedure at the initial session(s), then issues of confidentiality are less likely to become a problem as therapy progresses.

Haas and Alexander contend that family therapists are responsible for clarifying their basic ethical positions and must communicate their views to their clients. They write:

> The general guideline is that one's position should be articulated; if the therapist does not know where he or she stands on a given issue such as rights of women, proper role of secrets in the family, aspects of children's independence, etc. then it is incumbent upon that therapist to start the process of finding out [1981, p. 9].

We are in basic agreement with their position. We think that, if therapists are able to clarify their positions to all the family members from the outset of treatment, the chances are greatly increased that these members will be willing to cooperate in the therapy. At the least, any member of the family can then argue with the therapist's views.

Hare-Mustin (1980) has observed that family therapy may be dangerous to one's health. Since it requires the involvement of the entire family, it may not be in the best interests of individual family members. The priority placed on the good of the family as a unit may lead to individual risks. Further, by being required to participate in therapy, members may have to subordinate their own goals and give up limited confidentiality. Hare-Mustin suggests that ethical practice demands a method of minimizing these risks for individual members. This can be done by encouraging them to question the goals of family therapy, so that they can understand how their own needs relate to the family goals. Also, it is the therapist's responsibility to open for discussion the subject of how one member's goals are incompatible with family goals or perhaps even unacceptable to other members. She emphasizes the importance of discussing the limits of confidentiality and privacy at the beginning of family sessions. Members have the right to know the rules about disclosure and how this sharing of information will be used (both in the sessions and out of the sessions).

At this point we ask you to think of additional issues that you would want to discuss with your clients during the first few sessions. What factors might influence the relationship between you and your clients?

Ethical and legal issues in counseling children and adolescents

Consistent with the increasing concern over children's rights in general, more attention is being paid to such issues as the minor's right of informed consent. There are legal and ethical trends toward granting greater rights to children and adolescents in these areas (Glenn, C. M., 1980). According to G. P. Koocher (1976), ethical standards in counseling with minors deserve attention, because often "the standards of professional associations do not specifically address children as a unique subset of the population" (p. 3). Some of the legal and ethical questions faced by therapists who work with children and adolescents are as follows: Can minors consent to treatment without parental consent? Can minors consent to treatment without parental knowledge? To what degree should minors be allowed to participate in setting the goals of therapy and in providing consent to undergo it? What are the limits of confidentiality in counseling with minors? What does informed consent consist of in working with minors? In this section we consider some of these questions and focus on the rights of children when they are clients.

The right to treatment

In most states parental consent is legally required for minors to enter into a relationship with health-care professionals. There are exceptions to this general rule; some state statutes grant adolescents the right to seek counseling about birth control, abortion, substance abuse, and other crisis concerns. An example is a Virginia law of 1979 that is the broadest statute in the country on the rights of children and adolescents to consent to therapy. This law implies that "mature minors" should be able to consent to psychotherapy independently on grounds of personal privacy and liberty (Melton, 1981b). More specifically, a minor is deemed an adult for the purposes of consenting to:

1. health services needed to determine the presence of or to treat venereal disease or any infections or contagious disease that the State Board of Health requires to be reported
2. health services required in case of birth control, pregnancy, or family planning
3. health services needed in the case of outpatient care, treatment, or rehabilitation for substance abuse
4. health services needed in the case of outpatient care, treatment, or rehabilitation for mental or emotional illness

In keeping with this law, counselors in Virginia have the duty to keep information in the above areas confidential, even from parents. This duty challenges the commonly accepted premise that, before a counselor accepts a minor as a client, he or she is required to inform the parents and obtain their consent (Swanson, 1983b).

Like Virginia, California provides for certain exceptions. Minors who have reached the age of 12 may consent to mental-health treatment if certain conditions are met: The minors must be mature enough to participate intelligently in mental-health treatment on an outpatient basis (in the opinion of the therapist), *and* they must present a danger of serious physical or mental harm to themselves or others *or* have been the alleged victims of incest or child abuse. Minors who meet the above stipulations may consent to receive outpatient mental-health services from sources such as the following: licensed marriage and family counselors, licensed clinical social workers, licensed psychologists, or any governmental agency or community crisis center with qualified practitioners (Board of Medical Quality Assurance, 1980).

The justification for allowing children and adolescents to seek treatment without parental consent is that they might not obtain this needed treatment in some circumstances without such a right. There is some evidence that adolescents may seek help when given independent access, whereas they might not do so without the guarantee of privacy (Melton, 1981a). This is especially true in cases where the presenting problems involve family conflict, psychological or physical abuse, drug or alcohol abuse, and pregnancy or abortion counseling.

Counselors who are faced with the issue of when to accept minors as clients without parental consent must consider various factors. What is the competence level of the minor? What are the potential risks and consequences if treatment is denied? What are the chances that the minor will not seek help or will not be able to secure parental permission for needed help? How serious is the problem? What are the laws pertaining to providing therapy for minors without parental consent? Melton recommends to practitioners who must make decisions about accepting minors without parental consent that they seek legal advice about the relevant statutes in their states. He also advises them to consult with other professionals in weighing the ethical issues involved in each case.

Informed consent

Therapists who work with children and adolescents must often function as an advocate for these people. They have ethical responsibilities to provide information that will help minors become active participants in their treatment. On this matter, the guideline provided by the APA (1981a) is as follows: "When working with minors or other persons who are unable to give voluntary, informed consent, psychologists take special care to protect these persons' best interests."

Allowing children and adolescents to consent to therapy may have the benefits of increasing their participation in decision making about treatment when they enter *with* parental consent (Melton, 1981b). It is a good policy to provide children with treatment alternatives and enlist their participation in defining goals for their therapy. There are both ethical and therapeutic reasons for involving minors in their treatment. By giving them the maximum degree of autonomy within the therapeutic relationship, the therapist demonstrates respect for them. Also, it is likely that therapeutic change is promoted by informing children about the process and enlisting their involvement in it. On this issue, Melton (1981a) concludes: "Available research suggests that involvement of children in treatment planning increases the efficacy of treatment and that the presumption of incompetence to consent to treatment may be invalid for many adolescents" (p. 246).

In cases where children do not have the capacity to give full unpressured consent, some writers have recommended that there be a child advocate to examine and protect the child's interests, especially when the child is reluctant to participate in therapy (Koocher, G. P., 1976). This advocate should be a person other than the parent or the therapist. If children lack the background to weigh risks and benefits, and if they cannot give complete informed consent, therapists should still attempt to provide some understanding of the therapy process. If formal consent cannot be obtained, then even partial understanding is better than proceeding with therapy without any attempt to explain the goals and procedures of the process (Margolin, 1982).

At this point we suggest that you think about some of these legal and ethical considerations in providing therapy for minors.

• Some argue that it is the right of parents to know about matters that pertain to their adolescent daughters and sons. They assert, for example, that parents have a right to be involved in decisions about abortions. What is your position?

• There are those who argue for the right of minors to seek therapy without parental knowledge or consent, on the ground that needed treatment might not be given to them otherwise. When, if at all, do you think that you would counsel a minor without parental knowledge and consent?

• What are your thoughts on the kinds of information that should be provided to children and adolescents before they enter a therapeutic relationship?

• Do you think that therapists who do not provide minors with the information necessary to make informed choices are acting unethically? Why or why not?

• "The role of the traditional child psychotherapist must be modified to include the role of information provider to the children, so as to provide the children with informed consent" (Glenn, C. M., 1980, p. 617). Glenn also suggests that the child therapist should be able to function as the advocate of the child in certain legal situations and that he or she should be able to function as a social, political, and legal agent for change. What are your reactions to this viewpoint?

Involuntary commitment and human rights

The practice of involuntary commitment of people to mental institutions raises difficult professional, ethical, and legal issues. Practitioners must know their own state's laws pertaining to involuntary commitment. Our focus here is not specific legal provisions but, rather, the ethical aspects of involuntary commitment.

Jorgensen and Lyons (1972) indicate that 250,000 people are committed to mental institutions in the United States each year. They contend that the rights of people convicted of crimes are generally better protected than are the rights of people who undergo civil commitment to mental hospitals. They argue that "the person facing involuntary commitment is entitled to all the due process protections available for defendants in criminal trials" (p. 149).

In discussing the moral, legal, and ethical aspects of the civil rights of mental patients, Tolchin, Steinfeld, and Suchotliff (1970) claim that the laws protecting the rights of the mentally ill have lagged behind those that protect criminals. They further allege that psychologists have remained silent while the moral and legal rights of mental patients are being consistently violated. This silence, they argue, is both irresponsible and unethical. Their summary of some of the abuses of the human rights of those who are involuntarily hospitalized includes the following:

1. Patients may be held involuntarily and given no choice with respect to treatment or incarceration.
2. Patients are deprived of their freedom and autonomy within the institution on the ground that the psychiatrist knows what is best for them or under the guise of helping them or protecting them from themselves and others.
3. Generally, mental patients are the last persons to be consulted about the treatment they receive. They may not be informed of the nature of their treatment program or given the option of refusing treatment once a treatment plan has been formulated.
4. Patients are rarely given the results of psychological tests.
5. Patients may not be told the name or quantity of medication they receive.

White and White (1981) have explored the issue of whether the mental-health profession should impose treatment on unwilling patients who have run afoul of state commitment laws or should keep out of that conflict. In their article on the constitutional right of involuntarily committed patients to refuse treatment, they pose three questions: (1) Does the state have the power to commit people? (2) What are a person's rights pertaining to receiving treatment? (3) What are a person's rights pertaining to refusal of treatment? Briefly, their answers to these questions are:

1. The U.S. Supreme Court has held that the states do have a legitimate interest in providing care for people who are not able to care for themselves; the states also have the authority to protect the community from those individuals whose psychological condition makes them dangerous.

2. The legal issue of a committed mental patient's right to treatment is not settled. Although some lower courts have expressed support for such a right, no constitutional basis has been established by the Supreme Court to support this right.

3. Some patients may not be legally competent to exercise their right to decide whether to have treatment or what kind of treatment is in their best interests. Legal incompetence to make decisions concerning treatment hinges upon state laws, which vary.

What is the role of the mental-health profession in safeguarding the rights of the committed patient? In answering this question, White and White emphasize the role of informed consent. Their position is that committed patients must be given all the information necessary for them to make reasonable and intelligent decisions regarding choice of treatment. For example, patients should be given information about their diagnosis and condition. They should also be told about alternative courses of treatment and be able to discuss the benefits and risks of each approach to treatment. White and White's view is that the patient's informed consent to a specific treatment plan should be obtained and that treatment should be terminated at the patient's demand. They summarize the essence of the challenge for therapists in dealing with the involuntary patient:

> It is the responsibility of the mental health profession to make available to the patient all of the knowledge and skill it can marshal that might benefit that patient. The profession must recognize that the ultimate responsibility for treatment is with the individual, even when he or she decides to reject the help that is offered. The profession must grant the dignity of freedom of choice to the patient and then meet the patient on that basis [1981, p. 961].

Imagine yourself in the following situation. You're employed as a counselor at a state mental hospital. The ward on which you work is overcrowded, and there aren't nearly enough professionals on the staff to provide for much more than custodial services. You observe patients who seem to be psychologically deteriorating, and the unattractive surroundings reinforce the attitude of hopelessness that is so prevalent among the patients. You become aware that the rights of patients are often ignored, and you see many of the hospital's practices as destructive. For instance, when patients are given medication, there is rarely an ongoing evaluation of the effects of the drug treatment and whether it should be continued. Moreover, you recognize that some of the people who have been hospitalized against their will really don't belong there, yet institutional procedures and policies make it very difficult for them to be released or placed in a more appropriate agency. Finally, although some members of the staff are both competent and dedicated, others who hold positions of power are incompetent.

What do you think you might do if you were involved in this situation? What do you see as your responsibility, and what actions might you take? Check as many of the following statements as you think appropriate:

_____ Since I couldn't change the people in power, I'd merely do what I could to treat the patients with care and dignity.

_____ I'd bring the matter to public attention by writing to newspapers and talking with television reporters.

___ I'd attempt to rectify the situation by talking to the top administrators and telling them what I had observed.

___ I'd form a support group of my peers and see what we could do collectively.

___ I'd keep my views to myself, because the problem is too vast and complex for me to do anything about it.

___ I'd encourage the patients to revolt and demand their rights.

___ I'd directly confront the people I thought were incompetent or who were violating the rights of patients and attempt to change them.

What other courses of action might you take?

Handling client dependence as an ethical issue

Clients frequently experience a period of dependence on therapy or on their therapist. This temporary dependence isn't necessarily a bad thing. Some clients are people who have exaggerated the importance of being independent. They see the need to consult a professional as a sign of weakness. When these people do allow themselves to need others, their dependence doesn't necessarily present an ethical issue.

An ethical issue does arise, however, when counselors *encourage* dependence on the part of their clients. They may do so for any number of reasons. Counselor interns need clients, and sometimes they may keep clients coming to counseling longer than is necessary because they will look bad if they "lose" a client. Some therapists in private practice might fail to challenge clients who show up and pay regularly, even though they appear to be getting nowhere. Some therapists foster dependence in their clients in subtle ways out of a need to feel important. When clients play a helpless role and ask for answers, these counselors may readily tell them what to do. Dependent clients can begin to view their therapists as all-knowing and all-wise; therapists who have a need to be perceived in this way might act in ways that will keep their clients immature and dependent, thus feeding off the dependency needs of clients in order to gain a sense of significance.

A related issue involves attempts by professionals to keep the therapeutic process mysterious. This effort can have the result of encouraging clients to remain powerless. Mystification of the client/therapist relationship tends to intensify clients' dependence and also reduces their ability to assert their rights in the therapy process (Hare-Mustin et al., 1979). Gross (1979) also comments on ways in which therapists promote client dependency by keeping therapy a mysterious venture: "Professionals must keep clients mystified and dependent to maintain their power" (p. 36).

Stensrud and Stensrud (1981) observe that counseling can be hazardous to health, for it can teach people to be powerless instead of teaching them to trust themselves. They describe powerlessness as a "learned state of generalized helplessness in which clients (a) believe they are unable to have an impact on their environment, and (b) need some external force to intercede on their behalf" (p. 300). These authors note that clients can develop a self-fulfilling prophecy, whereby their expectation of powerlessness feeds into their experience of being powerless. They urge that clients participate actively in the entire therapy process. They also caution that, since people often produce the behavior that is expected of them, if therapists relate to clients in ways that tell the clients that they are not responsible for themselves, these clients are taught to feel dependent and helpless. Yet there are counselors who feel a sense of personal power and who do not need to keep clients dependent to maintain this power. Counselors who themselves feel a sense of powerlessness will have difficulty in preventing their clients from feeling powerless.

The ethical guidelines of the APGA (1981) warn about creating dependency: "The consulting relationship must be one in which client adaptability and growth toward self-direction are encouraged and cultivated. The member must maintain this role consistently and not become a decision maker for the client or create a future dependency on the consultant."

On the issue of termination of a therapeutic relationship, a matter that is related to client dependency, the code of ethics of the NASW (1979) states: "The social worker should terminate service to clients, and professional relationships with them, when such service and relationships are no longer required or no longer serve the clients' needs or interests."

In spite of the fact that most professional codes have guidelines that call for termination whenever further therapy will not bring significant gains, some therapists do have difficulty in letting go of their clients. They run the risk of unethical practice because of either financial or emotional needs. On the financial issue, we contend that ethical practitioners will continually examine whether they are resistant to termination because it would mean a decline in income. Obviously, termination cannot be mandated by ethical codes alone but rests on the honesty and goodwill of the therapist. We agree with Wolman's position (1982) that "every therapist has the moral obligation to terminate his or her work as soon as further work will not bring additional and significant therapeutic gains" (p. 195). Wolman contends that the therapist's need to feel useful can unconsciously cause him or her to postpone the end of therapy. He sees the mark of good therapists as the ability to help their clients reach the stage of autonomy, where they no longer need a therapist.

Like many of the other ethical issues discussed in this chapter, the issue of encouraging dependence in clients is often not a clear-cut one in practice. Since our main purpose here is to stimulate you to think of possible ways that you might foster dependence or independence in your clients, we'll present a couple of illustrative cases and ask you to respond to them.

Marcia is single and almost ready to graduate from college. She tells you that she has ambivalent feelings about graduating, because she feels that now she's expected to get a job and live on her own. This prospect frightens her, and she doesn't want to leave the security she has found as a college student. As she puts it, she doubts that she can "make it in the real world." Marcia doesn't trust her own decisions, because when she does make choices, the result, in her eyes, is disastrous. Her style is to plead with you to advise her whether she should date, apply for a job, leave home, go on to graduate school, and so forth. Typically, Marcia gets angry with you because you aren't being directive enough. She feels that you have more knowledge than she does and should therefore give her more guidance. She says: "Why am I coming here if you won't tell me what to do to straighten out my life? If I could make decent decisions on my own, I wouldn't need to come here in the first place!"

- How do you imagine you'd feel if Marcia were your client?
- How might you respond to her continual prodding for answers?
- How do you imagine you'd feel about Marcia's statement that you aren't doing your job and that you aren't being directive enough?
- What steps would you take to challenge her?
- In what ways do you think it would be possible for you to tie into her dependency needs and foster her dependence upon you for direction, instead of freeing her from you?
- How would you deal with Marcia if you eventually believed that you should terminate the relationship, and if she didn't feel ready to leave?

Ron, a young counselor, encourages his clients to call him at home at any time and as often as they feel like it. He frequently lets sessions run overtime, lends money to clients when they're "down and out," devotes many more hours to his job than he is expected to, and overtaxes himself by taking on an unrealistically large case load. Ron says that he lives for his work and that it gives him a sense of being a valuable person. The more he can do for people, the better he feels.

- In what ways could Ron's style keep his clients dependent on him?
- What could he be getting from being so "helpful"? What do you imagine his life would be like if there were no clients who needed him?
- If you were Ron's colleague and he came to you to talk about how "burnt out" he felt because he was "giving so much," what would you say to him?
- Can you identify with him in any ways? Do you see yourself as potentially needing your clients more than they need you?

Manipulation as unethical behavior

If psychotherapy is basically a process that teaches people how to be honest with themselves, then it is of the utmost importance for therapists to be honest with their clients. Unfortunately, there are many ways for therapists to deceive or manipulate clients, often under the guise of being helpful and concerned. Therapists who have plans for what they want their clients to do or to be and who keep these plans hidden are examples of manipulative therapists. Other therapists may attempt to control their relationships with their clients by keeping therapy a mysterious process and maintaining a rigid "professional stance" that excludes the client as a partner in the relationship. Therapy thus becomes a matter of the therapist's *doing* therapy on an unquestioning client.

To offset the danger of manipulating clients toward ends they have not chosen, some therapeutic approaches emphasize strategies designed to ensure that clients will have an active role in deciding what happens to them in the therapeutic relationship. As we saw in Chapter 4, many therapists use a contract as a basic prerequisite for continuing therapy. The contract contains a specific statement of goals and criteria for evaluating when these goals have been effectively met. The nature of the therapeutic relationship is thus defined by the contract, which is agreed upon by both the client and the therapist. Its proponents claim that this procedure emphasizes the partnership of client and therapist, demystifies the therapeutic process, and minimizes the chance that clients will be manipulated toward ends that well-intentioned therapists have for them.

Sidney Jourard contrasts manipulation with dialogue in counseling. He sees psychotherapy as "an invitation to authenticity" in which the therapist's role is to be an exemplar. Therapists can foster their clients' honesty and invite them to drop their pretenses only by dropping their own and meeting their clients in an honest manner. Jourard (1968) says "I believe that the psychotherapist is the teacher in the therapeutic dance, and the patient follows the leader" (pp. 64–65). One of the best ways for therapists to demonstrate their goodwill is by avoiding manipulation and being open, trusting, and thus vulnerable to their clients. If counselors manipulate their clients, they can expect manipulation in return; if they are open, however, their clients may be open as well. Jourard (1968) expresses this concept descriptively as follows:

> If I want him to be maximally open, but I keep myself fully closed off, peeking at him through chinks in my own armor, trying to manipulate him from a distance, then in due time he will discover that I am not in that same mode; and he will then put his armor back on and peer at me through chinks in it, and he will try to manipulate me [p. 64].

Manipulation can work in subtle ways. Consider the degree to which you think the behavior of the therapists in the following two examples are manipulative and unethical.

Joan, a wealthy, middle-aged widow, has been seeing Dr. Rupe on a regular basis for over three years because of her loneliness and depression. Much of the dialogue of the sessions is now social in nature. Joan continually tells Dr. Rupe how she enjoys the sessions and how meaningful they are to her. In one of these sessions Dr. Rupe mentions his interest in buying an antique Model A. That Christmas, Joan presents Dr. Rupe with the antique Ford.

- Is it ethical for the therapist to accept the gift?
- Did the therapist manipulate the situation by indicating his interest in antique cars?
- Was it unethical of the therapist to continue seeing a client with whom he was primarily engaging in social interchanges?
- Did the client's expressed appreciation warrant continuing the therapy? Was this alone a sufficient ground for continuing the professional relationship?
- Could this case be construed as manipulation of transference feelings?
- How could you defend Dr. Rupe's continuing the therapy and, even, his accepting the antique car?

Barbara is 20 years old and has been in therapy with Dr. Smart for over a year. She has developed a high degree of respect and fondness for her therapist, whom she sees as a father figure. She tells Dr. Smart that she is thinking of discontinuing therapy because she has lost her job and simply has no way of paying for the sessions. Barbara is obviously upset over the prospect of ending the relationship with her therapist, but she sees no alternative. Dr. Smart informs her that he is willing to continue her therapy even if she is unable to pay. He suggests that as an exchange of services Barbara can become the baby-sitter for his three children. She gratefully accepts this offer, only to find after a few months that the situation is becoming difficult for her. Eventually,

Barbara writes a note to Dr. Smart telling him that she cannot handle her reactions to his wife and their children. It makes her think of all the things that she missed in her own family. She writes that she has found this subject difficult to bring up in her sessions, so she is planning to quit both her services and her therapy.

- What mistakes, if any, do you think that Dr. Smart made?
- How would you have dealt with this situation? What might you have done differently?
- Do you think that it was unethical for the therapist to suggest that Barbara do baby-sitting for him? In doing so, to what degree did he take into consideration the nature of the transference relationship?

The issue of social and personal relationships with clients

Do social relationships with clients necessarily interfere with therapeutic relationships? Some would say no—that counselors and clients are able to handle a social relationship in conjunction with a therapeutic one, as long as it is clear where the priorities lie. They see this as being particularly true with clients who aren't deeply disturbed and who are seeking personal growth. Some peer counselors, for example, claim that the friendships they have had with people prior to or during counseling were actually positive factors in establishing trust and good, productive therapeutic relationships.

Other counselors take the position that counseling and friendship should not be mixed. They argue that attempting to manage a social and professional relationship simultaneously can negatively affect the therapy process, the friendship, or both. Some of the reasons they offer for discouraging the practice of accepting friends as clients or becoming socially involved with clients include: (1) counselors might not be as confrontive with clients they know socially; (2) counselors' own need to be liked and accepted may lead them to be less challenging, lest the friendship or social relationship be jeopardized; (3) counselors' own needs may interlock with those of their clients to the point that objectivity is lost; (4) by the very nature of the counseling relationship, counselors are in a more powerful position than clients, and the danger of exploiting clients becomes more likely when the relationship becomes other than a professional one.

Burton (1972) raises the question "Is it possible to meet clients socially and still carry interpersonal psychotherapy forward to completion?" Burton acknowledges the fact that some therapists have become life-long friends with, or even married, former clients. In general, however, he contends that therapists should avoid social relationships with clients on the ground that therapy does not usually leave the participants free to be friends.

Obviously, this is not a closed issue that can be resolved with a dogmatic answer. We question the assumption that, if counselors become socially involved with a client other than in the office, they are therefore less willing to risk challenging the client and are less objective. Although the danger exists that therapists may be less confrontive because of their fear of losing the relationship, we do not think that social involvements per se necessarily preclude honest and effective confrontation. We would ask therapists to consider if there is a discrepancy between the way they treat their clients and the way they treat their friends. It would be good to question our motives if we developed all our friends (or most of them) from our practices. Counselors need to be aware of their own motivations, as well as the motivations of their prospective clients, and they must honestly assess the impact a social relationship might have on the client/therapist relationship. This issue can take several forms. To illustrate, we'll ask you to respond to a specific case.

You are an intern in a college counseling center, and one of your clients says to you: "I really like working with you, but I hate coming over here to this cold and impersonal office. I always feel weird waiting in the lobby as if I were a 'case' or something. Why can't we meet outside on the lawn? Better yet, we could get away from campus and meet in the park nearby. I'd feel more natural and uninhibited in a more informal setting."

- Would you agree to meet your client outside of the office? Why or why not?
- Would your decision depend on how much you liked or were attracted to your client? Would your client's age and sex have much to do with your decision?

Later, your client invites you to a party that he or she is having and lets you know that it would mean a lot if you were to come. Your client says: "I'd really like to get to know you on a personal basis, because I'm being so deeply personal in here. I really like you, and I'd like more time with you than the hour we have each week."

- What are your immediate reactions? Assuming that you like your client and would like to go to the party, do you think it would be wise to attend? What would your decision be, and what would you say to your client?
- What effect do you think meeting your client on a social basis would have on the therapeutic process?

The therapeutic value of touching

Although we contend that erotic contact with clients is unethical, we do think that nonerotic contact is often appropriate and can have significant therapeutic value. It's important to stress this point, because there is a taboo against touching clients. Sometimes therapists hold back when they feel like touching their clients affectionately or compassionately. They may feel that touching can be misinterpreted as exploitative; they may be afraid of their impulses or feelings toward clients; they may be afraid of intimacy; or they may believe that to physically express closeness is unprofessional.

In a study by Holroyd and Brodsky (1977), 27% of the therapists who responded said they had occasionally engaged in nonerotic hugging, kissing, or affectionate touching with opposite-sex clients; 7% said they had done so frequently or always. The percentages varied with different kinds of therapists; 25% of humanistic therapists engaged in nonerotic contact frequently or always, but fewer than 10% of eclectic therapists and fewer than 5% of psychodynamic, behavior-modification, or rational-cognitive therapists did so. Approximately half of the therapists took the position that nonerotic physical contact would be beneficial for clients at least occasionally. Most of the suggestions fell into four categories of appropriate nonerotic contact: (a) with socially or emotionally immature clients, such as those with histories of maternal deprivation; (b) with people who were experiencing acute distress, such as grief, depression, or trauma; (c) for providing general emotional support; and (d) for greeting or at termination.

In a later study, Holroyd and Brodsky (1980) explore the question "Does touching patients lead to sexual intercourse?" The results of their study indicated that respondents who admitted having had sexual intercourse with their clients more often advocated and participated in nonerotic contact with opposite-sex clients but not with clients of the same sex. Also, male therapists who had had intercourse were likely to have used and to advocate affectionate touching with female but not male clients, even though the male clients might have initiated contact. Based on the data from questionnaires received from 347 male therapists and 310 female therapists, Holroyd and Brodsky came to the following conclusions:

- Touching that does not lead to intercourse is associated with older and more experienced therapists.
- It is the practice of restricting touching to opposite-sex clients, not touching itself, that is related to intercourse.

Holroyd and Brodsky observe that it is difficult to determine where "nonerotic hugging, kissing, and affectionate touching" leave off and "erotic contact" begins. They also suggest that any therapeutic technique that is reserved for one gender can be suspected of being sexist. They conclude: "The use of nonerotic touching as a mode of psychotherapeutic treatment requires further research. Moreover, the sexist implications of differential touching of male and female patients appear to be an important professional and ethical issue" (1980, p. 810).

Contending that the unexploitative touch is a "good discovery," Corlis and Rabe (1969) discuss touching as a potential therapeutic tool: "physical touch can open the road so often obscured by our thick growth of intellectual constructs, the road toward living with feeling again" (p. 102). We agree that touching can have therapeutic power, but we're convinced that touching should *not* be done as a technique or as something that therapists feel they're expected to do. Inauthentic physical contact is quickly detected and is likely to put distance between the client and the therapist. A client who senses that the touching isn't genuine is likely to distrust other things that the therapist says or does. Steinzor (1967) puts it well when he writes: "I will never embrace a patient for a technical reason or to assure him that I am not afraid of sensual contact. The fraudulence of such a meeting will be laid bare very soon by the patient's skin and muscles as they sense the manipulative turns of my arms" (p. 63).

In summary, we think that touching should be a spontaneous and honest expression of the therapist's feelings. Again, in this area therapists need to be aware of their own motives and to be honest with themselves about the meaning of the physical contact. They also need to be sensitive to each client's readiness for physical closeness and to the impact such contact may have on the client.

Think about your position on the ethical implications of the practice of touching as a part of the client/therapist relationship by answering these questions:

- What criteria could you use to determine whether touching your clients was therapeutic or countertherapeutic?
- How could you honestly answer the question "Are my own needs being met at the expense of my client's needs?"
- What factors do you need to consider in determining the appropriateness of touching clients? (Examples are age, gender, type of client, nature of client's problem, and setting in which therapy occurs.)
- Do you agree or disagree with the conclusions of Holroyd and Brodsky concerning the sexist implications of differential touching of male and female clients?
- If you are favorably inclined toward the practice of touching clients, are you likely to restrict this practice to: Any opposite-sex clients? Same-sex clients? Attractive opposite-sex clients? Explain.

The issue of erotic and sexual contact with clients

The issue of sexual relations with clients is a very controversial one that is frequently the subject of symposia or panels at professional conventions. Holroyd and Brodsky (1977) reported the results of a nationwide survey of 500 male and 500 female licensed psychologists, all Ph.D.s, which was conducted to assess their attitudes and practices with respect to erotic and nonerotic contact with clients. Holroyd and Brodsky reported a 70% return rate. Their findings included the following:

1. Erotic contact and intercourse are almost always between male therapists and female clients.
2. Therapists who crossed the sexual boundary once were likely to repeat this practice. Of those therapists who reported intercourse with patients, 80% repeated it.
3. Of the male therapists, 5.5% reported having had sexual intercourse with clients; for female therapists the figure was .6%.
4. Only 4% of the respondents thought that erotic contact might be beneficial. Seventy percent of male therapists and 88% of female therapists took the position that erotic contact is *never* beneficial to clients.

Most of the psychologists responding strongly disapproved of erotic contact in therapy and stated that it should never occur in a professional relationship. They took the position that such contact is totally inappropriate and is an exploitation of the relationship by the therapist. Erotic contact with clients was thus viewed as unprofessional, unethical, and antitherapeutic. One therapist made the comment "I feel without qualification that erotic patient-therapist contact is unethical at best and devastating at worst—it reflects pathological needs on the part of the therapist" (Holroyd & Brodsky, 1977, p. 848).

Professional opinion on this issue is not unanimous, however. Some therapists argue that erotic contact can help their clients feel validated as sexual persons, learn to free themselves of inhibitions and guilt feelings that keep them from enjoying their sexuality, and talk about other sexually taboo areas. Those who make this argument are generally male therapists who are speaking of the values of erotic contact for female clients. Such therapists might be asked "Would you be quite so willing to be helpful if your client were unattractive to you?" In writing on this issue, Lowry and Lowry (1975) make this comment:

> If a therapist finds that attractive patients need his "reassurance" more, he should question his motives to make sure that he provides sexual services to the elderly, ugly, to the crippled, to the incontinent, to the same sex, and to all races, creeds, and religions. We are not aware of a direct intervention sex therapist who meets these criteria [p. 233].

Ethical standards and sexual intimacies

Virtually all of the professional organizations now have a specific statement condemning sexual intimacies in the client/therapist relationship, as can be seen in the summary of relevant codes in the accompanying box.

Sexual Relations in Therapy: Summary of Codes of Ethics

American Personnel and Guidance Association (1981):
- "Dual relationships with clients that might impair the member's objectivity and professional judgment (e.g., as with close friends or relatives, sexual intimacies with any client) must be avoided and/or the counseling relationship terminated through referral to another competent professional."

American Psychological Association (1981a):
- "Psychologists are continually cognizant of their own needs and of their potentially influential position vis-à-vis persons such as clients, students, and subordinates. They avoid exploiting the trust and dependency of such persons. Psychologists make every effort to avoid dual relationships that could impair their professional judgment or increase the risk of exploitation. Examples of such relationships include, but are not limited to, research with and treatment of employees, students, supervisees, close friends, or relatives. Sexual intimacies with clients are unethical."

American Psychiatric Association (1981):
- "The necessary intensity of the therapeutic relationship may tend to activate sexual and other needs and fantasies on the part of both patient and therapist, while weakening the objectivity necessary for control. Sexual activity with a patient is unethical."

American Association for Marriage and Family Therapy (undated):
- "A therapist will attempt to avoid relationships with clients which might impair professional judgment or increase the risks of exploiting clients. Examples of such relationships include: treatment of family members, close friends, employees, or supervisees. Sexual intimacy with clients is unethical."

National Association of Social Workers (1979):
- "The social worker should under no circumstances engage in sexual activities with clients."

Standards for the Private Practice of Clinical Social Work (NASW, 1981):
- "The private practitioner shall not engage in sexual activities with clients."

It is clear from the statements of the major mental-health professional organizations that these principles go beyond merely condemning sexual relationships with clients. There are also implications for counseling with close friends or relatives, for forming social and personal relationships with clients, and for developing or maintaining any kind of relationship that is likely to impair one's ability to function in a professional manner. Further, it is clear that, if a client/therapist relationship does develop into a relationship that could potentially be countertherapeutic (or if there is a risk of exploiting the client), then ethical practice calls for a termination of the counseling relationship and a referral to another professional.

Those therapists who are convinced that sexual intimacy between a therapist and client is both unethical and professionally inappropriate state a number of grounds. The general argument typically involves the abuse of the power that therapists have by virtue of their function and role. Clients reveal deeply personal material about their hopes, sexual desires and struggles, and intimate relationships, and in many ways they become vulnerable to their therapists. It's easy to take advantage of this trust and exploit it for personal motives. Although it may be true that some clients provoke and tease their therapists, those who consider sexual intimacies to be unethical professional behavior contend that therapists should refuse to collaborate in such sexual game playing and instead confront their clients with what is occurring. Steinzor (1967) puts the point this way:

> To use the patient for my own persistent need for physical contact and sexual embrace would be an exploitation. As a therapist I have been sought out because I promise more and mean more to her than a transient affair. The possible moments of pleasure would soon give way to embarrassment and hurt [p. 63].

Another reason given by those who oppose erotic contact in therapeutic relationships is that it fosters dependence. Clients can easily come to think of their therapists as ideal persons when they see them only in the limited context of the office. Instead of forming meaningful relationships with others, clients may begin to live for the affection and attention they receive from their therapists once a week. Further, many would argue that, when sexual activity becomes a part of therapy, the objectivity of the therapist is lost. Therapists are likely to become more concerned about the feelings their clients have toward them than about challenging their clients to take an honest look at their own lives. Corlis and Rabe (1969) take a very clear stand that, when clients become sexual partners of therapists, they cease to be clients, and their therapists cease to be therapists: "The consuming concentration of the sexual encounter obviates any considerations but those which serve that particular partnership, with its physical power, and with its own personal merging. Sex may be therapeutic, but it is not therapy" (p. 99).

According to Lief (1982), the abuse of power is the core ethical issue in sexual misconduct. The power needs of exploitative therapists are met by clients who have a need to be desired and who want to overcome loneliness. Lief writes: "Power is an essential feature in erotic relationships between the doctor and the patient. While it is true that sexual gratification is a significant factor, in most instances it is less important than the unconscious desire to exert power and control over vulnerable and sometimes helpless patients" (p. 284).

A final argument against sexual involvement with clients is that they often feel taken advantage of and may discount the value of any part of their therapy. They may become embittered and angry, and they may terminate therapy with psychological scars. The problem is compounded if they are deterred from initiating therapy with anyone else because of the traumatic experience and thus feel stuck with their unresolved feelings.

Some states have legal sanctions in cases of sexual misconduct in the therapeutic relationship. For example, a California statute gives specific authority to all licensing and regulatory boards in the healing arts "to suspend or revoke the license of a person who has committed an act of sexual abuse, misconduct or sexual relations with a patient or client in the course of his/her professional duties" (Psychology Examining Committee Newsletter, 1980). Included under this law are psychologists, clinical social workers, marriage and family counselors, medical doctors and psychiatrists, dentists, nurses, and others. It is clear that professionals cannot argue that the client seduced them. The law states that the ultimate ethical and legal burden of responsibility to avoid such situations rests squarely on the licensed professional.

Filing ethics complaints.   There are definite procedures for filing and processing ethical complaints against psychologists, and such complaints are dealt with by the state professional associations and by the APA's Committee on Scientific and Professional Ethics and Conduct. Sanders and Keith-Spiegel (1980) present a summary of an investigation of a psychologist who was accused of becoming sexually involved with his female client after two years of therapy. The psychologist promptly terminated the therapeutic relationship, according to the client, yet no attempt was made to resolve the therapeutic issues remaining. The sexual relationship continued for about a year, on a weekly basis, until it was finally cut off by the client because of her guilt and disgust over the situation. The psychologist made two attempts to resume the affair, but the client refused to become involved.

Although the psychologist at first flatly denied the client's charges, he eventually admitted that they were true. He also said that he loved his client, that he was struggling with a mid-life crisis, and that he was having severe marital problems. He added that he was willing to seek personal therapy to work on his problems.

In this case, the state psychological association voted to monitor the psychologist's personal therapy and have his practice reviewed for one year. In his hearing before the APA's ethics committee, he gave a progress report on his personal therapy and attempted to convince the committee members that the insights he had gained would preclude the recurrence of this sort of ethical violation in the future. The committee offered a stipulated resignation from the APA for a period of five years, after which he might reapply if no further ethical violations had been brought to the APA. The committee concluded that this psychologist did appear remorseful, that he would be rehabilitated, and that he seemed to have the self-determination to do so.

In thinking about this case, attempt to answer these questions:

• Do you think that this psychologist should have been allowed to continue his professional practice? Why or why not?

- If you had been a member of the ethics committee that reviewed this case, what action would you have recommended?
- If the psychologist was aware that he had fallen in love with his client and wanted to become sexually involved with her (yet had not done so), what ethical course of action could he have taken? Is termination of the professional relationship enough?

In another case of an ethics complaint against a psychologist, Hare-Mustin and Hall (1981) report that a psychologist admitted to the APA committee that he had become sexually involved with a number of clients. As evidence of his rehabilitation, he said that he had joined a peer group. The committee questioned whether this was enough, in light of the nature of his unethical behavior. It offered him the opportunity to resign from the APA for five years and to seek treatment appropriate for his problems.

Legal restrictions

There are also legal issues involved in sexual relationships with clients. Therapists who have engaged in sex with their clients have been sued for malpractice. Psychologists found guilty, for example, have been given sanctions, have been expelled from membership in the APA, have had their licenses revoked or suspended by the state, and have been ordered to participate in their own personal therapy to resolve their problems.

Many cases of sexual misconduct probably go unreported because of the clients' shame and guilt, as well as their reluctance to pursue the matter in the courts. It appears, however, that female clients have recently become more willing to sue male therapists who take advantage of their professional position of power. The media have reported cases in which therapists exploited their clients; some of these therapists have taken the extreme position that the sexual involvement did not interfere with the therapy and often enhanced it. In talking with television reporters, one psychologist said that he felt strongly that his practices could be justified on the ground that his female clients were learning how to develop a loving relationship that included sex. A question here is: Whose needs were being met? It may be of interest to note that this psychologist was involved in a court action in which the judge found him guilty of gross negligence and recommended revocation of his license. The state accepted the judge's decision.

At this point we ask you to reflect on the following brief case and decide how you would respond to the situation.

For several months you've been working with a client whom you find attractive and exciting. You're aware that your client has loving feelings toward you and would be willing to become sexually involved with you. Your own feelings are growing in intensity, and you often have difficulty paying attention during sessions because of your own fantasies.

There are a number of different things you might do in this situation.

1. You could attempt to ignore your feelings for your client and your client's feelings toward you and focus on other aspects of the relationship. Do you

think that you'd be able to avoid dealing with these feelings? If you did, what effect might this have on your ability to pay attention to your client?

_____

_____

_____

2. You could tell your client that your feelings of attraction are strong enough that you don't want to continue the therapeutic relationship and that you think a referral to another therapist is in order. How ethical do you think this option is? Might your client feel abandoned? If you did make the referral, would you then be willing to enter into a sexual relationship with your former client? Why or why not?

_____

_____

_____

3. You could openly express your feelings toward your client and acknowledge his or her feelings toward you. For example, you might say: "I'm glad you find me an attractive person, and I'm strongly attracted to you as well. But I don't want to act on my sexual feelings, because I value our therapeutic relationship, and I feel pretty sure that such an involvement would get in the way of therapy. If you weren't my client, I could see myself being involved with you in this way." Can you imagine yourself saying this to a client? Why or why not? Might you also consult a colleague to discuss what you're feeling and to get feedback on your actions?

_____

_____

_____

4. You could consult with a colleague or you could seek professional supervision. Would you be inclined to do so? Why or why not?

_____

_____

_____

5. You could act on your feelings by getting sexually involved with your client, or you could terminate therapy and then begin another type of relationship. Is either of these alternatives acceptable to you? Why or why not?

_____

_____

_____

We agree with those therapists who contend that it is both unwise and unethical to become sexually involved with clients. This is not to say that counselors aren't human beings or will never have strong feelings of attraction toward certain clients. Counselors impose an unnecessary burden on themselves when they believe that they shouldn't have such feelings for clients or when they try to convince themselves that they should not have more feeling toward one client than toward another. What is important is how counselors decide to deal with these feelings as they affect the therapeutic relationship. Referral to another therapist isn't necessarily the best solution, unless it becomes clear that one can no longer be effective with a certain client. Instead, counselors may recognize a need for consultation or, at the very least, for an honest dialogue with themselves. It may also be appropriate to have a frank discussion with the client, explaining that the decision not to act on one's sexual feelings is based on a commitment to the primacy of the therapeutic relationship.

When we've discussed with students the issue of sexual involvement with clients, we've found that they almost universally see it as an unethical practice. However, we want to point out that the issue of erotic contact in therapy is not simply a matter of whether to have sexual intercourse with a client. Even if you decide intellectually that you wouldn't engage in sexual intimacies with a client, it's important to realize that the relationship between therapist and client can involve varying degrees of sexuality. Therapists may have sexual fantasies; they may behave seductively with their clients; they may influence clients to focus on romantic or sexual feelings toward them; or they may engage in physical contact that is primarily intended to arouse or satisfy their sexual desires. Although these therapists may not reach the point of having sexual intercourse with clients, their behavior is clearly sexual in nature and can have much the same effect as direct sexual involvement would have. Romantic overtones can easily distort the therapeutic relationship as the seductive play of the client and therapist becomes the real focus of the sessions. This is clearly an area in which counselors need to be able to recognize what they're doing. It's also crucial that they learn how to accept their sexual feelings and that they consciously decide how to deal with them in therapy.

Ethical and legal issues in clinical supervision

This chapter addresses ethical and legal issues that pertain to the client/therapist relationship. Since the relationship between the clinical supervisor and the trainee (or student of psychotherapy) is of such critical importance, however, we will at least raise some issues in connection with it and will draw some parallels between the supervision process and the therapy process.[1]

Although standards of ethical behavior between a therapist and client have been developed by the various professional organizations, specific guidelines for ethical behavior between a supervisor and trainee have not been delineated in all of these professional codes. If we take into consideration the importance of the supervisory relationship in the development of competent and responsible therapists, the depen-

---

[1] If you want to do further reading on these issues, we recommend G. Hart's *The Process of Clinical Supervision* (1982).

dent position of the trainee, and the similarities between the supervisory relationship and the therapy relationship, then the establishing of guidelines outlining the rights of trainees and the responsibilities of supervisors is very much needed (Newman, 1981).

The supervisor's responsibilities

Supervisors are responsible for the actions of the trainees they supervise. It is the supervisors' responsibility to check on the progress of their trainees and be familiar with their case loads. The trainee has the right to know about training objectives, assessment procedures, and evaluation criteria. It is the responsibility of supervisors to inform trainees about these matters at the beginning of supervision (Cormier & Bernard, 1982).

Supervisors also have the responsibility to monitor and assess the trainee's performance in a consistent and careful manner. Trainees have a legal right to periodic feedback and evaluation so that they have a basis for improving their clinical skills (Cormier & Bernard, 1982). Supervision is perhaps the most important component in the development of a competent practitioner. It is within the context of supervision that trainees begin to develop a sense of professional identity and to examine their own beliefs and attitudes regarding clients and therapy. Thus, the supervisor fosters the trainees' professional development by serving as teacher, role model, and evaluator (Newman, 1981).

Legal aspects of supervision

The legal considerations pertaining to the supervisory relationship involve informed consent, confidentiality and its limits, and the concept of liability.

First, supervisors must see that trainees provide the information to clients that is needed for them to make informed choices. This requirement implies that clients be made fully aware that the counselor they are seeing is a trainee; that he or she is meeting on a regular basis for supervision sessions; that the client's case may be discussed in group supervision meetings with other trainees; and that sessions may be taped or observed.

Second, supervisors have an ethical obligation to respect the confidentiality of client communications. There may be certain exceptions, however, such as cases when the supervisor determines that the client is potentially dangerous to himself or herself or to others. Supervisors must be sure that clients are fully informed about the limits of confidentiality.

Third, supervisors ultimately bear the legal responsibility for the welfare of those clients who are counseled by their trainees. Cormier and Bernard (1982) point out that supervisors must be familiar with each case of every supervisee, in order to prevent negligent supervision. This may not be practical in the sense that supervisors cannot be cognizant of all details of every case. But they should at least know the direction in which the cases are being taken. Cormier and Bernard add that the supervisor is legally responsible for knowing when counselors are involved in a case beyond their level of competence. Also, university training programs have a responsibility to clients to make some kind of formal assessment of each trainee before allowing the person to counsel clients.

Ethical aspects of supervision

Ethical standards for educators and supervisors of counselors were developed by the North Atlantic Association for Counselor Education and Supervision (NARACES) in 1980. Members of the association are engaged in the professional preparation of counselors or are responsible for supervising them. The accompanying box lists 15 guidelines pertaining to personnel administration as an illustration of these ethical standards.

Ethical Standards for Counselor Educators and Supervisors

(The standards include guidelines for the following areas: (1) counseling, (2) research, (3) personnel administration, and (4) supervision. As a sample, the ones pertaining to personnel administration are listed below [NARACES, 1980]):

1. Counselor educators and supervisors must pursue professional and personal in-service development through advanced course work, seminars, workshops, and professional conferences.
2. Counselor educators and supervisors should regularly submit their own work for review through supervision, peer evaluation, or consultation.
3. Counselor educators and supervisors have an obligation to inform their students and supervisees of the policies, goals, and programs toward which their institutional operations are oriented.
4. Counselor educators and supervisors should require that trainees and supervisors function in a competent manner, compatible with their skills and experiences.
5. Professional competencies expected of trainees shall be communicated in writing prior to admission to the graduate program and to individual courses.
6. Counselor educators and supervisors shall establish training programs which integrate academic study and supervised practice.
7. Counselor educators and supervisors, through continual trainee evaluation and appraisal, should be aware of the personal and professional limitations of the trainee which could impede future professional performance. Counselor educators and supervisors have the responsibility for assisting the trainee in securing remedial assistance and for screening those trainees who are unable to provide competent services.
8. Counselor educators and supervisors should make their trainees and supervisees aware of ethical standards and legal responsibilities of the profession which they are entering and in which they are functioning.
9. Counselor educators and supervisors should have the same respect for their trainees as counselors have for their counselees. Expectations should be made clear. Allowances should be made for freedom of choice. Under no circumstances should counselor educators and supervisors attempt to sway trainees to adopt a particular theoretical belief or point of view.
10. Counselor educators and supervisors are obligated to develop clear policies regarding field placement and the roles of the trainee and field supervisor.

11. Forms of training that focus on self-understanding/growth should be voluntary unless the experience is a required part of the training program and is made known to prospective trainees prior to entering the program. When the training program requires a growth experience involving self-disclosure or other relatively intimate or personal involvement, the counselor educators and supervisors should have no administrative, supervisory, or evaluative authority over the participants during the growth experience.

12. Counselor educators and supervisors are obligated to conduct training programs in keeping with the most current guidelines and/or standards of APGA, ACES and its various divisions and state guidelines.

13. Counselor educators and supervisors have responsibility for promoting and providing opportunities for counselor educator and supervisee growth and development. They must see that staff members are adequately supervised as to the quality of their functioning.

14. Counselor educators and supervisors should not teach or supervise in any area in which they are not competent. Furthermore, counselor educators and supervisors should have adequate experience in the areas in which they are teaching and supervising.

15. Copies of all notes, records, recommendations, and evaluations of supervisee and trainee performance should be made routinely available.

From *Ethical Standards for Counselor Educators and Supervisors*, by the North Atlantic Association for Counselor Education and Supervision (draft), 1980. Reprinted by permission.

Dual relationships and the supervision process.   Related to the issue of sexual contact between therapists and clients is the issue of sex in the supervisory relationship. As in the former situation, there can be an abuse of power because of the difference in status between supervisees and supervisors. Further, there is the matter of poor modeling for trainees for their future relationships with clients.

It can be argued that trainees are in a position of diminished consent. Thus, they are in a poor position to give voluntary consent to participate in any type of dual relationship. Other problems with dual relationships are pointed out by Cormier and Bernard (1982): there is the possibility of exploitation of trainees; there could be a reduction in the supervisor's power in some aspects of supervision; and the supervisor's objectivity can be impaired, thus clouding his or her ability to supervise effectively. (Such a situation might entail legal liability for failure to provide adequate supervision.)

Pope, Schover, and Levenson (1980) have discussed the multiple roles of clinical supervisors, including those of teacher, evaluator, and therapist. Considering the effects of each of these roles, we can see that ethical issues are raised when sexual intimacies become mixed up with the supervisory relationship.

• *Supervisors function as teachers.* It can easily be seen that teachers who gain sexual satisfaction through students are likely to have considerable difficulty in keeping their students' interests and welfare as primary.

• *Supervisors function as evaluators.* Sexual intimacy can obstruct the supervisor's ability to provide careful, objective, and valid evaluations.

• *Supervisors function as therapists.* Most training programs involve some type of experiential learning, as part of the supervision process and as a part of the trainee's personal-growth sessions. Thus, there are similarities between the supervisory relationship and the therapy relationship, in that both clients and trainees are likely to develop transference relationships. It is obvious that sexual relationships will increase feelings of transference and countertransference and will thus get in the way of effective personal learning.

Although the APA ethical principles (1981a) pertain primarily to the client/therapist relationship, there is one principle that has implications for professional conduct in the supervisory relationship:

> Psychologists do not exploit their professional relationships with clients, supervisees, students, employees, or research participants sexually or otherwise. Psychologists do not condone or engage in sexual harassment. Sexual harassment is defined as deliberate or repeated comments, gestures, or physical contacts of a sexual nature that are unwanted by the recipient.

What would you do in this situation?   You are a trainee, and your clinical supervisor consistently harasses you sexually, along with touching you in questionable ways. During your individual supervision sessions, the supervisor makes many comments with double meanings. The supervisor frequently looks at you in flirtatious ways. From what your supervisor says and does, you get the distinct impression that your evaluations will be more favorable if you engage in "playing the game." What course of action might you take in such a situation?

Some questions to consider

What is your position on some of the ethical and legal issues raised in this section? Specifically, take a stand on the following situations:

• Your supervisor does not provide what you consider to be adequate supervision. You are left mainly on your own with a difficult case load. The staff members where you work all are overloaded, and when you do get time with a supervisor, the person feels burdened with many responsibilities. Thus, you do not get quality time for supervision or for discussion of cases. What would you be inclined to do?

• You have a conflict with your supervisor over the ethical way to deal with a client. What would you do?

• You are aware that a clinical supervisor that you are scheduled to work with has a reputation of being sexually involved with supervisees. What course of action, if any, would you take?

• You do not get ongoing feedback on your performance as a trainee. At the end of the semester your supervisor gives you a negative evaluation. What are the ethical and legal issues involved? What might you do or say?

• Do you think it is unethical for a supervisor to initiate social or sexual relationships with trainees after they have graduated (and when the supervisor has no professional obligations to the trainee)? Explain your position.

Professional relationships and unethical behavior

Responsibilities to other therapists

You are seeing a client for the first time. During this session the client says that she is seeing another therapist but is not satisfied with her progress. She adds that she has been reluctant to bring up this matter with him. However, she has heard good things from her friends about you, and she would like to see you at the same time that she is seeing her other therapist. She says that this will give her a better idea of whether she should terminate her therapy with the other therapist.

- What would you say to this woman?
- Would you accept her as a client under these conditions? Why or why not?
- Would you encourage her to discuss this matter fully with her therapist before you saw her again? Why or why not?
- Would you see any ethical problems in taking the initiative and contacting her therapist? Is this your responsibility or her responsibility?

The Responsibility to Consult: Some Ethical Guidelines

National Association of Social Workers (1979):
- "The social worker should not assume professional responsibility for the clients of another agency or a colleague without appropriate communication with that agency or colleague."

American Personnel and Guidance Association (1981):
- "If an individual is already in a counseling relationship with another professional person, the member does not enter into a counseling relationship without first contacting and receiving the approval of that other professional. If the member discovers that the client is in another counseling relationship after the counseling relationship begins, the member must gain the consent of the other professional or terminate the relationship, unless the client elects to terminate the other relationship."

American Association for Marriage and Family Therapy (undated):
- "A therapist will not knowingly offer service to a client who is in treatment with another clinical professional without consultation among the parties involved."

American Psychological Association (1981a):
- "Psychologists know and take into account the traditions and practices of other professional groups with whom they work and cooperate fully with such groups. If a person is receiving similar services from another professional, psychologists do not offer their own services directly to such a person. If a psychologist is contacted by a person who is already receiving similar services from another professional, the psychologist carefully considers that professional relationship and proceeds with caution and sensitivity to the therapeutic issues as well as the client's welfare. The psychologist discusses these issues with the client so as to minimize the risk of confusion and conflict."

In clarifying your position on this case, consider the accompanying guidelines pertaining to the ethics of entering into a professional relationship with a client who is already involved in a therapeutic relationship.

Unethical behavior of colleagues

A particularly touchy issue relates to your obligation when you know of colleagues, peers, or supervisors who are engaging in unethical practices. In our classes and workshops many students have raised the question "What course of action should I take when I know of other therapists who consistently engage in unethical behavior?" To sharpen your thinking on this question, reflect for a few moments on the possibility of your being involved in the following situations:

- You know of a colleague who clearly lacks the competencies to effectively carry out therapeutic functions as a part of his placement in an agency. The person is employing techniques that he has not been trained to use in his therapy with psychotic patients. He is also not receiving adequate supervision. What would you do?
- You are aware of a therapist who charges sessions to a client's insurance that were not actually held. The therapist says that "double billing" is a common practice, and he sees nothing wrong with it. What would you do?
- You are aware that a clinical supervisor has made it a practice to have sexual relationships with several of her supervisees. Some of these students are friends of yours, and they tell you that they felt pressure to comply, since they were in a vulnerable position. What would you do?
- You know of a colleague who does not believe in informed consent. She tells you that it is counterproductive to give clients too much information about the therapy process. She admits that she strives to keep the therapeutic relationship a mysterious one, and she claims that it works for her. What would you do?
- A colleague has what you consider to be a rigid set of values, and he sees it as his function to impose them on his clients. He tells you that it is his job to "straighten out" his clients, that they typically do not know what is best for them, and that he finds many ways to indirectly move them in the direction of his thinking. What would you do?
- You know a student intern who makes it a practice to initiate social relationships with his clients. He says that this is acceptable, because his clients are consenting adults, and he argues that by dating some of his clients he actually gets to know them better, which helps him in his role as a therapist. What would you do?

No doubt you can come up with some other actions that you would consider unethical. You may find yourself uncertain of the appropriate course of action. You might wonder whether it is your place to judge the practices of colleagues or other practitioners whom you know. Even if you are convinced that there is a situation that involves clear ethical violations, you may be in doubt about the best way to deal with it. Should you first discuss the matter with the person? Assuming that you do and that the person becomes defensive, should you take any other action or simply

---

Unethical Behavior on the Part of Colleagues: Ethical Codes

American Psychological Association (1981a):

- "When psychologists know of an ethical violation by another psychologist, and it seems appropriate, they informally attempt to resolve the issue by bringing the behavior to the attention of the psychologist. If the misconduct is of a minor nature and/or appears to be due to lack of sensitivity, knowledge, or experience, such an informal solution is usually appropriate. Such informal corrective efforts are made with sensitivity to any rights to confidentiality involved. If the violation does not seem amenable to an informal solution, or is of a more serious nature, psychologists bring it to the attention of the appropriate local, state, and/or national committee on professional ethics and conduct."

American Professional Guidance Association (1981):

- "Ethical behavior among professional associates, both members and non-members, must be expected at all times. When information is possessed that raises doubt as to the ethical behavior of colleagues, whether Association members or not, the member must take action to attempt to rectify such a condition. Such action shall use the institution's channels first and then use procedures established by the state Branch, Division, or Association."

---

drop the matter? When would a violation be serious enough that you would consider it your obligation to bring it to the attention of an appropriate local, state, or national committee on professional ethics?

This section is likely to raise more questions than it provides answers for. While both the APA (1981a) and the APGA (1981) have ethical principles on this issue, you will ultimately be faced with the challenge of developing ethical decision-making skills to use in each case in which you are involved. Discussion in class on these issues can be the beginning of formulating alternative courses of action in situations where the unethical behavior of other practitioners is involved.

Ethical and professional issues in sex therapy

A relatively new issue in professional practice concerns the ethical and professional dimensions of sex therapy. There is some confusion regarding this issue, since clear standards have not been developed, and practitioners are frequently left to exercise their own judgment.

Reporting that the field of sex therapy is in enormous flux because innovative techniques are being used and because the field enters the realm of strongly held values, Lief (1982) asserts that ethical considerations are therefore of particular importance. He writes:

> In the absence of standards of treatment and with uncertain methods of accreditation, safeguarding the welfare of the patient through providing informed consent so that he knows and agrees in advance to the form of treatment, protecting his confidentiality and

rights of privacy, ensuring the patient's freedom from exploitation and assuring the competence of the therapist are much more difficult than is the case in types of psychotherapy which have been practiced for generations [p. 269].

Legislation in California mandates training in human sexuality as a condition of licensure, both for those being licensed for the first time and for those seeking renewal of their licenses. This legislation applies to the following licensed practitioners: marriage, family, and child counselors; social workers; and psychologists. The content and length of the required training is very unclear, but the law does illustrate the growing importance attached to sex therapy as a part of counseling and psychotherapy. In this section we briefly explore some of the central questions that need to be raised regarding ethical conduct in this specialized area of counseling.

Qualifications of sex therapists

One of the most basic issues that needs to be raised in this area is the question of who is qualified to do sex therapy. Ask yourself these questions:

- What personal and professional qualifications do I have that might eventually prepare me to do sex therapy?
- Is a single course in human sexuality enough course preparation to do this type of counseling?
- What preparation am I receiving in my training program to do this kind of therapy?
- What kind of practicum, specialized training, and supervision do I think is essential if I am to become involved in sex therapy?

In many programs students are exposed to no more than a single general course in human sexuality; yet, when they begin practicing, many of their clients will bring in sexual difficulties that demand attention. At the very least, counselors who lack the knowledge and skills needed to work in depth with sexual problems can be aware of their limitations and refuse to attempt counseling they're not competent to perform, even if their licenses allow them to counsel people with sexual dysfunctions. They can recognize the importance of referring clients who are in need of this specialized treament. To do so, they must be able to recognize when sex therapy is indicated, and they must be aware of good referral sources.

The scope of sex therapy

Some people criticize the sex-therapy movement on the grounds that too much attention is paid to "fixing plumbing" and not enough to the emotional aspects of sexuality. They argue that sex therapists focus too much on symptoms and physical functioning, whereas effective treatment must include a consideration of the individual's psychodynamics, the factors that led to the problem to begin with, and the nature of the relationship between the client and his or her sexual partner.

Therapy for sexual difficulties doesn't have to be mechanistic, however, or focused only on removal of symptoms. Some sex therapists are aware of the need for a more comprehensive approach. For example, they may stress the acquisition of more effective social skills at the same time as they work on sexual dysfunctions. Also, even though they may *begin* by working with obvious symptoms, they are fully aware that in-depth and meaningful treatment must go beyond symptoms and concern itself with the total life of the client.

Conjoint therapy as the preferred approach

Typically, the sex-therapy model prescribes working with both partners in a sexual relationship. The assumption is that one partner's sexual dysfunction is related in some way to the relationship with the other person. According to Kaplan (1974), the primary objective of sex therapy is to modify the couple's relationship and sexual life so that both persons are satisfied. Conjoint treatment, as opposed to separate treatment for each partner or for one partner alone, is also viewed as valuable because the shared sexual experiences of the couple become the central aspects of the treatment.

Of course, conjoint therapy depends on the willingness of both partners. What are the issues involved when one partner desires sex therapy and the other refuses to cooperate in any type of counseling? Suppose a woman wanted sex therapy and her husband refused treatment. Would it really help to work with her alone? Would any change occur? If she did become free of her sexual dysfunction, what kinds of problems might this pose for her if her husband had not been involved in the therapy? Would you refuse treatment for her until her husband agreed to participate in the program? Would you encourage her to change, even if her husband was rigid and would fight any of her changes? Would you consider employing a sex surrogate in this case? These are just some of the difficult questions that arise when conjoint therapy is not possible.

The use of sex surrogates

In some sex-therapy clinics, surrogates are used for clients who present themselves for treatment and are without partners. Kaplan (1974) indicates that a real dilemma is posed for sex therapists and clinics when these clients are told that a partner is necessary for successful treatment, especially when they say that they are too embarrassed by their problem to seek a partner. One answer to this dilemma is to use sex surrogates for working with clients without partners.

We think that there are a number of questions that need to be raised concerning the ethical and professional aspects of the use of surrogates as a standard practice. What are the motivations one might have in becoming a sex surrogate? Since it is crucial that surrogates serve the best interests of the client rather than their own needs, the issue of motivation assumes real importance. What are the standards of training for a surrogate? Who should be selected as a surrogate? Should a surrogate be used for a married person when the spouse refuses to be a part of the treatment? Finally, a question we think is extremely important is: Are the ethical and moral values of the client taken into consideration? The use of a surrogate may be contrary to the religious or moral beliefs of the client. These values need to be taken into account if the client is to be treated with respect.

We agree with Lief's position (1982) that sex therapists must be careful not to push their clients too far or too fast toward value changes that they are not ready for. As examples, Lief comments on the recommendation to masturbate (which some clients may see as reprehensible), or the recommendation to a couple that they engage in oral sex (when one or both of the partners find this repugnant). He sees it as unethical for therapists to disregard the values and morals of their clients by forcefully recommending practices that violate their beliefs. Surely, the decision whether to use sex surrogates must be made within the framework of the client's value system. Although Lief sees that surrogate partners may have a useful place in treating men with sexual dysfunctions, particularly for those men who are without available partners, he contends that there are certain reasons for the hesitations of practitioners to use surrogates:

- Some might see a moral and legal link between the practice of using sex surrogates and prostitution.
- Some therapists fear malpractice suits, since a number of court decisions have cautioned professionals not to depart from community values regarding appropriate treatment.
- There are sex surrogates who refuse to be supervised by a therapist, for they see themselves as more competent than "therapists."
- The client might encounter difficulty in applying what he has learned in the sex-therapy situation to another female partner.

Issues related to the therapeutic relationship

In Chapter 2 we discussed transference and countertransference as problems that most counselors and therapists eventually need to confront. In sex therapy these issues become even more vital. Because of the focus on the intimate details of the client's sexual behavior, feelings, and fantasies, there is a greater danger that the client will develop an erotic transference toward the therapist (Kaplan, 1974). This raises the ethical issue of therapists' encouragement of this erotic transference, which may be done seductively out of a need to be perceived as sexually attractive and desirable persons. Kaplan warns that, if therapists' clients fall in love with them with regularity, it can be inferred that the therapists' countertransference feelings are producing the situation.

Clearly, therapists' unawareness of their needs and their distorted vision because of their unresolved conflicts in regard to sex can greatly interfere with the therapy process. In order to achieve competence in the practice of sex therapy, Kaplan believes, therapists should be relatively free from their own sexual conflicts, guilt, and competitiveness, or at least be aware of how this personal material can influence the way they work with their clients in sex therapy. Therapists must be aware and responsive persons, not simply technicians:

> In sum, the therapist is not a treatment machine. His emotional responses are the indispensable instruments of superb therapy, and as such should be nurtured. On the other hand, he needs to guard against the emergence of neurotic countertransferential reactions, for these can lead to ineffective therapy or, even worse, to the destructive exploitation of his patients [Kaplan, 1974, p. 245].

Informed consent. In all forms of psychotherapy, the therapeutic relationship is determined to a large extent by informed-consent procedures. Some therapists structure the therapeutic relationship on the basis of a contract that spells out the rights and duties of both the client and the therapist. In the field of sex therapy, informed consent becomes particularly crucial, especially when the therapist assigns certain behavioral tasks to carry out at home. We are in agreement with Lief's position (1982) that it is essential for those practicing sex therapy to explain to the client or to the couple the nature of the therapy, the approximate number of sessions, the approximate length of time the therapy will take, the fees involved, and the specialized techniques that will be used. Part of informed consent involves a full discussion with clients about their feelings about expanding their sexual repertoire, with attention given to their values.

If you'd like to read a more in-depth treatment of ethical issues in sex therapy, we think that you'll find Lief (1982) especially meaningful.

Some comments on malpractice

Can practitioners be sued for failing to practice within the established ethical guidelines that have been discussed? How vulnerable are therapists to malpractice? What are some practical safeguards against being involved in a lawsuit?

Unless counselors take due care and act in good faith, they are liable to a civil suit for failing to do their duties as provided by law. When practitioners assume a professional role, they are expected to abide by legal standards and adhere to the ethical codes of their profession in providing care to their clients. Civil liability means that an individual can be sued for not doing right or for doing wrong to another. Malpractice can be seen as the opposite of acting in good faith. It is defined as the failure to render proper service, through ignorance or negligence, resulting in injury or loss to the client. Negligence consists of departing from usual practice; in other words, standards that are commonly accepted by the profession were not followed, and due care was not exercised.

There are three conditions that must be present in malpractice cases: (1) the defendant must have had a duty to the plaintiff, (2) damages must have resulted through negligence or improper action, and (3) a causal relationship must be established between damages and negligence (Burgum & Anderson, 1975). In his article on malpractice, Knapp (1980) points out that the courts do not assume malpractice or negligence if a therapist has made a mistake in judgment, for it is possible to make mistakes and exercise reasonable care at the same time. Knapp also comments that the courts generally accept any treatment as legitimate if a substantial minority of therapists practices it. Further, therapists are typically evaluated in accordance with their theoretical orientation. For example, a psychoanalytically oriented therapist would be measured according to acceptable standards in this theory and would not be assessed within the framework of practices typical in behavior therapy.

Some of the most frequent causes of malpractice action against therapists include the following:

- providing birth control and abortion counseling to minors
- prescribing and administering drugs inappropriately
- illegal search

- libel and slander
- violating the client's right of privacy
- physical injuries sustained by members in an encounter group
- striking or physically assaulting a client as a part of the treatment
- sexual relations with clients
- failure to exercise reasonable care in cases of suicide
- failure to warn and protect victims in cases involving violent clients
- misrepresentation of one's professional training

Recent cases have held counselors liable for damages when poor advice was given. If clients rely on the advice given by a professional and suffer damages as a result, they can initiate civil action. Professional health-care providers would do well to avoid the temptation to try to work with all clients, regardless of their level of competence to render appropriate service.

Some precautions

Below are a few safeguards against malpractice:

- Therapists protect both themselves and their clients by making use of informed-consent procedures and by using contracts to clarify the therapeutic relationship.
- Therapists are advised to become aware of local and state laws that limit their practice, as well as the policies of the agency that employs them.
- Openness in communications with clients and interest in their welfare are good defenses against malpractice suits (Van Hoose & Kottler, 1977).
- Therapists can use their skill in engendering positive feelings between themselves and their clients, since good relationships with clients substantially reduce the likelihood of a malpractice action (Knapp, 1980).
- It is a good practice to consult with colleagues or supervisors in cases involving difficult legal and ethical issues. It is foolhardy for practitioners to think that they should have all the answers and that they should not have to seek advice from other professionals.
- Having a theoretical orientation to guide one's practice, including a rationale for employing techniques, is an excellent way to assure responsible practice.
- Practitioners should familiarize themselves with statutes on privileged communication and general rules of confidentiality.
- It is a good practice to carefully document a client's treatment plan. Records might include notes of symptomatology, a diagnosis, treatment, documents verifying informed consent, relevant consultations and their outcomes, and a copy of the therapeutic contract (Knapp, 1980).
- Therapists are advised to create reasonable expectations about what psychotherapy can and cannot do. It is especially important for innovative therapeutic approaches to undergo research before they are used with the general public (Schutz, B., 1982).
- Since psychotherapy is in the legal limelight, training in graduate school and continuing education for licensed practitioners ought to include legal education. Special attention should be given to the ethical problems and other difficulties involved in the assessment and treatment of high-risk clients, such as people who pose a threat to themselves or to others (Schutz, B., 1982).

Trends in legal liability in therapy practice

According to Schutz (1982), legal liability for psychotherapy in the 1980s will change, partly due to the changes in the practice of psychotherapy. A few of the trends that he foresees are the following:

- There will be an increase in the use of the informed-consent doctrine in cases of negligence.
- Malpractice suits will be more effective against those therapeutic approaches that are highly directive and active, because of the ease of establishing proximate cause.
- As a result of the increase of therapy with elderly people, there will be an increase of undue-influence suits.
- There will be an increase in suits over therapeutic approaches that have not been as prompt and as effective as short-term therapies in achieving therapeutic results.
- If insurance claims are rejected because the treatment plan was found to be inadequate, clients might be allowed to recover the fees they paid for services.
- Family therapy will prompt suits by family members who are dissatisfied with the outcomes. Therapeutic approaches that focus solely on the family as a system will be particularly affected. With such a perspective it is possible to lose sight of the individual rights. Thus, these approaches involve more risk than those that focus on the individual.

Concluding comments

This brief discussion of malpractice is not aimed at increasing your anxiety level. Rather, we hope that this entire chapter has helped to familiarize you with legal and ethical standards as a guide to your practices. Although no professional is expected to be perfect, it is beneficial for practitioners to evaluate what they are doing and why they are practicing as they are. At this point you might be interested in further reading in the area of legal liability in counseling and psychotherapy, as well as malpractice issues. Sources to consider are Burgum and Anderson, 1975; Knapp, 1980; Schutz, B., 1980; and Van Hoose and Kottler, 1977.

Chapter summary

The underlying theme of this chapter has been the honesty and self-confrontation of therapists in determining the impact of their behavior on clients. Although certain behaviors are clearly unethical, most of the issues raised in this chapter are not cut-and-dried. Resolving them requires personal and professional maturity and a willingness to continue to question one's own motivations. A key question is: Whose needs are being met, the therapist's or the client's? Perhaps a sign of good faith on the part of therapists is their willingness to openly share their questions and struggles with colleagues. Such consultation may help to clear up many foggy issues or at least suggest a different perspective. We have discussed sexual involvement with clients, which is an obvious affront to their welfare. We should not overlook some of the more subtle and perhaps insidious behaviors of the therapist that may in the long run cause as much, or perhaps more, damage to clients.

Becoming a therapist doesn't make you perfect or superhuman. You'll make some mistakes. What we want to stress is the importance of reflecting on what you're doing and on whose needs are primary. A willingness to be honest with yourself in your self-examination is your greatest asset in becoming an ethical practitioner.

We suggest that you review your responses to the open-ended questions and cases presented in the last two chapters and make a list of the ethical issues that are most significant to you at this time. Bringing these issues up for discussion with fellow students can be an excellent way of beginning to clarify them for yourself.

Activities, exercises, and ideas for thought and discussion

1. As a practitioner, how would you determine what was ethical and what was unethical? Think about how you would go about developing your guidelines for ethical practice, and make up a list of behaviors that you judge to be unethical. After you've thought through this issue by yourself, you might want to explore your approach with fellow students.

2. Develop a panel in your class to explore the question of what unethical behavior in counseling is and what forms it can take. Try to select the issues that have the most significance to you and that you think will lead to a thought-provoking class discussion.

3. Working in small groups in class, explore the topic of the rights clients have in counseling and therapy. One person in each group can serve as a recorder. When the groups reconvene for a general class meeting, the recorders for the various groups can share their lists of clients' rights with the rest of the class. Then the class can rate each of these rights on a scale from "extremely important" to "very unimportant." What are the rights that your class agrees are the *most* important?

4. Review the cases and situations presented in this chapter, and role-play some of them in dyads. By actually experiencing these situations, you may be able to clarify some of your thoughts. If you do the role-play in your small group, the group members can give you valuable feedback concerning how they experienced you as a client or as a counselor.

5. Interview a practicing counselor about some of the most pressing ethical concerns he or she encounters as a counselor and how he or she has dealt with these concerns.

6. What are your views about forming social relationships with clients during the time they're in counseling with you? About touching clients in nonerotic ways out of affection or for support?

7. What guidelines do you think are important for those who claim to be qualified to offer sex therapy? What are some of the major professional and ethical issues involved in sex therapy?

8. In small groups in your class, examine some of the questions we raised in this chapter concerning sex therapy. For example, you might discuss the following: (a) When does a person know that he or she is adequately trained to do sex therapy? (b) What are some of the special problems that therapists must be alert to in regard to the therapist/client relationship in sex therapy?

What are the potential problems that can surface if transference and countertransference feelings are dealt with poorly? (c) What is your position on the use of sex surrogates for clients without partners? (d) How can the danger of treating only the symptoms of sexual problems be averted?

9. Several students can investigate ethical and legal issues pertaining to psychotherapy with children and adolescents and bring the findings to class. Some topics to consider might be: What are the rights of children in treatment? What legal considerations are involved in therapy with minors? What obligations does the therapist have toward the parents of these children? Should parental consent always be required?

10. In the practice of marital and family therapy, informed consent is especially important. As a class-discussion topic, explore some of these issues: What are the ethical implications of insisting that all members of a family participate in family therapy? What kind of information should a family therapist present from the outset to all those involved? Are there any ethical conflicts in focusing on the welfare of the entire family rather than on what might be in the best interests for an individual?

11. Interview several clinical supervisors to determine what they consider to be some of the most pressing ethical and legal issues in the supervisory relationship. Some questions you might ask of supervisors are: What are the rights of trainees? What are the main responsibilities of supervisors? To what degree should supervisors be held accountable for the welfare of the clients who are counseled by their trainees? What are some common problems faced by supervisors in effectively carrying out their duties?

12. Consider inviting an attorney who is familiar with the legal aspects pertaining to the client/therapist relationship to address your class. Possible topics for consideration are: What are the legal rights of clients in therapy? In working with children, what are some laws that can guide one's interventions? What are some legal issues pertaining to clinical supervisors and trainees? What are the most common grounds for malpractice suits?

13. Review that portion of the *Ethical Standards for Counselor Educators and Supervisors* (NARACES, 1980) that is given in this chapter. What are your reactions to the 15 points listed? Have you had any problems in your supervision? Are there any important changes you would like to make with respect to the supervision you have received in the past or are now receiving?

14. Assume that you are in a field placement as a counselor in a community agency. The administrators tell you that they do *not* want you to inform your clients that you are a student intern. They explain that your clients might feel that they are getting second-class service if they find out that you are in training. The administrators contend that your clients are paying for the services they receive (on a sliding scale, or ability-to-pay basis) and that it is not psychologically good to give them any information that might cause them to conclude that they are not getting the best help available. What would you say and do if you found yourself as an intern in this situation? Would it be ethical to follow this directive and not inform your clients that you were a trainee and that you were receiving supervision? Do you agree

or disagree with the rationale of the administrators? Might you accept the internship assignment under the terms outlined if you could not find any other field placements?

15. What kinds of unethical behavior of your colleagues, if any, do you think you would report? How might you proceed if you knew of the unethical practice of a colleague?

Suggested readings

Cormier, L. S., & Bernard, J. M. Ethical and legal responsibilities of clinical supervisors. *Personnel and Guidance Journal*, 1982, 60(8), 486–490. This article describes responsibilities of supervisors to counselors and to clients; examines such issues as due process, dual relationships, informed consent, confidentiality, and negligence in the context of supervision; and discusses several training methods that help prepare supervisors for handling their ethical and legal responsibilities effectively. The authors contend that supervision should be subject to greater professional scrutiny and that it is unwise for supervisors to isolate themselves.

Glenn, C. M. Ethical issues in the practice of child psychotherapy. *Professional Psychology*, 1980, *11*(4), 613–619. The author reviews literature relevant to the ethics of child psychotherapy, paying particular attention to the community mental health setting. Glenn says that current legal and ethical trends seem to grant greater rights to children in such areas as informed consent, confidentiality, testing and diagnosis, and treatment. He suggests that therapists who work with children should not only practice traditional therapy, but also assume the roles of child advocate, provider of information to children and the community, researcher, and change agent.

Hart, G. M. *The process of clinical supervision*. Baltimore: University Park Press, 1982. Hart describes and compares supervisory models and techniques in the human-service professions. Taking models from psychology, psychiatry, social work, and education, Hart compares them in terms of their assumptions, the relationship in each between supervisor and supervisee, and the content and hypothetical outcome of supervised sessions. This book offers readers specific conceptual frameworks, techniques for conducting supervision, and clear guidelines for selecting a model best suited to their needs.

Holroyd, J. C., & Brodsky, A. Does touching patients lead to sexual intercourse? *Professional Psychology*, 1980, *11*(5), 807–811. This article is based on a questionnaire about erotic and nonerotic contacts with clients. One conclusion is that nonerotic hugging, kissing, and touching of opposite-sex clients but not of same-sex clients is sex-biased behavior. Such practices present the risk of sexual intercourse with clients.

Newman, A. S. Ethical issues in the supervision of psychotherapy. *Professional Psychology*, 1981, *12*(6), 690–695. Newman argues that specific guidelines for ethical behavior between supervisors and trainees have not been delineated. The authors advocate creating guidelines that outline the rights of trainees and the responsibilities of supervisors. Specific ethical issues are raised and recommendations made.

White, M. D., & White, C. A. Involuntary committed patients' constitutional right to refuse treatment. *American Psychologist*, 1981, 36(9), 953–962. The authors address the issue of whether the mental-health profession should impose treatment on unwilling patients who have run afoul of state commitment laws or stand apart from that conflict. The federal courts concluded that individuals are protected by the Constitution from receiving unwanted psychotropic drugs. This is likely to result in patients' increased demand for nonmedical treatments for psychological disorders.

Ethical and Professional Issues Special to Group Work

Pre-chapter self-inventory

Directions: For each statement, indicate the response that most closely identifies your beliefs and attitudes. Use the following code:

5 = I *strongly agree* with this statement.
4 = I *agree*, in most respects, with this statement.
3 = I am *undecided* in my opinion about this statement.
2 = I *disagree*, in most respects, with this statement.
1 = I *strongly disagree* with this statement.

____ 1. A group leader's actual behavior in a group is more important than his or her theoretical approach.

____ 2. Ethical practice requires that prospective group members be carefully screened and selected.

____ 3. It's important to systematically prepare group members so that they can derive the maximum benefit from the group.

____ 4. Requiring people to participate in a therapy group raises ethical issues.

____ 5. It is unethical to allow a group to exert pressure on one of its members.

____ 6. Confidentiality is less important in groups than it is in individual therapy.

____ 7. Socializing among group members is almost always undesirable, since it inevitably interferes with the functioning of the group.

____ 8. Ethical practice requires making some provision for evaluating the outcomes of a group.

____ 9. A group leader has a responsibility to devise ways of minimizing any psychological risks associated with participation in the group.

____ 10. People are not competent to be group leaders until they have completed a structured program of education and training approved by one of the major mental-health professions.

____ 11. Trained group leaders should not have to follow formal guidelines for ethical practice; they should be free to practice according to their judgment.

___ 12. Verbal abuse and subsequent emotional casualties are more likely to occur in groups than in individual counseling.

___ 13. Ethical and professional codes alone will ensure professional leadership of groups.

___ 14. It is the group leader's responsibility to make prospective members aware of their rights and their responsibilities and to demystify the process of a group.

___ 15. Group members should know that they have the right to leave the group at any time.

___ 16. Before people enter a group, it is the leader's responsibility to discuss with them the personal risks involved, especially potential life changes, and help them explore their readiness to face these risks.

___ 17. It is a sound practice to provide written ethical guidelines to group members in advance and discuss them in the first meeting.

___ 18. Group therapists who do not keep the content of group sessions confidential are legally and ethically liable, and they can be sued for breach of confidence.

___ 19. Under certain circumstances, it may be ethical for a group leader to tape a group session without the prior knowledge and consent of the members, *if* the leader tells the members at the end of the session that they were taped.

___ 20. It is unethical for group leaders to employ a technique unless they are thoroughly trained in its use or under the supervision of an expert familiar with it.

___ 21. Ethical practice demands that leaders inform members about any research activities that might be a part of the group.

___ 22. Confrontation in groups is almost always destructive and generally inhibits the formation of trust and cohesion in the group.

___ 23. A group leader has a responsibility to teach members how to translate what they've learned in the group setting to their lives outside the group.

___ 24. A group leader has a responsibility to ask potential members who are already being counseled to consult with their therapists before joining the group.

___ 25. One way of minimizing the psychological risks of group participation is to negotiate contracts with group members.

Introduction

We are giving group therapy special attention, as we did with marital and family therapy, because it raises unique ethical concerns. Practitioners who work with groups encounter a variety of situations that differ from those encountered by therapists who work with individuals. Groups continue to increase in popularity, and in many agencies and institutions they are the primary therapeutic avenue. They are also considered the most cost effective.

Our illustrations of important ethical considerations are drawn from a broad spectrum of groups, including therapy groups, personal-growth groups, marathon groups, human-relations training groups, and different types of counseling groups. Obviously, these groups differ with respect to their member population, purpose, focus, and procedures, as well as in the level of training required for their leaders. Although these distinctions are important, the issues we discuss are common to most groups. For a more detailed description of the various groups and the differences among them, you may wish to consult *Groups: Process and Practice* (Corey & Corey, 1982) and *Developmental Groups for Children* (Duncan & Gumaer, 1980).

This chapter is to a large degree structured around the *Ethical Guidelines for Group Leaders*, as developed and approved by the Association for Specialists in Group Work (ASGW), which is a branch of the American Personnel and Guidance Association (APGA). The ASGW guidelines (1980) are intended to complement the broader APGA standards (1981) by clarifying the ethical responsibility of the counselor in a group setting and by stimulating a greater concern for competent group leadership. Roberts (1982) notes that one of the aims of the guidelines is to help practitioners neutralize personal values and biases and promote the good of the group or its individual members.

Theoretical assumptions and group work

Theoretical assumptions are no less important in group work than they are in individual counseling and psychotherapy. A basic theoretical question is: Why use a group approach? Group leaders need a rationale for putting people into groups, and they need to be aware of the advantages and limitations of group counseling. Some of the questions group leaders should be able to answer are:

- When is a group approach preferred over individual counseling?
- Are groups merely more convenient, financially and practically, than individual approaches are?
- What effect does the leader's ideological approach have on the group process?
- How do the differences between the educational, growth-oriented model and the medical model of group therapy affect group goals and processes?

In regard to the last of these questions, we want to note that the model from which a group leader operates has definite implications for practice. Typically, those practitioners who adhere to a personal-growth model are concerned with expanding awareness and helping participants learn skills to enhance their living, rather than with the treatment of disorders. Personal-growth models of group work are based on the assumption that people have within themselves the potential for growing as persons; recognizing blocks to personal growth is considered to be more important than merely solving problems. These models emphasize awareness, feelings, risk-taking behavior, experimentation with new behavior, here-and-now experiencing, and mutual feedback on the part of group members. The group leader's role is not to treat serious psychological disturbances but to act as a catalyst of meaningful group interaction.

In contrast, the medical-model approach to group work stresses treatment and the correction of problems. Group leaders may be less self-disclosing than those who follow a growth model, and comparatively more attention is given to understanding, conceptualizing, and becoming aware of how past history is manifested in present conflicts. Thus, there is a focus on defenses, resistances, and interpretation.

Although these basic orientations do influence the group process and the goals of a group, they are not incompatible. Many encounter-group leaders are coming to realize that the emphasis on here-and-now experiencing and open sharing of immediate feelings does have its limitations. They may therefore integrate the experiencing of intense emotions with some conceptualization. Participants can be encouraged to think about the meaning of their experiences, they can explore how their pasts are related to their present struggles, and they can work through conflicts and make new decisions. Cognitive awareness, which is so often neglected in encounter groups, can be integrated with feeling and doing to make the members' group experience more meaningful. Similarly, group therapists who are primarily concerned with treating deep personality problems can integrate many methods and techniques from the personal-growth model into their work.

Although we think it's important for group leaders to operate within a theoretical framework, we're not advocating rigid adherence to a single preexisting theory. We think it's valuable for group leaders to become familiar with a variety of theoretical models and then discover their own ways of blending concepts and techniques from several approaches. We see too many beginning group leaders who view theory as something abstract and impractical and who are excessively technique oriented. By studying various theories, group leaders may be stimulated to examine some of the following questions:

- What are the primary goals of each group, and how might they be met most effectively?
- Who should determine the group's goals? How should they be determined?
- What is the main role of the leader? How much responsibility does the leader have to structure and direct the group?
- What are the functions of the group members?
- Should the leader focus on individuals or on group interaction?
- Which techniques are most useful? Why use a particular technique? When should it be used?

We believe that, ultimately, a group leader's theory cannot be divorced from himself or herself as a person. The most meaningful theoretical perspective is one that is an extension of the leader's values and personality. However, it's unrealistic to expect that beginning group counselors will have developed and integrated well-defined personal theories to guide them in their practice. Rather, the development of a theoretical perspective is an ongoing task in which one's model undergoes continual revision. With new experience, new issues and questions are raised. Experiments can be tried to test out hunches, and ways of modifying old practices to fit new knowledge can be developed. Our main point is that group leaders need to constantly question how they practice and be open to changes in their theories and styles.

Yalom (1975) contends that, although the behavior of group leaders is not predictable from their particular ideological schools, their behaviors and leadership styles seem to be the critical variables in determining the effectiveness of a group. Yalom cites research demonstrating that four leadership functions have a direct relationship to the outcomes of group work. First, *caring* is essential; the greater the amount of caring, the greater the chance of positive outcomes. Second, *meaning attribution* (explaining, clarifying, providing a cognitive framework for change) is also directly related to positive outcome. Third, *emotional stimulation* (challenging, risk taking, self-disclosure, activity) is important to give vitality to a group; however, too much of this stimulation tends to result in more emotional interaction than members can integrate. Fourth, the leader's *executive function*, which includes structuring, developing norms, and suggesting procedures, is valuable in providing the group with enough direction that the members do not flounder needlessly. However, excessive direction deprives members of their autonomy and restricts the free-flowing nature of a group.

Developing a sound theory to guide one's practice is necessary for effective and ethical group work. For a comprehensive discussion of the major contemporary theories of group counseling, you might consult *Theory and Practice of Group Counseling* (Corey, 1981b); *Basic Approaches to Group Psychotherapy and Group Counseling* (Gazda, 1982); and *Group Counseling: Theory and Process* (Hansen, Warner, & Smith, 1980).

Training and supervision of group leaders

For some time, administrators of the ASGW have been convinced that, since group counseling entails distinct problems, skills, and training issues, leaders deserve special training standards. One reason group leaders need their own guidelines is that they practice in such diverse settings as private practice, prisons, schools, university counseling centers, mental-health centers, agencies, industry, and the military (Kottler, 1982).

Training of group leaders is a professional issue because the various disciplines have differing views and standards. For example, group workers in psychology receive different training from psychiatric workers. Social workers are taught group work from a perspective that is sometimes different from that of counselors. The activities and minimum number of hours suggested for clinical training and supervision in group work differ from one professional organization to another.

Kottler (1982) gives a description of the ASGW *Guidelines for Training Group Leaders*, which set out the minimum abilities required of leaders. A well-qualified leader must:

- have a clear definition of group counseling
- screen clients and assess their readiness to participate productively in a group
- be able to use major strategies and techniques in group counseling
- diagnose self-defeating behaviors in group members
- model appropriate behavior
- interpret nonverbal behavior accurately
- intervene during critical incidents in the group process
- deal constructively with disruptive group members
- be able to work effectively with a co-leader
- know how to close a group session and terminate the group process

The ASGW guidelines also cover training in clinical practice. They suggest the minimum and ideal number of hours that should be devoted to supervised experience in the following areas:

- critiquing group tapes
- observing group counseling in action
- participating as a group member
- leading a group under supervision
- leading a group with a partner and receiving constructive feedback from both partner and supervisor
- completing a practicum in group leadership, with the opportunity to lead a group alone and then to get feedback from a supervisor
- completing an internship in group leadership, with practice as a group leader in an on-the-job situation
- continuing education and training, including leading groups under supervision during the first three years and ongoing self-scrutiny throughout one's professional career

Yalom (1975) suggests supervised clinical group experience or participation in a training and supervision group, contending that mere experience is not enough without ongoing evaluation and feedback. As to the specifics of supervised practice, the American Group Psychotherapy Association's (1978) training model for group therapists requires a minimum two-year program with 120 hours of clinical experience leading or co-leading a therapy group, plus at least 75 hours of supervised group experience.

Paradise and Siegelwaks (1982) believe that continuing exposure to ethical inquiry will foster ethical behavior among group workers. They contend that systematic ethical training should be included in formal course work to help trainees deal effectively with the following major concerns (p. 164):

- issues of group leadership
- responsibilities toward participants
- screening of potential group members
- relationships among participants outside the group
- confidentiality
- permissible behavior within the group
- uses of undue pressure within the group
- multiple relationships between participants and leaders

Kottler (1983) also argues that ethics should be brought into clearer focus for group leaders. He maintains that practitioners must ultimately answer to themselves for their actions. He gives special attention to the common unethical behaviors of group workers, as well as to the problems that make practitioners vulnerable to error. He lists the following problems as special to group work (p. 288):[1]

---

[1] From *Pragmatic Group Leadership*, by J. A. Kottler. Copyright © 1983 by Wadsworth, Inc. This and all other quotations from the same source are reprinted by permission of Brooks/Cole Publishing Company, Monterey, California.

1. Verbal abuse and subsequent casualties are more likely to occur in groups than in individual treatment.
2. The therapist has less control over proceedings and client behavior. Potentially more things can go wrong before the leader can intervene.
3. The therapist has more control in influencing capabilities, a power that can be used for better or for worse.
4. Confidentiality can be neither guaranteed nor enforced because other group members don't necessarily live by the same moral code that group leaders do.
5. Many group leaders practice without benefit of training, education, or supervision. There are no standardized criteria for acceptable qualifications. In the same city, a psychiatrist, psychologist, astrologer, palm reader, and prostitute can all label their professional activities as "group therapy."
6. Because groups are such intense environments, the risks for each member are greater. Change *and* damage are accelerated.
7. The screening of clients is frequently haphazard. Clients are often required to participate in the experience involuntarily.
8. Group work presents special re-entry problems for participants when the sessions have ended.
9. Dependency effects are more pronounced in groups.
10. There is no licensure, certification, or regulation that can effectively enforce the practice of responsible group leadership.

Our views on training

We are in basic agreement with Kottler's views that professional codes, legislative mandates, peer practices, and institutional policies alone will not ensure professional group leadership. We think that students in group-leadership training must be presented with the typical dilemmas they will face in practice and must learn ways to clarify their views on these issues. This can best be done by including ethics in the formal content of the trainees' academic program as well as discussing ethical issues that grow out of the students' experiences in practicum, internship, and field work. We have found that one effective way to teach the process of ethical decision making is presenting trainees with case vignettes of typical problems that occur in group situations and then encouraging open discussion of the ethical issues and the pertinent guidelines for these situations (Corey, Corey, & Callanan, 1982). In our own approach to training and supervising group leaders, we emphasize that they will not have the answers to many of the ethical dilemmas that they encounter in practice, because ethical decision making is an ongoing process that takes on a new form and increased meaning as the practitioner gains experience. What is critical is that group leaders develop a receptivity to self-examination and to questioning the professionalism of their group practice.

We highly recommend at least three experiences as adjuncts to a training program for group workers: personal (private) psychotherapy, experience in group therapy or as a member of a personal-growth group, and participation in a supervision and training group.

Personal psychotherapy for group leaders.   We agree with Yalom's (1975) recommendation that extensive self-exploration is necessary if trainees are to perceive countertransference feelings, recognize blind spots and biases, and use their personal attributes effectively in groups. Group leaders should demonstrate the courage and willingness to do for themselves what they expect members in their groups to do—expand their awareness of self and the effect of that self on others.

Self-exploration groups for group leaders.   As an adjunct to a group leader's formal course work and internship training, participation in some kind of therapeutic group can be extremely valuable. In addition to helping interns resolve personal conflicts and develop increased self-understanding, a personal-growth group can be a powerful teaching tool. One of the best ways to learn how to assist group members in their struggles is to work yourself as a member of a group. Yalom (1975) and the ASGW also recommend personal-group experience as a part of a comprehensive training program for group counselors.

Training workshops for group leaders.   We have found workshops most useful in helping group trainees develop the skills necessary for effective intervention. Also, the interns can learn a great deal about their response to criticism, their competitiveness, their need for approval, their concerns over being competent, and their power struggles. In working with both university students learning about group approaches and with professionals who want to upgrade their group skills, we have found an intensive weekend workshop to be effective and dynamic. In these workshops the participants have ample opportunity to lead their small group for a designated period of time. After a segment in which the participants lead their group, we intervene by giving feedback and by prompting a discussion by the entire group. By the end of the weekend, each participant has led the group at least twice (for an hour each time) under direct supervision.

As you consider issues related to group leaders' competence, answer these questions for yourself:

- Who is qualified to lead groups? What are the criteria for determining the competence of group leaders?
- What do you think of the training in clinical practice suggested in the ASGW's *Guidelines for Training Group Leaders?*
- Does ethical practice demand that group leaders receive some form of personal therapy? Should this be group therapy or experience in a personal-growth group? How important are continuing education and training once one has completed a professional program?
- What are your reactions to the suggestions we offered for the training of group workers?

Co-leaders

If you should decide to get involved in groups, it's likely that you'll work with a co-leader at some time or other. We think there are many advantages to the co-leader model. The group can benefit from the insights and feedback of two leaders. The leaders can complement and balance each other. They can grow by discussing what goes on in the group and by observing each other's style, and together they can evaluate what has gone on in the group and plan for future sessions. Also, with co-leaders the total burden does not rest with one person. While one leader is working with a particular member, the other can be paying attention to others in the group.

The choice of a co-leader is crucial. A group can suffer if its leaders are not working together harmoniously toward a common goal. If much of the leaders' energy is directed at competing with each other or at some other power struggle or hidden agenda, there is little chance that the group will be effective.

We think that the selection of a co-leader should involve more than attraction and liking. Each of the leaders should be secure enough that the group won't have to suffer as one or both of them try to "prove" themselves. We surely don't think it's essential that co-leaders always agree or share the same perceptions or interpretations; in fact, a group can be given vitality if co-leaders feel trusting enough to express their differences of opinion. Mutual respect and the ability to establish a relationship based upon trust, cooperation, and support are most important. Also, each person should be autonomous and have his or her own style yet be able to work with the other leader as a team.

In our view, it's essential for co-leaders to spend some time together immediately following a group to assess what happened. Similarly, we believe that they should meet at least briefly before each group session to talk about anything that might affect their functioning in the group.

The three of us have worked as a team leading groups for 11 years. Philosophically we share a set of common values that have an impact on our view of group work. We're fortunate in this regard; if we had divergent philosophical and theoretical orientations, it would be difficult, if not impossible, to work together as an effective team. Our styles are very different, and the ways in which we each work and participate in our groups reflect our particular personalities. However, we have a high degree of respect and liking for one another, and our differences in style and personality actually seem to enhance our functioning in our groups. Before a group session, we do spend time together to prepare ourselves psychologically for the group. We meet again after each session to share our perceptions, discuss what is occurring in the group, talk about what we're feeling, challenge one another, and plan for future sessions. Working together in this way has been most rewarding for us and has enhanced the quality of our leadership abilities.

At this point, we ask you to draw up your own guidelines for selecting a co-leader.

- What are the qualities you'd look for in a co-leader?
- What kind of person would you *not* want to lead with?
- If you found that you and your co-leader clashed on many issues and approached groups very differently, what do you think you'd do?
- What ethical implications are involved when a great deal of time during the sessions is taken up with power struggles and conflicts between the co-leaders?
- In what ways could you be most helpful to your co-leader?

Recruitment and informed consent

Professional issues are involved in publicizing a group and recruiting members. How can group leaders make potential members aware of the services available? What information do clients have a right to expect before they decide to attend a group?

The ASGW ethical standards (1980) clarify the group leader's responsibility for providing information about services to prospective clients. Two of the guidelines that are relevant here are: (1) "Group leaders shall fully inform group members, in advance and preferably in writing, of the goals in the group, qualifications of the leader, and procedures to be employed." (2) "Group leaders shall explain, as realistically as possible, exactly what services can and cannot be provided within the particular group structure offered."

We take the position that people have a right to know what they are getting into before they make a commitment to become a part of any group. It is the group leader's responsibility to make prospective members aware of their rights and their responsibilities and to demystify the process of a group. Some of the things that it is important for people to know before they decide to join a group are the fees and any other related expenses; the division of responsibility of the leader and the participants; any experimental techniques or any research that might be a part of the group; the potential risks involved in group participation; notice of any observations of the group through one-way mirrors or any recording of group sessions; the duration of the group and the number of participants; whether follow-up service is included in the fee; the education, training, and special group qualifications of the leader; and the limitations of confidentiality, including the use of information acquired during sessions outside the group structure.

Personal contact is the ideal way to inform potential members about the details of a group. The leader can enthusiastically and directly demonstrate the potential values of participating in a group. At times, personal contact is not possible, and leaders may rely on printed announcements. If flyers are used, ethical practice dictates that professional standards (not commercial ones) be used. For example, a flyer might contain some basic information that we've just described, including a brief statement of the purpose of the group, background of the leader, and so forth. This can be the first step in the process of getting members; people interested in learning more about the group can arrange for a private screening-and-orientation session. In written announcements, no claims should be made that cannot be substantiated. Global promises have no place on a professional announcement. Likewise, testimonials from satisfied members of other groups should be avoided.

Screening and selection of group members

Group leaders are faced with the difficult task of determining who should be included in a group and who should not. Are groups appropriate for all people? To put the question in another way, is it appropriate for *this* person to become a participant in *this* type of group, with *this* leader, at *this* time?

There are many groups whose leaders do not screen prospective participants. This is particularly true of weekend workshops that are essentially experiential groups and of marathon groups where strangers meet for one intensive weekend. Assuming that not everyone will benefit from a group experience—and that some people will be psychologically harmed by certain group experiences—is it unethical to fail to screen prospective group candidates? Some writers argue that truly effective screening is impossible. Others take the position that ethical practice demands the careful screening and preparation of all candidates.

Eric Berne (1961) views the selection of patients as a sign of professional inadequacy. His bias is toward a group approach to treatment. He contends that transactional analysis has been adequately tested with groups of neurotics, psychotics, sexual psychopaths, people with character disorders, and borderline cases and that groups can be formed of any of these types of people with some confidence. Berne's position on screening is well summed up in the following words:

> In general, the behavior of a patient in a group cannot be reliably predicted from his behavior in daily life or in individual interviews. A retarded depressive will not necessarily remain retarded in a group, nor will a deluded paranoid necessarily bring his delusions into the group as an unmanageable, disturbing factor. The only way to settle this in a given case is to try it [pp. 169–170].

In discussing the issue of screening people for an *encounter group*, William Schutz (1971) frankly admits that he is not sure what kind of participant he would include or exclude if he did screen. He says: "I think it would be marvelous if people were screened so that those who would profit most would be admitted to encounter groups and those who would not profit, or who would be damaged, would be excluded. But I have very little idea of how to do this" (p. 313).

Others maintain that group leaders have a clear responsibility to determine what types of people should be excluded from a group. In its guidelines for psychologists conducting *growth groups*, the American Psychological Association (1973b) takes the position that screening interviews should be conducted by group leaders prior to the acceptance of any participant. Further, the APA statement says that group leaders are responsible for screening out those individuals they judge to be inappropriate for a given group.

Gazda and Mack (1982) agree with the APA position and add that screening procedures should be designed to ensure that prospective participants understand what is expected of them and that only those members will be selected who are likely to benefit from the group experience. Prospective group members should be told of the limits of confidentiality, and, if the group will be used for research purposes, the members should be informed. In addition, Gazda and Mack believe, members should be told:

- that membership is voluntary
- that complete confidentiality cannot be guaranteed
- that certain situations may require the group leader to break confidences
- that members will be informed of any research that may be a part of the group
- that recording of group sessions will be done only with the consent of the members
- that members have the "freedom of exit" from the group

- that participants may need to be removed from the group if the leader determines that they are being harmed by the experience
- that any member who is in treatment with another professional should obtain clearance from that person to participate in the group

In the context of *group psychotherapy*, Yalom (1975) argues that, unless careful selection criteria are employed, clients may end up discouraged and unhelped. Yalom maintains that it is easier to identify the kinds of people who should be excluded from therapy groups than it is to identify those who should be included. Citing clinical studies, Yalom lists the following as poor candidates for outpatient, intensive group therapy: schizoid, paranoid, or sociopathic personalities; brain-damaged persons; monopolists (incessant talkers); depressives; people addicted to drugs or alcohol; people who are suicidal; and extremely narcissistic people.

In describing the kinds of people she would exclude from a *marathon therapy group*, Mintz (1971) lists people who have poor reality testing, people who are currently showing overt psychotic symptoms, and people who are extremely withdrawn. Mintz believes that therapists are ethically obliged to tactfully explain reasons for excluding a person and to make specific suggestions concerning where the person can obtain individual psychotherapy. She adds that people who are currently in individual therapy should not be accepted for a marathon without the knowledge and consent of their therapists.

Lakin (1972) contends that three types of people should be screened from *sensitivity training groups:* (1) people who will become too defensive under stress to listen to what others say to them, (2) people who tend to project their feelings onto others and to feel victimized by them, and (3) people whose self-esteem is so low that they need constant reassurance. Lakin points to the danger of accepting dominant people who would deal with their anxiety by monopolizing the group's time and draining its energy.

In the *Ethical Guidelines for Group Leaders* (ASGW, 1980) the following principle is given:

> The group leader shall conduct a pre-group interview with each prospective member for purposes of screening, orientation, and, in so far as possible, shall select group members whose needs and goals are compatible with the established goals of the group; who will not impede the group process; and whose well-being will not be jeopardized by the group experience.[2]

What should a leader do when conducting private screening interviews is not possible or realistic? Some practitioners meet their groups without screening or orienting the members. Are they behaving unethically? We think that one alternative is to use the initial session for screening and informed consent. Our position is that screening is most effective when the leader interviews the members and the members also have an opportunity to interview the leader. While prospective group members are being screened, they should be deciding whether they want to work with a particular leader and whether the group in question is suitable for them. Group candi-

---

[2] From *Ethical Guidelines for Group Leaders*, by the Association for Specialists in Group Work. Copyright 1980 by the American Personnel and Guidance Association. This and all other quotations from the same source are reprinted by permission.

dates should not passively allow the matter to be decided for them by an expert. Group leaders should welcome the opportunity to respond to any questions or concerns prospective members have, and they should actively encourage prospective participants to raise questions about matters that will affect their participation.

In our own approach to screening, we've often found it difficult to predict who will benefit from a group experience. We realize that pre-group screening interviews are like any interviews in that people may tend to say what they think the interviewer expects. Often people who are interviewed for a group feel that they must sell themselves or that they are being evaluated and judged. Perhaps these feelings can be lessened somewhat if leaders take the initiative to emphasize that these interviews are really designed as a two-way process in which leaders and prospective members can decide together whether a particular group, with a particular leader, at a particular time, is in the best interests of all concerned. Although we do have difficulty in predicting who will benefit from a group, we have found screening interviews most helpful in excluding some people who we believed would probably have left the group with negative feelings or who would have drained and sapped the group of the energy necessary for productive work.

It often happens that both the prospective member and the group leader are unsure whether a particular group is indicated for that person. For this reason, in a group that will be meeting several times, the first few sessions can be considered exploratory in nature. Members can be encouraged to come to the first session or two and then consider whether the group is what they're looking for. In this way, leaders encourage a process of self-selection that gives members the responsibility of deciding what is right for them. Actually experiencing the group for a time enables members to make an informed decision about participation. If, after a few sessions, either the leader or a particular member has any reservations, they can arrange a private meeting to explore these concerns and come to some agreement.

Pause a moment now to reflect on this issue of screening candidates for group participation.

1. If you were to organize a specific type of group and you decided to screen potential members, what are some characteristics or attitudes that you would *most* look for in accepting a person?

_____

_____

_____

_____

2. What kinds of persons might you exclude from your group? Why? How would you handle the matter of informing them that you would not accept them into your group?

_____

_____

_____

_____

_____

_____

3. If you were looking for a group for yourself, what are some of the characteristics of a *leader* that you would want to avoid? Check any of the following that apply.

___ rigid orientation
___ defensiveness
___ dogmatic attitude
___ lack of clarity about group goals
___ technique-oriented approach
___ aloofness
___ charismatic personality
___ warmth and possessiveness
___ lack of caring
___ aggressiveness

Others:

_____

_____

The group leader conducts screening interviews for a group whose goal is to become aware of personal styles in relating to one another. During one private session, she has some strong reservations about including the interviewee. She observes the candidate as being an extremely frightened person. However, this candidate is very insistent on being included in the group. He says: "I really want this group, and I'm sure that it will help me. If you don't let me in, it will just be one more rejection in my life." The group leader has real reservations about including this person, because she does not think her group is appropriate for him. However, she does not express her reservations, and she accepts the person against her better judgment. In the course of the group this member becomes an obstacle to group cohesion and group progress.

- How much should a leader trust his or her own intuition about excluding a member, particularly in the absence of clinical data to support the intuition?
- If you have a feeling that a candidate should be excluded, do you think it is wise to express your reservations? Why or why not?
- How might you tell a person that you would not let him or her into the group? How might you deal sensitively, yet directly, with such a candidate who you thought would not benefit from your group (or who would be a potential burden to the group)?

The preparation of group participants

To what extent are group leaders responsible for preparing participants to get the maximum benefit from their group experience? Many group practitioners do very little to systematically prepare members for a group. In fact, some therapists and group leaders are opposed to systematic preparation on the ground that it will bias the members' experience. Many encounter-group leaders assume that part of the task of group members is to flounder and struggle and eventually define their own goals and give their group direction without much intervention by the leader. These leaders think that preparation and structuring on the part of the leader inhibits a group's spontaneity and autonomy.

Others take the position that members must be given some preparation in order to derive the maximum gains from a group experience. As we saw in the previous section, the ASGW's ethical guidelines (1980) emphasize the importance of both screening and orientation in helping members gain the maximum benefit from a group experience.

Yalom (1975) is an advocate of systematic preparation for people in group therapy. His preparation includes exploring misconceptions and expectations, predicting early problems, and providing a conceptual framework that includes guidelines for effective group behavior. His preparatory interviews contain some of the following elements:

1. A brief explanation of the interpersonal theory of psychiatry is given.
2. Members are given guidelines for how they can best help themselves. This step includes talking about trust, self-disclosure, members' rights to privacy, risk taking, and experimentation with new behavior.
3. Stumbling blocks are predicted.
4. Members are told that the goal of the therapy group is to change behavior and attitudes, that treatment will take at least a year, and that significant changes should not be expected for months.
5. Members are told about the history of group therapy.
6. Confidentiality and extragroup socializing are discussed.

Yalom views this preparatory process as more than the dissemination of information. He claims that it reinforces the therapist's respect for the client, demonstrates that therapy is a collaborative venture, and shows that the therapist is willing to share his or her knowledge with the client.

In his skills/contract approach to *human-relations training groups*, Egan (1976) endorses the idea of systematic preparation of group members. Egan tells his readers: "The more clearly you understand the experience before you embark upon it, the more intelligently you will be able to give yourself to it and the more valuable it will be to you" (p. 3). Research cited by Egan suggests that a lack of structure during initial group sessions tends to intensify participants' fears and leads to unrealistic expectations. The research also indicates that groups are more effective if participants clearly understand group goals and processes, as well as what is expected of them.

In Egan's approach to groups, members begin by learning the elements of human-relations training. They learn that the group is a laboratory, that it is a place that encourages experimentation, that the focus is on the here-and-now, that self-disclosure is expected, that they will be giving and receiving feedback, that "cultural permission" is given to learn how to interact with others in new ways, and that interpersonal skills will be practiced and learned in the group.

It is our practice to systematically prepare participants, whether they are in weekly therapy groups, ongoing growth groups, or residential weekend or week-long personal-growth workshops. In our training workshops we have seen much resistance that can be attributed to a lack of knowledge of group process and a lack of clarity of goals. What we say here applies to all types of groups, with some modifications. At both the screening session and the initial group meeting, we explore the members' expectations, clarify goals and objectives, discuss procedural details, explore possible risks and values of group participation, and discuss guidelines for getting the most from a group experience (see Corey & Corey, 1982, pp. 88–97; Corey, Corey, Callanan, & Russell, 1982b, pp. 46–51). As part of member preparation, we like to include a discussion of the values and limitations of groups, the psychological risks involved in group participation, and ways of minimizing these risks. We also allow time for dealing with misconceptions that people have of groups and for exploring any fears or resistances the members may have. In most of our groups members do have certain fears about what they will experience, and, until we acknowledge these fears and talk about them, very little other productive work can occur. Further, we ask members to spend time before they come to the group defining for themselves what they most want to get from the group experience. To make their goals more concrete, we usually ask them to develop a contract that entails areas of concern that they're willing to work on in the group. We also ask them to do some reading and to write about their goals and about the significant turning points in their lives.

At this point, we ask you to write down a few things you might want to do to prepare people for a group.

_____

_____

_____

_____

_____

What is your position on the ethical aspects of failing to prepare group members for their experience in the group? What do you think would occur if you did little in the way of preparing group members?

Voluntary and involuntary participation in groups

Should group membership always be voluntary? Are there situations in which it is ethical to require or coerce people to participate in a group? What are the problems involved in mandatory group participation? How is informed consent especially critical in groups where attendance is mandatory?

The ASGW's (1980) guideline is: "Group leaders shall inform members that participation is voluntary and that they may exit from the group at any time." We have some reservations about this guideline. First, some practitioners lead groups that are composed of involuntary clients. Second, once members make a commitment to the group, they also have responsibilities to the group, and it is not responsible simply to drop out without any discussion.

Involuntary clients.   When group participation is mandatory, much effort needs to be directed toward fully informing members of the nature and goals of the group, procedures to be used, the rights of members to decline certain activities, the limits of confidentiality, and what effect their level of participation in the group will have on critical decisions about them outside of the group. An example will help make our point. The three of us provide in-service training workshops for staff members who lead involuntary groups at a state mental hospital. Groups are the basic type of treatment for "those incompetent to stand trial," "sociopathic criminals," and "mentally disordered sex offenders." One of the factors involved in the determination of patients' release from the hospital and return to the community is their cooperation in the treatment program, which includes participation in regular group-therapy sessions. If patients do not show up for a group, they are likely to have their "hall cards" taken from them, which means that they are restricted to their wards. In such cases where attendance at group sessions is mandatory, informed consent implies that leaders explore with members, during an orientation session, what the group will be about, so that members will understand clearly what their rights and responsibilities are.

The freedom to leave a group.   We contend that the leader's attitudes and policies about the freedom of exit should be spelled out and discussed at the onset of a group or, better, at a preliminary meeting. Corey, Corey, Callanan, and Russell (1982b) take the position that clients have a responsibility to the leader and other members to explain why they want to leave. There are several reasons for this policy. It can be deleterious to members to leave without being able to discuss what they considered threatening or negative in the experience. Further, it is unfortunate for members to leave a group because of a misunderstanding about some feedback they have received. It can surely be harmful in terms of developing group cohesion, for the members who remain may think that they "caused" a particular member's departure. We tell our members that they have an obligation to attend all sessions and to inform us and the group should they decide to withdraw. If members even consider withdrawing, we encourage them to bring this up for exploration in a session. We do not think that it is ethical to use undue pressure to keep these members, and we are alert to other members' pressuring a person to stay.

In a prison group, an inexperienced leader senses how counterproductive the therapy is in an involuntary group. In an attempt to lessen the members' resistances, she tells them that she does not want anybody in the group who is not willing to participate freely in the sessions. She neglects to inform them that their refusal to attend group sessions will be documented and will be considered in the decision about their release. Thus, the members are operating under the false assumption that they have freedom of choice, yet they do not have all the information they need to make a real choice.

- What do you think of the ethics of this leader?
- Did this leader's desire for an effective group justify her practice? Explain.
- Do you think that members can benefit from a group experience even if they are required to attend? Why or why not?
- What strategy might she have used that would have enabled her to have more effective group participation while still giving the patients true freedom of choice?

Psychological risks in groups

The fact that groups can be powerful catalysts of personal change means that they are also risky. We don't think groups should be free of risk, because learning how to grow entails taking risks. In our view, however, ethical practice demands that group leaders at least inform prospective participants of the potential risks involved in the group experience. We also believe that group leaders have an ethical responsibility to take precautionary measures to reduce unnecessary psychological risks. Our view is that merely informing participants of the possible risks does not absolve leaders of all responsibility. Certain safeguards can be taken during the course of a group to avoid disastrous outcomes. In this section we discuss some of the risks that we believe participants should know about.

1. One risk of group participation is that members may experience major disruptions in their lives as a result of their work in the group. Of course, this risk is present in any type of therapy, not simply in groups. Members should be aware, however, that others in their lives may not appreciate their changes. This situation could lead to decisions that will change their life-styles. On this point of discussion of risks, the ASGW's (1980) guideline is as follows: "Group leaders shall stress the personal risks involved in any group, especially regarding potential life-changes, and help group members explore their readiness to face these risks."

2. Often group participants are encouraged to "let it all hang out." In this quest for complete self-revelation, privacy is sometimes invaded. Participants must learn the difference between appropriate and facilitative self-disclosure and disclosure that leaves nothing private. Group leaders need to be alert to attempts to force people to disclose more than they are ready to share. Otherwise participants may withdraw, feeling a sense of shame for having said more than they were ready and willing to say.

3. The risk of invasion of privacy brings up the related risk of group pressure. In most groups there are pressures to be open, to be honest, to take risks, to talk about personal matters, and to try new behavior. These behaviors are then positively reinforced. At times group pressure to get people to join in certain activities or to change their ideas and behavior can be very strong. More often it appears as a subtle pressure to conform unquestioningly to group norms and expectations. Can you imagine the reactions members would receive who did not conform to any of the group norms?

We think it's important to recognize that group pressure is inevitable and that it can even be useful in encouraging participants to take an honest look at themselves. However, even though not all group pressure is bad, it can be misused. In our view, the participants' right not to explore certain issues or to stop at a certain point should be respected. Also, members should not be coerced into participating in an exercise if they're unwilling to do so. One of the ASGW's (1980) guidelines is relevant here: "Group leaders shall protect member rights against physical threats, intimidation, coercion, and undue peer pressure insofar as it is reasonably possible."

4. Scapegoating is another potential hazard in groups. We question the ethical sensitivity of leaders who fail to intervene actively when they see participants "ganging up" on a certain group member. Unchallenged projection and dumping can have dire effects on the person who is under attack.

5. Confrontation can be used or misused in groups. At times participants may view confrontation in a negative way, seeing it as a destructive tearing down of defenses that leaves a person in a highly vulnerable place. To be sure, confrontation can be done in a way that results in a devastating attack. Leaders and participants alike need to learn how to recognize this destructive type of behavior and prevent it from going on in a group. On the other hand, confrontation can be an act of caring, and it can be done in such a way that a member is *challenged*, without the hit-and-run effect of destructive confrontation. As Egan (1976) puts it, confrontation can be an *invitation* for people to examine their behavior and its consequences more carefully. When confrontation is positive, it occurs in such a way that confronters share their reactions to the person being confronted. Harmful attacks on others should not be permitted under the guise of "sharing."

6. Another risk involved in groups is that what members disclose may not always be kept confidential. Even though a leader may continue to stress the necessity of not discussing what goes on in the group with outsiders, there is no guarantee that all members will respect the confidential nature of what occurs in their group.

7. On occasion people have been physically injured in groups as a result of such activities as wrestling, pushing, holding down, fighting with bataccas (soft, felt-covered clubs), and other forms of releasing aggression. We have seen irresponsible leaders goad participants to "let out your anger" and then watch helplessly, clearly unprepared for the ensuing violent outbursts of rage. In short, we think that it's unethical for leaders to work toward eliciting aggressive feelings unless they are competent to deal with the likely results. One safeguard is to tell members not to strike one another but to beat a pillow to release aggressive feelings in a symbolic way.

There are several guidelines for preventing injury when using certain physical techniques (see Corey, Corey, Callanan, & Russell, 1982b):

- Leaders should protect group members from harm; they should be prepared to deal with unforeseen directions that the physical exercise might take.
- Such techniques should not be used with clients whom the group leader does not know well. The nature of the client/therapist relationship and the client's personality are critical variables in deciding whether to use physical techniques and exercises.
- Beginning group leaders should use physical techniques only when direct supervision is available or when they are co-leading with an experienced group leader.

- It is both unethical and unwise to push members into physical exercises. It is essential that members be invited to participate in an exercise and given the clear option of refraining. If the leader explains the general purpose of such exercises and asks whether members want to participate, the chance of a negative outcome is minimized.

One way of minimizing psychological risks in groups is to use a contract approach, whereby leaders specify what their responsibilities are and members specify what their commitment to the group is by declaring what they're willing to explore and what they're willing to do. Goldberg (1977), who makes a strong case for contract negotiation as the basis for a group, believes that this device can reduce psychological risks. He adds the important point that leaders need to *respect* their contracts with the participants in terms of what they have agreed to do and what they have agreed not to do.

Egan (1976) uses the contract approach to ensure that participants know what they are agreeing to when they become members of a skills-training group. The contract states that participants will use group time to explore their own interpersonal styles and to alter these styles in ways *they* deem appropriate. Other aspects of the contract include:

- working with others to achieve the goals of the group
- learning how to listen to others
- responding to others concretely
- letting others into your "world"
- letting others know what you like about them or what keeps you at a distance from them
- sharing what you learn about yourself in the group
- giving and asking for feedback

If such a contract approach is used, many of the risks we've mentioned can be reduced. If members and leaders operate under a contract that clarifies expectations, we believe there is less chance for members to be exploited or to leave a group feeling that they've had a bad experience.

Of course, a contract approach is not the only way to reduce potential risks; nor is it sufficient, by itself, to do so. Probably one of the most important safeguards is the leader's training in group processes. Group leaders have the major responsibility for preventing needless harm to members, and to fulfill this role they need to have a clear grasp of the boundaries of their competence. This implies that leaders conduct only those types of groups for which they have been sufficiently prepared. A group leader may be trained to lead a group of peers in a personal-growth or consciousness-raising group yet be ill prepared to embark on a marathon or therapy group. Sometimes people who have attended a few marathon groups become excited about doing this type of group as leaders, even though they have little or no training and no opportunity for supervision. They soon find that they are in over their heads and are unable to cope with what emerges in the group. Working with an experienced co-leader is one good way to learn and also a way of reducing some potential risks.

Gumaer (1982, p. 160) identified some helpful hints that can do a lot to avoid the psychological risks that we have discussed in this section:

1. Be very familiar with codes of ethics in professional group associations.
2. Be preventive and identify and react to typical dilemmas before leading groups.
3. Discuss ethical issues and your reactions with colleagues who have many years of group work experience.
4. Provide written ethical guidelines to group members in advance and discuss them in the first meeting.
5. Consult expert opinions immediately when difficult decisions have to be made.
6. Periodically seek supervision by experts.
7. Be assertive of your support of ethical behavior in group work.

Confidentiality in groups

In Chapter 5 we discussed the ethical, legal, and professional aspects of confidentiality in the practice of counseling and psychotherapy. We come back to this issue because there are special implications of confidentiality in group situations. Some key questions that need to be raised are:

- Is confidentiality a prerequisite for the development of the trust needed for productive work to occur in a group?
- Are confidences that are divulged in group therapy protected under the laws of privileged communication?
- What are the ethical responsibilities of group leaders with respect to safeguarding the confidentiality of the disclosures made in groups?

Does the legal concept of privileged communication apply to group work? Meyer and Smith (1977) indicate that in almost *no* jurisdiction in the United States may psychotherapists guarantee their group-therapy clients that their communications are privileged. Even in jurisdictions that grant a client/therapist privilege, there is no certainty that this privilege applies to *group* therapy. Meyer and Smith suggest that new or remedial legislation at the state and national levels is needed. They also make the point that the silence of the therapist is not adequate, since the silence of the group members must also be assured. A possible approach mentioned is allowing civil suits by group members against other members who disclose information about group-therapy discussions.

Bindrim (1977) describes a $50,000 judgment awarded in his favor by a California Superior Court. A member of one of his groups wrote a book about the experience, and, even though the names of the therapist and all the participants had been changed, the jury determined that the main character was identifiable as Bindrim and that the writer had presented a distorted picture of what occurred in the therapy session.

Bindrim also describes the procedures he uses to safeguard confidentiality. He asks all the participants in his groups to sign a contract in which they agree not to discuss or write about what transpired in the sessions or to talk about who was present. In addition, with the knowledge of the participants, he keeps tape recordings of all the group sessions. Like Meyer and Smith, Bindrim believes that further legislation is obviously needed. It is his position that participants in therapy groups conducted by licensed professionals should have the right to civil action whether the statements made about them are libelous or not. Further, they should not have to prove that they are identifiable by other persons or that they have suffered actual financial damage. According to Bindrim, legislation is sorely needed that will extend to therapy groups the same right of privileged communication that now exists for individual therapy.

Pinney (1983) observes that group therapists are ethically and legally bound to keep confidential the material of group sessions. Those who do not are legally liable, for they can be sued for a breach of confidence.

In his article *Confidentiality in Group Counseling*, Plotkin (1978) raises these critical questions: Are the members of a group under the same ethical and legal obligation as the group leader not to disclose the identities of other members or the content of what was shared in the group? If there is any obligation, how can it be enforced? Plotkin contends that most texts in group counseling are silent on these issues and that the professional and legal literature is unclear and unhelpful. He states that the maintenance of confidentiality by group members has not been recognized as an ethical problem either for the members or the group leader. Plotkin also observes that there are no judicial decisions, and little legal commentary, concerning breaches of confidentiality or invasion of privacy as a result of group experiences. For legal reasons alone, then, it's important for therapists to raise the issue of confidentiality in their groups. As Plotkin indicates, it is possible that therapists who fail to advise their groups about confidentiality obligations may eventually be sued for professional negligence.

With regard to the ethics of confidentiality in group work, we agree with Plotkin that confidentiality is the "ethical cornerstone" of the client/therapist relationship and that the same assurance of confidentiality must be extended to all the participants in a group situation. Plotkin believes that a persuasive argument can be made that, since group members are a "necessary and customary" part of the therapist's procedures and treatment approach, they have the same obligation as the therapist to maintain the confidential character of their group. In any event, as Plotkin maintains, these problems should be given serious professional attention before clients are injured or the integrity of group therapy is compromised. We like Plotkin's suggestions to group leaders:

> Group leaders are well advised to rethink the contracts they enter into with their clients. These contracts should specify in writing, at a minimum, the therapist's duty to maintain the confidentiality of the relationship and should include those situations in which the law or ethics may require the therapist to reveal certain confidences. They should also spell out the client's obligation to maintain the confidentiality of any group session in which he or she participates [p. 14].

How to encourage confidentiality

Although most writers on ethical issues in group work make the point that confidentiality cannot be guaranteed, most of them also talk about the importance of teaching the members ways to avoid breaking confidences. Davis and Meara (1982) make the point that group confidentiality is difficult to enforce. Since group members cannot assume that anything they say or hear in the group will remain confidential, they should be able to make an informed choice about how much to reveal to the group. According to Davis and Meara, members should know about the difficulties in enforcing confidentiality, and leaders must spend time on this issue beyond merely discussing the topic at the initial sessions. They draw the following conclusion: "There are many reasons members break confidentiality and the leader cannot prevent all violations. If confidentiality becomes a norm for a cohesive group, there is a greater likelihood that members' secrets will remain in the group; however, there still are no guarantees" (p. 153).

It is our position that leaders need to periodically reaffirm to group members the importance of not discussing with others what occurs in the group. In our own groups we talk with each prospective member about the necessity of confidentiality in establishing the trust and cohesion required if participants are to risk revealing themselves in significant ways. We discuss this point during the screening interviews, again during the pre-group or initial group meetings, at times during the course of a group when it seems appropriate, and again at the termination of the group. Since the three of us have done many intensive residential groups in which as many as 16 participants live together for an entire week, we have been concerned about maintaining the confidential character of the group. It has been our experience that most people in our groups do not maliciously attempt to hurt others by talking with people outside the group about specific members. However, it's tempting for members to share the nature of their experience with other people, and in so doing they sometimes make inappropriate disclosures. This is particularly true of participants in intensive, time-extended (marathon) groups, who are likely to be asked many questions when they return home about what it was like. Because of this tendency to want to share with outsiders, we repeatedly caution participants in any type of group about how easily and unintentionally the confidentiality of the group can be broken.

If you were to lead any type of group, which of the following measures might you take to ensure confidentiality? Check any of the following statements that apply:

___ I'd repeatedly mention the importance of confidentiality.

___ I'd require group members to sign a statement saying that they would maintain the confidential character of the group.

___ I'd let members know that they would be asked to leave the group if they violated confidentiality.

___ I'd have a written document on hand describing the dimensions of confidentiality that all the members could refer to.

___ With the permission and knowledge of the members, I'd tape-record all the sessions.

___ I'd say very little about confidentiality and leave it up to the group members to decide how they would deal with the issue.

Other:

_____

_____

_____

_____

Exceptions to confidentiality

The APGA (1981) cautions counselors that they must set a norm of confidentiality regarding all group participants' disclosures. But the APGA does make exceptions. "When the client's condition indicates that there is clear and imminent danger to the client or others, the counselor must take reasonable personal action or inform responsible authorities. Consultation with other professionals must be used where possible."

In basic agreement with the APGA position is the APA's ethical standard of the obligation of psychologists to respect the confidentiality of clients. The APA (1981a) qualifies this position with:

> They reveal information to others only with the consent of the person or the person's legal representative, except in those unusual circumstances in which not to do so would result in clear danger to the person or to others. Where appropriate, psychologists inform their clients of the legal limits of confidentiality.

About halfway into the life span of a group, around the seventh week, a male member expresses his rage toward his ex-wife. He gives indications that he has plans for inflicting grave harm on her and her boyfriend as a means of righting the wrong done to him. The group leader treats this as a symptom of repressed anger and has the member act out his fantasies in a group, on the assumption that this will defuse his anger. The leader fails to notice that the member is still agitated when the session is over. He assumes that this release of anger has made the man safe. The group leader did not tell members during the first group session of a therapist's obligation to inform potential victims, and at no time during this group session does the leader tell this angry member of the legal "duty to warn" in such cases.

- The member in fact does not harm his ex-wife and the boyfriend. Does this make the leader's behavior ethical and legal?
- If you were the leader in this case, what guidelines would you use to determine whether the member would be likely to act out his violent fantasies?
- If you had a similar situation occur in a group you were leading, how might you proceed?

The use of tapes

In the *Ethical Guidelines for Group Leaders* (ASGW, 1980) there are two principles related to the issue of confidentiality: (1) "Group leaders shall protect members by defining clearly what confidentiality means, why it is important, and the difficulties involved in enforcement." (2) "Group leaders shall inform members about recording of sessions and how tapes will be used." The use of videotapes and audio tapes of group sessions adds another dimension to the matter of confidentiality. Members have the right to know of any recordings that might occur and what use will be made of the tapes, and their written permission should be secured before any recording of a session. Consider the issues involved in this case:

A student leader who is under supervision tape-records the sessions with the permission of the members, but she fails to tell them who may listen to the tapes. This leader does not tell the members that not only will her supervisor listen to the tape but so will her fellow trainees, who are meeting in a group-supervision class each week. The following week one of the trainees meets a member of the group, whom she knows, and says "I like what I heard you say on the tape at one of your group sessions."

Making tapes for supervision purposes is an acceptable practice, both for training leaders and for giving feedback to members. We think that it is essential that no recording be made without the knowledge and consent of the members of the group. Further, they should also be told why the session is being recorded, who will be listening to the tapes, how the tapes will be used, and whether the tapes will be erased or stored. If the tapes will be used for research purposes or will be critiqued by a supervisor or other students in a group-supervision session, then the members have a right to be informed.

How might the situation in the case above have been handled differently? The leader could have told her group that she would be listening to the tape after the session and that later her supervisor and fellow students would also hear portions of the tape. She could have clearly mentioned the purposes of the group-supervision session and then opened the group to a discussion of any reservations or reactions concerning the practice of taping. As another preventive step to ward off possible problems such as the one in this case, the group leader could have named the trainees in her supervision group. Then she could have asked if anyone in her group knew any trainee and, if so, if this would cause any problems.

The key point is that taping broadens the base of confidentiality and requires more precautions. Members have a right to know of any possible uses of the tapes and should be asked for permission for any such use. It would be a good practice to ask for this permission in writing. Another good practice is to begin each recording with a statement to the effect that what follows is confidential material.

Uses and abuses of group techniques

Group techniques can be used to facilitate the movement of a group and as catalysts to deepen and intensify certain feelings. We think it's important for leaders to use only those techniques that they have experienced personally and to have a clear rationale for using each technique. This is an area in which theory can be a useful guide for practice.

Techniques can also be abused or used in unethical ways. Some of the ways in which leaders can use techniques unprofessionally are:

- springing any and all kinds of techniques on groups without knowing their potential impact
- using techniques merely as gimmicks
- using techniques to serve their own hidden agendas or to enhance their power
- using techniques whose sole purpose is to create an explosive atmosphere
- using techniques to pressure members or in other ways rob them of dignity or the respect of others

There are various views on the values and limitations of techniques and exercises in group work. In our own work, we have gradually come to agree in part with the position of Carl Rogers (1970). Rogers avoids using planned procedures, because he believes that group members have the resources within themselves to eventually find their own direction without structured exercises imposed on them by the group leader. Rogers writes that, on those occasions when he *has* resorted to using techniques to get groups moving, they have rarely worked. He admits that the reason planned techniques fail for him is because of his lack of faith in their usefulness. On the other hand, according to Rogers, nothing is a gimmick if it occurs with real spontaneity. Thus, he sees a wide range of exercises such as role playing, psychodrama, and body contact as being useful when they are appropriate—that is, when they grow out of natural occurrences within the group and when they are expressions of what people are feeling at the time.

Like Rogers, we value techniques when they are appropriate ways of intensifying the experience of group participants. When we began leading groups together, we experimented with a variety of planned exercises that were designed to stimulate interactions and to elicit certain intense feelings. In fact, we were tempted to judge the effectiveness of these groups by the intensity of the feelings that were stirred up and expressed. We discovered, however, that significant learning and change occurred among people who did not have cathartic experiences. We also discovered that cathartic experiences *in and of themselves* did not seem sufficient to produce long-term changes. We therefore began to resist initiating many planned exercises designed to bring out certain feelings or to make things happen in the group. Still, we remain willing to invent techniques or to draw upon techniques we've borrowed from others when these procedures seem appropriate to what a participant is experiencing and when we think they will help a person work through some conflict. This kind of appropriateness has become our guideline for using techniques effectively. Of course, each group leader will need to develop his or her own guidelines for determining whether and when to use techniques.

Therapist competence.   The ASGW's (1980) basic principle is that "group leaders shall not attempt any technique unless thoroughly trained in its use or under supervision by an expert familiar with the intervention." How can leaders determine whether they have the competence to use a certain technique? Although some leaders who have received training in the use of a technique may hesitate to use it (out of fear of making a mistake), other overly confident leaders without training may not have any reservations about trying out new techniques. It is a good policy for leaders to have a clear rationale for any technique they use. Further, it is useful if leaders have experienced these techniques as members of a group.

The case of an inexperienced leader.   An inexperienced group leader has recently graduated from a master's-degree program in counseling. As a part of his job as a community mental-health counselor, he organizes a weekly two-hour group. He realizes that his training in group approaches is limited, so he decides to attend a weekend workshop on body therapy. He does some intensive personal work himself at the workshop, and he comes away impressed with the power of what he has witnessed. He is eager to meet his group on Tuesday evening so that he can try out some of these body-oriented techniques designed to "open the feelings." (He has not been trained in these techniques in graduate school, nor is he receiving any direct supervision in the group that he is leading.)

At the next session of the group, a member says "I feel choked up with pain and anger, and I don't know how to deal with my feelings." The leader intervenes by having the member lie down, while he pushes on the client's abdomen and encourages her to scream, kick, shout, and release all the feelings that she's been keeping locked up inside of her. The client becomes pale and her breathing becomes shallow and fast. She describes tingling sensations in her arms, a numbness, and a tight mouth, and she says that she is scared and cannot breathe. The leader encourages her to stay with it and get out all those pent-up feelings that are choking her up. At the same time, others in the group seem frightened, and some are angry with the leader for pushing the client.

- Do you think that most leaders would be competent to use body-oriented techniques after one weekend workshop?
- Was this leader's behavior inappropriate, unethical, or both? If the leader had had a qualified supervisor at the session, would your answer be different?
- How can a conscientious group leader determine when he or she is "thoroughly trained" in the use of a technique?
- Do you agree with the ASGW guideline that group leaders should not use *any* technique without being "thoroughly trained"? Why or why not?

Unfinished business.   Another major issue pertaining to the use of group techniques relates to providing immediate help for any group member who shows extreme distress at the end of a group session, especially if techniques were used to elicit intense emotions. Although some "unfinished business" promotes growth, there is an ethical issue in the use of a technique that incites strong emotional reactions if the client is abandoned at the end of a session because time has run out. Leaders must take care to allow enough time to deal adequately with the reactions that were stimulated in a session. Techniques should not be introduced in a session when there is not enough time to work through the feelings that might result or in a setting where there is no privacy or where the physical setup is such that it would be physically harmful to employ certain techniques.

Our position on the ethical use of techniques is that group leaders must learn about their potential effects. One way for leaders to learn is by taking part in group therapy themselves. By being group members and experiencing a range of techniques, they can come to appreciate the appropriate use of techniques for the client's needs, not for the enhancement of the therapist's ego. In our training workshops for group leaders we encourage spontaneity and inventiveness in the use of techniques, but we also stress the importance of striking a balance between creativity and lack of caution.

In our opinion, the reputation of group work has suffered because of irresponsible practitioners, mostly those who use techniques as gimmicks without the backing of a clear rationale. We believe that, if the group leader has a sound academic background, has had extensive supervised group experience, has experienced his or her own therapy or some type of personal-growth experience, and has a basic respect for clients, he or she is not likely to abuse techniques (Corey, Corey, Callanan, & Russell, 1982a).

Issues concerning termination and reentry

The final phase of a group and the departure to the outside world are among the most important stages of the group experience. This is true for therapy groups as well as for encounter groups, and it is true for groups that meet on an ongoing basis as well as for concentrated group experiences such as marathon or residential groups. The final stage of a group provides an opportunity for members to clarify the meaning of their experience, to consolidate the gains they've made, and to make decisions about the kinds of new behavior they want to carry away from the group and apply to their everyday lives. We see the following professional issues involved in the termination of a group:

- What responsibilities do group leaders have for assisting participants to develop a conceptual framework that will make sense of, integrate, and consolidate what they've learned in their group?
- To what degree is it the leader's responsibility to ensure that members aren't stuck with unnecessary psychological turmoil at the end of the group?
- How can group leaders help participants translate what they've learned as a result of the group into their daily lives? Should leaders assume that this translation will occur automatically, or must they prepare members for maximizing their learning?
- What are some ways of minimizing postgroup depression?

A common criticism of groups is that people are often stuck with feelings of depression, resentment, and anger after a group ends, without any means of dealing with and resolving these feelings. However, our contention that group members should not be left with unnecessary psychological turmoil does *not* mean that we think they should be comfortable and free of conflict when they leave. On the contrary, we're convinced that a certain amount of anxiety due to unfinished business can be a stimulus for continued growth. It is the leader's task to recognize when anxiety is counterproductive.

Group leaders have other tasks to perform when a group ends. They can minimize postgroup depression by pointing out that members often experience a sense of loss and depression after a group ends. Further, they need to prepare members for dealing with those they are intimate with. The group should be reminded that others in their lives may not have changed as they have and may not be ready for their changes. We routinely caution people in our groups to give people on the outside a chance to get used to their changes. Before the group ends, we do much role playing to give members an opportunity to practice responding to others   different ways. They have the advantage of receiving feedback from the rest of the group on how they come across. We also announce to our groups our availability for some individual sessions at no extra fee after the conclusion of a group, should members feel the need for such consultation. Finally, we spend time talking about where they can continue their personal work. Many group participants become aware of areas in their lives that they want to explore in more depth in individual sessions. Others may want to pursue specific types of groups or workshops. For this reason, we mention specific referral resources where participants can continue working on making the changes they've begun.

As a stage in the life of the group, termination has its own meaning and significance. Yalom (1975) observes that therapy groups tend to avoid the difficult work of terminating by ignoring or denying their concerns. Yalom sees it as the therapist's responsibility to keep group members focused on the reality and meaning of the ending of their group. He describes the termination of a group as a real experience of loss and suggests that therapists can assist members to deal with this reality by disclosing their own feelings about separating.

> The therapist, no less than the patients, will miss the group. For him, too, it has been a place of anguish, conflict, fear, and also of great beauty; some of life's truest and most poignant moments occur in the small and yet limitless microcosm of the therapy group [p. 374].

Issues related to follow-up and evaluation

What kind of follow-up should be provided after the termination of any group? What professional obligation does the group leader have to systematically evaluate the outcomes of a group? How can leaders assist members to evaluate the effectiveness of their group experience?

Gazda and Mack (1982) point out that a major criticism of the way in which leaders handle the termination of groups concerns the sudden ending of weekend encounter groups without any provisions for follow-up. According to Gazda and Mack, group leaders are responsible for the following services:

- planning a follow-up session for short-term groups
- becoming acquainted with professionals to whom they can refer group participants when they cannot continue a professional involvement themselves
- informing participants of referral sources where they can obtain the assistance they might need

Follow-up services are suggested by the ASGW (1980) in the following guideline: "Group leaders shall provide between-session consultation to group members and follow-up after termination of the group, as needed or requested." We support this guideline, for we think it is a good practice for leaders to provide between-session intervention in cases where this is justified. Further, we agree that follow-up procedures are especially important for marathon groups or residential groups that meet for a few days to a week and then disband. Follow-up can be done in a number of ways. Both short-term (one-month) and long-term (three months to a year) follow-up group sessions can be invaluable accountability measures. Since the members know that they will come together to evaluate their progress toward their stated goals, they are frequently more willing to work actively at making changes. Participants can develop contracts at the final sessions that involve action between the termination and the follow-up session (or sessions). These sessions are valuable not only because they offer the leader an opportunity to evaluate the effectiveness of the group but also because they provide members with the opportunity to gain a more realistic assessment of the impact the group had upon them. If a meeting of the entire group is impractical, one-to-one sessions can be scheduled with each member of the group or as many members as can be contacted. In this postgroup interview the participants can discuss what the group meant to them in retrospect. In addition, this private session provides an ideal opportunity to discuss referral resources, should they be indicated. As another alternative (or in conjunction with the group follow-up and the private interview), questionnaires can be sent to members at some point after the termination of a group as a method of evaluating a group experience (see Corey & Corey, 1982, pp. 180–182; Corey, Corey, Callanan, & Russell, 1982b, pp. 154–157).

In the week-long groups the three of us lead together, we have made it a practice to schedule a follow-up session around three months after the group ends. These sessions have been most valuable both for the group members and for ourselves. Through these sessions we get a more realistic picture than we would otherwise have of the impact of the group on the members' everyday lives; the postsessions enable us to see whether members have actually applied what they learned in the group. For their part, members can share what their reentry was like for them and discuss any problems they're having in implementing what they learned in the group in their transactions with others. They have a chance to express and work through any after-thoughts or feelings left over from the group experience, and they can report on the degree to which they have fulfilled their contracts since they left the group. They also have a chance to receive additional feedback and reinforcement from the other members. Even for groups that meet on a weekly basis, we think it's wise to set a time for a group follow-up session to discuss the experience and put it in perspective.

On the question of evaluating the results of a group, we admit that we find it difficult to objectively assess outcomes. Generally, we've relied on subjective measures; for example, after our groups terminate, we ask the members to write reaction papers in which they evaluate what the experience meant for them. We do think it's important to teach members how to recognize the ongoing changes they're making that are partially the result of what they learned in the group. Members have a tendency to discount what they actually did in a group, and they may not be aware of the subtle changes they continue to make after the group ends. We think it's our responsibility to teach them how to evaluate the nature and degree of their changes.

Some other ethical guidelines for group work

In this section we list some other ethical guidelines as developed by the ASGW (1980) and briefly comment on these issues.

Experimentation and research

"Group leaders shall provide prospective clients with specific information about any specialized or experimental activities in which they may be expected to participate" (ASGW, 1980). Group members should be informed of any research involving the group, and their consent should be obtained in writing (Gazda & Mack, 1982). If leaders intend to write journal articles or books, then it is essential that they take measures to adequately safeguard the confidentiality of the material explored in the group. The same care should be taken to disguise identities if the leaders talk with colleagues about the progress of their groups. For those who conduct group work in institutions, such as community mental-health clinics and schools, they will probably face the issue of preparing written reports for the institution. The members have a right to know what kinds of information will appear in an institutional report.

Videotape techniques.   In writing on ethical problems of group psychotherapy, Rosenbaum (1982a) observes that there is an increasing trend toward using videotape recordings and one-way screens in training and research. Patients often give "informed consent" to such procedures out of their anxiety and their need to please the therapist. Rosenbaum asks whether it is ethical to exploit this need of the client. He also cites a study in which the researcher did not make any mention of the ethics of the procedures involved. Rosenbaum writes that "it would appear fair to patients to inform them of the research that is part of the psychotherapy process" (p. 253).

Milton Berger (1982) emphasizes that therapists who want to use video with clients in individual, couple, family, or group psychotherapy must seek training in this specialized technique. Berger makes a strong case that great care needs to be taken in playing back sessions to clients, for they might not be psychologically ready to see what transpired and to integrate these events. He discusses the powerful impact of confronting one's videotaped image and the importance of preparing clients. Berger gives an example of nonethical use of video playback that he observed in a psychiatric center. A dance therapist videotaped a session with an acutely psychotic patient and then arranged to have the tape played back to the patient. When the patient saw herself on videotape, she became extremely agitated and ran into the corridor in great distress. The dance therapist had no prior training or experience in the use of video replay self-confrontation techniques with patients.

Issues in research.   In writing on the ethical implications of research in group work, R. W. Brown (1982) mentions the protection of human rights as a critical factor. Some of these rights are the right of participants to privacy and confidentiality; the right to terminate participation at any time without being subject to implicit sanctions; and the right to informed consent and deception-free therapy.

In a broader context Brown discusses the ethical issue of evaluating the effectiveness of various approaches and programs for group workers. He maintains that innovative programs in group work need to be documented by clear and compelling data that have been soundly and ethically collected. "Such program effectiveness data are needed by decision makers to robustly substantiate the productive impact of group work. Those programs that fail to be evaluated positively must be viewed with skepticism" (p. 171). Brown advocates full disclosure of the results of research studies and sees a professional responsibility to present the results of evaluation studies in journals and at conventions. Being an ethical and professional group practitioner involves making an effort to evaluate the effectiveness of groups and thus to increase accountability.

Goal development

"Group leaders shall make every effort to assist clients in developing their personal goals" (ASGW, 1980). How group leaders deal with the matter of goals is a function of their theoretical stance on group work. Although some groups are highly structured around specific goals, others seem to function without any explicit statement of goals. Some group leaders insist on behavioral contracts as a way of organizing a group. They expect members to develop specific and clear contracts that include a statement of what the member is willing to change. Other group leaders are opposed to a contract approach, because they think that it is too limiting and imposes too much structure on the members. They also maintain that what members initially present during early sessions is not their significant problem. Also, there are leaders who have no specific goals for a particular group and genuinely want the group to develop its own direction. They have faith in the group to move in a positive and constructive way without directive intervention on their part. Thus, they help members clarify their own goals, but they do not impose goals. The key issue is: Is it ethical to conduct a group in the absence of clearly stated goals?

Imposition of values

"Group leaders shall refrain from imposing their own agendas, needs, and values on group members" (ASGW, 1980). The critical word in this guideline is *imposing*. We think that the leader's function is to challenge members to find their own values, not to impose his or her values upon the members. We don't think that leaders always need to express their personal views on value-laden situations during a session, yet at times it may be critical to do so. We are particularly inclined to tell members about our values in cases where there is a conflict, rather than blandly giving our acceptance or pretending that no difference of opinion exists. Expressed values are less likely to interfere with the process in a group than values that are concealed, and they usually allow us to work more effectively with members. In some cases it might be in order to refer clients to someone else, because the conflict inhibits the leader's objectivity. The crux of the ethical concern here is that group leaders are behaving unethically when they use their groups as a forum for "advancing" their personal agendas or when they seek to meet their own needs at the expense of the welfare of the members. Ethical practice requires that leaders assist the participants in clarifying and defining their own values.

Utilization of group resources

"Group leaders shall insure to the extent that it is reasonably possible that each member has the opportunity to utilize group resources and interact within the group by minimizing barriers such as rambling and monopolizing time" (ASGW, 1980). It is the leader's responsibility to help members use the resources within the group to an optimal degree. At times, certain members may display problematic behaviors (such as monopolizing time, engaging in storytelling, asking many questions and making interpretations for others, chronically jumping in and giving advice or reassurance when it is not appropriate, and so forth). The group leader does not have to take full responsibility for these interventions with difficult members, for the group, too, has a share of the responsibility. However, it is the leader's task to make certain interventions so that some members do not sap the energy of the group and make it difficult for others to do productive work or to meet their needs.

Individual treatment

"Group leaders shall make every reasonable effort to treat each member individually and equally" (ASGW, 1980). Leaders sometimes burden themselves with the unrealistic expectation that they should be absolutely impartial at all times to all members. They may think that they should like each member to the same degree, give each member equal time, and be equally interested in each. If they do not feel this universal caring, some leaders develop guilt feelings.

What seems most important in reference to this guideline is that leaders do not cling to initial impressions of a member and that they do keep themselves open to changing their reactions. Although it is true that some members may present themselves in ways that make it difficult for them to be liked or interesting, a leader who hopes to have a therapeutic effect on these members will be willing to look at each of them as a unique person and will give each an equal chance of getting attention and fair treatment in the group setting.

Kottler (1983) asserts that most group leaders engage in subtle forms of unethical behavior, one of which is having definite preferences and at times treating people in preferential ways. Although we might attempt to hide our biases, they are bound to come out in a group. Some clients are given less time than others and are simply not treated equally. Kottler makes the following generalization, which surely deserves some thought:

> Inevitably, we all act unethically because we are all imperfect beings, inconsistent, hypocritical. We muddle in the dark doing our best to be genuinely helpful but knowing that we can't possibly please everyone all the time. This confession can only be admitted by pragmatic group leaders who need no longer to prove their competence [p. 294].

Personal relationships

"Group leaders shall abstain from inappropriate personal relationships with members throughout the duration of the group and any subsequent professional involvement" (ASGW, 1980). What criteria can a group leader use to determine the degree of appropriateness of personal and social relationships with group members? A key question that leaders need to ask of themselves is whether the social relationship is interfering with the therapeutic relationship. The crux of the matter is to avoid abusing one's power and misusing one's professional role to make personal or social contacts. Although what constitutes "inappropriate personal relationships" is not always clear, trying to determine it does demand honesty in examining one's own motivations and needs.

In the process of being honest about one's motivations, a group leader needs to keep in mind that there is a tendency on the part of some members to glorify the group leader and, in doing so, to lessen their own power. Ethical group leaders do not take advantage of this tendency, nor do they exploit group members in the service of their ego needs.

You are working with an ongoing group for a period of several months. The members have occasional parties, and they inform you that these informal gatherings have drawn them closer together. However, they feel a separation from you, because they see you only in a professional role as their "group leader." They tell you that they miss you at these social events and invite you to attend these parties once in a while. They tell you that your presence would increase the cohesion of their group, for they would all feel as if they were working together. In short, they clearly express their desire for more personal contact with you, as they want to get to know you in a more informal situation outside of the professional role that you've established with them.

- How would you respond to the invitation?
- How would your willingness or unwillingness to accept be a function of your theory of group leadership? How would you explain your decision to them?
- If you accepted the invitation, what might be some of the potential results, both positive and negative?
- If you refused, how willing would you be to deal with this issue at the subsequent group meeting?
- How might you explore the possible demand to make yourself known to them on their terms and their motivations for wanting you to attend their party?
- How might this be a different situation in a group in which a member said: "You know everything about us; we know nothing of you. Why don't you tell us something personal about yourself?"

Promoting autonomy of members

"Group leaders shall help promote independence of members from the group in the most efficient period of time" (ASGW, 1980). Ultimately, the goal of group participation is to assist members to make their own decisions and to function as autonomous people. However, some group leaders actually promote the dependence of their members. Some of the reasons for this practice are the need to be needed; the need to depend on their work as a confirmation of their worth; and the need to make money. Whatever the reason or reasons for keeping group members dependent, group leaders need to continually look at their practices to determine whether they are fostering the growth of their clients or are encouraging their members to rely upon them for direction.

Case vignette.   A group leader is conducting an ongoing group with no termination date in sight. Whenever a member wants to quit, he or she is reminded that there is more in-depth work to be done. The leader maintains that dependence on the leader is an expected part of the process of group therapy, which itself is a long and arduous process. Personality change is not necessarily accomplished in 12 months of therapy, this leader contends. She sees nothing wrong in having people come to the group for long periods of time. She gives the analogy of the person with diabetes who needs to take insulin for life. She assumes that there are always issues to be worked through and that eventually the members will be able to overcome their dependency if they are willing to work through the feelings of transference they have toward the group leader and perhaps toward other members.

Commentary.   It is our view that the leader's assumptions about group process should be stated at the outset. These assumptions include the duration of therapy, especially in the case of this leader, whose bias is toward long-term therapy. The psychoanalytic orientation justifies the development of transference and promotes dependency upon the leader for a time. However, the members have a right to know what they are getting themselves involved in before they commit themselves to such an intensive group.

Alcohol and drugs

"Group leaders shall not condone the use of alcohol or drugs directly prior to or during group sessions" (ASGW, 1980). Although many group leaders agree that using alcohol or drugs before or during group sessions is not productive and do not condone such practices, they may have some difficulty in dealing with members who come to a session under the influence. It is possible that leaders may not take a stand out of the fear of being seen as authoritarian. Or they may simply decide to tolerate members who come to sessions under the influence of drugs or alcohol because they feel powerless to change the situation. It is important that group leaders be prepared to give a rationale for any "no-drugs-or-alcohol" rule, rather than simply laying it down as an edict. Members might be testing the limits of the leader by coming to a session somewhat inebriated or stoned. If leaders give in to the pressure and do not challenge this testing, they are likely to lose the respect of the members. The setting of realistic limits by leaders, including the prohibition of coming to sessions under the influence of drugs or alcohol, can be one way to gain the respect that is necessary to conduct an effective group.

Questions for review and reflection

The following questions can help clarify how you see your role as a professional and your responsibilities as a group practitioner. Think carefully, and answer these questions sincerely.

- Do you have an effective method for screening potential group members? Can you confidently differentiate between those who are suitable for a group and those who are not?
- Do you adequately prepare people for group membership? Do you routinely inform prospective participants of their rights and obligations, of the goals of the group, of the procedures and techniques you intend to use, of the expectations you have, of the possible psychological risks involved in group participation, and of any other factors that might affect the prospective members in deciding whether to become involved in the group?
- Do you stress the importance of confidentiality before members enter the group, at appropriate times during the group process, and on termination of the group? Do you take adequate steps to increase the probability that members will maintain confidences?
- Are you alert to symptoms of psychological debilitation in group members, indicating that they should not continue in the group? Are you available for individual consultations? Do you have referral resources?
- Do you have a rationale for the group exercises, techniques and procedures you employ?

- Do you help participants apply what they learn in the group to their everyday lives?
- Do you arrange follow-up group sessions to determine the impact the group experience had on the members? Do you hold individual interviews after the group ends to discuss and evaluate what the experience meant privately to each member?
- Do you have procedures for improving your groups? How do you get feedback, and what do you do with it? What research and evaluation methods do you use to assess the processes and outcomes of the groups you lead?
- What do you do to enhance your skills as a leader? Do you attend ongoing training programs? Do you get adequate supervision and consultation from other professionals when you need them? If you work with a co-leader, do you take the time to exchange ideas?
- How often do you think about the ethical and professional issues of group leadership that have been raised or implied here? What are you doing to clarify your position on specific moral issues that emerge in your groups?

Chapter summary

Along with the impetus for group approaches to counseling and therapy comes a need for ethical and professional guidelines for those who lead groups. In this chapter we have focused on what we consider to be some of the most important issues in group work, and we have encouraged you to take your own position on these issues.

There are many types of groups, and there are many possible uses of groups in various settings. Our attempt has been to select the issues that are related to most types of groups. Some of these questions are: How does a leader's theoretical view of groups influence the way that a group is structured? What are some key elements in recruiting, screening, selecting, and preparing group members? What ethical, professional, legal, and practical issues concerning confidentiality are involved in any type of group? To what degree should participants be prepared for a group before the group begins? What are some ethical issues in the selection and training of group leaders? In what ways can group techniques be used or abused? What responsibility do group leaders have in terms of follow-up and evaluation? With respect to these and other issues, we have stressed the importance of formulating your own guidelines for ethical practice in leading groups.

Activities, exercises, and ideas for thought and discussion

1. In your own class, you can experience the initial session of a group. Two students can volunteer to be co-leaders, and approximately ten other students can become group members. Assume that the group is a personal-growth group that will meet for a predetermined number of weeks. The co-leaders' job is to orient and prepare the members by describing the group's purpose, by giving an overview of group-process concepts, and by talking about ground rules for effective group participation. If time allows, members can express any fears and expectations they have about being involved in

the group, and they can also raise questions they would like to explore. This exercise is designed to give you practice in dealing with concerns that both group leaders and members often have at the beginning of a group.

2. This classroom exercise can be done in subgroups. One person develops a proposal for a group and presents this proposal to the people in the subgroup. The proposal should spell out the goals of the group, the rationale for doing the group, the people the group is intended for, the guidelines for participation, the screening and selection methods, the techniques that may be used, and the way the outcomes of the group will be evaluated. The members can give feedback and also ask questions about the proposal.

3. This exercise is designed to give you practice in conducting screening interviews for potential group members. One person volunteers to conduct interviews, and another student can role-play a potential group member. Allow about ten minutes for the interview. Afterwards, the prospective client can talk about what it was like to be interviewed, and the group leader can share his or her experience. This exercise can be done with the entire class watching, in small groups, or in dyads.

4. Suppose you're expected as part of your job to lead a group composed of people who are *required* to be part of the group and who really don't want to be there. How will the nature of the group affect your approach? What might you do differently with this group, compared to a group of people who requested the experience? This is a good situation to role-play in class, with several students role-playing the reluctant members while others practice dealing with them.

5. Assume that you're a group leader. A member comes to you to say that another member is gossiping about details that have been divulged in the group. The person who tells you this is quite upset over the disclosure of confidences. How will you deal with this situation? You can role-play this kind of case in small groups to demonstrate how you'd deal with the matter.

6. You're leading a counseling group with high school students on their campus. One day a member comes to the group obviously under the influence of drugs. He is incoherent and disruptive. How do you deal with him? What might you say or do? Discuss how you would deal with this situation in class, or demonstrate how you might respond by having a fellow student role-play the part of the adolescent.

7. Again, assume that you're leading a high school counseling group. An angry father who gave written permission for his son's participation comes to your office and demands to know what's going on in your group. He is convinced that his son's participation in the group is an invasion of family privacy. As a group leader, how would you deal with this angry father? To make the situation more real and interesting, someone in class can role-play the father.

8. Often group leaders neglect to pay sufficient attention to what happens to the participants when they leave a group. Assume that you're leading a group and that the group will soon end. What are some things you will do or say to increase the chances that the participants will apply what they've learned to their daily lives?

9. The issue of selecting a co-leader for a group is an important one, for not all matches of co-leaders are productive. For this exercise, form dyads and negotiate with your partner to determine whether the two of you would be effective if you were to lead a group together. You might discuss matters such as potential power struggles, competitiveness, compatibility of views and philosophy, your differing styles and how they might complement or interfere with each other, and other issues that you think would have a bearing on your ability to work together well as a team.

10. In small groups, explore your ideas about what you consider to be unethical behavior in group settings. Try to come up with specific behaviors and practices that you think are unethical. If time permits, discuss how you might deal with unethical behavior on the part of a co-leader or members of the group.

11. You become aware that certain members of your group are using one person in the group as a scapegoat. There is a tendency to gang up on this member and to dump feelings on the person. How will you deal with this situation?

12. What are your ideas about the kind of training you would like to see group leaders receive before they lead groups? Assume that you're asked to design a training program for group leaders. What will the key features of your program be? In small groups, discuss the designs you and your fellow students formulate. Then the class can reconvene to share and compare results.

13. Form a panel in class to explore the topic of the uses and abuses of group techniques. The panel can look at specific ways in which group techniques can be used to enhance learning, as well as ways in which they can be misused.

14. What are some ethical issues pertaining to involuntary groups? Do you think that there are special issues applying to mandatory groups that would not apply to groups composed of voluntary members?

15. Review the excerpts from *Ethical Guidelines for Group Leaders* (ASGW, 1980) that are listed in this chapter. Which of these guidelines do you consider to be most important? Are there any guidelines with which you do not agree? We suggest that you form small groups in your class to discuss specific guidelines that stimulate the greatest controversy.

Suggested readings

Corey, G., & Corey, M. S. *Groups: Process and practice* (2nd ed.). Monterey, Calif.: Brooks/ Cole, 1982. Part One of this new edition has been reorganized and now emphasizes the key tasks of group members and leaders during each stage of the group process. There is also a chapter on ethical and professional issues for group leaders. Part Two describes working with specific populations, such as groups for children, adolescents, adults, and the elderly. The focus is on practical experiences in group counseling, and there are exercises and activities throughout.

The International Journal of Group Psychotherapy. This official quarterly of the American Group Psychotherapy Association is another excellent resource for group practitioners. The articles deal primarily with the practice of group therapy in a variety of settings. For information about subscribing, write the American Group Psychotherapy Association, 1995 Broadway, New York, New York 10023.

The Journal for Specialists in Group Work. Published four times a year by the Association for Specialists in Group Work, a division of the American Personnel and Guidance Association, this is an excellent journal for students and practitioners who wish to keep current in the field of group work. Articles discuss innovations and ideas and their practical applications in groups, group-counseling research, and special topics of interest to group leaders. Students who join the ASGW will receive the journal. Information about joining is available from the Association for Specialists in Group Work, 2 Skyline Place, Suite 400, 5203 Leesburg Pike, Falls Church, Virginia 22041.

Kottler, J. A. *Pragmatic group leadership.* Monterey, Calif.: Brooks/Cole, 1983. This readable and informative text describes useful traditional concepts and practical subjects such as risk-taking strategies, creative metaphors, uses of humor, co-leadership, and common unethical situations. Kottler discusses significant dimensions of group leadership and specific techniques and strategies for the pragmatic group leader, explaining how the consequent behavior of individuals in the group can change.

Special issue: Ethical issues in group work. *The Journal for Specialists in Group Work,* 1982, 7(3). The ASGW ethical guidelines for group leaders that were cited in this chapter are listed in this special issue. Other articles on the ethics of group work include ethical considerations in using group techniques, confidentiality in groups, ethics and the experts, issues in evaluating group work, and the unethical behaviors we are all guilty of and try to conceal.

Yalom, I. D. *The theory and practice of group psychotherapy* (2nd ed.). New York: Basic Books, 1975. This is an excellent, well-written, and comprehensive text on the conceptual bases and clinical practices of group therapy. Yalom provides guidelines for handling most of the technical problems encountered in organizing and leading therapy groups. There are detailed discussions of such topics as the curative factors in groups, the tasks and roles of the group therapist, problem patients in groups, and the training of group therapists.

The Counselor in the Community and in the System

Pre-chapter self-inventory

Directions: For each statement, indicate the response that most closely identifies your beliefs and attitudes. Use the following code:

5 = I *strongly agree* with this statement.
4 = I *agree*, in most respects, with this statement.
3 = I am *undecided* in my opinion about this statement.
2 = I *disagree*, in most respects, with this statement.
1 = I *strongly disagree* with this statement.

_____ 1. In general, it's important to include members of the client's environment in his or her treatment.

_____ 2. Counselors ought to take an active role in dealing with the social and political conditions that are related to human suffering.

_____ 3. Mental-health experts should devote more of their energies to prevention of emotional and behavioral disorders, rather than treatment.

_____ 4. With increasing attention being paid to the community mental-health approach, the role of the professional must be expanded to include a variety of indirect services to clients as well as direct clinical services.

_____ 5. The community mental-health emphasis on the wider community makes more sense than the earlier focus on individual problems.

_____ 6. The use of paraprofessionals is a valuable and effective way of dealing with the shortage of professional help.

_____ 7. Paraprofessionals who receive adequate training and close supervision are capable of providing most of the direct services that professionals now provide.

_____ 8. Current therapeutic strategies and approaches are adequate and appropriate for working with various minority groups.

We wish to thank Jerry Wright, Ph.D., and Myron Orleans, Ph.D., both at California State University at Fullerton, who read this chapter and provided useful comments.

——— 9. To practice ethically with a minority group, the counselor must possess specific knowledge and information about the group.

——— 10. In working with minority groups in the community, counselors must be skilled in out-of-office strategies such as outreach, consulting, and working as an agent for change. They must view some counseling problems as residing outside of the minority clients themselves.

——— 11. I generally don't like to challenge the people I work for.

——— 12. It's possible to work within the framework of a system and still do the things I'm convinced are most important to do.

——— 13. When I think of working in some agency or institution, I feel a sense of powerlessness about initiating any real change in that organization.

——— 14. It's important to continually ask myself "What makes me think I have the right to counsel anybody?"

——— 15. I see myself as basically cooperative in working with colleagues.

——— 16. I frequently have good ideas and proposals, and I see myself as willing to do the work necessary to translate these plans into actual programs.

——— 17. If I'm honest with myself, I can see that I might have a tendency to blame external sources for a failure on my part to do more professionally.

——— 18. I see myself as a fighter in a system, in the sense that I'll work to change things I don't approve of.

——— 19. Although I might be unable to bring about drastic changes in an institution or system, I do feel confident that I can make changes within the boundaries of my own position.

——— 20. I can see that I might fall into complacency and rarely question what I'm doing or how I could do my work more effectively.

——— 21. Counselors who no longer raise questions or struggle with ethical concerns have stopped growing professionally.

——— 22. It would be unethical to accept a position with an agency whose central aims I disagreed with philosophically.

——— 23. Ethical concerns are not simply answered once and for all; to become an ethical practitioner, I must be willing to continually raise questions about what I'm doing.

——— 24. As a counselor, I'm part of a system, and I have a responsibility to work toward changing those aspects of the system that I think need changing.

——— 25. I feel a personal need for meaningful contact with colleagues so that I don't become excessively narrow in my thinking.

Introduction

Working with people who come to them for counseling is only one way in which professionals can use their skills to promote mental and emotional health. It can be easy to neglect the fact that the aspirations and difficulties of clients intertwine with those of many other people in their lives and, ultimately, with those of the community at large. Many people would argue that professional helpers can foster real and lasting changes only if they have an impact on this social setting of people's lives.

Part of this chapter is concerned with the community mental-health movement, which originated in the mid-1960s in the United States. According to Iscoe (1982), this movement resulted in part from a recognition that mental hospitals had departed radically from their original functions of asylum and treatment. This approach to mental health also grew out of a conviction that individual and group psychotherapy were not appropriate in developing and applying a model based upon health and prevention. Iscoe observes that the community mental-health thrust arose as a strong protest against orthodox clinical methods, which aimed at curing disorders but lacked proper attention to their prevention. Thus, the goal of the community perspective to mental health was to apply the knowledge of behavioral science to improving the functioning of people in their environments and to preventing serious emotional dysfunction.

Taking a community approach to mental health involves abandoning the view that the role of practitioners is to sit back and wait for people to come to them for help. A broader conception of the practitioner's role might include the following:

- using informal groups in cross-cultural counseling
- developing social-support networks
- being aware of cross-cultural issues in counseling and being willing to modify traditional therapeutic practices to meet the needs of diverse ethnic and cultural groups
- developing abilities that will lead to one's being better able to reach minority groups in the community
- actively reaching out to potential clients
- initiating programs aimed at preventing problems rather than merely treating them
- drawing upon and improving the skills of paraprofessionals and laypeople to meet the many different needs of clients
- educating consumers about existing resources
- developing strategies to effectively deal with problems such as drug and alcohol abuse, child abuse, violence, and sexual abuse
- attempting to restructure society in such a way that power and control are redistributed so that the "disenfranchised" are helped to develop and use their combined strengths (Goldenberg, 1983)
- consulting with a variety of social agencies about programs in gerontology, welfare, child care, and rehabilitation and helping community workers apply psychological knowledge in their work
- evaluating human-services programs by designing research to assess agencies' intervention efforts
- functioning as a liaison with community agencies so that services can be best delivered to those who need help

In this chapter we explore these possibilities in the context of the counselor's responsibility to the community. We'll begin by looking at the community mental-health movement, an approach that emphasizes the social setting of the counselor's work. Then we'll focus on an issue of particular importance to the community mental-health worker—namely, how the system affects the counselor.

In addition to their degrees, training, and professional competencies, counselors working in the community must also have the ability to deal with the rules and regulations of agencies. Such counselors typically have little say in the formulation of agency policies. As opposed to private practice, where practitioners deliver their services directly to their clientele, practitioners working in agency settings must mediate not only with clients but also with the system. The following are some examples of the organizations we are talking about:

- a city or county mental-health agency
- a free clinic
- a church counseling agency
- a school system, including a college counseling center
- a state mental hospital
- a community halfway house

One of the reasons that these various systems put an added strain on the counselor is that the providers of their funding may require monumental amounts of paperwork to justify their continued existence. Another source of strain is counselors' relations with the power structure of the institution. The people who administer the agency or institution may have long forgotten the practicalities involved in providing direct services to a range of clients. On the other hand, practitioners who deal with clients directly may have little appreciation for the struggles of administrators who must fight for the continued funding of their programs. Thus, if there is inadequate communication, as there often is, tension is inevitable.

Many professionals struggle with the issue of how to work within a system while retaining their dignity, vitality, and convictions. Although working in any organization can be frustrating, we've observed a tendency on the part of some counselors to put the blame too readily on institutions when their efforts to help others don't succeed. Although bureaucratic obstacles can certainly make it difficult to implement sound ideas, we assume that it's possible to learn ways of working within an institution with dignity and self-respect. Consequently, we emphasize the need for honest self-examination in determining the degree to which the "system" is actually hindering you as you try to put your ideas into practice.

As counselors, we each need to determine how much responsibility we have for the outcomes of our projects. We also need to decide what our styles for working within a system will be and how we can be most effective. Some counselors who are dissatisfied with the system decide to subvert it in as many ways as they can. Others conform to institutional policies for fear of losing their positions. Some counselors find ways of making compromises between institutional demands and their personal requirements; others find it impossible to retain their personal and professional dignity and still work within an institutional framework. It will be up to you to find your own answers to questions such as these:

- What stance will I take in dealing with the system?
- How can I meet the requirements of an institution and at the same time do what I most believe in?
- In what ways can I work to change the system?

- At what point does the price of attempting to work within an organized structure become too high? Can I work within an institutional framework and still retain my dignity?

The community mental-health orientation

Many therapists see a need for new approaches to augment the process of individual therapy. Since only a relatively small number of people can be effectively reached by traditional therapeutic approaches, these practitioners support the idea of innovative measures that will make maximum use of the professional resources available. The need for diverse and readily accessible treatment programs has been a key factor in the development of the community mental-health orientation.

Whitlock (1978) describes the "revolution" in community psychology:

> The present revolution involves psychological counselors and the new professionals who are trained in crisis intervention, as well as other mental-health and allied professions. This revolution consists of discarding the constraints of the doctor-patient medical model and abandoning the idea that an emotional problem is a private matter between doctor and patient or between counselor and client. Personality disturbance is no longer a matter of private misery. Both the disturbance itself and the therapeutic efforts to alleviate it are related to the network of relationships in which an individual is involved [p. 9].

Goldenberg (1983) observes that the community mental-health orientation represents a shift in focus from the individual to the wider community. Rather than replacing individual approaches, the community orientation aims at supplementing psychotherapy by stressing the prevention of disorders and by offering a wide variety of programs for education and rehabilitation. This emphasis involves a change in the roles and functions of counselors and therapists, who must be equipped to offer a broader range of psychological services for a larger segment of the population.

Goldenberg describes the community mental-health orientation as more an attitude than a body of knowledge. The approach emphasizes the development of innovative treatment methods and a commitment to reach those segments of the population that are often neglected. Further, community mental health has a "seeking orientation," in that there is a process of actively reaching out of traditional settings (clinics, private offices) to render services to specific populations within the community. Goldenberg writes:

> Ideally, the long-standing imbalance in the delivery of mental-health services, benefiting White middle- or upper-class neurotic adults almost exclusively, would be partly corrected by such an approach, by providing inexpensive, easily available mental-health services through clinics distributed throughout the community, particularly in large urban centers [p. 344].

Another major factor in the development of the community mental-health viewpoint is the notion that people can be helped more effectively in their communities than in mental institutions. Returning psychiatric patients to the community, it is hoped, will lead to their reintegration into society. On this issue, Bloom (1983) commented "The community-mental-health movement grew out of the conviction that mental hospitals were as much a cause of chronic mental disorder as a cure and that hospitalization was probably as often harmful as it was helpful" (p. 42).

It is our view that an increasing number of people are unable to cope with the demands of their environment and are receptive to the idea of professional assistance. As more people overcome the stigma attached to seeking psychological help, the demand for community services increases. In our opinion, psychotherapy can no longer afford to be tailor-made for the upper-middle-class group. People who are unable to afford the services of professionals in private practice are entitled to adequate treatment programs. Consequently, community clinics are needed to serve people of all ages and backgrounds and with all types and degrees of problems.

The need for community mental-health programs is compounded by such problems of our contemporary society as poverty, absent parents, broken homes, child abuse, unemployment, tension and stress, alienation, addictions to drugs and alcohol, delinquency, and neglect of the elderly. These are merely a few of the areas that pose a formidable challenge for the community approach to the prevention and treatment of human problems.

Operation outreach

We are supportive of the "outreach" approach to mental health, which demands that counselors have the courage to leave their offices and work with people in various community settings. We think the following statement by Drum and Figler (1977) merits careful reflection:

> Many helpers realized that services could not only be successfully provided outside of the office, but that in many cases they were more successful because they were now able to "draw the unreachables" and focus on some of the needs unique to people who lived in a certain part of the community or shared a common life-style [p. 25].

Outreach strategies are particularly important in reaching ethnic minorities. The complex issues involved in working with minority groups within the framework of the majority community have been well-documented in the literature (Atkinson, Morten, & Sue, 1979; Levine & Padilla, 1980; Pedersen, Draguns, Lonner, & Trimble, 1981; Sue, D.W., 1981). If practitioners hope to reach and effectively deal with a cultural group different from their own, they must acquire a broad understanding of the group and begin to study the subtle factors that affect the interpersonal interactions within it. In other words, they need to understand how various behaviors and attitudes are viewed within specific populations (Blustein, 1982). Blustein makes a case for using indigenous support systems and informal groups to reach minority groups. Examples include peer groups in schools, self-help groups, church groups, street-corner groups, and work groups. People in minority groups often turn to members of their own and extended families, to friends, and to community members when they need help, rather than turning to professional practitioners within the dominant culture. As Blustein notes, these indigenous networks of support are particularly important to groups living in a culture that is inconsistent with their own. Thus, he encourages counselors to create interventions that are a natural extension of the informal helping networks of their client population.

> Informal groups can also be a valuable asset in outreach attempts. As counselors increase their understanding of the dynamics of informal groups, they may be able to set up systems to attract resistant clients. A possible implementation of this approach might

occur in an institutional setting where intracultural support is a primary influence; in this case, a counselor can use informal leaders of a group or peer counselors as outreach workers in drawing in the passive or withdrawn client [1982, p. 263].

Brooks (1977a) makes the point that professionals need to think of ways of actively reaching people who otherwise might not take advantage of available resources: "Counselors must leave their pleasant or semipleasant offices, and base their offerings in locations that are more readily accessible for the clientele being served" (p. 365). Thus, mental-health practitioners are asked to imagine themselves doing more outreach work in the territory of their clients. They might function on the steps of a tenement, in a data-processing lab, at a hospital bedside, in a school locker room, in a business setting, or in other places where their clients live, work, and play.

The outreach approach includes developmental and educational efforts aimed at the prevention of unnecessary life problems. Drum and Figler (1977) argue that clients should not have to experience real turmoil before they are willing to ask for the help they need. Rather, the outreach approach focuses on growth and developmental needs and aims at prevention, not just remediation. Preventive outreach entails programs that people can use to anticipate and thus deal more effectively with the hazards of living. Such programs might include psychological education, environmental engineering, education of the community concerning mental health, and consultation in a variety of systems, among others. According to Drum and Figler, counselors who involve themselves in community programs will need to be skillful in planning, managing, persuading, suggesting, politicking, training, advocating, speaking to groups, writing, and organizing people. This shift in the counselor's role truly involves a real challenge!

Characteristics of community mental-health programs

The community mental-health orientation is based upon concepts from fields such as psychology, sociology, social welfare, education, mental hygiene, and public health. The characteristics of the comprehensive mental-health center, as described by Bloom (1983), Dugger (1980), and Goldenberg (1983), include the following:

- Focus is on the interaction a person has with others in the environment and on the impact of social forces on behavior. Emphasis of treatment should be on linking individuals with their communities through the use of new kinds of facilities, such as day-treatment and other outpatient centers.
- Treatment is available to a wide range of people with all types of problems.
- The term *comprehensive* implies a wide range of services, including consultation, direct care, education, and prevention.
- The center's programs should reach people who have previously been unreached, particularly those in the low-income groups.
- A major emphasis should be on the provision of services for children.
- A variety of treatment approaches should be offered, including crisis intervention, groups, therapeutic communities, and family therapy.
- Community control of the centers is important.
- Fees should be charged on an ability-to-pay basis.
- The center should develop a program of in-service education for the staff.

- Roles and leadership should be determined more by competence than by professional identification.
- Training and supervision of paraprofessionals is an important function of the center. Paraprofessionals can frequently assume roles previously limited to professionals.
- Periodic program evaluation is necessary to determine the degree to which the center is meeting the needs of the community.
- In terms of planning, focus is on designing programs to meet the unmet needs of high-risk populations.
- In terms of delivery of services, the strategies are aimed at reaching large numbers of people through the use of brief therapies and crisis intervention.
- Behavior disorders are studied from the vantage point of environmental factors that contribute to these problems, rather than the inner conflicts of individuals.

Services of community mental-health programs. Community mental-health centers provide a new mechanism for organizing and delivering psychological services. Such services are flexible, so that programs can be adapted to the unique needs of a particular group within the community. Goldenberg (1983) mentions that no two centers are exactly alike, because a mental-health center is a program of coordinated services in a community rather than a physical structure. For example, one center might give priority to organizing social-action programs within the community. Another center might focus on providing crisis counseling, family therapy, and other traditional clinical services. However, even though these programs are unique in some ways, they have some common denominators in terms of the scope of services provided. Goldenberg notes that community mental-health centers are required to provide, at a minimum, the following five services:

1. inpatient care: brief hospitalization for diagnosis and treatment, with the aim of rapid discharge
2. outpatient care: rendering direct psychological services in a nonresidential setting on an ongoing basis
3. partial hospitalization: providing flexible part-time care for people in day-treatment centers and encouraging them to return home in the evenings and on weekends
4. emergency care: providing crisis intervention as needed on a 24-hour basis
5. consultation, education, and information: indirect services to community agencies with the goal of prevention

Levels of prevention

A central feature of the community mental-health approach is preventive intervention—that is, reducing unnecessary environmental stresses while building individual, group, and community coping skills. We think that Goldenberg (1983) makes an excellent point when he writes:

> Just as public health workers organize programs to combat the spread of infectious diseases by attacking agents known to cause physical diseases wherever they can be found in the

community, so mental-health workers believe that similar attacks can be made on agents known to cause psychological disturbances within the community [p. 358].

This posture includes actively seeking out vulnerable people who are subjected to heavy environmental stresses and who are considered to be candidates for developing dysfunctional behavior. Also, a preventive orientation involves a commitment to work toward curing the social system of certain ills, such as racism, sexism, and poverty.

Three levels of prevention are generally described. *Primary prevention* is aimed at reducing the incidence of a disorder in a community through counseling and intervention methods employed *before* the disorder is evidenced. For example, people, especially those "at risk," can be taught ways of dealing with stress in their lives. They can learn how to recognize their level of tension through the use of biofeedback devices and can learn to reduce it through relaxation exercises. Meditation is another example of a way to reduce the level of stress. Other activities that are aimed at primary prevention include developmental counseling, personal-growth groups, courses and workshops designed for enhancing skills in living, premarital counseling, parenting groups, child guidance, and other programs for those who are facing major changes in life-style.

Secondary prevention involves treating an existing disorder before it becomes severe and prolonged. Since intervention is more likely to be successful during the beginning stages of a disorder than after it has become ingrained, early detection is important (Goldenberg, 1983). Suicide-prevention centers, for example, are designed to diagnose personality patterns where suicide is likely and to intervene with supportive and reeducative measures.

Tertiary prevention is the maintenance of a maximal level of functioning after a chronic condition becomes evident. Like secondary-prevention programs, tertiary prevention is aimed at reducing the impairment from existing disorders. Some think that tertiary prevention should be the major goal of community mental-health programs. As Aguilera and Messick (1982) indicate, however, a great number of rehabilitation services still take place in institutions, with a minimum of community involvement.

The following example, as described by Conyne (1983), should make more concrete the three types of prevention defined above. Consider a class of entering freshmen at a university, and think about the developmental tasks that are facing them as they leave their home, family, and friends and enter an unfamiliar situation. A *primary* prevention program could consist of providing early information to these freshmen about what they could expect at the university, where needed resources are, and how to make use of the resources. A *secondary* prevention intervention might consist of a coordinated referral and treatment program. For example, a counseling center could develop a program designed to detect potential adjustment problems and a system of referral and counseling for such concerns. A *tertiary* prevention program could involve developing approaches for rehabilitating students who have serious emotional, social, and psychological problems. For example, such a rehabilitation program might combine the university counseling center, appropriate members of the residential housing staff, and those faculty members who are teaching students that require hospitalization. The goal here would be to coordinate efforts so that these students could reenter the university as soon as possible.

Pause a moment now to reflect on ways of implementing preventive efforts. What part might you want to play in developing or implementing preventive measures?

1. Too often the people who seek psychological help are in a state of crisis. What are some ways of reaching these people before their situations become critical? How can people be encouraged to be open to prevention of emotional problems?
2. If you were asked to develop some specific programs aimed at primary prevention of emotional and behavioral disorders, what are some of the features you'd include?

The use of paraprofessionals

The question of how best to deliver psychological services to the people who are most in need of them is a controversial one. It is clear that there are not enough professionally trained people to meet the demand for psychological assistance. Faced with this reality, many people in the mental-health field have concluded that nonprofessionals should be given the training and supervision they need to provide some psychological services that only professionals have previously been allowed to provide. There has therefore been a trend toward the increased use of paraprofessionals in counseling and related fields.

One important reason for the increasing use of paraprofessionals is economic. Service agencies have discovered that paraprofessionals can indeed provide some services as effectively as full professionals, for much lower salaries. However, as Goldenberg (1983) observes, this is not the only advantage to the use of paraprofessionals: "Many paraprofessionals are being trained for new service functions and roles that some psychologists believe they are better able than professionals to fulfill because of their special relationships, as residents, to the communities they serve" (p. 366).

A training model for paraprofessionals as educator consultants is described in *A Symposium on Skill Dissemination for Paraprofessionals* (Danish, D'Augelli, Brock, Conter, & Meyer, 1978). The symposium touched on empirical studies that underscored an important point: many jobs could be done equally well by helpers who were less highly trained than professional specialists. In some cases, paraprofessionals appeared to have greater success than professionals with institutionalized people who were once considered hopeless. Programs aimed at training peer counselors in the mental-health field indicate that informal helpers are becoming a valuable resource for professional practitioners (Blustein, 1982).

Not all mental-health professionals are enthusiastic about the potential of the paraprofessional movement. Some point to the danger that inadequately trained people might do more harm than good; others claim that the poor who need treatment will receive inferior service; still others fear that more and more paraprofessionals will be allowed to practice without the close supervision and intensive training they need. In addition, as Goldenberg (1983) points out, paraprofessionals represent a threat to the economic interests of some professionals. Despite the opposition of some professionals, however, there seems to be little chance that the trend toward the use of paraprofessionals will be reversed. We are in agreement with Goldenberg when he says: "Professionals have a social responsibility to train paraprofessionals. If they fail to carry out this responsibility, the public will turn to individuals with little or no training and the results may in the long run prove to be most unfortunate for all" (p. 370).

Types of nontraditional mental-health workers

Currently, there are three general types of nontraditional mental-health workers.

1. Many community colleges offer two-year programs in the human services. Students in these programs receive specialized training that is aimed at preparing them to work in community mental-health centers, hospitals, and other human-services agencies. In addition, many colleges and universities have established four-year undergraduate programs in human services that stress practical experience, training, and supervision in mental-health work.

2. Lay volunteers from the community are also receiving training and supervision in therapeutic intervention with a wide range of clients. These volunteers work on hot lines, co-lead groups, and engage in other types of supportive activities. Many professionals contend that, although the use of community volunteers is not a cure-all for the problem of the shortage of available personnel, trained volunteers can make a contribution in augmenting the work of professional therapists.

3. The use of former patients is another promising way of meeting the increasing demand for mental-health services. Former addicts play a role through substance-abuse programs in rehabilitating others who are addicted to drugs. Alcoholics Anonymous is well known for its contributions in keeping alcoholics sober through the efforts of people who have learned that they can no longer handle alcohol. In many places, former mental patients are helping others make the transition from state hospitals to their communities. Besides helping to alleviate the shortage of personnel in the mental-health field, these nonprofessionals may actually be more effective in reaching certain people, because they have experienced similar problems and learned to deal with them successfully.

Looking at the community mental-health approach in retrospect, Iscoe (1982) contends that one of its failures is that it has not developed sufficient understanding of the daily lives and values of lower-middle-class groups, nor has it developed interventions and approaches to meet the psychological needs of these people. He adds that many paraprofessionals (drug and alcohol counselors, crisis workers, mental-health workers, and community specialists) have not been traditionally trained and typically work without supervision from professionals. It appears that a large part of the success of community mental-health programs will depend upon these nontraditional workers' receiving the training and supervision they need to develop the skills for effective intervention. Mental-health professionals can be expected to spend less time in providing direct services to clients so that they will have time for teaching and consulting with community workers.

The trend toward the increased use of paraprofessionals means that professionals will have to assume new and expanding roles. Rather than devoting the bulk of their time to direct services, such as one-to-one counseling, they may need to spend considerable time offering in-service workshops for paraprofessionals and volunteer workers. Other activities that could assume priority include educating the public about the nature of mental health, consulting, working as change agents in the community, designing new programs, conducting research, and evaluating existing programs.

Other ways of becoming involved in the community

It is relatively easy for counselors to believe that they can effectively meet the needs of their clients through one-to-one sessions in the office. We have indicated in this chapter, however, that many problems demand a broader approach if real change is to occur. We suggest that you consider the responsibility you may have to teach clients to use the resources available to them in their communities.

What follows is a list of things you might do to link your clients to the community in which they live. Rate each of these activities, using the following code: A = I would do this routinely; B = I would do this occasionally; C = I would do this rarely.

_____ 1. Familiarize myself with available community resources so that I could refer my clients to appropriate sources of further help.

_____ 2. With my clients' permission, contact people who have a direct influence in their lives.

_____ 3. Try to arrange sessions that would involve both a client and the significant people in his or her life so that we could explore ways of changing certain relationships.

_____ 4. As a part of the counseling process, teach my clients how to take advantage of the auxiliary support systems in the community.

_____ 5. Suggest homework assignments or use other techniques to get my clients thinking about ways that they could apply what they learn in the individual sessions to their everyday lives.

_____ 6. Use natural leaders as a part of outreach work in setting up a liaison with professional practitioners and agencies.

_____ 7. Train natural leaders of various cultural groups in peer-counseling skills so that they could work with groups that might resist seeking professional services from an agency.

_____ 8. Connect with informal groups and social networks by becoming a participant/observer in a variety of these groups.

_____ 9. After observing a variety of informal groups to learn about the values and beliefs of a given culture, design outreach programs that are a natural extension of these informal helping networks.

_____ 10. Consider joining some type of informal group of another culture so that I could better understand a different world. (Examples: a church group, a community group, a social group.)

Now think of other options for encouraging your clients to find other ways of meeting their needs besides the traditional approaches of individual and group counseling.

The professional's role in educating the community

Too often counselors wait for clients to come to them in their offices. As a consequence many prospective clients never appear. There are many reasons why people do not make use of available resources: they may not be aware of their existence; they may have misconceptions about the nature and purpose of counseling; they may be reluctant to recognize their problems; or they may harbor the attitude that they should be able to take charge of their lives on their own.

For these reasons, we think that educating the public and thus changing the attitudes of the community toward mental health is a primary responsibility of professionals. Perhaps the most important task in this area is to demystify the notion of mental illness. Unfortunately, many people still cling to archaic notions of mental illness. They may make a clear demarcation between people they perceive as "crazy" and those they perceive as "normal." Some of the misconceptions that are still widespread are these: that, once people suffer from mental illness, they can never be cured; that people with emotional or behavioral disorders are merely deficient in "will power"; and that the mentally ill are always dangerous and should be separated from the community lest they "contaminate" or harm others. Professionals face a real challenge in combating these faulty notions.

Psychotherapy is another area that needs to be demystified. Some of the misconceptions people have of psychotherapy include these: that it is some form of magic; that it is only for people with extreme problems; that therapists provide clients with answers; that therapy is only for weak people; and that people should be able to solve their problems without professional help. These misconceptions often reinforce the resistance people already have toward seeking professional help. Unless professionals actively work on presenting psychotherapy in a way that is intelligible to the community at large, many people who could benefit from professional help may not seek it out.

To illustrate how widespread ignorance concerning available resources can be, one of us regularly asks upper-division classes of students in human services and counseling whether they know where the college counseling center is located. Generally, only about a quarter of the class members know where the center is; even fewer are aware of the kinds of services offered. If this lack of knowledge is common among people who will eventually be involved in community mental health, how much more common must it be among the general public? And if future professionals are not aware of available resources, how can they educate others to use them? Moreover, we've found that these students, who might be expected to be somewhat sophisticated regarding psychological counseling, often have misconceptions about therapy and resist seeking help when they need it for themselves.

Of course, the problem does not originate entirely with students. We've found that many college counselors are unwilling to do much public-relations work. They tend to resist going outside their offices and making themselves known to students through direct contacts. Some of these counselors assume that it's up to the students to take the initiative to find help if they want it. This same attitude is shared by many counselors who work in community agencies. They stay within the agency and do very little to develop a public-relations program that will make the community more aware of existing services and how to utilize them. It is hardly surprising that many people who need psychological help never get it if no one has set up an effective program to educate the public and deal with people's resistance in getting the help they need.

Meeting the needs of diverse ethnic and cultural groups

Germane to the discussion of reaching the maximum number of people in the community is the issue of finding effective ways to provide psychological services that meet the special needs of diverse cultural groups. The development of a cross-cultural counseling perspective is essential for counselors working in the community. This section looks at the knowledge, abilities, and attitudes needed by the culturally skilled counselor.

During the 1960s and 1970s the appropriateness of the services being offered to minority clients was challenged. Traditional therapeutic practices were criticized as irrelevant for and oppressive toward the culturally different. Practitioners were challenged to develop new methods, concepts, programs, and services that are suited to the life experiences of minority clients (Sue, D.W., Bernier, Durran, Feinberg, Pedersen, Smith, & Nuttall, 1982).

Graduate programs are also coming under criticism for inadequate treatment of the mental-health issues of ethnic minorities. Frequently, minority-group issues are dealt with from a White-middle-class perspective.

Wrenn (1983) takes the position that counselors must fight politically and professionally for their continued existence. He calls for a "fighting, risk-taking counselor," who is aware of major social ills and is willing to take an active stance in alleviating some of them. For Wrenn, risk-taking counselors must know the cultural groups with which they work and be sensitive to their pressing problems. He contends that counselors can have a significant impact on the plight of oppressed groups only if they know the minority group's language and family culture. He writes:

> The need is great. The Native Americans have lived for over 300 years in this country within an alien culture. Some of their humanitarian and spiritual values are superior to the savagely competitive and materialistic values of the dominant Anglo culture. Yet we do not know their language; we do not profit from their nature lore and gentleness [p. 326].

According to Wrenn, the largest ethnic minority is the Hispanics, numbering 12 million in 1980. Hispanic school enrollment has risen significantly in New Mexico, Texas, and Arizona. A projection is that by 1990 one-half of the school enrollment in California and one-third of the enrollment in Texas will be Hispanic. Wrenn asserts that few counselors have the attitudes, knowledge, and skills to work effectively with Hispanics. Since the demand for counselors with such abilities will increase, Wrenn poses the question "What greater opportunity than this for counselors who want to risk, to grow, and to live compassionately?" (p. 326).

Characteristics of the culturally skilled counselor

D.W. Sue (1981) has pointed out that cross-cultural counseling implies not only major cultural differences between the counselor and the client but also differences associated with the client's minority status in the United States. Therefore, Sue contends, the counselor is likely to be continually tested by the minority client, and matters of expertness, trustworthiness, and similarity of world view are thus extremely important to consider. He makes a case for burying the assumption that the same therapeutic approaches will be effective with all clients, regardless of their cultural backgrounds. In reviewing studies pertaining to cross-cultural counseling, Sue lists the following key points:

- Minority clients may not be oriented toward traditional verbal therapies.
- Self-disclosure may be incompatible with the cultural values of Asian Americans, Chicanos, and other groups.
- The sociopolitical environment may dictate against self-disclosure.
- The ambiguous nature of counseling may not be compatible with the value systems of certain ethnic and cultural groups.
- Many minority clients may prefer active/directive approaches rather than a person-centered approach to counseling.

Sue (1981) has developed several propositions that are critical in determining the effectiveness of cross-cultural counseling. Two of them are:

- Cross-cultural counseling effectiveness is most likely to be enhanced when the counselor and client share the same world view. World views are frequently correlated with a person's cultural/racial heritage, ethnic identification, and experiences in society. As a result, the credibility and attractiveness of the counselor is likely to be high [p. 104].
- Cross-cultural counseling effectiveness is most likely to be enhanced when the counselor uses counseling modalities and defines goals consistent with the life experiences/cultural values of the client [pp. 106–107].

Sue argues that equal treatment in counseling may be discriminatory treatment. From his perspective, differential approaches are needed that are compatible with the life experiences of the clients.

Sue and his colleagues (1982) recommend that counselor-education programs be redesigned so that students are able to come to grips with the feelings experienced by those from diverse cultures. These issues must be dealt with in more meaningful ways than simply on a cognitive level. For example, students must be aided to appreciate feelings of helplessness and powerlessness, as well as to learn how these factors contribute to low motivation, frustration, hatred, ambivalence, and a general sense of apathy. The authors' recommendation includes focusing on the unique contributions of the various ethnic groups. Attention needs to be given to the value of indigenous help-giving networks. They also suggest that a graduate program in counseling should deal with consciousness-raising knowledge and skills.

With these recommendations in mind, Sue and his associates developed minimal cross-cultural counseling competencies to be incorporated into training programs. The characteristics in the accompanying box are based on an adaptation of their position paper and on other sources (Atkinson et al., 1979; Levine & Padilla, 1980; Pedersen et al., 1981; Sue, D.W., 1981).

The case of John O'Brien.   John O'Brien, who comes from a lower-middle-class neighborhood in an Eastern city, has struggled to get a college degree and finally

Essential Components of Cross-Cultural Counseling

1. *Beliefs and attitudes of culturally skilled counselors*
   - They are aware of their own values, attitudes, and biases and of how they are likely to affect minority clients. As a check on this process, they monitor their functioning through consultation, supervision, and continuing education.
   - They can appreciate diverse cultures, and they feel comfortable with differences that exist between themselves and their clients in terms of race and beliefs.
   - They believe that there can be a unique integration of different value systems that can contribute to both therapist and client growth.
   - If necessary, they are willing to refer a client because of their limitations in cross-cultural counseling.
2. *Knowledge of culturally skilled counselors*
   - They understand the impact of oppression and racist concepts on the mental-health professions and on their personal and professional lives.
   - They are aware of institutional barriers that prevent minorities from making full use of psychological services in the community.
   - They understand how the value assumptions of the major theories of counseling may interact with the values of different cultural groups.
   - They are aware of culture-specific (or indigenous) methods of helping.
   - They possess specific knowledge about the historical background, traditions, and values of the group they are working with.
3. *Skills of culturally skilled counselors*
   - They are able to utilize counseling styles that are congruent with the value systems of different minority groups.
   - They are able to modify and adapt conventional approaches to counseling and psychotherapy in order to accommodate cultural differences.
   - They are able to send and receive both verbal and nonverbal messages accurately and appropriately.
   - They are able to employ institutional intervention skills on behalf of their clients when necessary or appropriate.
   - They are able to make out-of-office interventions when necessary by assuming the role of consultant and agent for change.

We thank Noreen Matsushima, D.S.W., who helped us to revise and refine these guidelines from the various sources.

has attained a master's degree in counseling. He has moved to the West Coast, proud of his accomplishments, yet he considers himself sensitive to his own background and to those who struggle with similar problems. He has been hired to work in a clinic in a neighborhood with a large minority population.

At the clinic, John starts a group for troubled adolescents. His goals for this group are as follows: (1) to instill pride in his group members so that they will see that their present environment is an obstacle to be overcome, not to suffer with; (2) to increase self-esteem in his group members and to challenge them to fight the negativism they may encounter in their home environments; (3) to teach them to minimize their differences in terms of the larger community (for example, he points out how some of their idioms and ways of speaking separate them from the majority and reinforce differences and stereotypes); and (4) to teach them how one can overcome obstacles and achieve a graduate degree with minimal help from one's environment. He tells them, not in an arrogant way, "If I can do it, you can do it too."

John does not work very closely with the other staff members. He views them as being more interested in politics and red tape and as actually giving very little energy to working in the community. He has little to do with the families of the adolescents, because he sees them as being too willing to accept handouts and welfare and not very interested in being self-sufficient and independent. He tells his group members: "What you have at home with your families has obviously not worked for you. What you have in this group is the opportunity to change and to have that change appreciated."

- Do you see John O'Brien as possessing the competencies necessary to qualify as a cross-cultural counselor? Why or why not?
- Does he demonstrate an understanding of the unique needs of this minority group? If so, how?
- What, if any, cultural prejudices does John exhibit in the way he deals with his group members? What prejudices, if any, do his goals for his adolescent group imply?
- What effect might it have had on John's goals if he had become familiar with the environment of his group?
- In what position do you think that John put himself in order to learn something about the culture with which he is working?
- What potential risks has John exposed his group members to after the group is finished?
- What difficulties do you anticipate John might encounter because of his attitude toward his colleagues in the clinic? Do you think he might be open to criticism from the parents? Explain.
- What stereotyping might John be doing in terms of his attitudes toward the parents of his adolescents?
- What reactions do you have to the manner in which John set up group goals?
- If you were a colleague of John's, what trouble might you have with him? If you were a member of John's group, what difficulties might you encounter?
- If you had no major differences with John's goals for his adolescent group, would you go about implementing the project any differently? What might you do differently, and why?

Commentary. John O'Brien is an illustration of a well-intentioned counselor who demonstrates in so many ways an almost complete lack of sensitivity to the particular needs of this minority community. We disagree with his axiom that, simply because he could obtain a graduate degree (against difficult odds), anybody could meet with the same degree of success. John made no attempt to become aware of the unique struggles or values of his clients. An obvious oversight is that he failed to include the adolescents in the development of goals that would guide their group. He stereotyped in a very indirect, but powerful, fashion the parents of his group members. John imposed majority values in terms of language and upward mobility. He set up potential conflict between his members and their families by the way he downplayed and labeled their families' value systems.

The point we wish to make is that, even though this may be an extreme example of a well-intentioned, but nevertheless insensitive, counselor, John's attitude typifies the mentality of many of those who come from the community majority to work with the community minority. The counselor's own struggles to achieve his goals do not necessarily make him competent to deal with another's life situation. The counselor entering the minority community has at least as much to learn as to teach, and if any real work is to be done, it must be accomplished on a cooperative basis.

Working within the system

The tendency to avoid responsibility

We've alluded to the tendency to blame institutions for failing to implement effective programs. So often we hear the "If only it weren't for——" argument, which absolves the speaker of responsibility and diminishes his or her personal power at the same time. Take a moment now to reflect on some typical statements of this kind and apply them to yourself. How likely are you to resort to these statements as a way of deflecting responsibility to external sources? Rate each one, using the following code:

A = I feel this way often, and I can hear myself making this statement frequently.
B = I feel this way at times, and I might be inclined to say this occasionally.
C = I rarely feel this way.
D = I can't see myself using this statement as a way of absolving myself of personal responsibility.

_____ 1. You have to play politics if you want to get your programs through.
_____ 2. I can't do what I really want to do, because my director or supervisor wouldn't allow it.
_____ 3. If the community were more receptive to mental-health programs, my proposals and projects would be far more successful than they are.
_____ 4. I'm not succeeding because my clients aren't motivated.
_____ 5. I can't really say what I think, because I'd lose my job.
_____ 6. The bureaucratic system makes it almost impossible to develop innovative and meaningful programs.
_____ 7. If I were given more time off, I could develop exciting projects; as it is now, all my time is consumed by busywork.
_____ 8. I'm not free to pursue my own interests in my job, because the institution dictates what my interests will be.
_____ 9. The system makes it difficult to engage in the kind of counseling that would produce real change.
_____ 10. My own individuality and professional identity must be subordinate to the policies of the institution if I expect to survive in the system.

What other statements might you make in order to blame the system for the difficulties you encounter as a professional?

_____

_____

_____

_____

The reality of working in the system. Edelwich and Brodsky (1980) identify several "givens of the system." These are real sources of frustration, but they are part of the reality that all concerned must learn to work with:

- The system is not responsive to client needs. It seems that clients are neglected in favor of administrative requirements and the politics of power.
- The system is typically not responsive to the people working in it. Workers are often not given responsibility or consulted about decisions, and they are overlooked in many ways.
- Workers are often not appreciated by their clients. This lack of appreciation occurs most frequently when the clients do not want the help of the worker to begin with. It leads workers to wonder what their purpose is and why they continue in a situation in which they do not seem to be making any significant differences in the lives of their clients.
- There is too much paper work, which distracts workers from what they most want to do.
- Many workers complain that they are not adequately trained for the difficult jobs they are expected to do.

If you accept this description of the "givens of the system," the question is: How can you constructively deal with these real barriers that make your job difficult?

The results of evading personal responsibility. Counselors who put the blame on the "system" when they fail to act in accordance with their beliefs are bound to experience a growing sense of powerlessness. This feeling is sometimes expressed in words such as "I really can't change anything at all! I may as well just do what's expected and play the game." We think that the temptation to submit to this stance of professional impotence constitutes a real ethical concern. It is the kind of attitude that feeds on itself.

Another way of evading personal responsibility is to settle into a comfortable rut. We've seen many counselors who have found a niche in the system and who have learned to survive with a minimum of effort. In order to remain comfortable, they continue to do the same thing over and over for weeks, months, and years. They rarely question the effectiveness of their efforts or give much thought to ways of reaching a greater number of people more effectively. They neither question the system in which they're involved nor develop new projects that would give them a change of pace. Although we appreciate their difficulties, we think that this kind of complacency is just as deadly a form of powerlessness as the defeated feeling of those who decide they can't really change things.

Defeatism and complacency are both attitudes that cheat the *clients* whom counselors are trying to serve. For this reason, we ask you to consider how ethical it is for counselors to give in to these feelings. We believe that counselors have a responsibility to look at their own tendency to become comfortable to the degree that they make the system work for them instead of those it is intended to serve.

Assuming power within the system

If counselors recognize that there are obstacles to overcome in any system, they may be able to acquire a sense of personal power to make significant changes. Our central aim in the rest of this chapter is to encourage you to define a style of working within a system that suits your personality. Although we cannot prescribe a universal method of getting along in an institution, we can present some strategies that we have found helpful and ask you to determine how appropriate these strategies are for you. In addition, we hope that you can think of other ways of preserving your individuality while working as part of a system.

Your first opportunity to assert your individuality is in the job interview. Often people being interviewed for a position confine themselves to answering the questions that are asked of them. However, job interviews can be mutual exchanges in which you can explore the requirements and expectations of a position and assess its suitability for yourself. It's important to recognize that accepting a position with an agency entails agreeing to work within a certain philosophical framework. By asking relevant questions, you begin to assume a stance of power, for you are exploring how much you want a particular job and what price you're willing to pay for it.

Our experience has been that most established organizations resist change but that small and subtle changes can be significant. If you devote most of your energy to trying to change the people who defend the status quo, your positive programs may become a lesser priority. You'll need to decide for yourself how much energy you're willing to expend on dealing with the resistive forces you encounter. If you attempt radical, system-wide changes, you might feel overwhelmed or paralyzed. If you focus instead on making changes within the scope of your position, you'll stand a better chance of extending your influence. For instance, a social worker whose goal is to correct fundamental inequities in the social-welfare system may soon feel discouraged and helpless. By directing his attention to ways of dealing more humanely with the people he comes into contact with, he may experience a sense of power and accomplishment as he makes less grandiose, but still significant, changes. To take another example, a school counselor may give up in exasperation if she directs most of her efforts to changing her colleagues' view of their role. If she concentrates instead on defining her own role so that she can do the kind of counseling she believes in, she may succeed in making a smaller but still meaningful change.

Another way to assume power to make changes is to learn the reasons for the policies of the organization you work for. Perhaps there are good reasons why certain policies have been established, even if they seem to restrict your freedom in your job.

On the other hand, if a policy is not in the best interest of the clients, you can begin to challenge the assumptions on which the policy is based. You can suggest alternative policies, and you can find out whether others on the staff share your view. A sound understanding of the aims of the agency can strengthen your assessment of existing policies and make your suggestions more acceptable to those in charge. Consulting with colleagues can put you in a better position to suggest changes than operating in isolation.

Often people remain powerless because they don't make the effort to order their priorities and work on them systematically. We've found it helpful to determine what we *most* wanted to accomplish in a given position. We recognize that we don't have total autonomy while we're associated with a system, and so at times we're willing to negotiate and compromise. By ordering our priorities, we can decide which compromises we can make without sacrificing our integrity and which positions cannot be compromised in good faith. Knowing what we consider to be most important puts us in a much better position to ask for what we want. In conjunction with this, good communication with directors and supervisors is essential. We try to keep the people to whom we report informed about how we're using our time and why. Many times a proposal fails to be accepted, not because it's unsound, but because the person responsible for approving it has not been adequately informed of its rationale or design. Since supervisors or directors are the ones who will be on the receiving end of any complaints, they may thwart a plan or block certain activities because they haven't been convinced of their merit.

One essential element in learning how to work effectively within a system is to realize that you're a vital part of that system, that "the institution" is not something that can be divorced from you. This implies that your relationships with other staff members are a central part of the system. Ignoring this reality and attempting to function in isolation will probably diminish your effectiveness. More positively, colleagues can be nourishing and supportive, and your interactions with them can give you a fresh perspective on some of your activities. Furthermore, genuine relationships with your coworkers can be a way of gaining power to make changes with the help of others who share your cause.

Unfortunately, although interactions with others in the institution can be energizing, they can also be debilitating. Instead of developing support groups within an agency, some people develop cliques, harbor unspoken hostility, and generally refuse to confront the conflicts or frictions that keep the staff divided. Often there are hidden agendas at staff meetings, and only superficial matters are discussed while real issues are kept secret. We want to underscore the importance of finding ays to establish working relationships that enrich your professional life instead of draining your energy. It's strange that counselors, who are supposed to be experts in helping others to establish nourishing relationships, often complain that they miss meaningful contacts with their colleagues. If you feel isolated, you can decide to take the initiative and arrange for fruitful interactions with others on the staff. For example, you could suggest a regular meeting time during which several colleagues could share their concerns and experiences. In addition, we think that working with others on special projects is a good way to renew yourself and a source of inspiration that can suggest new directions.

Some questions for reflection and discussion. In thinking about the questions we pose below, clarify your position on ways that you could increase your chances of assuming power within the system.

- What are some questions that you would want to raise in a job interview?
- What experiences have you had in encountering resistance to ideas that you wanted to put into practice?
- What would you do if the organization you worked for instituted some policies to which you were strongly opposed?
- What would you do if you strongly believed that some fundamental changes needed to be made in your institution but your colleagues disagreed?
- What would you do if your supervisor continually blocked most of your activities, despite your efforts to keep him or her informed of the reasons for them?
- How would you attempt to make contact with other colleagues if members of your staff seemed to work largely in isolation from one another?
- If your staff seemed to be divided by jealousies, hostilities, or unspoken conflicts, what do you think you would do about the situation?
- What do you consider to be the ethics involved in staying with a job after you've done everything you can to bring about change, but to no avail? (Consider that you are being asked to do things that are against your basic philosophy.)

Two case examples

The following two case examples are designed to illustrate some of the issues we've discussed in this chapter. Try to imagine yourself in each of these situations, and ask yourself how you would deal with them.

Sarah works in a community mental-health clinic, and most of her time is devoted to dealing with immediate crisis situations. The more she works with people in crises, the more she is convinced that the focus of her work should be on preventive programs designed to educate the public. Sarah comes to believe strongly that there would be far fewer clients in a state of crisis if people were effectively contacted and motivated to participate in growth-oriented educational programs. She develops detailed, logical, and convincing proposals for programs she would like to implement in the community, but they are consistently rejected by the director of her center on the ground that the primary purpose of the clinic is to intervene in crisis situations. Because the clinic is partially funded by the government for the expressed purpose of crisis intervention, the director feels uneasy about approving any program that doesn't relate directly to this objective.

If you were in Sarah's place, what do you think you would do? Which of the following courses of action would you be likely to take?

___ I'd probably do what the director expected and complain that the bureaucratic structure inhibited the implementation of imaginative programs.

___ Rather than take the director's no as a final answer, I'd try to work toward a compromise. I'd do what was expected of me while finding some way to make room for my special project. I'd work with the director until I convinced her to permit me to launch my program in some form.

___ If I couldn't do what I deemed important, I'd look for another job.

___ I'd get several other staff members together in order to pool our resources and look for ways to implement our program as a group.

Other:

_____

_____

_____

George is a social worker in a school district. He is expected to devote most of his time to checking on children who are habitually truant and to doing social-welfare work with dependent families. Although he knew his job description before he accepted the position, George now feels that his talents could be put to better use if he were allowed to do intensive counseling with families as units. Referral sources in the area are meager, and the families he works with cannot afford private treatment. Although George has the training to do the type of family counseling that he thinks is sorely needed, his school administrator makes it clear that any kind of therapy is outside the province of the school's responsibility. George is told to confine himself to tracking down truant children, doing legal work, and processing forms.

If you were in George's position, what do you think you would do?

___ I'd present a written plan to the local school board, showing that family counseling is needed and that public facilities are inadequate to meet this need.

___ I'd go ahead and do the family counseling without telling my administrator.

___ I wouldn't make waves, because I wouldn't want to lose my job.

Other:

_____

_____

_____

Professional burn-out

Nature and scope of the problem

The phenomenon of professional burn-out has been the topic of numerous publications and is receiving increasing attention at professional conferences and conventions. What is professional burn-out? What are its causes? How are professionals who work in institutions particularly susceptible to losing their vitality? What can be done to prevent burn-out? How can counselors stay alive personally and professionally?

Burn-out is a state of physical, emotional, and mental exhaustion. It is the result of repeated emotional pressures, often associated with intense involvement with people over long periods of time. Professionals who are burned out are characterized by physical depletion and by feelings of hopelessness and helplessness. They tend to develop negative attitudes toward themselves, others, work, and life (Pines & Aronson, with Kafry, 1981).

Professionals who limit their work to one type of activity are particularly suscepible to burn-out. Many therapists who work alone in their own practice report that they often get caught in the routine of seeing client after client. They find it increasingly difficult to be fully present for their clients, especially when it seems that they are dealing with the same kind of problem over and over again. After a while they may well find themselves responding almost mechanically. It may be very difficult to deal with this kind of situation if one's livelihood seems to depend on maintaining one's own private practice. Nevertheless, therapists can question whether sticking to one kind of practice is worth the price they're paying in deadness and lack of excitement.

The problem of burn-out is particularly critical for people working in systems in the human-services field. With the emphasis in this kind of work on giving to others, there is often not enough focus on giving to oneself. According to Pines and her associates (1981), people who perform human services share three basic characteristics: (1) they are involved in emotionally taxing work; (2) they tend to be sensitive to others' problems and have a desire to relieve suffering; and (3) they often see their work as a calling to be givers to those who feel powerless and helpless. Unfortunately, some who enter the helping professions have high hopes that are never realized. If they meet with constant frustration, see almost no positive change in their clients, and encounter obstacles to meeting their goals of helping others, their hopes may eventually be replaced by the hopelessness and powerlessness that are prime characteristics of many of the clients they see. Farber and Heifetz (1982) note the following basic characteristics associated with burned-out professionals: they lose concern for clients; they come to treat the people they work with in ways that are detached and even dehumanizing; they become cynical toward their clients and often blame them for creating their own problems; and they experience a wide range of symptoms, such as emotional frustration and psychosomatic ailments.

Causes of burn-out

Farber and Heifetz found that therapists had the following perceptions of the causes of burn-out:

- The majority of the therapists interviewed (54.7%) felt that burn-out resulted from the nonreciprocated attentiveness, giving, and responsibility demanded by the therapeutic relationship.
- Other causes of burn-out included overwork (22.2%), the general difficulty in dealing with patient problems (20.4%), discouragement as a function of tedious work tasks (18.5%), the tendency of therapeutic work to bring out their own personal conflicts (13%), the general passivity of counseling work (13%), and the isolation involved in therapy (11.1%).
- If they experienced stresses at home, therapists felt that they were particularly prone to transient feelings of burn-out. Their own family problems lowered their threshold for the demanding work of therapy and impaired their ability to attend effectively to the needs of their clients.
- Most practitioners (73.7%) cited "lack of therapeutic success" as the single most stressful aspect of their work.

The Farber and Heifetz study suggests that therapists expect their work to be difficult and even stressful, but that they also expect that their efforts will be appreciated and that they will see positive results. Constant giving without the reinforcement of some measure of success apparently produces burn-out. Although working conditions, such as excessive work load and organizational politics, can create an added burden of stress for therapists who work in institutions, many therapists can accept these realities of working in the system. When therapeutic work is only minimally successful and often frustrating, however, the chances of experiencing disillusionment are particularly high. For example, therapists who work primarily with suicidal, homicidal, depressed, severely regressed, and chronically resistant clients are likely to experience signs of burn-out.

We encourage you now to look at the factors that are most likely to cause burn-out in you. A common denominator in many cases of burn-out is the question of *responsibility*. Counselors may feel responsible for what their clients do or don't do; they may assume total responsibility for the direction of therapy; or they may have extremely high expectations of themselves. How does this apply to you? In what ways could your assumption of an inordinate degree of responsibility contribute to your burn-out?

There are other causes of burn-out besides an excessive sense of responsibility. Consistently working with clients whom you don't like, who are unmotivated and yet demanding, or who don't appreciate or value you can cause burn-out. How would working with such clients affect you? What other factors can you think of that would lead to your burn-out?

Staying alive personally and professionally

Since professional burn-out is an internal phenomenon that becomes obvious to others only in its advanced stages, you should take special care to recognize your own limits. How you approach your tasks and what you get from doing them are more important than how much you're doing. Some people are able to put much more of themselves into a project than others without feeling drained. One person, for example, may feel exhausted after conducting a group-therapy session, whereas another may come out of it energized and excited. One helpful suggestion is to find what Jourard (1971) calls a "check out" place where you can briefly meditate and experiment with different ways of living without pressure from others. Ultimately, whether you experience burn-out depends on how well you monitor your own responses to the stresses of your work and the effects these stresses have on you and on the quality of your counseling.

Ways of preventing burn-out.   Perhaps the most basic way to retain your vitality as a person and as a professional is to realize that you are not a bottomless pit that can give and give without replenishing yourself. Counselors often ignore signs that they are becoming depleted. They may view themselves as having unlimited capacities to give, and at the same time they may not pay attention to taking care of their own needs for nurturing, recognition, and support. However, simply recognizing that they cannot be universal givers without getting something in return is not enough to keep them alive as people and professionals. What follows are some specific suggestions for preventing burn-out. As you read them, apply them to yourself to see how they might fit for you. Although there are no sure ways to avoid feelings of disillusionment and fatigue at times, there are practices and attitudes that can be learned to reduce the risk of being chronically burned out.

• Learn to set limits with demanding clients; take care to avoid overextending yourself in a system.

• Learn the value of a sense of humor. Some therapists adopt a "heavy" attitude toward life and forget how to laugh. Humor may be one of the best ways to keep matters in perspective.

• Develop a circle of associates and colleagues whom you can trust. Meetings can be used to discuss difficult cases, personal concerns, and ways of surviving with dignity in a system.

• It is a good idea to have activities and interests besides therapy as a way of renewing yourself. These diversions can serve as a temporary escape from the stresses of therapeutic work and can prevent the therapeutic mode from totally dominating your perspective. Also, related activities (such as consulting, teaching, supervising, or working with colleagues) can give you a new perspective on therapeutic work. Of course, hobbies and recreational activities apart from work can be valuable sources of replenishing you personally.

• Keeping in mind your most important professional objectives is helpful. We often get involved in unrewarding tasks and forget to pay attention to our priorities. We can at least learn to ask ourselves: "Is what I am doing now really important? Are there ways I can learn to delegate certain tasks? Do I need to learn to say no more often?"

• Learn the value of expressing negative feelings about your work, rather than keeping all your reactions to yourself. Unfortunately, we may not often hear or read about the fears, failures, and doubts experienced by colleagues.

• Attending some exciting seminars, conferences, and conventions (especially workshops on ways to stay alive as a person and as a professional) can keep you vital.

• Professionals in public agencies and institutions have adopted various ways of lessening the pressures inherent in their environments. Some vary their activities by teaching, supervising and training interns, doing public-relations work in the community, consulting with other colleagues or agencies, or working on their own special projects. Exchanging positions with someone from a different agency is another way of generating new vitality. Counselors from different agencies can trade places with one another for periods varying from a week to several months. This procedure allows counselors to share their special talents with another staff and to work with new people for a time. It can thus benefit both the counselors who make the exchange and the staffs that play host to the visiting counselors.

As a further strategy to prevent burn-out, graduate training programs in therapy should prepare students for the realities they will face when they work in a system. Counselor-education programs should also teach their graduates the skills they must have in order to make appropriate changes within their service-delivery system (Warnath, 1979). Along this same line, Farber and Heifetz (1982) call for graduate training programs that actively prepare students for the inevitable disappointments they will encounter in the course of their training, as well as in the jobs they eventually secure. If students are not given adequate preparation, they may be especially vulnerable to early disenchantment and high rates of burn-out, for they are saddled with unrealistic expectations. Watkins (1983) maintains that counselors have given inadequate attention to burn-out and its consequences. Although he agrees that there are many ways of preventing it, he advocates three specific approaches: (1) undertaking personal therapy as a means of reconstitution, (2) creating free time for self-regeneration, and (3) associating with "healthy souls," especially by making time for family and friends as a way of bolstering and enriching life.

Your personal strategy.   Now think of some ways of preventing burn-out or regaining your vitality. The following is a list of suggestions for dealing with burn-out. Of course, counselors need to find their own way of remaining vital as professionals; our purpose in presenting this list is simply to stimulate you to think of your own ways of preventing or treating burn-out. After you think about each suggestion, rate each one by using the following code: A = this approach would be very meaningful to me; B = this approach would have some value for me; C = this approach would have little value for me.

____ Think of ways to bring variety into my work.
____ Become involved in peer-group meetings where a support system is available.
____ Find other interests besides my work.
____ Attend to my health and take care of my body by exercising and eating well.
____ Take stock of what I'm doing to determine whether it is meaningful or draining.
____ Do some of the things now that I plan to do when I retire.
____ Take time for myself to do some of the things that I enjoy doing.
____ Refuse to get caught in the trap of assuming an inordinate amount of responsibility.
____ Attend a personal-growth group or some type of personal-therapy experience to work on my level of vitality.
____ Travel or seek new experiences.
____ Read stimulating books and do some personal writing.
____ Exchange jobs for a time with a colleague.

_____ Find nourishment with family and friends.

_____ Find a person who will confront and challenge me and who will encourage me to look at what I'm doing.

Now list some other personal solutions to the problem of burn-out.

_____

_____

_____

_____

_____

Chapter summary

The primary thrust of this chapter has been to suggest ways of going beyond the limitations of one-to-one counseling. We've suggested that counselors not only need to get involved in the community but also need to find ways of helping their clients make the transition from individual counseling to their everyday lives. In discussing the community mental-health orientation, we described this approach as an example of *one* way to meet the increasing demand for psychological services. We suggested that it's important to think of ways to educate the community about available resources and to broaden the range of these resources. Too often mental-health professionals have not been creative in devising programs that are addressed to the diverse needs of the community. For this reason we discussed some alternatives to conventional therapy and the new roles implied by these alternatives for professional counselors and therapists.

Many of you who are reading this book may be looking forward to a full-time career in the system. We think it is essential to consider how to make the system work *for* you, rather than *against* you. We have challenged you to think of ways to accept the responsibility of surviving and working effectively in an organization and thus increase your power as a person. Finally, we've asked you to reflect on the major causes of the disillusionment that often accompanies working in the system and to find creative ways to remain vital as a person and as a professional.

Some concluding ideas

In these chapters we've raised some of the ethical and professional issues that you will be most likely to encounter in your counseling practice. Instead of providing answers, we've tried to stimulate you to think about your own guidelines for professional practice and to initiate a process of reflection that you can apply to the many other issues you will face as a counselor.

If there is one fundamental question that can serve to tie together all the issues we've discussed, it is this: Who has the right to counsel another person? This question can be the focal point of your reflection on ethical and professional issues. It can also be the basis of your self-examination each day you meet with clients. You can continue to ask yourself: What makes me think I have a right to counsel others? What do I have to offer the people I'm counseling? Am I doing in my own life what I'm encouraging my clients to do? At times, if you answer these questions honestly, you may be troubled. There may be times when you feel that you have no ethical right to counsel others, perhaps because your own life isn't always the model you would like it to be for your clients. Yet this occasional self-doubt is far less damaging, in our view, than a failure to examine these questions. Complacency will stifle your growth as a counselor; honest self-examination, though more difficult, will make you a more effective helper.

We want to close our discussion by returning to the theme that has guided us throughout this book—namely, that developing a sense of professional and ethical responsibility is a task that is never really finished. There are no final or universal answers to many of the questions we have posed. For ourselves, we hope we never fall into the deadening trap of thinking that we "have it made" and no longer need to reexamine our assumptions and practices. We've found that the kinds of issues raised in this book have demanded periodic reflection and an openness to change. Thus, although we hope you've given careful thought to your own ethical and professional guidelines, we also hope that you'll be willing to rethink your positions as you gain more experience.

So where can you go from here? How can you maintain the process of reflection that you've begun in this course? One excellent way to keep yourself alive intellectually is to develop a reading program. We suggest that you begin by selecting some of the books that we've listed in the References and Reading List. We'd also like to suggest that you re-read this book from time to time. We hope that it has become more than an impersonal textbook and that, by writing your responses in the text, you've made it your own personal manual. It can be most valuable for you to re-read various chapters as you take different courses that deal with the issues we've considered. In addition, periodically reexamining your responses can stimulate your thinking and provide a measure of your professional and intellectual growth. We hope you'll find other ways to make this book meaningful for yourself as you continue your search for your own direction.

Activities, exercises, and ideas for thought and discussion

1. Invite people who are involved in community mental health to speak to your class about the services they provide, the population they serve, and the current problems and trends in community mental health.
2. In small subgroups, explore specific ways of getting involved in your clients' lives beyond the office. What are some ways of becoming involved in the community or using community resources to assist you in working with your clients? After you've explored these issues, the class can reconvene to pool ideas.
3. Wrenn (1983) identifies the following areas as some of the major "emerging faces of counseling":
   • counseling those concerned with midlife vocational and life-style changes
   • counseling the older adult

- counseling men and women on assuming new and expanding sex-role identities
- counseling couples and the family
- counseling in business and industry
- counseling in professional teams from a holistic view
- counseling within cultures
- counseling for creative use of leisure time

How do you see these areas as related to changes in society? How do you see these social changes as having an impact on the role and function of the counselor? What is your reaction to this statement by Wrenn: "As important as it is to help clients think futuristically, to dare to cast their lot with an emerging vocation, it is more important for the counselor, himself or herself, to move with change" (p. 324)?

4. Several students who are interested in the use of paraprofessionals in the human-services field can investigate the issue and present their results in the form of a panel discussion. The discussion can focus on the advantages and disadvantages of the use of paraprofessionals, current trends, and other issues the panel deems important.

5. Assume that you're the director of a mental-health center in your community. Your project is funded by the government, and you're given the freedom to design and implement any type of program you think is appropriate and innovative. What would your program be designed to do? What would some of its innovative features be? What kinds of services would you offer to the community? What kinds of people would be working at the center? This exercise has many possibilities, a few of which include:
   - It can be the basis of a reaction or position paper.
   - It can be explored in class in small groups.
   - It can be the basis for a panel discussion.
   - Members of the class can interview mental-health workers or clinic directors.
   - You can invite the director of a mental-health center to explore this issue with your class.
   - Several students can work on this project as a team and present their findings to the class.

6. Design ways of informing and educating the community about what psychological services are, who they are for, and how people can make maximum use of the resources available to them.

7. An issue you may well face in your practice is how to get through the resistance that people have toward asking for psychological assistance. Ask yourself how you should respond to clients who have questions such as these: "What will people think if they find out that I'm coming for professional help?" "Shouldn't I really be able to solve my problems on my own? Isn't it a sign of weakness that I need others to help me?" "Aren't most people who come to a community clinic really sick?" "Will I really be able to resolve my problems by consulting a mental-health professional?" After you've thought through your own responses, you can share them in dyads or in small groups.

8. For this exercise, begin by working in dyads. One student assumes the role of a person in some type of crisis. The student who will role-play the client should be able to identify in some way with the crisis situation. The other student becomes the crisis counselor and conducts an intake interview that does not exceed 30 minutes. Alternatively, a crisis situation can be presented to the entire class, and several students can show what immediate interventions they would make. An example would be working on a hot line with a teenage caller who is frightened because of a bad trip with LSD. Students who participate as counselors should be given feedback, and alternative intervention techniques should be discussed.

9. Assume that you want to become a change agent in your community and that one of your goals is to deal with social and political factors associated with the problems that people bring to your clinic. What are some things you can imagine doing? This is a good topic for brainstorming in class.

10. Groups of students can visit a private clinic, a day-treatment center, a state hospital, a family-guidance clinic, a free clinic, a comprehensive community mental-health center, and other human-services agencies. The groups can share their observations and reactions in class. This is an excellent way to directly experience the workings of a mental-health facility and to learn about the functioning of other agencies by hearing what other students observed.

11. How aware are you of the resources that exist in your community? Would you know where to refer clients for special help? How aware are you of the support systems that exist in your community? Individually or with other students, investigate a comprehensive community mental-health center in your area. In doing so, find the answers to questions such as these:
    • Where would you send a family who needed help?
    • What facilities are available to treat drug and alcohol abuse?
    • What kinds of crisis intervention are available? What are some common crises that are encountered?
    • Are health and medical services available at the center?
    • What kinds of groups are offered?
    • Is individual counseling available? For whom? At what fee? Long-term? Short-term?
    • Where would you refer a couple seeking marital counseling?
    • Are hot-line services available?
    • What provisions are there for emergency situations?
    • What do people have to do to qualify for help at the center?

12. As a small-group discussion activity, explore the topic of how you see yourself in relation to the educational system of which you are a part. Discuss the implications your style as a learner may have for the style you'll develop when you work for some institution or agency. Some questions for exploration are: How active are you in the process of your own education? What specific things do you do to make your education more meaningful? Are you willing to talk with instructors if you feel that they aren't offering you a valuable course? Are you willing to suggest constructive alternatives if

you're dissatisfied with a class or with your program? Do you often feel powerless as a student and thus assume the stance that there's nothing you can do to really change the things you think most need changing?

After you've had enough time to discuss this issue in small groups, the class can reconvene and compare results. Are there any common characteristics in the learning styles of the class members? How might these characteristics affect the way you work in a system as a professional?

13. With another student, role-play a job interview. One person is the director of a counseling center, and the other is the applicant. After about 10 to 15 minutes, switch roles. Discuss how you felt in each position, and get feedback from your partner after both of you have had a chance to play each role. Some questions the interviewer might ask include:
    - Why are you applying for this job?
    - What are your expectations if you get the position?
    - Since there are many applicants and only a few positions, tell me why we should select you for the job. What do you have to offer that is unique?
    - Could you briefly describe your philosophy of counseling?
    - What do you most hope to accomplish as a counselor, and how would you evaluate whether you were accomplishing your goals?
    - What kinds of clients could you *least* effectively counsel? What kinds of clients would you be *most* effective with?

14. Invite an administrator of a mental-health facility to address your class on ways of working creatively within a system. You can also invite people in nonadministrative positions to talk about how they have dealt with institutional barriers. Have they had to make compromises? Have they given up their identities to remain in their positions? Have they ever found it necessary to quit a certain job in order to keep their identities?

15. Several students can interview a variety of professionals in the mental-health field about the major problems they encounter in their institution. What barriers do they meet when they attempt to implement programs? How do they deal with obstacles or red tape? How does the system affect them? You can divide this task up so that a wide range of professionals and paraprofessionals are interviewed, including some who have been in the same job for a number of years and others who are just beginning. It would be interesting to compare the responses of experienced and inexperienced personnel. The students who do the interviewing can share their impressions and reactions without revealing the identities of the persons interviewed.

16. Look at your life so far. Has there ever been a time—in school, at home, at work—when you have experienced the symptoms that indicate burn-out? Can you determine the events leading up to the situation, the unique aspects of your environment that contributed to it, and the strategies you used to deal with it?

17. What cross-cultural life experiences have you had? Did you learn anything about your potential prejudices? What prejudices, if any, did you feel directed at you? You might bring your experiences to class. Also, we suggest that you interview other students or faculty members who identify themselves as

ethnically or culturally different from you. What might they teach you about differences that you as a counselor would need to take into consideration in order to work more effectively with them?

18. This exercise deals with the fundamental question: Who has a right to counsel anybody? Form small groups of perhaps three people. Take turns briefly stating the personal and professional qualities that give something to offer people. The others give feedback. Afterwards, you explore any self-doubts you have concerning your ethical right to counsel others.

19. Refer to the multiple-choice survey at the end of Chapter 1 on attitudes and beliefs regarding ethical and professional issues. We suggest that you cover your initial answers and retake the inventory now that you've come to the end of the course. Then you can compare your responses to see whether your thinking has changed. In addition, we suggest that you circle the ten questions that are most significant to you or that you're most interested in pursuing further. Bring these to class, and discuss them in small groups. Afterwards a survey can be conducted to get some idea of the issues that were most important to the students in your class.

20. As a way to review this book and the course you are completing, write down a few of the most important things you have learned. You might also write down some of the questions that this book and your course have left unanswered for you. After you've made your two lists, form small groups and exchange ideas with other students. This can be an excellent way to get some sense of the most crucial areas and topics that were explored by your fellow students and a fine way to wrap up the course.

Suggested readings

Aguilera, D., & Messick, J. *Crisis intervention: Theory and methodology* (4th ed.). St. Louis: C. V. Mosby, 1982. This book contains a clear discussion of brief psychotherapies, crisis intervention, and prevention. It covers basic theory and principles for working with a variety of client problems. The authors describe a useful model of intervention that involves specific steps leading to crisis resolution. Many examples of situational and maturational crises are given.

Bloom, B. *Community mental health: A general introduction* (2nd ed.). Monterey, Calif.: Brooks/Cole, 1983. Bloom discusses topics such as preventive programs, mental-health consultation, crisis intervention, and other aspects of the community mental-health movement. This is a useful book for those interested in current practices in the community approach.

Hatcher, C., Brooks B., & Associates. *Innovations in counseling psychology: Developing new roles, settings, techniques.* San Francisco: Jossey-Bass, 1977. The authors look at new roles in which counselors move beyond traditional functions to initiate change and prevent problems. They show how counselors are making use of recent knowledge concerning the effects of environment on behavior. They examine new developments in counseling the elderly, minority-group students, and those with drug-related problems. And they investigate new settings such as community centers and free clinics.

Iscoe, I. Toward a viable community health psychology: Caveats from the experiences of the community mental health movement. *American Psychologist*, 1982, 37(8), 961–965. Opportunities and pitfalls in the development of a health psychology are discussed in this article, with particular reference to the community mental-health movement. The author develops the point that a health psychology should adopt a community perspective rather than an individual one. The preventive aspects of mental health are stressed.

Levine, E. S., & Padilla, A. M. *Crossing cultures in therapy: Pluralistic counseling for the Hispanic.* Monterey, Calif.: Brooks/Cole, 1980. This book begins with a discussion of the relationship between culture and personality and then proceeds to an examination of the elements of pluralistic counseling. The authors suggest methods of intervention from a pluralistic perspective in dealing with problems of stress. The many case histories and examples give a concrete and real-life quality to the principles explored. This is a useful book for professionals and others who work with Hispanics and other minority groups.

Sue, D. W. *Counseling the culturally different: Theory and practice.* New York: Wiley, 1981. This excellent book presents an integrated framework for viewing cross-cultural counseling issues. The author's theory is useful for understanding counseling issues relating to all minority groups. The book identifies similarities and differences among the various ethnic groups as they relate to mental-health practices, and it provides a wide focus on how the social and political systems affect minorities and counseling. The concept of the culturally skilled counselor is especially well done. Sue offers perspectives for understanding Asian Americans, Blacks, and Hispanics and provides recommendations for counseling them.

References and Reading List

Abroms, G. M. The place of values in psychotherapy. *Journal of Marriage and Family Counseling*, 1978, 4(4), 3–17.

Agel, J. *The radical therapist*. New York: Ballantine, 1971.

Aguilera, D., & Messick, J. *Crisis intervention. Theory and methodology* (4th ed.). St. Louis: C. V. Mosby, 1982.

Alexander, F. *Psychoanalysis and psychotherapy*. New York: Norton, 1956.

American Association for Marriage and Family Therapy. *Code of professional ethics*. Claremont, Calif.: Author, undated.

American College Personnel Association. *Statement of ethical and professional standards*. Falls Church, Va.: American Personnel and Guidance Association, 1980.

American Group Psychotherapy Association. *Guidelines for the training of group psychotherapists*. New York: Author, 1978.

American Mental Health Counselors Association. *Code of ethics for certified clinical mental health counselors*. Falls Church, Va.: Author, 1980.

American Personnel and Guidance Association. *Ethical standards* (Rev. ed.). Falls Church, Va.: Author, 1981.

American Personnel and Guidance Association. *Guidepost*, 1982, 25(9).

American Psychiatric Association. *Diagnostic and statistical manual of mental disorders* (3rd ed.). Washington, D.C.: Author, 1980.

American Psychiatric Association. *The principles of medical ethics, with annotations especially applicable to psychiatry*. Washington, D.C.: Author, 1981.

American Psychological Association. *Casebook on ethical standards of psychologists*. Washington, D.C.: Author, 1967.

American Psychological Association. *Ethical principles in the conduct of research with human participants*. Washington, D.C.: Author, 1973. (a)

American Psychological Association. Guidelines for psychologists conducting growth groups. *American Psychologist*, 1973, 28(10), 933. (b)

American Psychological Association. *Standards for educational and psychological tests*. Washington, D.C.: Author, 1977. (a)

American Psychological Association. Standards for providers of psychological services. *American Psychologist*, 1977, 32, 495–505. (b)

American Psychological Association. Guidelines for therapy with women. *American Psychologist*, 1978, 30, 1122–1123.

American Psychological Association, Council of Representatives. *Criteria for accreditation of doctoral training programs and internships in professional psychology*. Washington, D.C.: Author, 1979 (amended 1980).

American Psychological Association. *Ethical principles of psychologists* (Rev. ed.). Washington, D.C.: Author, 1981. (a)

American Psychological Association. Specialty guidelines for the delivery of services. *American Psychologist*, 1981, 36(6), 639–681. (b)

American Psychological Association. *Specialty guidelines for the delivery of services by clinical psychologists.* Washington, D.C.: Author, 1981. (c)

American Psychological Association. *Specialty guidelines for the delivery of services by counseling psychologists.* Washington, D.C.: Author, 1981. (d)

American Psychological Association. *Specialty guidelines for the delivery of services by industrial/organizational psychologists.* Washington, D.C.: Author, 1981. (e)

American Psychological Association. *Specialty guidelines for the delivery of services by school psychologists.* Washington, D.C.: Author, 1981. (f)

American Psychological Association, Committee on Professional Standards. Casebook for providers of psychological services. *American Psychologist,* 1982, 37(6), 698–701.

American Psychological Association, Division of Counseling Psychology. Counseling women III. *The Counseling Psychologist,* 1979, 8(1). (a)

American Psychological Association, Division of Counseling Psychology. Principles concerning the counseling and therapy of women. *The Counseling Psychologist,* 1979, 8(1), 21. (b)

Anderson, J. K., Parenté, F. J., & Gordon, C. A forecast of the future for the mental health profession. *American Psychologist,* 1981, 36(8), 848–855.

Anderten, P., Staulcup, V., & Grisso, T. On being ethical in legal places. *Professional Psychology,* 1980, 11(5), 764–773.

Anschuetz, N. Marketing psychology. *Professional Psychology,* 1979, 10(2), 154–160.

Appelbaum, P. *Tarasoff:* An update on the duty to warn. *Hospital and Community Psychiatry,* 1981, 32, 14–15.

Arbuckle, D. *Counseling and psychotherapy: An existential-humanistic view* (3rd ed.). Boston: Allyn & Bacon, 1975.

Association for Specialists in Group Work. *Ethical guidelines for group leaders.* Falls Church, Va.: Author, 1980.

Association for Specialists in Group Work. *Guidelines for training group leaders.* Falls Church, Va.: Author, 1983.

Atkinson, D. R., Morten, G., & Sue, D. W. *Counseling American minorities.* Dubuque, Iowa: William C. Brown, 1979.

Bass, S., & Dole, A. Ethical leader practices in sensitivity training for prospective professional psychologists. *Journal Supplement Abstract Service,* 1977, 7(2), 47–66.

Bazelon, D. L. Veils, values, and social responsibility. *American Psychologist,* 1982, 37(2), 115–121.

Berger, Milton. Ethical problems in the use of videotape. In M. Rosenbaum (Ed.), *Ethics and values in psychotherapy: A guidebook.* New York: Free Press, 1982.

Berger, Morton. Ethics and the therapeutic relationship: Patient rights and therapist responsibilities. In M. Rosenbaum (Ed.), *Ethics and values in psychotherapy: A guidebook.* New York: Free Press, 1982.

Berman, A. L., & Cohen-Sandler, R. Suicide and malpractice: Expert testimony and the standard of care. *Professional Psychology: Research and Practice,* 1983, 14(1), 6–19.

Bernard, J. M. Inservice training for clinical supervisors. *Professional Psychology,* 1981, 12(6), 740–748.

Berne, E. *Transactional analysis in psychotherapy.* New York: Grove, 1961.

Berne, E. *Sex in human loving.* New York: Simon & Schuster, 1970.

Berne, E. *What do you say after you say hello?* New York: Grove, 1972.

Bernstein, B. L. Ignorance of the law is no excuse. In J. C. Hansen (Ed.), *Values, ethics, legalities and the family therapist.* Rockville, Md.: Aspen, 1982.

Bernstein, B. L., & Lecomte, C. *Licensing of practitioners in psychology: Current status and critical analysis.* Paper presented at the meeting of the American Psychological Association, Toronto, September 1978.

Bernstein, B. L., & Lecomte, C. Licensure in psychology: Alternative direction. *Professional Psychology,* 1981, 12(2), 200–208.

Bindrim, P. Confidentiality in group therapy sessions upheld by judgment rendered in California Superior Court. *Newsletter,* Group Psychotherapy Association of Southern California, November/December 1977.

Bloom, B. *Community mental health: A general introduction* (2nd ed.). Monterey, Calif.: Brooks/Cole, 1983.

Blustein, D. L. Using informal groups in cross-cultural counseling. *Journal for Specialists in Group Work*, 1982, 7(4), 260–265.

Board of Medical Quality Assurance, Psychology Examining Committee, State of California Department of Consumer Affairs. *Newsletter*. Sacramento, Calif.: Author, January 1980.

Bouhoutsos, J., Holroyd, J., Lerman, H., Forer, B. R., & Greenberg, M. Sexual intimacy between psychotherapists and patients. *Professional Psychology: Research and Practice*, 1983, *14*(2), 185–196.

Brammer, L., & Shostrom, E. *Therapeutic psychology: Fundamentals of counseling and psychotherapy* (4th ed.). Englewood Cliffs, N.J.: Prentice-Hall, 1982.

Brickman, P., Rabinowitz, V., Karuza, J., Coates, D., Cohn, E., & Kidder, L. Models of helping and coping. *American Psychologist*, 1982, 37(4), 368–384.

Brodsky, A. M., & Hare-Mustin, R. T. (Eds.). *Women and psychotherapy: An assessment of research and practice*. New York: Guilford Press, 1980.

Brooks, B. Directions for tomorrow. In C. Hatcher & B. Brooks (Eds.), *Innovations in counseling psychology*. San Francisco: Jossey-Bass, 1977. (a)

Brooks, B. Training models for tomorrow. In C. Hatcher & B. Brooks (Eds.), *Innovations in counseling psychology*. San Francisco: Jossey-Bass, 1977. (b)

Brown, F. The ethics of psychodiagnostic assessment. In M. Rosenbaum (Ed.), *Ethics and values in psychotherapy: A guidebook*. New York: Free Press, 1982.

Brown, R. W. Ethics and evaluation: Implications for group work. *The Journal for Specialists in Group Work*, 1982, 7(3), 167–173.

Bugental, J. *The search for existential identity*. San Francisco: Jossey-Bass, 1976.

Burgum, T., & Anderson, S. *The counselor and the law*. Washington, D.C.: APGA Press, 1975.

Burton, A. *Interpersonal psychotherapy*. Englewood Cliffs, N.J.: Prentice-Hall, 1972.

California Association of Marriage and Family Counselors. *Newsletter*. Los Angeles: Author, January 1978.

Carkhuff, R., & Berenson, G. *Beyond counseling and psychotherapy*. New York: Holt, Rinehart & Winston, 1967.

Claiborn, W. L., Stricker, G., & Bent, R. J. (Eds.). Special issue: Peer review and quality assurance. *Professional Psychology*, 1982, *13*(1).

Conyne, R. K. Two critical issues in primary prevention: What it is and how to do it. *Personnel and Guidance Journal*, 1983, 61(6), 331–334.

Corey, G. Description of a practicum course in group leadership. *The Journal for Specialists in Group Work*, 1981, 6(2), 100–108. (a)

Corey, G. *Theory and practice of group counseling*. Monterey, Calif.: Brooks/Cole, 1981. (b)

Corey, G. *Manual for theory and practice of group counseling*. Monterey, Calif.: Brooks/Cole, 1981. (c)

Corey, G. *Case approach to counseling and psychotherapy*. Monterey, Calif.: Brooks/Cole, 1982. (a)

Corey, G. Practical strategies for planning therapy groups. In P. Keller (Ed.), *Innovations in clinical practice: A sourcebook*. Sarasota, Fla.: Professional Resource Exchange, 1982. (b)

Corey, G. *Theory and practice of counseling and psychotherapy* (2nd ed.). Monterey, Calif.: Brooks/Cole, 1982. (c)

Corey, G. *Manual for theory and practice of counseling and psychotherapy* (2nd ed.). Monterey, Calif.: Brooks/Cole, 1982. (d)

Corey, G. An introduction to group counseling. In B. Pate & J. Brown (Eds.), *Being a counselor: Directions and challenges*. Monterey, Calif.: Brooks/Cole, 1983.

Corey, G., & Corey, M. *Groups: Process and practice* (2nd ed.). Monterey, Calif.: Brooks/Cole, 1982.

Corey, G., with Corey, M. *I never knew I had a choice* (2nd ed.). Monterey, Calif.: Brooks/Cole, 1983.

Corey, G., Corey, M., & Callanan, P. In-service training for group leaders in a prison hospital: Problems and prospects. *The Journal for Specialists in Group Work*, 1981, 6(3), 130–135.

Corey, G., Corey, M., & Callanan, P. *A casebook of ethical guidelines for group leaders.* Monterey, Calif.: Brooks/Cole, 1982.

Corey, G., Corey, M., Callanan, P., & Russell, J. M. A residential workshop for personal growth. *The Journal for Specialists in Group Work,* 1980, 5(4), 205–215.

Corey, G., Corey, M. S., Callanan, P., & Russell, J. M. Ethical considerations in using group techniques. *The Journal for Specialists in Group Work,* 1982, 7(3), 140–148. (a)

Corey, G., Corey, M., Callanan, P., & Russell, J. M. *Group techniques.* Monterey, Calif.: Brooks/Cole, 1982. (b)

Corlis, R., & Rabe, P. *Psychotherapy from the center: A humanistic view of change and of growth.* Scranton, Pa.: International Textbook, 1969.

Cormier, L. S., & Bernard, J. M. Ethical and legal responsibilities of clinical supervisors. *Personnel and Guidance Journal,* 1982, 60(8), 486–490.

Corsini, R. (Ed.). *Current psychotherapies* (2nd ed.). Itasca, Ill.: F. E. Peacock, 1979.

Corsini, R. (Ed.). *Handbook of innovative psychotherapies.* New York: Wiley, 1981.

Cottingham, H. F. Some broader perspectives on credentialing counseling psychologists. *The Counseling Psychologist,* 1980, 9(1), 19–22.

Council for the National Register of Health Service Providers in Psychology. *National register of health service providers in psychology.* Washington, D.C.: Author, 1980.

Courtois, C. A. Victims of rape and incest. *The Counseling Psychologist,* 1979, 8(1), 38–40.

Cowen, E. L. Help is where you find it: Four informal helping groups. *American Psychologist,* 1982, 37(4), 385–395.

Daniel, R. W., & Weikel, W. J. Trends in counseling: A Delphi study. *Personnel and Guidance Journal,* 1983, 61(6), 327–331.

Danish, S. J., D'Augelli, A., Brock, G., Conter, K., & Meyer, R. A symposium on skill dissemination for paraprofessionals: Models of training, supervision, and utilization. *Professional Psychology,* 1978, 9(1), 16–37.

Danish, S. J., & Smyer, M. A. Unintended consequences of requiring a license to help. *American Psychologist,* 1981, 36(1), 13–21.

Davis, J. W. Counselor licensure: Overskill? *Personnel and Guidance Journal,* 1981, 60(2), 83–85.

Davis, K. L., & Meara, N. M. So you think it is a secret. *The Journal for Specialists in Group Work,* 1982, 7(3), 149–153.

DeKraai, M. B., & Sales, B. D. Privileged communications of psychologists. *Professional Psychology,* 1982, 13(3), 372–388.

Denkowski, K. M., & Denkowski, G. C. Client-counselor confidentiality: An update of rationale, legal status, and implications. *Personnel and Guidance Journal,* 1982, 60(6), 371–375.

Dörken, H., & Webb, J. T. Licensed psychologists on the increase, 1974–1979. *American Psychologist,* 1981, 36(11), 1419–1426.

Drum, D., & Figler, H. Outreach in counseling. In C. Hatcher & B. Brooks (Eds.), *Innovations in counseling psychology.* San Francisco: Jossey-Bass, 1977.

Dugger, J. *The new professional: Introduction for the human services/mental health worker* (2nd ed.). Monterey, Calif.: Brooks/Cole, 1980.

Duncan, J., & Gumaer, J. *Developmental groups for children.* Springfield, Ill.: Charles C Thomas, 1980.

Edelwich, J., with Brodsky, A. *Burn-out: Stages of disillusionment in the helping professions.* New York: Human Sciences Press, 1980.

Egan, G. *Interpersonal living: A skills/contract approach to human-relations training in groups.* Monterey, Calif.: Brooks/Cole, 1976.

Egan, G. *The skilled helper: A model for systematic helping and interpersonal relating.* Monterey, Calif.: Brooks/Cole, 1982.

Ellis, A. *Humanistic psychotherapy: The rational-emotive approach.* New York: McGraw-Hill, 1973.

Ellis, A. Rational-emotive therapy. In A. Ellis & J. Whitely (Eds.), *Theoretical and empirical foundations of rational-emotive therapy.* Monterey, Calif.: Brooks/Cole, 1979.

Ellis, A., & Grieger, R. *Handbook of rational-emotive therapy.* New York: Springer, 1977.

Erikson, E. H. *Childhood and society* (2nd ed.). New York: Norton, 1963.

Everstine, L., Everstine, D. S., Heymann, G. M., True, R. H., Frey, D. H., Johnson, H. G., & Seiden, R. H. Privacy and confidentiality in psychotherapy. *American Psychologist,* 1980, 35(9), 828–840.

Farber, B. A., & Heifetz, L. J. The process and dimensions of burnout in psychotherapists. *Professional Psychology,* 1982, 13(2), 293–301.

Fieldsteel, N. Ethical issues in family therapy. In M. Rosenbaum (Ed.), *Ethics and values in psychotherapy: A guidebook.* New York: Free Press, 1982.

Fishman, D. B., & Neigher, W. D. American psychology in the eighties. Who will buy? *American Psychologist,* 1982, 37(5), 533–546.

Fitting, M. *Autonomy and the welfare of elderly clients: A dilemma for psychologists.* Paper presented at the meeting of the American Psychological Association, Washington, D.C., August 1982.

Flanagan, S., & Liberman, R. Ethical issues in the practice of behavior therapy. In M. Rosenbaum (Ed.), *Ethics and values in psychotherapy: A guidebook.* New York: Free Press, 1982.

Fox, R. E., Barclay, A. G., & Rodgers, D. A. The foundations of professional psychology. *American Psychologist,* 1982, 37(3), 306–312.

Frankl, V. *Man's search for meaning.* New York: Pocket Books, 1963.

Franks, V., & Burtle, V. (Eds.). *Women in therapy: New psychotherapies for a changing society.* New York: Brunner/Mazel, 1974.

Fretz, B. R., & Mills, D. H. *Licensing and certification of psychologists and counselors.* San Francisco: Jossey-Bass, 1980. (a)

Fretz, B. R., & Mills, D. H. Professional certification in counseling psychology. *The Counseling Psychologist,* 1980, 9(1), 2–17. (b)

Garfield, S. L. *Psychotherapy: An eclectic approach.* New York: Wiley, 1980.

Garfield, S. L. Effectiveness of psychotherapy: The perennial controversy. *Professional Psychology: Research and Practice,* 1983, 14(1), 35–43.

Gazda, G. *Basic approaches to group psychotherapy and group counseling* (3rd ed.). Springfield, Ill.: Charles C Thomas, 1982.

Gazda, G., & Mack, S. Ethical practice guidelines for group work practitioners. In G. M. Gazda (Ed.), *Basic approaches to group psychotherapy and group counseling* (3rd ed.). Springfield, Ill.: Charles C Thomas, 1982.

Gehring, D. D. The counselor's "duty to warn." *Personnel and Guidance Journal,* 1982, 61(4), 208–210.

Gilbert, L. A. Feminist therapy. In A. M. Brodsky & R. T. Hare-Mustin (Eds.), *Women and psychotherapy: An assessment of research and practice.* New York: Guilford Press, 1980.

Gill, S. J., Professional disclosure and consumer protection in counseling. *Personnel and Guidance Journal,* 1982, 60(7), 443–446.

Glasser, W. *Reality therapy.* New York: Harper & Row, 1965.

Glenn, C. M. Ethical issues in the practice of child psychotherapy. *Professional Psychology,* 1980, 11(4), 613–619.

Glenn, M., & Kunnes, R. *Repression or revolution? Therapy in the United States today.* New York: Harper & Row, 1973.

Goldberg, C. *Therapeutic partnership: Ethical concerns in psychotherapy.* New York: Springer, 1977.

Goldenberg, H. *Abnormal psychology: A social/community approach.* Monterey, Calif.: Brooks/Cole, 1977.

Goldenberg, H. *Contemporary clinical psychology* (2nd ed.). Monterey, Calif.: Brooks/Cole, 1983.

Goldfried, M. R. Toward the delineation of therapeutic change principles. *American Psychologist,* 1980, 35(11), 991–999.

Goldstein, A. Behavior therapy. In R. Corsini (Ed.), *Current psychotherapies.* Itasca, Ill.: F. E. Peacock, 1973.

Goulding, M., & Goulding, R. *Changing lives through redecision therapy.* New York: Brunner/ Mazel, 1979.

Goulding, R., & Goulding, M. *The power is in the patient: A TA/Gestalt approach to psychotherapy.* San Francisco: TA Press, 1978.

Grayson, H. Ethical issues in the training of psychotherapists. In M. Rosenbaum (Ed.), *Ethics and values in psychotherapy: A guidebook.* New York: Free Press, 1982.

Gross, S. Professional disclosure: An alternative to licensure. *Personnel and Guidance Journal,* 1977, *55,* 586–588.

Gross, S. J. The myth of professional licensing. *American Psychologist,* 1978, *33,* 1009–1016.

Gross, S. J. Comment on licensing. *APA Monitor,* September/October 1979, p. 15.

Gumaer, J. Ethics and the experts: Insight into critical incidents. *The Journal for Specialists in Group Work,* 1982, *7*(3), 154–161.

Haas, L. J., & Alexander, J. F. *Ethical and legal issues in family therapy.* Paper presented at the meeting of the American Psychological Association, Los Angeles, 1981.

Hansen, J. C. (Ed.). *Values, ethics, legalities and the family therapist.* (Family Therapy Collection: No. 1. L. L'Abate, issue editor.) Rockville, Md.: Aspen, 1982.

Hansen, J., Stevic, R., & Warner, R. *Counseling: Theory and process* (2nd ed.). Boston: Allyn & Bacon, 1977.

Hansen, J., Warner, R., & Smith, E. *Group counseling: Theory and process* (2nd ed.). Chicago: Rand McNally, 1980.

Hare-Mustin, R. T. Family therapy and sex-role stereotypes. *The Counseling Psychologist,* 1979, *8*(1), 31–32.

Hare-Mustin, R. T. Family therapy may be dangerous to your health. *Professional Psychology,* 1980, *11*(6), 935–938.

Hare-Mustin, R. T. An appraisal of the relationship between women and psychotherapy: 80 years after the case of Dora. *American Psychologist,* 1983, *38*(5), 593–601.

Hare-Mustin, R. T., & Hall, J. E. Procedures for responding to ethics complaints against psychologists. *American Psychologist,* 1981, *36*(12), 1494–1505.

Hare-Mustin, R. T., Marecek, J., Kaplan, A. G., & Liss-Levinson, N. Rights of clients, responsibilities of therapists. *American Psychologist,* 1979, *34*(1), 3–16.

Hart, G. M. Continuing professional development. Outlook for counselor educators and supervisors. *Counselor Education and Supervision,* December 1978, pp. 116–125. (a)

Hart, G. M. *Values clarification for counselors.* Springfield, Ill.: Charles C Thomas, 1978. (b)

Hart, G. M. *The process of clinical supervision.* Baltimore: University Park Press, 1982.

Hatcher, C., Brooks, B., & Associates. *Innovations in counseling psychology: Developing new roles, settings, techniques.* San Francisco: Jossey-Bass, 1977.

Hendrickson, R. M. Counselor liability: Does the risk require insurance coverage? *Personnel and Guidance Journal,* 1982, *61*(4), 205–207.

Herink, R. (Ed.). *The psychotherapy handbook.* New York: New American Library, 1980.

Hines, P. M., & Hare-Mustin, R. T. Ethical concerns in family therapy. *Professional Psychology,* 1978, *9,* 165–171.

Hogan, D. B. *The regulation of psychotherapists: A handbook of state licensure laws* (4 vols.). Cambridge, Mass.: Ballinger, 1979.

Holroyd, J., & Brodsky, A. Psychologists' attitudes and practices regarding erotic and nonerotic physical contact with patients. *American Psychologist,* 1977, *32*(10), 843–849.

Holroyd, J. C., & Brodsky, A. Does touching patients lead to sexual intercourse? *Professional Psychology,* 1980, *11*(5), 807–811.

Iscoe, I. Toward a viable community health psychology: Caveats from the experiences of the community mental health movement. *American Psychologist,* 1982, *37*(8), 961–965.

Ivey, A. E. Counseling 2000: Time to take charge. *The Counseling Psychologist,* 1980, *8*(4), 12–16.

Ivey, A., & Authier, J. *Microcounseling: Innovations in interviewing, counseling, psychotherapy, and psychoeducation.* Springfield, Ill.: Charles C Thomas, 1978.

Ivey, A., & Simek-Downing, L. *Counseling and psychotherapy: Skills, theories, and practice.* Englewood Cliffs, N.J.: Prentice-Hall, 1980.

Jensen, R. E. Competent professional service in psychology: The real issue behind continuing education. *Professional Psychology*, 1979, *10*(3), 381–389.

Jorgensen, F., & Lyons, D. Human rights and involuntary civil commitment. *Professional Psychology*, 1972, *3*(2), 143–150.

Jorgensen, F., & Weigel, R. Training psychotherapists: Practices regarding ethics, personal growth, and locus of responsibility. *Professional Psychology*, 1973, *4*(1), 23–27.

Jourard, S. *Disclosing man to himself*. Princeton, N.J.: Van Nostrand, 1968.

Jourard, S. *The transparent self* (Rev. ed.). New York: Van Nostrand, 1971.

Kahn-Edrington, M. Abortion counseling. *The Counseling Psychologist*, 1979, *8*(1), 37–38.

Kalish, R. A., & Collier, K. W. *Exploring human values: Psychological and philosophical considerations*. Monterey, Calif.: Brooks/Cole, 1981.

Kane, M. T. The validity of licensure examinations. *American Psychologist*, 1982, *37*(8), 911–918.

Kaplan, H. S. *The new sex therapy*. New York: Brunner/Mazel, 1974.

Kaplan, H., & Sadock, B. (Eds.). *Comprehensive group psychotherapy* (2nd ed.). Baltimore: Williams & Wilkins, 1983.

Kaslow, F., & Steinberg, J. Ethical divorce therapy and divorce proceedings: A psycholegal perspective. In J. C. Hansen (Ed.), *Values, ethics, legalities and the family therapist*. Rockville, Md.: Aspen, 1982.

Kempler, W. Gestalt therapy. In R. Corsini (Ed.), *Current psychotherapies*. Itasca, Ill.: F. E. Peacock, 1973.

Kingdon, M. A. Lesbians. *The Counseling Psychologist*, 1979, *8*(1), 44–45.

Klagsbrun, S. C. Ethics in hospice care. *American Psychologist*, 1982, *37*(11), 1263–1265.

Klenowski, J. R. Adolescents' rights of access to counseling. *Personnel and Guidance Journal*, 1983, *61*(6), 365–367.

Knapp, S. A primer on malpractice for psychologists. *Professional Psychology*, 1980, *11*(4), 606–612.

Knapp, S., & Vandecreek, L. *Tarasoff*: Five years later. *Professional Psychology*, 1982, *13*(4), 511–516.

Koch, J., & Koch, L. A consumer's guide to therapy for couples. *Psychology Today*, March 1976, pp. 33–40.

Koocher, G. P. A bill of rights for children in psychotherapy. In G. P. Koocher (Ed.), *Children's rights and the mental health professions*. New York: Wiley, 1976.

Koocher, G. P. Credentialing in psychology: Close encounters with competence? *American Psychologist*, 1979, *34*(8), 696–702.

Korchin, S. J., & Schuldberg, D. The future of clinical assessment. *American Psychologist*, 1981, *36*(10), 1147–1158.

Korelitz, A., & Schulder, D. The lawyer-therapist consultation team. *Journal of Marital and Family Therapy*, 1982, *8*(1), 113–119.

Kosinski, F. A. Standards, accreditation, and licensure in marital and family therapy. *Personnel and Guidance Journal*, 1982, *60*(6), 350–352.

Kottler, J. A. Unethical behaviors we all do and pretend we do not. *The Journal for Specialists in Group Work*, 1982, *7*(3), 182–186.

Kottler, J. A. *Pragmatic group leadership*. Monterey, Calif.: Brooks/Cole, 1983.

Krasner, L. The reinforcement machine. In B. Berenson & R. Carkhuff (Eds.), *Sources of gain in counseling and psychotherapy*. New York: Holt, Rinehart & Winston, 1967.

Laing, R. D. *The politics of experience*. New York: Pantheon, 1967.

Lakin, M. *Interpersonal encounter: Theory and practice in sensitivity training*. New York: McGraw-Hill, 1972.

Landman, J. T., & Dawes, R. M. Psychotherapy outcome. *American Psychologist*, 1982, *37*(5), 504–516.

Lazarus, A. A. Divorce counseling or marriage therapy? A therapeutic option. *Journal of Marital and Family Therapy*, 1981, *7*(1), 15–22.

Levine, E. S., & Padilla, A. M. *Crossing cultures in therapy: Pluralistic counseling for the Hispanic*. Monterey, Calif.: Brooks/Cole, 1980.

Lewinsohn, P., & Pearlman, S. Continuing education for psychologists. *Professional Psychology*, 1972, *3*(1), 48–52.

Lief, H. Ethical problems in sex therapy. In M. Rosenbaum (Ed.), *Ethics and values in psychotherapy: A guidebook*. New York: Free Press, 1982.

Lindsey, R. T. Informed consent and deception in psychotherapy research: An ethical analysis. *The Counseling Psychologist*, in press.

Liss-Levinson, N. Women with sexual concerns. *The Counseling Psychologist*, 1979, *8*(1), 36–37.

Lowe, C. M. *Value orientation in counseling and psychotherapy: The meanings of mental health*. San Francisco: Chandler, 1969.

Lowry, T., & Lowry, T. Ethical considerations in sex therapy. *Journal of Marriage and Family Counseling*, 1975, *1*(3), 229–236.

Manthei, R. J. Client choice of therapist or therapy. *Personnel and Guidance Journal*, 1983, *61*(6), 334–340.

Margolin, G. Ethical and legal considerations in marital and family therapy. *American Psychologist*, 1982, *37*(7), 788–801.

Maslow, A. *Toward a psychology of being* (2nd ed.). New York: Van Nostrand, 1968.

Maslow, A. *Motivation and personality* (2nd ed.). New York: Harper & Row, 1970.

May, R. *Psychology and the human dilemma*. Princeton, N.J.: Van Nostrand, 1967.

McConnell, L. G. The sexual value system. *Journal of Marriage and Family Counseling*, 1977, *3*(1), 55–67.

Melton, G. B. Children's participation in treatment planning: Psychological and legal issues. *Professional Psychology*, 1981, *12*(2), 246–252. (a)

Melton, G. B. Effects of a state law permitting minors to consent to psychotherapy. *Professional Psychology*, 1981, *12*(5), 647–654. (b)

Meyer, R., & Smith, S. A crisis in group therapy. *American Psychologist*, 1977, *32*(8), 638–643.

Miller, J. Cultural and class values in family process. *Journal of Marital and Family Therapy*, 1981, *7*(4), 467–473.

Miller, L. S., Bergstrom, D. A., Cross, H. J., & Grube, J. W. Opinions and use of the DSM system by practicing psychologists. *Professional Psychology*, 1981, *12*(3), 385–390.

Mintz, E. *Marathon groups: Reality and symbol*. New York: Avon, 1971.

Minuchin, S. *Families and family therapy*. Cambridge, Mass.: Harvard University Press, 1974.

Moreland, J., Schwebel, A. I., Fine, M. A., & Vess, J. D. Postdivorce family therapy: Suggestions for professionals. *Professional Psychology*, 1982, *13*(5), 639–646.

Morrison, J., Layton, B., & Newman, J. Ethical conflict in clinical decision making: A challenge for family therapists. In J. C. Hansen (Ed.), *Values, ethics, legalities and the family therapist*. Rockville, Md.: Aspen, 1982.

Moses, A. E., & Hawkins, R. O. *Counseling lesbian women and gay men: A life-issues approach*. St. Louis: C. V. Mosby, 1982.

Muehleman, T., & Kimmons, C. Psychologists' views on child abuse reporting, confidentiality, life, and the law: An exploratory study. *Professional Psychology*, 1981, *12*(5), 631–638.

Myers, R. A. Education and training: The next decade. *The Counseling Psychologist*, 1982, *10*(2), 39–44.

National Association of Social Workers. *Code of ethics*. Washington, D.C.: Author, 1979.

National Association of Social Workers. *Standards for the private practice of clinical social work*. Washington, D.C.: Author, 1981.

Newman, A. S. Ethical issues in the supervision of psychotherapy. *Professional Psychology*, 1981, *12*(6), 690–695.

North Atlantic Association for Counselor Education and Supervision. *Ethical standards for counselor educators and supervisors* (draft). Falls Church, Va.: Author, 1980.

Nutt, R. L. Review and preview of attitudes and values of counselors of women. *The Counseling Psychologist*, 1979, *8*(1), 18–20.

O'Leary, K. D., & Borkovec, T. D. Conceptual, methodological, and ethical problems of placebo groups in psychotherapy research. *American Psychologist,* 1978, *33,* 821–830.

O'Shea, A. T., & Connery, M. G. The child advocate attorney–the mental health professional: A current "courtship." *Journal of Marital and Family Therapy,* 1980, *6*(3), 277–283.

O'Shea, M., & Jessee, E. Ethical, value, and professional conflicts in systems therapy. In J. C. Hansen (Ed.), *Values, ethics, legalities and the family therapist.* Rockville, Md.: Aspen, 1982.

Palmer, J. O. *A primer of eclectic psychotherapy.* Monterey, Calif.: Brooks/Cole, 1980.

Paradise, L., & Siegelwaks, B. Ethical training for group leaders. *The Journal for Specialists in Group Work,* 1982, *7*(3), 162–166.

Parloff, M. B. Can psychotherapy research guide the policymaker? *American Psychologist,* 1979, *34*(4), 296–306.

Patterson, C. H. *Theories of counseling and psychotherapy* (3rd ed.). New York: Harper & Row, 1980.

Pedersen, P. B., Draguns, J., Lonner, W., & Trimble, J. (Eds.). *Counseling across cultures* (Rev. ed.). Honolulu: University Press of Hawaii, 1981.

Pedersen, P. B., & Marsella, A. J. The ethical crisis for cross-cultural counseling and therapy. *Professional Psychology,* 1982, *13*(4), 492–500.

Perls, F. *Gestalt therapy verbatim.* Moab, Utah: Real People Press, 1969.

Phillips, B. N. Regulation and control in psychology: Implications for certification and licensure. *American Psychologist,* 1982, *37*(8), 919–926.

Pines, A., & Aronson, E., with Kafry, D. *Burnout: From tedium to personal growth.* New York: Free Press, 1981.

Pinney, E. L. Ethical and legal issues in group psychotherapy. In H. Kaplan & B. Sadock (Eds.), *Comprehensive group psychotherapy* (2nd ed.). Baltimore: Williams & Wilkins, 1983.

Plotkin, R. Confidentiality in group counseling. *APA Monitor,* March 1978, p. 14.

Pope, K. S., Levenson, H., & Schover, L. R. Sexual intimacy in psychology training: Results and implications of a national survey. *American Psychologist,* 1979, *34*(8), 682–689.

Pope, K. S., Schover, L. R., & Levenson, H. Sexual behavior between clinical supervisors and trainees: Implications for professional standards. *Professional Psychology,* 1980, *10,* 157–162.

Portwood, D. A right to suicide? *Psychology Today,* January 1978, pp. 66–74.

Powell, C. J. *Adolescence and the right to die: Issues of autonomy, competence and paternalism.* Paper presented at the meeting of the American Psychological Association, Washington, D.C., August 1982.

Prochaska, J. *Systems of psychotherapy: A transtheoretical analysis.* Homewood, Ill.: Dorsey, 1979.

Rice, D. G., & Rice, J. K. Non-sexist "marital" therapy. *Journal of Marriage and Family Counseling,* 1977, *3*(1), 3–10.

Rinella, V. J., & Goldstein, M. R. Family therapy with substance abusers: Legal considerations regarding confidentiality. *Journal of Marital and Family Therapy,* 1980, *6*(3), 319–326.

Roberts, A. L. Ethical guidelines for group leaders. *The Journal for Specialists in Group Work,* 1982, *7*(3), 174–181.

Rogers, C. *Counseling and psychotherapy.* Cambridge, Mass.: Houghton Mifflin, 1942.

Rogers, C. *Client-centered therapy.* Boston: Houghton Mifflin, 1951.

Rogers, C. *On becoming a person.* Boston: Houghton Mifflin, 1961.

Rogers, C. *Freedom to learn.* Columbus, Ohio: Charles E. Merrill, 1969.

Rogers, C. *Carl Rogers on encounter groups.* New York: Harper & Row, 1970.

Rogers, C. Some new challenges. *American Psychologist,* 1973, *28,* 379–387.

Rogers, C. *Carl Rogers on personal power: Inner strength and its revolutionary impact.* New York: Delacorte, 1977.

Rogers, C. *A way of being.* Boston: Houghton Mifflin, 1980.

Rosenbaum, M. Ethical problems of group psychotherapy. In M. Rosenbaum (Ed.), *Ethics and values in psychotherapy: A guidebook.* New York: Free Press, 1982. (a)

Rosenbaum, M. (Ed.). *Ethics and values in psychotherapy: A guidebook.* New York: Free Press, 1982. (b)

Roth, L. H., & Meisel, A. Dangerousness, confidentiality and the duty to warn. *American Journal of Psychiatry,* 1977, *134,* 508–511.

Ruback, R. B. Issues in family law: Implications for therapists. In J. C. Hansen (Ed.), *Values, ethics, legalities and the family therapist.* Rockville, Md.: Aspen, 1982.

Sampson, J. P., & Pyle, K. R. Ethical issues involved with the use of computer-assisted counseling, testing, and guidance systems. *Personnel and Guidance Journal,* 1983, *61*(5), 283–287.

Sanders, J. R. Complaints against psychologists adjudicated informally by APA's Committee on Scientific and Professional Ethics and Conduct. *American Psychologist,* 1979, *34*(12), 1139–1144.

Sanders, J. R., & Keith-Spiegel, P. Formal and informal adjudication of ethics complaints against psychologists. *American Psychologist,* 1980, *35*(12), 1096–1105.

Scarato, A. M., & Sigall, B. A. Multiple role women. *The Counseling Psychologist,* 1979, *8*(1), 26–27.

Schacht, T., & Nathan, P. But is it good for the psychologists? Appraisal and status of DSM III. *American Psychologist,* 1977, *32*(12), 1017–1025.

Schofield, W. *Psychotherapy: The purchase of friendship.* Englewood Cliffs, N.J.: Prentice-Hall (Spectrum), 1964.

Schutz, B. *Legal liability in psychotherapy.* San Francisco: Jossey-Bass, 1982.

Schutz, W. *Here comes everybody.* New York: Harper & Row, 1971.

Schwitzgebel, R. L., & Schwitzgebel, R. K. *Law and psychological practice.* New York: Wiley, 1980.

Secrest, L., & Hoffman, P. E. The philosophical underpinnings of peer review. *Professional Psychology,* 1982, *13*(1), 14–18.

Seymour, W. Counselor/therapist values and therapeutic style. In J. C. Hansen (Ed.), *Values ethics, legalities and the family therapist.* Rockville, Md.: Aspen, 1982.

Shah, S. Privileged communications, confidentiality, and privacy: Privileged communications. *Professional Psychology,* 1969, *1*(1), 56–69.

Shah, S. Privileged communications, confidentiality, and privacy: Confidentiality. *Professional Psychology,* 1970, *1*(2), 159–164. (a)

Shah, S. Privileged communications, confidentiality, and privacy: Privacy. *Professional Psychology,* 1970, *1*(3), 243–252. (b)

Sheridan, K. Sex bias in therapy: Are counselors immune? *Personnel and Guidance Journal,* 1982, *61*(2), 81–83.

Shimberg, B. Testing for licensure and certification. *American Psychologist,* 1981, *36*(10), 1138–1146.

Siegel, M. Privacy, ethics and confidentiality. *Professional Psychology,* 1979, *10*(2), 249–258.

Slimak, R. E., & Berkowitz, S. R. The university and college counseling center and malpractice suits. *Personnel and Guidance Journal,* 1983, *61*(5), 291–295.

Smith, D. Unfinished business with informed consent procedures. *American Psychologist,* 1981, *36*(1), 220–226.

Smith, D. Trends in counseling and psychotherapy. *American Psychologist,* 1982, *37*(7), 802–809.

Smith, M. L., & Glass, G. V. Meta-analysis of psychotherapy outcome studies. *American Psychologist,* 1977, *32,* 752–760.

Smith, M. L., Glass, G. V., & Miller, T. I. *The benefits of psychotherapy.* Baltimore: Johns Hopkins University Press, 1980.

Sophie, J. Counseling lesbians. *Personnel and Guidance Journal,* 1982, *60*(6), 341–345.

Spiegel, S. B. Separate principles for counselors of women: A new form of sexism. *The Counseling Psychologist,* 1979, *8*(1), 49–50.

Spitzer, R. L., Skodol, A. E., Gibbon, M., & Williams, J. *DSM-III Case Book.* Washington, D.C.: American Psychiatric Association, 1981.

Sporakowski, M. J. The regulation of marital and family therapy. In J. C. Hansen (Ed.), *Values, ethics, legalities and the family therapist.* Rockville, Md.: Aspen, 1982.

Sporakowski, M. J., & Staniszewski, W. P. The regulation of marriage and family therapy: An update. *Journal of Marital and Family Therapy,* 1980, *6*(3), 335–348.

Spotnitz, H. Ethical issues in the treatment of psychotics and borderline psychotics. In M. Rosenbaum (Ed.), *Ethics and values in psychotherapy: A guidebook.* New York: Free Press, 1982.

Steinberg, J. L. Towards an interdisciplinary commitment: A divorce lawyer proposes attorney-therapist marriages or, at the least, an affair. *Journal of Marital and Family Therapy,* 1980, *6*(3), 259–268.

Steiner, J. Ethical issues in the institutionalization of patients. In M. Rosenbaum (Ed.), *Ethics and values in psychotherapy: A guidebook.* New York: Free Press, 1982.

Steinzor, B. *The healing partnership: The patient as colleague in psychotherapy.* New York: Harper & Row, 1967.

Stensrud, R., & Stensrud, K. Counseling may be hazardous to your health: How we teach people to feel powerless. *Personnel and Guidance Journal,* 1981, *59*(5), 300–304.

Stolz, S., & Associates. *Ethical issues in behavior modification.* San Francisco: Jossey-Bass, 1978.

Stricker, G. Ethical issues in psychotherapy research. In M. Rosenbaum (Ed.), *Ethics and values in psychotherapy: A guidebook.* New York: Free Press, 1982.

Stricker, G., Claiborn, W. L., & Bent, R. J. Peer review: An overview. *Professional Psychology,* 1982, *13*(1), 5–8.

Stude, E. W., & McKelvey, J. Ethics and the law: Friend or foe? *Personnel and Guidance Journal,* 1979, *57*(9), 453–456.

Sue, D. W. *Counseling the culturally different: Theory and practice.* New York: Wiley, 1981.

Sue, D. W., Bernier, J. E., Durran, A., Feinberg, L., Pedersen, P., Smith, E. J., & Nuttall, E. V. Position paper: Cross-cultural counseling competencies. *The Counseling Psychologist,* 1982, *10*(2), 45–52.

Sue, S. Community mental health services to minority groups. *American Psychologist,* 1977, *32*(8), 616–624.

Sue, S. Ethnic minority issues in psychology. *American Psychologist,* 1983, *38*(5), 583–592.

Swanson, C. Ethics and the counselor. In B. Pate & J. Brown (Eds.), *Being a counselor: Directions and challenges.* Monterey, Calif.: Brooks/Cole, 1983. (a)

Swanson, C. The law and the counselor. In B. Pate & J. Brown (Eds.), *Being a counselor: Directions and challenges.* Monterey, Calif.: Brooks/Cole, 1983. (a)

Szasz, T. *The myth of mental illness: Foundations of a theory of personal conduct* (Rev. ed.). New York: Harper & Row, 1974.

Taggart, M. Linear versus systemic values: Implications for family therapy. In J. C. Hansen (Ed.), *Values, ethics, legalities and the family therapist.* Rockville, Md.: Aspen, 1982.

Talbutt, L. C. Ethical standards: Assets and limitations. *Personnel and Guidance Journal,* 1981, *60*(2), 110–112.

Tolchin, G., Steinfeld, G., & Suchotliff, L. The mental patient and civil rights: Some moral, legal, and ethical considerations. *Professional Psychology,* 1970, *1*(3), 212–216.

Torrey, E. F. *The death of psychiatry.* Radnor, Pa.: Chilton, 1974.

Tymchuk, A. J. A perspective on ethics in mental retardation. *Mental Retardation,* 1976, *14*(6), 44–47.

Tymchuk, A. J. Ethical decision making and psychological treatment. *Journal of Psychiatric Treatment and Evaluation,* 1981, *3*, 507–513.

Tymchuk, A. J., & Associates. Survey of training in ethics in APA-approved clinical psychology programs. *American Psychologist,* 1979, *34*(12), 1168–1170.

Tymchuk, A. J., Drapkin, R., Major-Kingsley, S., Ackerman, A. B., Coffman, E. W., & Baum, M. S. Ethical decision making and psychologists' attitudes toward training in ethics. *Professional Psychology,* 1982, *13*(3), 412–421.

Van Hoose, W., & Kottler, J. *Ethical and legal issues in counseling and psychotherapy.* San Francisco: Jossey-Bass, 1977.

Vitulano, L. A., & Copeland, B. A. Trends in continuing education and competency demonstration. *Professional Psychology*, 1980, *11*(6), 891–897.

Wagner, C. A. Confidentiality and the school counselor. *Personnel and Guidance Journal*, 1981, *59*(5), 305–310.

Warnath, C. F. Counselor burnout: Existential crisis or a problem for the profession? *Personnel and Guidance Journal*, 1979, *57*(7), 325–330.

Watkins, C. E. Burnout in counseling practice: Some potential professional and personal hazards of becoming a counselor. *Personnel and Guidance Journal*, 1983, *61*(5), 304–308.

Wayne, G. An examination of selected statutory licensing requirements for psychologists in the United States. *Personnel and Guidance Journal*, 1982, *60*(7), 420–425.

White, M. D., & White, C. A. Involuntary committed patients' constitutional right to refuse treatment. *American Psychologist*, 1981, *36*(9), 953–962.

Whitlock, G. *Understanding and coping with real-life crises*. Monterey, Calif.: Brooks/Cole, 1978.

Winkelpleck, J. M., & Westfeld, J. S. Counseling considerations with gay couples. *Personnel and Guidance Journal*, 1982, *60*(5), 294–345.

Wolman, B. Ethical problems in termination of psychotherapy. In M. Rosenbaum (Ed.), *Ethics and values in psychotherapy: A guidebook*. New York: Free Press, 1982.

Woodman, N. J., & Lenna, H. R. *Counseling with gay men and women*. San Francisco: Jossey-Bass, 1980.

Wrenn, C. G. Two psychological worlds: An attempted rapprochement. In J. Krumboltz (Ed.), *Revolution in counseling*. Boston: Houghton Mifflin, 1966.

Wrenn, C. G. *The world of the contemporary counselor*. Boston: Houghton Mifflin, 1973.

Wrenn, C. G. The fighting, risk-taking counselor. *Personnel and Guidance Journal*, 1983, *61*(6), 323–326.

Wright, R. H. What to do until the malpractice lawyer comes: A survivor's manual. *American Psychologist*, 1981, *36*(12), 1535–1541.

Wyman, E., & McLaughlin, M. E. Traditional wives and mothers. *The Counseling Psychologist*, 1979, *8*(1), 24–25.

Yalom, I. D. *The theory and practice of group psychotherapy* (2nd ed.). New York: Basic Books, 1975.

Yalom, I. *Existential psychotherapy*. New York: Basic Books, 1980.

Zimpfer, D. G. Professional issues in groups. In D. G. Zimpfer (Ed.), *Group work in the helping professions: A bibliography*. Washington, D.C.: Association for Specialists in Group Work, 1976.

Professional Codes of Ethics

A. Ethical Standards,
American Personnel and Guidance Association

(Approved by Executive Committee upon referral of the Board of Directors, January 17, 1981.)

PREAMBLE

The American Personnel and Guidance Association is an educational, scientific, and professional organization whose members are dedicated to the enhancement of the worth, dignity, potential, and uniqueness of each individual and thus to the service of society.

The Association recognizes that the role definitions and work settings of its members include a wide variety of academic disciplines, levels of academic preparation and agency services. This diversity reflects the breadth of the Association's interest and influence. It also poses challenging complexities in efforts to set standards for the performance of members, desired requisite preparation or practice, and supporting social, legal, and ethical controls.

The specification of ethical standards enables the Association to clarify to present and future members and to those served by members, the nature of ethical responsibilities held in common by its members.

The existence of such standards serves to stimulate greater concern by members for their own professional functioning and for the conduct of fellow professionals such as counselors, guidance and student personnel workers, and others in the helping professions. As the ethical code of the Association, this document establishes principles that define the ethical behavior of Association members.

Section A: General

1. The member influences the development of the profession by continuous efforts to improve professional practices, teaching, services, and research. Professional growth is continuous throughout the member's career and is exemplified by the development of a philosophy that explains why and how a member functions in the helping relationship. Members must gather data on their effectiveness and be guided by the findings.

2. The member has a responsibility both to the individual who is served and to the institution within which the service is performed to maintain high standards of professional conduct. The member strives to maintain the highest levels of professional services offered to the individuals to be served. The member also strives to assist the agency, organization, or institution in providing the highest caliber of professional services. The acceptance of employment in an institution implies that the member is in agreement with the general policies and principles of the institution. Therefore the professional activities of the member are also in accord with the objectives of the institution. If, despite concerted efforts, the member cannot reach agreement with the employer as to acceptable standards of conduct that allow for changes in institutional policy conducive to the positive growth and development of clients, then terminating the affiliation should be seriously considered.

3. Ethical behavior among professional associates, both

members and nonmembers, must be expected at all times. When information is possessed that raises doubt as to the ethical behavior of professional colleagues, whether Association members or not, the member must take action to attempt to rectify such a condition. Such action shall use the institution's channels first and then use procedures established by the state Branch, Division, or Association.

4. The member neither claims nor implies professional qualifications exceeding those possessed and\ is responsible for correcting any misrepresentations of these qualifications by others.

5. In establishing fees for professional counseling services, members must consider the financial status of clients and locality. In the event that the established fee structure is inappropriate for a client, assistance must be provided in finding comparable services of acceptable cost.

6. When members provide information to the public or to subordinates, peers or supervisors, they have a responsibility to ensure that the content is general, unidentified client information that is accurate, unbiased, and consists of objective, factual data.

7. With regard to the delivery of professional services, members should accept only those positions for which they are professionally qualified.

8. In the counseling relationship the counselor is aware of the intimacy of the relationship and maintains respect for the client and avoids engaging in activities that seek to meet the counselor's personal needs at the expense of that client. Through awareness of the negative impact of both racial and sexual stereotyping and discrimination, the counselor guards the individual rights and personal dignity of the client in the counseling relationship.

Section B: Counseling relationship

This section refers to practices and procedures of individual and/or group counseling relationships.

The member must recognize the need for client freedom of choice. Under those circumstances where this is not possible, the member must apprise clients of restrictions that may limit their freedom of choice.

1. The member's *primary* obligation is to respect the integrity and promote the welfare of the client(s), whether the client(s) is (are) assisted individually or in a group relationship. In a group setting, the member is also responsible for taking reasonable precautions to protect individuals from physical and/or psychological trauma resulting from interaction within the group.

2. The counseling relationship and information resulting therefrom [must] be kept confidential, consistent with the obligations of the member as a professional person. In a group counseling setting, the counselor must set a norm of confidentiality regarding all group participants' disclosures.

3. If an individual is already in a counseling relationship with another professional person, the member does not enter into a counseling relationship without first contacting and receiving the approval of that other professional. If the member discovers that the client is in another counseling relationship after the counseling relationship begins, the member must gain the consent of the other professional or terminate the relationship, unless the client elects to terminate the other relationship.

4. When the client's condition indicates that there is clear and imminent danger to the client or others, the member must take reasonable personal action or inform responsible authorities. Consultation with other professionals must be used where possible. The assumption of responsibility for the client's behavior must be taken only after careful deliberation. The client must be involved in the resumption of responsibility as quickly as possible.

5. Records of the counseling relationship, including interview notes, test data, correspondence, tape recordings, and other documents, are to be considered professional information for use in counseling and they should not be considered a part of the records of the institution or agency in which the counselor is employed unless specified by state statute or regulation. Revelation to others of counseling material must occur only upon the expressed consent of the client.

6. Use of data derived from a counseling relationship for purposes of counselor training or research shall be confined to content that can be disguised to ensure full protection of the identity of the subject client.

7. The member must inform the client of the purposes, goals, techniques, rules of procedure and limitations that may affect the relationship at or before the time that the counseling relationship is entered.

8. The member must screen prospective group participants, especially when the emphasis is on self-understanding and growth through self-disclosure.

The member must maintain an awareness of the group participants' compatibility throughout the life of the group.

9. The member may choose to consult with any other professionally competent person about a client. In choosing a consultant, the member must avoid placing the consultant in a conflict of interest situation that would preclude the consultant's being a proper party to the member's efforts to help the client.

10. If the member determines an inability to be of professional assistance to the client, the member must either avoid initiating the counseling relationship or immediately terminate that relationship. In either event, the member must suggest appropriate alternatives. (The member must be knowledgeable about referral resources so that a satisfactory referral can be initiated.) In the event the client declines the suggested referral, the member is not obligated to continue the relationship.

11. When the member has other relationships, particularly of an administrative, supervisory and/or evaluative nature with an individual seeking counseling services, the member must not serve as the counselor but should refer the individual to another professional. Only in instances where such an alternative is unavailable and where the individual's situation warrants counseling intervention should the member enter into and/or maintain a counseling relationship. Dual relationships with clients that might impair the member's objectivity and professional judgment (e.g., as with close friends or relatives, sexual intimacies with any client) must be avoided and/or the counseling relationship terminated through referral to another competent professional.

12. All experimental methods of treatment must be clearly indicated to prospective recipients and safety precautions are to be adhered to by the member.

13. When the member is engaged in short-term group treatment/training programs (e.g., marathons and other encounter-type or growth groups), the member ensures that there is professional assistance available during and following the group experience.

14. Should the member be engaged in a work setting that calls for any variation from the above statements, the member is obligated to consult with other professionals whenever possible to consider justifiable alternatives.

Section C: Measurement and evaluation

The primary purpose of educational and psychological testing is to provide descriptive measures that are objective and interpretable in either comparative or absolute terms. The member must recognize the need to interpret the statements that follow as applying to the whole range of appraisal techniques including test and nontest data. Test results constitute only one of a variety of pertinent sources of information for personnel, guidance, and counseling decisions.

1. The member must provide specific orientation or information to the examinee(s) prior to and following the test administration so that the results of testing may be placed in proper perspective with other relevant factors. In so doing, the member must recognize the effects of socioeconomic, ethnic and cultural factors on test scores. It is the member's professional responsibility to use additional unvalidated information carefully in modifying interpretation of the test results.

2. In selecting tests for use in a given situation or with a particular client, the member must consider carefully the specific validity, reliability, and appropriateness of the test(s). *General* validity, reliability and the like may be questioned legally as well as ethically when tests are used for vocational and educational selection, placement, or counseling.

3. When making any statements to the public about tests and testing, the member must give accurate information and avoid false claims or misconceptions. Special efforts are often required to avoid unwarranted connotations of such terms as *IQ* and *grade equivalent scores*.

4. Different tests demand different levels of competence for administration, scoring, and interpretation. Members must recognize the limits of their competence and perform only those functions for which they are prepared.

5. Tests must be administered under the same conditions that were established in their standardization. When tests are not administered under standard conditions or when unusual behavior or irregularities occur during the testing session, those conditions must be noted and the results designated as invalid or of questionable validity. Unsupervised or inadequately supervised test-taking, such as the use of tests through the mails, is considered unethical. On the other hand, the use of instruments that are so designed or standardized to be self-adminis-

tered and self-scored, such as interest inventories, is to be encouraged.

6. The meaningfulness of test results used in personnel, guidance, and counseling functions generally depends on the examinee's unfamiliarity with the specific items on the test. Any prior coaching or dissemination of the test materials can invalidate test results. Therefore, test security is one of the professional obligations of the member. Conditions that produce most favorable test results must be made known to the examinee.

7. The purpose of testing and the explicit use of the results must be made known to the examinee prior to testing. The counselor must ensure that instrument limitations are not exceeded and that periodic review and/or retesting are made to prevent client stereotyping.

8. The examinee's welfare and explicit prior understanding must be the criteria for determining the recipients of the test results. The member must see that specific interpretation accompanies any release of individual or group test data. The interpretation of test data must be related to the examinee's particular concerns.

9. The member must be cautious when interpreting the results of research instruments possessing insufficient technical data. The specific purposes for the use of such instruments must be stated explicitly to examinees.

10. The member must proceed with caution when attempting to evaluate and interpret the performance of minority group members or other persons who are not represented in the norm group on which the instrument was standardized.

11. The member must guard against the appropriation, reproduction, or modifications of published tests or parts thereof without acknowledgment and permission from the previous publisher.

12. Regarding the preparation, publication and distribution of tests, reference should be made to:
    a. *Standards for Educational and Psychological Tests and Manuals*, revised edition, 1974, published by the American Psychological Association on behalf of itself, the American Educational Research Association and the National Council on Measurement in Education.
    b. The responsible use of tests: A position paper of AMEG, APGA, and NCME. *Measurement and Evaluation in Guidance*, 1972, 5, 385–388.
    c. "Responsibilities of Users of Standardized Tests," APGA, *Guidepost*, October 5, 1978, pp. 5–8.

Section D: Research and publication

1. Guidelines on research with human subjects shall be adhered to, such as:
    a. *Ethical Principles in the Conduct of Research with Human Participants*, Washington, D.C.: American Psychological Association, Inc., 1973.
    b. Code of Federal Regulations, Title 45, Subtitle A, Part 46, as currently issued.

2. In planning any research activity dealing with human subjects, the member must be aware of and responsive to all pertinent ethical principles and ensure that the research problem, design, and execution are in full compliance with them.

3. Responsibility for ethical research practice lies with the principal researcher, while others involved in the research activities share ethical obligation and full responsibility for their own actions.

4. In research with human subjects, researchers are responsible for the subjects' welfare throughout the experiment and they must take all reasonable precautions to avoid causing injurious psychological, physical, or social effects on their subjects.

5. All research subjects must be informed of the purpose of the study except when withholding information or providing misinformation to them is essential to the investigation. In such research the member must be responsible for corrective action as soon as possible following completion of the research.

6. Participation in research must be voluntary. Involuntary participation is appropriate only when it can be demonstrated that participation will have no harmful effects on subjects and is essential to the investigation.

7. When reporting research results, explicit mention must be made of all variables and conditions known to the investigator that might affect the outcome of the investigation or the interpretation of the data.

8. The member must be responsible for conducting and reporting investigations in a manner that minimizes the possibility that results will be misleading.

9. The member has an obligation to make available sufficient original research data to qualified others who may wish to replicate the study.

10. When supplying data, aiding in the research of another person, reporting research results, or in making original data available, due care must be taken to disguise the identity of the subjects in the absence of specific authorization from such subjects to do otherwise.

11. When conducting and reporting research, the member must be familiar with, and give recognition to, previous work on the topic, as well as to observe all copyright laws and follow the principles of giving full credit to all to whom credit is due.

12. The member must give due credit through joint authorship, acknowledgment, footnote statements, or other appropriate means to those who have contributed significantly to the research and/or publication, in accordance with such contributions.

13. The member must communicate to other members the results of any research judged to be of professional or scientific value. Results reflecting unfavorably on institutions, programs, services, or vested interests must not be withheld for such reasons.

14. If members agree to cooperate with another individual in research and/or publication, they incur an obligation to cooperate as promised in terms of punctuality of performance and with full regard to the completeness and accuracy of the information required.

15. Ethical practice requires that authors not submit the same manuscript or one essentially similar in content, for simultaneous publication consideration by two or more journals. In addition, manuscripts published in whole or in substantial part in another journal or published work should not be submitted for publication without acknowledgment and permission from the previous publication.

Section E: Consulting

Consultation refers to a voluntary relationship between a professional helper and help-needing individual, group or social unit in which the consultant is providing help to the client(s) in defining and solving a work-related problem or potential problem with a client or client system. (This definition is adapted from Kurpius, DeWayne. Consultation theory and process: An integrated model. *Personnel and Guidance Journal*, 1978, 56.)

1. The member acting as consultant must have a high degree of self-awareness of his-her own values, knowledge, skills, limitations, and needs in entering a helping relationship that involves human and-or organizational change and that the focus of the relationship be on the issues to be resolved and not on the person(s) presenting the problem.

2. There must be understanding and agreement between member and client for the problem definition, change goals, and predicated consequences of interventions selected.

3. The member must be reasonably certain that she/he or the organization represented has the necessary competencies and resources for giving the kind of help that is needed now or may develop later and that appropriate referral resources are available to the consultant.

4. The consulting relationship must be one in which client adaptability and growth toward self-direction are encouraged and cultivated. The member must maintain this role consistently and not become a decision maker for the client or create a future dependency on the consultant.

5. When announcing consultant availability for services, the member conscientiously adheres to the Association's *Ethical Standards*.

6. The member must refuse a private fee or other remuneration for consultation with persons who are entitled to these services through the member's employing institution or agency. The policies of a particular agency may make explicit provisions for private practice with agency clients by members of its staff. In such instances, the clients must be apprised of other options open to them should they seek private counseling services.

Section F: Private practice

1. The member should assist the profession by facilitating the availability of counseling services in private as well as public settings.

2. In advertising services as a private practitioner, the member must advertise the services in such a manner so as to accurately inform the public as to services, expertise, profession, and techniques of counseling in a professional manner. A member who assumes an executive leadership role in the organization shall not permit his/her name to be used in professional notices during periods when not actively engaged in the private practice of counseling.

   The member may list the following: highest relevant degree, type and level of certification or license, type and/or description of services, and other relevant information. Such information must not contain false, inaccurate, misleading, partial, out-of-context, or deceptive material or statements.

3. Members may join in partnership/corporation with other members and-or other professionals provided that each member of the partnership or corporation makes clear the separate specialties by name in compliance with the regulations of the locality.

4. A member has an obligation to withdraw from a counseling relationship if it is believed that employment will result in violation of the *Ethical Standards*. If the mental or physical condition of the member renders it difficult to carry out an effective professional relationship or if the member is discharged by the client because the counseling relationship is no longer productive for the client, then the member is obligated to terminate the counseling relationship.
5. A member must adhere to the regulations for private practice of the locality where the services are offered.
6. It is unethical to use one's institutional affiliation to recruit clients for one's private practice.

Section G: Personnel administration

It is recognized that most members are employed in public or quasi-public institutions. The functioning of a member within an institution must contribute to the goals of the institution and vice versa if either is to accomplish their respective goals or objectives. It is therefore essential that the member and the institution function in ways to (a) make the institution's goals explicit and public; (b) make the member's contribution to institutional goals specific; and (c) foster mutual accountability for goal achievement.

To accomplish these objectives, it is recognized that the member and the employer must share responsibilities in the formulation and implementation of personnel policies.

1. Members must define and describe the parameters and levels of their professional competency.
2. Members must establish interpersonal relations and working agreements with supervisors and subordinates regarding counseling or clinical relationships, confidentiality, distinction between public and private material, maintenance, and dissemination of recorded information, work load and accountability. Working agreements in each instance must be specified and made known to those concerned.
3. Members must alert their employers to conditions that may be potentially disruptive or damaging.
4. Members must inform employers of conditions that may limit their effectiveness.
5. Members must submit regularly to professional review and evaluation.
6. Members must be responsible for inservice development of self and-or staff.
7. Members must inform their staff of goals and programs.

8. Members must provide personnel practices that guarantee and enhance the rights and welfare of each recipient of their service.
9. Members must select competent persons and assign responsibilities compatible with their skills and experiences.

Section H: Preparation standards

Members who are responsible for training others must be guided by the preparation standards of the Association and relevant Division(s). The member who functions in the capacity of trainer assumes unique ethical responsibilities that frequently go beyond that of the member who does not function in a training capacity. These ethical responsibilities are outlined as follows:

1. Members must orient students to program expectations, basic skills development, and employment prospects prior to admission to the program.
2. Members in charge of learning experiences must establish programs that integrate academic study and supervised practice.
3. Members must establish a program directed toward developing students' skills, knowledge, and self-understanding, stated whenever possible in competency or performance terms.
4. Members must identify the levels of competencies of their students in compliance with relevant Division standards. These competencies must accommodate the para-professional as well as the professional.
5. Members, through continual student evaluation and appraisal, must be aware of the personal limitations of the learner that might impede future performance. The instructor must not only assist the learner in securing remedial assistance but also screen from the program those individuals who are unable to provide competent services.
6. Members must provide a program that includes training in research commensurate with levels of role functioning. Para-professional and technician-level personnel must be trained as consumers of research. In addition, these personnel must learn how to evaluate their own and their program's effectiveness. Graduate training, especially at the doctoral level, would include preparation for original research by the member.
7. Members must make students aware of the ethical responsibilities and standards of the profession.
8. Preparatory programs must encourage students to value the ideals of service to individuals and to soci-

ety. In this regard, direct financial remuneration or lack thereof must not influence the quality of service rendered. Monetary considerations must not be allowed to overshadow professional and humanitarian needs.

9. Members responsible for educational programs must be skilled as teachers and practitioners.

10. Members must present thoroughly varied theoretical positions so that students may make comparisons and have the opportunity to select a position.

11. Members must develop clear policies within their educational institutions regarding field placement and the roles of the student and the instructor in such placements.

12. Members must ensure that forms of learning focusing on self-understanding or growth are voluntary, or if required as part of the education program, are made known to prospective students prior to entering the program. When the education program offers a growth experience with an emphasis on self-disclosure or other relatively intimate or personal involvement, the member must have no administrative, supervisory, or evaluating authority regarding the participant.

13. Members must conduct an educational program in keeping with the current relevant guidelines of the American Personnel and Guidance Association and its Divisions.

B. Code of Professional Ethics, *American Association for Marriage and Family Therapy*

Section I: Code of personal conduct

1. A therapist provides professional service to anyone regardless of race, religion, sex, political affiliation, social or economic status, or choice of lifestyle. When a therapist cannot offer service for any reason, he or she will make proper referral. Therapists are encouraged to devote a portion of their time to work for which there is little or no financial return.

2. A therapist will not use his or her counseling relationship to further personal, religious, political, or business interests.

3. A therapist will neither offer nor accept payment for referrals, and will actively seek all significant information from the source of referral.

4. A therapist will not knowingly offer service to a client who is in treatment with another clinical professional without consultation among the parties involved.

5. A therapist will not disparage the qualifications of any colleague.

6. Every member of the AAMFT has an obligation to continuing education and professional growth in all possible ways, including active participation in the meetings and affairs of the Association.

7. A therapist will not attempt to diagnose, prescribe for, treat, or advise on problems outside the recognized boundaries of the therapist's competence.

8. A therapist will attempt to avoid relationships with clients which might impair professional judgment or

increase the risks of exploiting clients. Examples of such relationships include: treatment of family members, close friends, employees, or supervisees. Sexual intimacy with clients is unethical.

9. The AAMFT encourages its members to affiliate with professional groups, clinics, or agencies operating in the field of marriage and family life. Similarly, interdisciplinary contact and cooperation are encouraged.

Section II: Relations with clients

1. A therapist, while offering dignified and reasonable support, is cautious in prognosis and will not exaggerate the efficacy of his or her services.

2. The therapist recognizes the importance of clear understandings on financial matters with clients. Arrangements for payments are settled at the beginning of a therapeutic relationship.

3. A therapist keeps records of each case and stores them in such a way as to insure safety and confidentiality, in accordance with the highest professional and legal standards.

   a. Information shall be revealed only to professional persons concerned with the case. Written and oral reports should present only data germane to the purposes of the inquiry; every effort should be made to avoid undue invasion of privacy.

   b. The therapist is responsible for informing clients of the limits of confidentiality.

Code of Professional Ethics, by the American Association for Marriage and Family Therapy. Copyright by the American Association for Marriage and Family Therapy (no date). Reprinted by permission.

c. Written permission shall be granted by the clients involved before data may be divulged.

d. Information is not communicated to others without consent of the client unless there is clear and immediate danger to an individual or to society, and then only to the appropriate family members, professional workers, or public authorities.

4. A therapist deals with relationships at varying stages of their history. While respecting at all times the rights of clients to make their own decisions, the therapist has a duty to assess the situation according to the highest professional standards. In all circumstances, the therapist will clearly advise a client that the decision to separate or divorce is the responsibility solely of the client. In such an event, the therapist has the continuing responsibility to offer support and counsel during the period of readjustment.

Section III: Research and publication

1. The therapist is obligated to protect the welfare of his or her research subjects. The conditions of the Human Subjects Experimentation shall prevail, as specified by the Department of Health, Education and Welfare guidelines.

2. Publication credit is assigned to those who have contributed to a publication, in proportion to their contribution, and in accordance with customary publication practices.

Section IV: Implementation

1. In accepting membership in the Association, each member binds himself or herself to accept the judgment of fellow members as to standards of professional ethics, subject to the safeguards provided in this section. Acceptance of membership implies consent to abide by the acts of discipline herein set forth and as enumerated in the Bylaws of the Association. It is the duty of each member to safeguard these standards of ethical practice. Should a fellow member appear to violate this Code, he or she may be cautioned through friendly remonstrance, colleague consultation with the party in question, or formal complaint may be filed in accordance with the following procedure:

a. Complaint of unethical practice shall be made in writing to the Chairperson of the Standing Committee on Ethics and Professional Practices and to the Executive Director. A copy of the complaint shall be furnished to the person or persons against whom it is directed.

b. Should the Standing Committee decide the complaint warrants investigation, it shall so notify the charged party(ies) in writing. When investigation is indicated, the Standing Committee shall constitute itself an Investigating Committee and shall include in its membership at least one member of the Board and at least two members (other than the charging or charged parties or any possible witnesses) from the local area involved. This Investigating Committee or representatives thereof shall make one or more local visits of investigation of the complaint. After full investigation following due process and offering the charged party(ies) opportunity to defend him or herself, the Committee shall report its findings and recommendations to the Board of Directors for action.

c. The charged party(ies) shall have free access to all charges and evidence cited against him or her, and shall have full freedom to defend himself or herself before the Investigating Committee and the Board, including the right to legal counsel.

d. Recommendation made by the Committee shall be:
   1. Advice that the charges be dropped as unfounded.
   2. Specified admonishment.
   3. Reprimand.
   4. Dismissal from membership.

2. Should a member of this Association be expelled, he or she shall at once surrender his or her membership certificate to the Board of Directors. Failure to do so shall result in such action as legal counsel may recommend.

3. Should a member of this Association be expelled from another recognized professional association or his/her state license revoked for unethical conduct, the Standing Committee on Ethics shall investigate the matter and, where appropriate, act in the manner provided above respecting charges of unethical conduct.

4. The Committee will also give due consideration to a formal complaint by a non-member.

Section V: Public information and advertising

All professional presentations to the public will be governed by the Standards on Public Information and Advertising.

STANDARDS ON PUBLIC INFORMATION AND ADVERTISING

Section I: General principles

The practice of marriage and family therapy as a mental health profession is in the public interest. Therefore, it is appropriate for the well-trained and qualified practitioner to inform the public of the availability of his/her services. However, much needs to be done to educate the public as to the services available from qualified marriage and family therapists. Therefore, the clinical members of AAMFT have a responsibility to the public to engage in appropriate informational activities and to avoid misrepresentation or misleading statements in keeping with the following general principles and specific regulations.

Selection of a marriage and family therapist

A. At a time when the Human Services field is burgeoning and becoming increasingly complex and specialized, few marriage and family therapists are willing and competent to deal with every kind of marital or family problem, and many laypersons have difficulty in determining the competence of psychotherapists in general and marriage and family therapists in particular to render different types of services. The selection of a marriage and family therapist is particularly difficult for transients, persons moving into new areas, persons of limited education or means, and others who have had no previous experience or the degree of sophistication required to evaluate training and competence or because they are in some sort of crisis.

B. Selection of a marriage and family therapist by a layperson should be made on an informed basis. Advice and recommendation of third parties—physicians, other professionals, relatives, friends, acquaintances, business associates—and restrained publicity may be helpful. A marriage and family therapist should not compensate another person for recommending him/her, for influencing a prospective client to employ him/her, or to encourage future recommendations. Advertisements and public communications, whether in directories, announcement cards, newspapers, or on radio or television, should be formulated to convey information that is necessary to make an appropriate selection. Self-praising should be avoided. Information that may be helpful in some situations would include: (1) office information, such as name, including a group name and names of professional associates, address, telephone number, credit card acceptability, languages spoken and written, and office hours; (2) earned degrees, state licensure and/or certification, and AAMFT clinical membership status; (3) description of practice, including a statement that practice is limited to one or more fields of marriage and family therapy; and (4) permitted fee information.

C. The proper motivation for commercial publicity by marriage and family therapists lies in the need to inform the public of the availability of competent, independent marriage and family therapists. The public benefit derived from advertising depends upon the usefulness of the information provided to the community to which it is directed. Advertising marked by excesses of content, volume, scope, or frequency, or which unduly emphasizes unrepresentative biographical information, does not provide that public benefit. The use of media whose scope or nature clearly suggests that the use is intended for self-praising of the therapist without concomitant benefit to the public distorts the legitimate purpose of informing the public and is clearly improper. Indeed, this and other improper advertising may hinder informed selection of a competent, independent professional and advertising that involves excessive cost may unnecessarily increase fees for marriage and family therapy.

D. Advertisements and other communications should make it apparent that the necessity [for] and advisability of marriage and family therapy depend on variant factors that must be evaluated individually. Because fee information frequently may be incomplete and misleading to a layperson, a marriage and family therapist should exercise great care to assure that fee information is complete and accurate. Because of the individuality of each problem, public statements regarding average, minimum, or estimated fees may be deceiving as will commercial publicity conveying information as to results previously achieved, general or average solutions, or expected outcomes. It would be misleading to advertise a set fee for a specific type of case without adhering to the stated fee in charging clients. Advertisements or public claims that use statistical data or other information based on past performance or prediction of future success may be deceptive if they ignore important variables. Only factual assertions, and not opinions, should be made in public communications. Not only must commercial publicity be truthful but its accurate meaning must be apparent to the average layperson. No guarantees about the outcomes of therapy should be made or implied. Any commercial publicity or advertising for which payment is made should so indicate unless it is apparent from the context that it is paid publicity or an advertisement.

E. The desirability of affording the public access to information relevant to their needs and problems has resulted in some relaxation of the former restrictions against advertising by marriage and family therapists. Historically, those restrictions were imposed to prevent deceptive publicity that would mislead laypersons, cause distrust of the profession, and undermine public confidence in the profession, and all marriage and family therapists should remain vigilant to prevent such results. Ambiguous information relevant to a layperson's decision regarding his/her selection of a marriage and family therapist, provided in ways that do not comport with the dignity of the profession or which demean the amelioration of human problems, is inappropriate in public communications. The regulation of advertising by marriage and family therapists is rooted in the public interest. Advertising through which a marriage and family therapist seeks business by use of extravagant or brash statements or appeals to fears could mislead and harm the layperson. Furthermore, public communications that would produce unrealistic expectations in particular cases and bring about distrust of the profession would be harmful to society. Thus, public confidence in our profession would be impaired by such advertisements of professional services. The therapist-client relationship, being personal and unique, should not be established as the result of pressures, deceptions, or exploitation of the vulnerability of clients frequently experiencing significant stress at the time they seek help.

F. The Regulations recognize the value of giving assistance in the selection process through forms of advertising that furnish identification of a marriage and family therapist while avoiding falsity, deception, and misrepresentation. All publicity should be evaluated with regard to its effects on the layperson. The layperson is best served if advertisements contain no misleading information or emotional appeals, and emphasize the necessity of an individualized evaluation of the situation before conclusions as to need for a particular type of therapy and probable expenses can be made. The therapist-client rela-

tionship should result from a free and informed choice by the layperson. Unwarranted promises of benefits, over-persuasion, or vexatious or harassing conduct is improper.

G. The name under which a marriage and family therapist conducts his/her practice may be a factor in the selection process. The use of a name which could mislead laypersons concerning the identity, responsibility, source, and status of those practicing thereunder is not proper. Likewise, one should not hold oneself out as being a partner or associate of a firm if he/she is not one in fact.

H. In order to avoid the possibility of misleading persons with whom he/she deals, a marriage and family therapist should be scrupulous in the representation of his/her professional background, training, and status. In some instances a marriage and family therapist confines his/her practice to a particular area within the field of marriage and family therapy. However, a member should not hold himself/herself out as a specialist without evidence of training, education, and supervised experience in settings which meet recognized professional standards. A marriage and family therapist may, however, indicate, if it is factual, a limitation of his/her practice or that he/she practices within one or more particular areas of marriage and family treatment in public pronouncements which will assist laypersons in selecting a marriage and family therapist and accurately describe the limited area in which the member practices.

I. The marriage and family therapist should support the creation and evolution of ethical, approved plans (such as marriage and family therapist referral systems) which aid in the selection of qualified therapists.

Section II: Regulations

A. The American Association for Marriage and Family Therapy is the sole owner of its name, its logo, and the abbreviated initials AAMFT. Use of the name, logo, and initials is restricted to the following conditions.

1. Only individual clinical members may identify their membership in AAMFT in public information or advertising materials, not associates or students of organizations.

2. The initials AAMFT may not be used following one's name in the manner of an academic degree because this is misleading.

3. Use of the logo is limited to the association, its committees and regional divisions when they are

engaged in bona fide activities as units or divisions of AAMFT.

4. A regional division or chapter of AAMFT may use the AAMFT insignia to list its individual members as a group (e.g., in the Yellow Pages). When all Clinical Members practicing within a directory district have been invited to list, any one or more member may do so.

B. A marriage and family therapist shall not knowingly make a representation about his/her ability, background, or experience, or that of a partner or associate, or about the fee or any other aspect of a proposed professional engagement, that is false, fraudulent, misleading, or deceptive, and that might reasonably be expected to induce reliance by a member of the public.

C. Without limitation, a false, fraudulent, misleading, or deceptive statement or claim includes a statement or claim which:

1. Contains a material misrepresentation of fact;

2. Omits to state any material fact necessary to make the statement, in light of all circumstances, not misleading;

3. Is intended or is likely to create an unjustified expectation;

4. Relates to professional fees other than:

   a. a statement of the fee for an initial consultation; a statement of the fee charges for a specific service, the description of which would not be misunderstood or be deceptive;

   b. a statement of the range of fees for specifically described services, provided there is a reasonable disclosure of all relevant variables and considerations so that the statement would not be misunderstood or be deceptive;

   c. a statement of specified hourly rates, provided the statement makes clear that the total charge will vary according to the number of hours devoted to the matter;

   d. the availability of credit arrangements; or

5. Contains a representation or implication that is likely to cause an ordinary prudent person to misunderstand or be deceived or fails to contain reasonable warnings or disclaimers necessary to make a representation or implication not deceptive.

D. A member shall not, on his/her own behalf or on behalf of a partner or associate or any other therapist associated with the firm, use or participate in the use of any form of advertising of services which:

1. Contains statistical data or other information based on past performance or prediction of future success;

2. Contains a testimonial about or endorsement of a therapist;

3. Contains a statement of opinion as to the quality of the services or contains a representation or implication regarding the quality of services, whether therapeutic or educational, which is not susceptible of reasonable verification by the public;

4. Is intended or is likely to attract clients by use of showmanship or self-praising.

E. A member shall not compensate or give anything of value to a representative of the press, radio, television, or other communication medium in anticipation of or in return for professional publicity in a news item. A paid advertisement must be identified as such unless it is apparent from the context that it is a paid advertisement. If the paid advertisement is communicated to the public by use of radio or television, it shall be prerecorded, approved for broadcast by the therapist, and a recording of the actual transmission shall be retained by the therapist.

PROFESSIONAL NOTICES, LETTERHEADS, OFFICES, AND DIRECTORY LISTINGS

F. A member or group of members shall not use or participate in the use of a professional card, professional announcement card, office sign, letterhead, telephone directory listing, association directory listing, or a similar professional notice or device if it includes a statement or claim that is false, fraudulent, misleading, or deceptive within the meaning of Section II, C or that violates the regulations contained in Section II, D.

G. A member shall not practice under a name that is misleading as to the identity, responsibility, or status of those practicing thereunder, or is otherwise false, fraudulent, misleading, or deceptive within the meaning of Section II, C or is contrary to law. However, the name of a professional corporation or professional association may contain "P.C." or "P.A." or similar symbols indicating the nature of the organization.

H. A member shall not hold himself/herself out as having a partnership with one or more other qualified therapists unless they are in fact partners.

I. A partnership shall not be formed or continued between or among members in different geographical locations unless all enumerations of the members or associates of the firm on its letterhead and in other permissible listings make clear the limitations due to geographical separation of the members or associates of the firm.

J. Academic degrees earned from institutions accredited by regionally or nationally recognized accrediting agencies or associations may be used or permitted to be used provided that the statement or claim is neither false, fraudulent, misleading, or deceptive within the meaning of Section II, C.

SOLICITATION OF PROFESSIONAL EMPLOYMENT

K. A member shall not seek, by in-person contact, his/her employment as a therapist (or employment of a partner or associate) by a client who has not sought his/her advice regarding employment of a marriage and family therapist if:

1. The solicitation involves use of a statement or claim that is false, fraudulent, misleading, or deceptive within the meaning of Section II, C; or

2. The solicitation involves the use of undue influence; or

3. The potential client is apparently in a physical or mental condition which would make it unlikely that he or she could exercise reasonable, considered judgment as to the selection of a marriage and family therapist.

L. A member shall not compensate or give anything of value to a person or organization to recommend or secure his/her employment by a claim or as a reward for having made a recommendation resulting in his/her employment by a client.

M. A member shall not accept employment when he/she knows or it is obvious that the person who seeks his/her service does so as a result of conduct prohibited by this Section.

SUGGESTION OF NEED OF MARRIAGE OR FAMILY THERAPY

N. A member who has given unsolicited advice to a layperson that he/she/they should obtain marriage or family therapy shall not accept employment results from that advice if:

1. The advice embodies or implies a statement or claim that is false, fraudulent, misleading, or deceptive within the meaning of Section II, C or that violates the regulations contained in Section II, D; or

2. The advice involves the use by the marriage and family therapist of coercion, duress, compulsion, intimidation, unwarranted promises of benefits, overreaching, [or] vexatious or harassing conduct.

C. Code of Ethics,
National Association of Social Workers

I. The social worker's conduct and comportment as a social worker

A. *Propriety.* The social worker should maintain high standards of personal conduct in the capacity or identity as social worker.

1. The private conduct of the social worker is a personal matter to the same degree as is any other person's, except when such conduct compromises the fulfillment of professional responsibilities.
2. The social worker should not participate in, condone, or be associated with dishonesty, fraud, deceit, or misrepresentation.
3. The social worker should distinguish clearly between statements and actions made as a private individual and as a representative of the social work profession or an organization or group.

B. *Competence and professional development.* The social worker should strive to become and remain proficient in professional practice and the performance of professional functions.

1. The social worker should accept responsibility or employment only on the basis of existing competence or the intention to acquire the necessary competence.
2. The social worker should not misrepresent professional qualifications, education, experience, or affiliations.

C. *Service.* The social worker should regard as primary the service obligation of the social work profession.

1. The social worker should retain ultimate responsibility for the quality and extent of the service that individual assumes, assigns, or performs.
2. The social worker should act to prevent practices that are inhumane or discriminatory against any person or group of persons.

D. *Integrity.* The social worker should act in accordance with the highest standards of professional integrity and impartiality.

1. The social worker should be alert to and resist the influences and pressures that interfere with the exercise of professional discretion and impartial judgment required for the performance of professional functions.
2. The social worker should not exploit professional relationships for personal gain.

E. *Scholarship and research.* The social worker engaged in study and research should be guided by the conventions of scholarly inquiry.

1. The social worker engaged in research should consider carefully its possible consequences for human beings.
2. The social worker engaged in research should ascertain that the consent of participants in the research is voluntary and informed, without any implied deprivation or penalty for refusal to participate, and with due regard for participants' privacy and dignity.
3. The social worker engaged in research should

Reprinted with permission, *Code of Ethics* of the National Association of Social Workers as adopted by the 1979 NASW Delegate Assembly, effective July 1, 1980.

protect participants from unwarranted physical or mental discomfort, distress, harm, danger, or deprivation.

4. The social worker who engages in the evaluation of services or cases should discuss them only for the professional purposes and only with persons directly and professionally concerned with them.

5. Information obtained about participants in research should be treated as confidential.

6. The social worker should take credit only for work actually done in connection with scholarly and research endeavors and credit contributions made by others.

II. The social worker's ethical responsibility to clients

F. *Primacy of clients' interests.* The social worker's primary responsibility is to clients.

1. The social worker should serve clients with devotion, loyalty, determination, and the maximum application of professional skill and competence.

2. The social worker should not exploit relationships with clients for personal advantage, or solicit the clients of one's agency for private practice.

3. The social worker should not practice, condone, facilitate, or collaborate with any form of discrimination on the basis of race, color, sex, sexual orientation, age, religion, national origin, marital status, political belief, mental or physical handicap, or any other preference or personal characteristic, condition, or status.

4. The social worker should avoid relationships or commitments that conflict with the interests of clients.

5. The social worker should under no circumstances engage in sexual activities with clients.

6. The social worker should provide clients with accurate and complete information regarding the extent and nature of the services available to them.

7. The social worker should apprise clients of their risks, rights, opportunities, and obligations associated with social service to them.

8. The social worker should seek advice and counsel of colleagues and supervisors whenever such consultation is in the best interest of clients.

9. The social worker should terminate service to clients, and professional relationships with them,

when such service and relationships are no longer required or no longer serve the clients' needs or interests.

10. The social worker should withdraw services precipitously only under unusual circumstances, giving careful consideration to all factors in the situation and taking care to minimize possible adverse effects.

11. The social worker who anticipates the termination or interruption of service to clients should notify clients promptly and seek the transfer, referral, or continuation of services in relation to the clients' needs and preferences.

G. *Rights and prerogatives of clients.* The social worker should make every effort to foster maximum self-determination on the part of clients.

1. When the social worker must act on behalf of a client who has been adjudged legally incompetent, the social worker should safeguard the interests and rights of that client.

2. When another individual has been legally authorized to act in behalf of a client, the social worker should deal with that person always with the client's best interest in mind.

3. The social worker should not engage in any action that violates or diminishes the civil or legal rights of clients.

H. *Confidentiality and privacy.* The social worker should respect the privacy of clients and hold in confidence all information obtained in the course of professional service.

1. The social worker should share with others confidences revealed by clients, without their consent, only for compelling professional reasons.

2. The social worker should inform clients fully about the limits of confidentiality in a given situation, the purposes for which information is obtained, and how it may be used.

3. The social worker should afford clients reasonable access to any official social work records concerning them.

4. When providing clients with access to records, the social worker should take due care to protect the confidences of others contained in those records.

5. The social worker should obtain informed consent of clients before taping, recording, or permitting third party observation of their activities.

I. *Fees.* When setting fees, the social worker should ensure that they are fair, reasonable, considerate, and commensurate with the service performed and with due regard for the clients' ability to pay.

1. The social worker should not divide a fee or accept or give anything of value for receiving or making a referral.

III. The social worker's ethical responsibility to colleagues

J. *Respect, fairness, and courtesy.* The social worker should treat colleagues with respect, courtesy, fairness, and good faith.

1. The social worker should cooperate with colleagues to promote professional interests and concerns.
2. The social worker should respect confidences shared by colleagues in the course of their professional relationships and transactions.
3. The social worker should create and maintain conditions of practice that facilitate ethical and competent professional performance by colleagues.
4. The social worker should treat with respect, and represent accurately and fairly, the qualifications, views, and findings of colleagues and use appropriate channels to express judgments on these matters.
5. The social worker who replaces or is replaced by a colleague in professional practice should act with consideration for the interest, character, and reputation of that colleague.
6. The social worker should not exploit a dispute between a colleague and employers to obtain a position or otherwise advance the social worker's interest.
7. The social worker should seek arbitration or mediation resolution for compelling professional reasons.
8. The social worker should extend to colleagues of other professions the same respect and cooperation that is extended to social work colleagues.
9. The social worker who serves as an employer, supervisor, or mentor to colleagues should make orderly and explicit arrangements regarding the conditions of their continuing professional relationship.
10. The social worker who has the responsibility for employing and evaluating the performance of other staff members should fulfill such responsibility in a fair, considerate, and equi-

table manner, on the basis of clearly enunciated criteria.

11. The social worker who has the responsibility for evaluating the performance of employees, supervisees, or students should share evaluations with them.

K. *Dealing with colleagues' clients.* The social worker has the responsibility to relate to the clients of colleagues with full professional consideration.

1. The social worker should not solicit the clients of colleagues.
2. The social worker should not assume professional responsibility for the clients of another agency or a colleague without appropriate communication with that agency or colleague.
3. The social worker who serves the clients of colleagues, during a temporary absence or emergency, should serve those clients with the same consideration as that afforded any client.

IV. The social worker's ethical responsibility to employers and employing organizations

L. *Commitments to employing organization.* The social worker should adhere to commitments made to the employing organization.

1. The social worker should work to improve the employing agency's policies and procedures, and the efficiency and effectiveness of its services.
2. The social worker should not accept employment or arrange student field placements in an organization which is currently under public sanction by NASW for violating personnel standards, or imposing limitations on or penalties for professional actions on behalf of clients.
3. The social worker should act to prevent and eliminate discrimination in the employing organization's work assignments and in its employment policies and practices.
4. The social worker should use with scrupulous regard, and only for the purpose for which they are intended, the resources of the employing organization.

V. The social worker's ethical responsibility to the social work profession

M. *Maintaining the integrity of the profession.* The social worker should uphold and advance the values, ethics, knowledge, and mission of the profession.

1. The social worker should protect and enhance the dignity and integrity of the profession and should be responsible and vigorous in discussion and criticism of the profession.
2. The social worker should take action through appropriate channels against unethical conduct by any other member of the profession.
3. The social worker should act to prevent the unauthorized and unqualified practice of social work.
4. The social worker should make no misrepresentation in advertising as to qualifications, competence, service, or results to be achieved.

N. *Community service.* The social worker should assist the profession in making social services available to the general public.

1. The social worker should contribute time and professional expertise to activities that promote respect for the utility, the integrity, and the competence of the social work profession.
2. The social worker should support the formulation, development, enactment, and implementation of social policies of concern to the profession.

O. *Development of knowledge.* The social worker should take responsibility for identifying, developing, and fully utilizing knowledge for professional practice.

1. The social worker should base practice upon recognized knowledge relevant to social work.
2. The social worker should critically examine and keep current with emerging knowledge relevant to social work.
3. The social worker should contribute to the knowledge base of social work and share research knowledge and practice wisdom with colleagues.

VI. The social worker's ethical responsibility to society

P. *Promoting the general welfare.* The social worker should promote the general welfare of society.

1. The social worker should act to prevent and eliminate discrimination against any person or group on the basis of race, color, sex, sexual orientation, age, religion, national origin, marital status, political belief, mental or physical handicap, or any other preference or personal characteristic, condition, or status.
2. The social worker should act to ensure that all persons have access to the resources, services, and opportunities which they require.
3. The social worker should act to expand choice and opportunity for all persons, with special regard for disadvantaged or oppressed groups and persons.
4. The social worker should promote conditions that encourage respect for the diversity of cultures which constitute American society.
5. The social worker should provide appropriate professional services in public emergencies.
6. The social worker should advocate changes in policy and legislation to improve social conditions and to promote social justice.
7. The social worker should encourage informed participation by the public in shaping social policies and institutions.

D. Standards for the Private Practice of Clinical Social Work, *National Association of Social Workers*

Qualifications for the clinical social worker in private practice

I. The clinical social worker in private practice shall meet the educational and practice requirements of the National Association of Social Workers, shall maintain current knowledge of scientific and professional developments, and shall obtain additional training when required for effective practice.

A. The practitioner shall have a Master's or Doctoral degree from an accredited school of social work plus two years or 3,000 hours of post-degree direct practice experience, supervised by a Master's level clinical social worker, in a hospital, clinic, agency, or other institutional setting.

B. The practitioner shall abide by NASW's continuing education requirements and other standards relating to competence in clinical practice which shall be established by the Association.

C. The clinical social worker practicing privately for the first time should obtain consultation from an experienced clinical social worker.

D. The practitioner shall limit the practice to demonstrated areas of professional competence.

E. When using specialized methods of practice which range beyond those normally learned in a school of social work or social work practice setting, the practitioner shall obtain training or professional supervision in the modalities employed.

Legal aspects of private clinical practice

II. The clinical social worker in private practice shall comply with the laws of the jurisdiction within which s/he practices. The practitioner shall adhere to the educational, experiential, and other practice requirements of law in those jurisdictions which regulate clinical social work.

Professional identification and commitment

III. The privately practicing clinician whose training is in social work: (a) identifies himself/herself as a member of the social work profession, regardless of clinical orientation; and (b) is committed to the profession.

A. Commitment to the profession is demonstrated through organizational participation, teaching, writing, and other activities.

B. The practitioner should belong to the NASW, ACSW, the NASW Register of Clinical Social Workers and shall adhere to the NASW Code of Ethics.

C. The privately practicing clinical social worker, like all social workers, should seek modification within the client and within those societal systems and institutions which affect the client.

D. The practitioner shall be subject to NASW standards and grievance procedures and to peer and utilization review depending upon state and local law and customary professional practice.

Standards for the Private Practice of Clinical Social Work, by the National Association of Social Workers (draft of April 22, 1981). Reprinted with permission from the NASW Policy Statement Series.

The maintenance of confidentiality

IV. The clinical social worker in private practice shall abide by the provisions of confidentiality in the NASW Code of Ethics. (See Appendix I.)

   A. The social worker should share with others confidences revealed by clients, without their consent, only for compelling professional reasons.

   1. The clinical social worker in private practice may find it necessary to reveal confidential information disclosed by the patient to protect the patient or the community from imminent danger.

   2. When the clinical social worker in private practice is ordered by the court to reveal the confidences entrusted by patients, the practitioner may comply or may ethically hold the right to dissent within the framework of the law.

The management aspects of a private clinical practice

V. To render the best possible service to the client, the clinical social worker shall be capable of managing the business aspects of a private practice.

   A. The clinical practitioner shall be familiar with relevant state and local laws on the conduct of a business.

   B. The practitioner should carry malpractice and premises liability insurance.

   C. The practitioner shall deal expediently and efficiently with insurance companies covering clinical social work services. This includes maintenance of records and the use of diagnostic categories in billing private and governmental carriers.

   D. The private practitioner and client shall agree to a contract during the initial visit(s). Conditions of the contract shall be clear and explicit. These shall include:

   1. Agreement about fees; insurance; length, frequency, and location of sessions; appointments missed or cancelled without adequate notice; vacation coverage during an absence; collateral contacts. (The foregoing information may be provided on a standardized form.)

   2. Agreement regarding goals of treatment.

   3. Informing the client of his/her rights.

   E. Private clinical practitioners shall keep up-to-date, accurate records on the treatment of the client. (Records should protect confidentiality while recording subjects discussed in sufficient detail to justify therapeutic action.)

   F. Offices in which services are rendered shall be located for client safety, accessibility, and privacy.

   G. A social worker in private practice may advertise. The advertisement should clearly inform a prospective client of the nature of the services to be received. Advertisements shall not misrepresent qualifications, competence, service, or results to be achieved. (See Code of Ethics V.M.4.)

   H. When a clinical social worker terminates a private practice, there is a responsibility to refer clients elsewhere. If the clinical social worker chooses, s/he may carefully select a successor to whom the practice may be sold. Clients should be given the choice of transferring to the successor or to another clinician. The responsible practitioner collaborates with the successor for the maximum benefit of their mutual clients.

   I. The privately practicing clinical social worker's rates shall be commensurate with services performed and with fees charged by mental health professionals practicing in the community. Clients who cannot pay the practitioner's fee should be referred to a mental health or family agency or to a private practitioner with lower rates.

   J. The practitioner's bill shall reflect services actually rendered.

   K. The clinical social worker shall not divide a fee or accept or give anything of value for receiving or making a referral. (See Code of Ethics II.I.1.)

   L. Unpaid accounts may be collected through a collection agency [or] small claims court or through other legal action when efforts to collect directly from the client have failed.

Modalities and methods of treatment

VI. A variety of professionally acceptable and ethically sanctioned modalities and methods of treatment may be used in the private practice of clinical social work.

   A. The practitioner shall be familiar with the client's physical condition, collaborating with a physician when the client is chronically ill or disabled and/or using medication. The practitioner shall refer the client to a physician for treatment or medication when necessary.

B. The privately practicing clinical social worker may certify or admit clients to institutional facilities depending upon state or local practice.

C. An appointment with a relative or collateral shall be made only when the client's permission has been obtained.

D. The privately practicing clinical social worker shall not discriminate against or refuse to treat a client because of race, sex, color, sexual orientation, religion, lifestyle, mental or physical handicap. (See Code of Ethics II.F.3.)

E. The private practice may be limited to certain specialties but clients outside the practitioner's area of expertise should be referred to appropriate resources.

F. The private practitioner shall not engage in sexual activities with clients. (See Code of Ethics II.F.5.)

G. Clients should be treated as expeditiously as possible. Consultation should be sought when there is a lack of progress in treatment.

Relationships with other professionals and community agencies

VII. The privately practicing clinical social worker shall maintain the highest professional and business ethics in dealing with other professionals and community agencies.

A. The practitioner shall be familiar with the network of professional and self-help systems in the community and shall link clients with relevant services and resources.

B. When the client is referred to another resource, the role of the primary provider of care and the specific responsibility of each party concerned with the client should be delineated clearly.

C. When the clinical social worker is unable to continue service to an individual(s), there is a responsibility to offer suitable referral(s).

D. The practitioner shall cooperate with professionals who subsequently treat former clients.

E. The clinical social worker leaving an agency for private practice shall abide by that agency's explicit policy regarding transfer of clients. If the agency permits transfer of the client to a private practice, there shall be advance agreement between the agency and the practitioner before discussing options with the client.

F. The clinical social worker employing others in the private practice shall assume professional responsibility and accountability for all services provided.

APPENDIX I: CONFIDENTIALITY AND PRIVACY

The social worker should respect the privacy of clients and hold in confidence all information obtained in the course of professional service.

The social worker should share with others confidences revealed by clients, without consent, only for compelling professional reasons.

The social worker should inform clients fully about the limits of confidentiality in a given situation, the purposes for which information is obtained, and how it may be used.

The social worker should afford clients reasonable access to any official social work records concerning them.

When providing clients with access to records, the social worker should take due care to protect the confidences of others contained in those records.

The social worker should obtain informed consent of clients before taping, recording, or permitting third party observation of their activities.

E. Principles of Medical Ethics, with Annotations Especially Applicable to Psychiatry, American Psychiatric Association

Section 1

A physician shall be dedicated to providing competent medical service with compassion and respect for human dignity.

1. The patient may place his/her trust in his/her psychiatrist knowing that the psychiatrist's ethics and professional responsibilities preclude him/her gratifying his/her own needs by exploiting the patient. This becomes particularly important because of the essentially private, highly personal, and sometimes intensely emotional nature of the relationship established with the psychiatrist.

2. A psychiatrist should not be a party to any type of policy that excludes, segregates, or demeans the dignity of any patient because of ethnic origin, race, sex, creed, age, socioeconomic status, or sexual orientation.

3. In accord with the requirements of law and accepted medical practice, it is ethical for a physician to submit his/her work to peer review and to the ultimate authority of the medical staff executive body and the hospital administration and its governing body. In case of dispute, the ethical psychiatrist has the following steps available:

   a. Seek appeal from the medical staff decision to a joint conference committee, including members of the medical staff executive committee and the executive committee of the governing board. At this appeal, the ethical psychiatrist could request that outside opinions be considered.

   b. Appeal to the governing body itself.

   c. Appeal to state agencies regulating licensure of hospitals if, in the particular state, they concern themselves with matters of professional competency and quality of care.

   d. Attempt to educate colleagues through development of research projects and data and presentations at professional meetings and in professional journals.

   e. Seek redress in local courts, perhaps through an enjoining injunction against the governing body.

   f. Public education as carried out by an ethical psychiatrist would not utilize appeals based solely upon emotion, but would be presented in a professional way and without any potential exploitation of patients through testimonials.

4. A psychiatrist should not be a participant in a legally authorized execution.

Section 2

A physician shall deal honestly with patients and colleagues, and strive to expose those physicians deficient in character or competence, or who engage in fraud or deception.

1. The requirement that the physician conduct himself with propriety in his/her profession and in all the actions of his/her life is especially important in the case of the psychiatrist because the patient tends to model his/her behavior after that of his/her therapist by identification. Further, the necessary intensity of the therapeutic relationship may tend to activate sexual and other needs and fantasies on the part of both patient and therapist, while weakening the objectivity necessary for control. Sexual activity with a patient is unethical.

2. The psychiatrist should diligently guard against exploiting information furnished by the patient and should not use the unique position of power afforded him/her by the psychotherapeutic situation to influence the patient in any way not directly relevant to the treatment goals.

3. A psychiatrist who regularly practices outside his/her area of professional competence should be considered unethical. Determination of professional competence should be made by peer review boards or other appropriate bodies.

4. Special consideration should be given to those psychiatrists who, because of mental illness, jeopardize the welfare of their patients and their own reputations and practices. It is ethical, even encouraged, for another psychiatrist to intercede in such situations.

5. Psychiatric services, like all medical services, are dispensed in the context of a contractual arrangement between the patient and the treating physician. The provisions of the contractual arrangement, which are binding on the physician as well as on the patient, should be explicitly established.

6. It is ethical for the psychiatrist to make a charge for a missed appointment when this falls within the terms of the specific contractual agreement with the patient. Charging for a missed appointment or for one not cancelled 24 hours in advance need not, in itself, be considered unethical if a patient is fully advised that the physician will make such a charge. The practice, however, should be resorted to infrequently and always with the utmost consideration of the patient and his/her circumstances.

7. An arrangement in which a psychiatrist provides supervision or administration to other physicians or nonmedical persons for a percentage of their fees or gross income is not acceptable; this would constitute fee-splitting. In a team of practitioners, or a multidisciplinary team, it is ethical for the psychiatrist to receive income for administration, research, education, or consultation. This should be based upon a mutually agreed upon and set fee or salary, open to renegotiation when a change in the time demand occurs. (See also Section 5, Annotations 2, 3, and 4.)

8. When a member has been found to have behaved unethically by the American Psychiatric Association or one of its constituent district branches, there should not be automatic reporting to the local authorities responsible for medical licensure, but the decision to report should be decided upon the merits of the case.

Section 3

A physician shall respect the law and also recognize a responsibility to seek changes in those requirements which are contrary to the best interests of the patient.

1. It would seem self-evident that a psychiatrist who is a lawbreaker might be ethically unsuited to practice his/her profession. When such illegal activities bear directly upon his/her practice, this would obviously be the case. However, in other instances, illegal activities such as those concerning the right to protest social injustices might not bear on either the image of the psychiatrist or the ability of the specific psychiatrist to treat his/her patient ethically and well. While no committee or board could offer prior assurance that any illegal activity would not be considered unethical, it is conceivable that an individual could violate a law without being guilty of professionally unethical behavior. Physicians lose no right of citizenship on entry into the profession of medicine.

2. Where not specifically prohibited by local laws governing medical practice, the practice of acupuncture by a psychiatrist is not unethical per se. The psychiatrist should have professional competence in the use of acupuncture. Or, if he/she is supervising the use of acupuncture by nonmedical individuals, he/she should provide proper medical supervision. (See also Section 5, Annotations 3 and 4.)

Section 4

A physician shall respect the rights of patients, of colleagues, and of other health professionals, and shall safeguard patient confidences within the constraints of the law.

1. Psychiatric records, including even the identification of a person as a patient, must be protected with extreme care. Confidentiality is essential to psychiatric treatment. This is based in part on the spe-

cial nature of psychiatric therapy as well as on the traditional ethical relationship between physician and patient. Growing concern regarding the civil rights of patients and the possible adverse effects of computerization, duplication equipment, and data banks makes the dissemination of confidential information an increasing hazard. Because of the sensitive and private nature of the information with which the psychiatrist deals, he/she must be circumspect in the information that he/she chooses to disclose to others about a patient. The welfare of the patient must be a continuing consideration.

2. A psychiatrist may release confidential information only with the authorization of the patient or under proper legal compulsion. The continuing duty of the psychiatrist to protect the patient includes fully apprising him/her of the connotations of waiving the privilege of privacy. This may become an issue when the patient is being investigated by a government agency, is applying for a position, or is involved in legal action. The same principles apply to the release of information concerning treatment to medical departments of government agencies, business organizations, labor unions, and insurance companies. Information gained in confidence about patients seen in student health services should not be released without the student's explicit permission.

3. Clinical and other materials used in teaching and writing must be adequately disguised in order to preserve the anonymity of the individuals involved.

4. The ethical responsibility of maintaining confidentiality holds equally for the consultations in which the patient may not have been present and in which the consultee was not a physician. In such instances, the physician consultant should alert the consultee to his/her duty of confidentiality.

5. Ethically the psychiatrist may disclose only that information which is relevant to a given situation. He/she should avoid offering speculation as fact. Sensitive information such as an individual's sexual orientation or fantasy material is usually unnecessary.

6. Psychiatrists are often asked to examine individuals for security purposes, to determine suitability for various jobs, and to determine legal competence. The psychiatrist must fully describe the nature and purpose and lack of confidentiality of the examination to the examinee at the beginning of the examination.

7. Careful judgment must be exercised by the psychiatrist in order to include, when appropriate, the parents or guardian in the treatment of a minor. At the same time the psychiatrist must assure the minor proper confidentiality.

8. Psychiatrists at times may find it necessary, in order to protect the patient or the community from imminent danger, to reveal confidential information disclosed by the patient.

9. When the psychiatrist is ordered by the court to reveal the confidences entrusted to him/her by patients, he/she may comply or he/she may ethically hold the right to dissent within the framework of the law. When the psychiatrist is in doubt, the right of the patient to confidentiality and, by extension, to unimpaired treatment should be given priority. The psychiatrist should reserve the right to raise the question of adequate need for disclosure. In the event that the necessity for legal disclosure is demonstrated by the court, the psychiatrist may request the right to disclosure of only that information which is relevant to the legal question at hand.

10. With regard for the person's dignity and privacy and with truly informed consent, it is ethical to present a patient to a scientific gathering, if the confidentiality of the presentation is understood and accepted by the audience.

11. It is ethical to present a patient or former patient to a public gathering or to the news media only if that patient is fully informed of enduring loss of confidentiality, is competent, and consents in writing without coercion.

12. When involved in funded research, the ethical psychiatrist will advise human subjects of the funding source, retain his/her freedom to reveal data and results, and follow all appropriate and current guidelines relative to human subject protection.

13. Ethical considerations in medical practice preclude the psychiatric evaluation of any adult charged with criminal acts prior to access to, or availability of, legal counsel. The only exception is the rendering of care to the person for the sole purpose of medical treatment.

Section 5

A physician shall continue to study, apply, and advance scientific knowledge, make relevant information available to patients, colleagues, and the public, obtain consultation, and use the talents of other health professionals when indicated.

1. Psychiatrists are responsible for their own continuing education and should be mindful of the fact that theirs must be a lifetime of learning.

2. In the practice of his/her specialty, the psychiatrist consults, associates, collaborates, or integrates his/her work with that of many professionals, including psychologists, psychometricians, social workers, alcoholism counselors, marriage counselors, public health nurses, etc. Furthermore, the nature of modern psychiatric practice extends his/her contacts to such people as teachers, juvenile and adult probation officers, attorneys, welfare workers, agency volunteers, and neighborhood aids. In referring patients for treatment, counseling, or rehabilitation to any of these practitioners, the psychiatrist should ensure that the allied professional or paraprofessional with whom he/she is dealing is a recognized member of his/her own discipline and is competent to carry out the therapeutic task required. The psychiatrist should have the same attitude toward members of the medical profession to whom he/she refers patients. Whenever he/she has reason to doubt the training, skill, or ethical qualifications of the allied professional, the psychiatrist should not refer cases to him/her.

3. When the psychiatrist assumes a collaborative or supervisory role with another mental health worker, he/she must expend sufficient time to assure that proper care is given. It is contrary to the interests of the patient and to patient care if he/she allows himself/herself to be used as a figurehead.

4. In relationships between psychiatrists and practicing licensed psychologists, the physician should not delegate to the psychologist or, in fact, to any nonmedical person any matter requiring the exercise of professional medical judgment.

5. The psychiatrist should agree to the request of a patient for consultation or to such a request from the family of an incompetent or minor patient. The psychiatrist may suggest possible consultants, but the patient or family should be given free choice of the consultant. If the psychiatrist disapproves of the professional qualifications of the consultant or if there is a difference of opinion that the primary therapist cannot resolve, he/she may, after suitable notice, withdraw from the case. If this disagreement occurs within an institution or agency framework, the difference should be resolved by the mediation or arbitration of higher professional authority within the institution or agency.

Section 6

A physician shall, in the provision of appropriate patient care, except in emergencies, be free to choose whom to serve, with whom to associate, and the environment in which to provide medical services.

1. Physicians generally agree that the doctor-patient relationship is such a vital factor in effective treatment of the patient that preservation of optimal conditions for development of a sound working relationship between a doctor and his/her patient should take precedence over all other considerations. Professional courtesy may lead to poor psychiatric care for physicians and their families because of embarrassment over the lack of a complete give-and-take contract.

Section 7

A physician shall recognize a responsibility to participate in activities contributing to an improved community.

1. Psychiatrists should foster the cooperation of those legitimately concerned with the medical, psychological, social, and legal aspects of mental health and illness. Psychiatrists are encouraged to serve society by advising and consulting with the executive, legislative, and judiciary branches of the government. A psychiatrist should clarify whether he/she speaks as an individual or as a representative of an organization. Furthermore, psychiatrists should avoid cloaking their public statements with the authority of the profession (e.g., "Psychiatrists know that . . .").

2. Psychiatrists may interpret and share with the public their expertise in the various psychosocial issues that may affect mental health and illness. Psychiatrists should always be mindful of their separate roles as dedicated citizens and as experts in psychological medicine.

3. On occasion psychiatrists are asked for an opinion about an individual who is in the light of public attention, or who has disclosed information about himself/herself through public media. It is unethical for a psychiatrist to offer a professional opinion unless he/she has conducted an examination and has been granted proper authorization for such a statement.

4. The psychiatrist may permit his/her certification to be used for the involuntary treatment of any person only following his/her personal examination of that person. To do so, he/she must find that the person, because of mental illness, cannot form a judgment as to what is in his/her own best interests and that, without such treatment, substantial impairment is likely to occur to the person or others.

F. Ethical Principles of Psychologists, *American Psychological Association*

PREAMBLE

Psychologists respect the dignity and worth of the individual and strive for the preservation and protection of fundamental human rights. They are committed to increasing knowledge of human behavior and of people's understanding of themselves and others and to the utilization of such knowledge for the promotion of human welfare. While pursuing these objectives, they make every effort to protect the welfare of those who seek their services and of the research participants that may be the object of study. They use their skills only for purposes consistent with these values and do not knowingly permit their misuse by others. While demanding for themselves freedom of inquiry and communication, psychologists accept the responsibility this freedom requires: competence, objectivity in the application of skills, and concern for the best interests of clients, colleagues, students, research participants, and society. In the pursuit of these ideals, psychologists subscribe to principles in the following areas: 1. Responsibility, 2. Competence, 3. Moral and Legal Standards, 4. Public Statements, 5. Confidentiality, 6. Welfare of the Consumer, 7. Professional Relationships, 8. Assessment Techniques, 9. Research with Human Participants, and 10. Care and Use of Animals.

Acceptance of membership in the American Psychological Association commits the member to adherence to these principles.

Psychologists cooperate with duly constituted committees of the American Psychological Association, in particular, the Committee on Scientific and Professional Ethics and Conduct, by responding to inquiries promptly and completely. Members also respond promptly and completely to inquiries from duly constituted state association ethics committees and professional standards review committees.

Ethical Principles of Psychologists (revised edition), by the American Psychological Association. Copyright 1981 by the American Psychological Association. Reprinted by permission of the publisher.

This version of the *Ethical Principles of Psychologists* (formerly entitled *Ethical Standards of Psychologists*) was adopted by the American Psychological Association's Council of Representatives on January 24, 1981. The revised *Ethical Principles* contain both substantive and grammatical changes in each of the nine ethical principles constituting the *Ethical Standards of Psychologists* previously adopted by the Council of Representatives in 1979, plus a new tenth principle entitled "Care and Use of Animals." Inquiries concerning the *Ethical Principles of Psychologists* should be addressed to the Administrative Officer for Ethics, American Psychological Association, 1200 Seventeenth Street, N.W., Washington, D.C., 20036.

These revised *Ethical Principles* apply to psychologists, to students of psychology, and to others who do work of a psychological nature under the supervision of a psychologist. They are also intended for the guidance of nonmembers of the Association who are engaged in psychological research or practice.

Any complaints of unethical conduct filed after January 24, 1981, shall be governed by this 1981 revision. However, conduct (a) complained about after January 24, 1981, but which occurred prior to that date, and (b) not considered unethical under prior versions of the principles but considered unethical under the 1981 revision, shall not be deemed a violation of ethical principles. Any complaints pending as of January 24, 1981, shall be governed either by the 1979 or by the 1981 version of the *Ethical Principles*, at the sound discretion of the Committee on Scientific and Professional Ethics and Conduct.

Principle 1: Responsibility

In providing services, psychologists maintain the highest standards of their profession. They accept responsibility for the consequences of their acts and make every effort to ensure that their services are used appropriately.

a. As scientists, psychologists accept responsibility for the selection of their research topics and the methods used in investigation, analysis, and reporting. They plan their research in ways to minimize the possibility that their findings will be misleading. They provide thorough discussion of the limitations of their data, especially where their work touches on social policy or might be construed to the detriment of persons in specific age, sex, ethnic, socioeconomic, or other social groups. In publishing reports of their work, they never suppress disconfirming data, and they acknowledge the existence of alternative hypotheses and explanations of their findings. Psychologists take credit only for work they have actually done.

b. Psychologists clarify in advance with all appropriate persons and agencies the expectations for sharing and utilizing research data. They avoid relationships that may limit their objectivity or create a conflict of interest. Interference with the milieu in which data are collected is kept to a minimum.

c. Psychologists have the responsibility to attempt to prevent distortion, misuse, or suppression of psychological findings by the institution or agency of which they are employees.

d. As members of governmental or other organizational bodies, psychologists remain accountable as individuals to the highest standards of their profession.

e. As teachers, psychologists recognize their primary obligation to help others acquire knowledge and skill. They maintain high standards of scholarship by presenting psychological information objectively, fully, and accurately.

f. As practitioners, psychologists know that they bear a heavy social responsibility because their recommendations and professional actions may alter the lives of others. They are alert to personal, social, organizational, financial, or political situations and pressures that might lead to misuse of their influence.

Principle 2: Competence

The maintenance of high standards of competence is a responsibility shared by all psychologists in the interest of the public and the profession as a whole. Psychologists

recognize the boundaries of their competence and the limitations of their techniques. They only provide services and only use techniques for which they are qualified by training and experience. In those areas in which recognized standards do not yet exist, psychologists take whatever precautions are necessary to protect the welfare of their clients. They maintain knowledge of current scientific and professional information related to the services they render.

a. Psychologists accurately represent their competence, education, training, and experience. They claim as evidence of educational qualifications only those degrees obtained from institutions acceptable under the Bylaws and Rules of Council of the American Psychological Association.

b. As teachers, psychologists perform their duties on the basis of careful preparation so that their instruction is accurate, current, and scholarly.

c. Psychologists recognize the need for continuing education and are open to new procedures and changes in expectations and values over time.

d. Psychologists recognize differences among people, such as those that may be associated with age, sex, socioeconomic, and ethnic backgrounds. When necessary, they obtain training, experience, or counsel to assure competent service or research relating to such persons.

e. Psychologists responsible for decisions involving individuals or policies based on test results have an understanding of psychological or educational measurement, validation problems, and test research.

f. Psychologists recognize that personal problems and conflicts may interfere with professional effectiveness. Accordingly, they refrain from undertaking any activity in which their personal problems are likely to lead to inadequate performance or harm to a client, colleague, student, or research participant. If engaged in such activity when they become aware of their personal problems, they seek competent professional assistance to determine whether they should suspend, terminate, or limit the scope of their professional and/or scientific activities.

Principle 3: Moral and legal standards

Psychologists' moral and ethical standards of behavior are a personal matter to the same degree as they are for any other citizen, except as these may compromise the fulfillment of their professional responsibilities or reduce the public trust in psychology and psychologists. Regard-

ing their own behavior, psychologists are sensitive to pre-vailing community standards and to the possible impact that conformity to or deviation from these standards may have upon the quality of their performance as psychologists. Psychologists are also aware of the possible impact of their public behavior upon the ability of colleagues to perform their professional duties.

a. As teachers, psychologists are aware of the fact that their personal values may affect the selection and presentation of instructional materials. When dealing with topics that may give offense, they recognize and respect the diverse attitudes that students may have toward such materials.

b. As employees or employers, psychologists do not engage in or condone practices that are inhumane or that result in illegal or unjustifiable actions. Such practices include, but are not limited to, those based on considerations of race, handicap, age, gender, sexual preference, religion, or national origin in hiring, promotion, or training.

c. In their professional roles, psychologists avoid any action that will violate or diminish the legal and civil rights of clients or of others who may be affected by their actions.

d. As practitioners and researchers, psychologists act in accord with Association standards and guidelines related to practice and to the conduct of research with human beings and animals. In the ordinary course of events, psychologists adhere to relevant governmental laws and institutional regulations. When federal, state, provincial, organizational, or institutional laws, regulations, or practices are in conflict with Association standards and guidelines, psychologists make known their commitment to Association standards and guidelines and, wherever possible, work toward a resolution of the conflict. Both practitioners and researchers are concerned with the development of such legal and quasi-legal regulations as best serve the public interest, and they work toward changing existing regulations that are not beneficial to the public interest.

Principle 4: Public statements

Public statements, announcements of services, advertising, and promotional activities of psychologists serve the purpose of helping the public make informed judgments and choices. Psychologists represent accurately and objectively their professional qualifications, affiliations, and functions, as well as those of the institutions or organizations with which they or the statements may be associated. In public statements providing psychological information or professional opinions or providing information about the availability of psychological products, publications, and services, psychologists base their statements on scientifically acceptable psychological findings and techniques with full recognition of the limits and uncertainties of such evidence.

a. When announcing or advertising professional services, psychologists may list the following information to describe the provider and services provided: name, highest relevant academic degree earned from a regionally accredited institution, date, type, and level of certification or licensure, diplomate status, APA membership status, address, telephone number, office hours, a brief listing of the type of psychological services offered, an appropriate presentation of fee information, foreign languages spoken, and policy with regard to third-party payments. Additional relevant or important consumer information may be included if not prohibited by other sections of these Ethical Principles.

b. In announcing or advertising the availability of psychological products, publications, or services, psychologists do not present their affiliation with any organization in a manner that falsely implies sponsorship or certification by that organization. In particular and for example, psychologists do not state APA membership or fellow status in a way to suggest that such status implies specialized professional competence or qualifications. Public statements include, but are not limited to, communication by means of periodical, book, list, directory, television, radio, or motion picture. They do not contain (i) a false, fraudulent, misleading, deceptive, or unfair statement; (ii) a misinterpretation of fact or a statement likely to mislead or deceive because in context it makes only a partial disclosure of relevant facts; (iii) a testimonial from a patient regarding the quality of a psychologist's services or products; (iv) a statement intended or likely to create false or unjustified expectations of favorable results; (v) a statement implying unusual, unique, or one-of-a-kind abilities; (vi) a statement intended or likely to appeal to a client's fears, anxieties, or emotions concerning the possible results of failure to obtain the offered services; (vii) a statement concerning the comparative desirability of offered services; (viii) a statement of direct solicitation of individual clients.

c. Psychologists do not compensate or give anything of

value to a representative of the press, radio, television, or other communication medium in anticipation of or in return for professional publicity in a news item. A paid advertisement must be identified as such, unless it is apparent from the context that it is a paid advertisement. If communicated to the public by use of radio or television, an advertisement is prerecorded and approved for broadcast by the psychologist, and a recording of the actual transmission is retained by the psychologist.

d. Announcements or advertisements of "personal growth groups," clinics, and agencies give a clear statement of purpose and a clear description of the experiences to be provided. The education, training, and experience of the staff members are appropriately specified.

e. Psychologists associated with the development or promotion of psychological devices, books, or other products offered for commercial sale make reasonable efforts to ensure that announcements and advertisements are presented in a professional, scientifically acceptable, and factually informative manner.

f. Psychologists do not participate for personal gain in commercial announcements or advertisements recommending to the public the purchase or use of proprietary or single-source products or services when that participation is based solely upon their identification as psychologists.

g. Psychologists present the science of psychology and offer their services, products, and publications fairly and accurately, avoiding misrepresentation through sensationalism, exaggeration, or superficiality. Psychologists are guided by the primary obligation to aid the public in developing informed judgments, opinions, and choices.

h. As teachers, psychologists ensure that statements in catalogs and course outlines are accurate and not misleading, particularly in terms of subject matter to be covered, bases for evaluating progress, and the nature of course experiences. Announcements, brochures, or advertisements describing workshops, seminars, or other educational programs accurately describe the audience for which the program is intended as well as eligibility requirements, educational objectives, and nature of the materials to be covered. These announcements also accurately represent the education, training, and experience of the psychologists presenting the programs and any fees involved.

i. Public announcements or advertisements soliciting research participants in which clinical services or other professional services are offered as an inducement make clear the nature of the services as well as the costs and other obligations to be accepted by participants in the research.

j. A psychologist accepts the obligation to correct others who represent the psychologist's professional qualifications, or associations with products or services, in a manner incompatible with these guidelines.

k. Individual diagnostic and therapeutic services are provided only in the context of a professional psychological relationship. When personal advice is given by means of public lectures or demonstrations, newspaper or magazine articles, radio or television programs, mail, or similar media, the psychologist utilizes the most current relevant data and exercises the highest level of professional judgment.

l. Products that are described or presented by means of public lectures or demonstrations, newspaper or magazine articles, radio or television programs, or similar media meet the same recognized standards as exist for products used in the context of a professional relationship.

Principle 5: Confidentiality

Psychologists have a primary obligation to respect the confidentiality of information obtained from persons in the course of their work as psychologists. They reveal such information to others only with the consent of the person or the person's legal representative, except in those unusual circumstances in which not to do so would result in clear danger to the person or to others. Where appropriate, psychologists inform their clients of the legal limits of confidentiality.

a. Information obtained in clinical or consulting relationships, or evaluative data concerning children, students, employees, and others, is discussed only for professional purposes and only with persons clearly concerned with the case. Written and oral reports present only data germane to the purposes of the evaluation, and every effort is made to avoid undue invasion of privacy.

b. Psychologists who present personal information obtained during the course of professional work in writings, lectures, or other public forums either obtain adequate prior consent to do so or adequately disguise all identifying information.

c. Psychologists make provisions for maintaining confidentiality in the storage and disposal of records.

d. When working with minors or other persons who are unable to give voluntary, informed consent, psychologists take special care to protect these persons' best interests.

Principle 6: Welfare of the consumer

Psychologists respect the integrity and protect the welfare of the people and groups with whom they work. When conflicts of interest arise between clients and psychologists' employing institutions, psychologists clarify the nature and direction of their loyalties and responsibilities and keep all parties informed of their commitments. Psychologists fully inform consumers as to the purpose and nature of an evaluative, treatment, educational, or training procedure, and they freely acknowledge that clients, students, or participants in research have freedom of choice with regard to participation.

a. Psychologists are continually cognizant of their own needs and of their potentially influential position vis-à-vis persons such as clients, students, and subordinates. They avoid exploiting the trust and dependency of such persons. Psychologists make every effort to avoid dual relationships that could impair their professional judgment or increase the risk of exploitation. Examples of such dual relationships include, but are not limited to, research with and treatment of employees, students, supervisees, close friends, or relatives. Sexual intimacies with clients are unethical.

b. When a psychologist agrees to provide services to a client at the request of a third party, the psychologist assumes the responsibility of clarifying the nature of the relationships to all parties concerned.

c. Where the demands of an organization require psychologists to violate these Ethical Principles, psychologists clarify the nature of the conflict between the demands and these principles. They inform all parties of psychologists' ethical responsibilities and take appropriate action.

d. Psychologists make advance financial arrangements that safeguard the best interests of and are clearly understood by their clients. They neither give nor receive any remuneration for referring clients for professional services. They contribute a portion of their services to work for which they receive little or no financial return.

e. Psychologists terminate a clinical or consulting relationship when it is reasonably clear that the consumer is not benefiting from it. They offer to help the consumer locate alternative sources of assistance.

Principle 7: Professional relationships

Psychologists act with due regard for the needs, special competencies, and obligations of their colleagues in psychology and other professions. They respect the prerogatives and obligations of the institutions or organizations with which these other colleagues are associated.

a. Psychologists understand the areas of competence of related professions. They make full use of all the professional, technical, and administrative resources that serve the best interests of consumers. The absence of formal relationships with other professional workers does not relieve psychologists of the responsibility of securing for their clients the best possible professional service, nor does it relieve them of the obligation to exercise foresight, diligence, and tact in obtaining the complementary or alternative assistance needed by clients.

b. Psychologists know and take into account the traditions and practices of other professional groups with whom they work and cooperate fully with such groups. If a person is receiving similar services from another professional, psychologists do not offer their own services directly to such a person. If a psychologist is contacted by a person who is already receiving similar services from another professional, the psychologist carefully considers that professional relationship and proceeds with caution and sensitivity to the therapeutic issues as well as the client's welfare. The psychologist discusses these issues with the client so as to minimize the risk of confusion and conflict.

c. Psychologists who employ or supervise other professionals or professionals in training accept the obligation to facilitate the further professional development of these individuals. They provide appropriate working conditions, timely evaluations, constructive consultation, and experience opportunities.

d. Psychologists do not exploit their professional relationships with clients, supervisees, students, employees, or research participants sexually or otherwise. Psychologists do not condone or engage in sexual harassment. Sexual harassment is defined as deliberate or repeated comments, gestures, or physical contacts of a sexual nature that are unwanted by the recipient.

e. In conducting research in institutions or organizations, psychologists secure appropriate authorization to conduct such research. They are aware of their obligations to future research workers and ensure that host institutions receive adequate information about the research and proper acknowledgment of their contributions.

f. Publication credit is assigned to those who have contributed to a publication in proportion to their professional contributions. Major contributions of a professional character made by several persons to a common project are recognized by joint authorship, with the individual who made the principal contribution listed first. Minor contributions of a professional character and extensive clerical or similar nonprofessional assistance may be acknowledged in footnotes or in an introductory statement. Acknowledgment through specific citations is made for unpublished as well as published material that has directly influenced the research or writing. Psychologists who compile and edit material of others for publication publish the material in the name of the originating group, if appropriate, with their own name appearing as chairperson or editor. All contributors are to be acknowledged and named.

g. When psychologists know of an ethical violation by another psychologist, and it seems appropriate, they informally attempt to resolve the issue by bringing the behavior to the attention of the psychologist. If the misconduct is of a minor nature and/or appears to be due to lack of sensitivity, knowledge, or experience, such an informal solution is usually appropriate. Such informal corrective efforts are made with sensitivity to any rights to confidentiality involved. If the violation does not seem amenable to an informal solution, or is of a more serious nature, psychologists bring it to the attention of the appropriate local, state, and/or national committee on professional ethics and conduct.

Principle 8: Assessment techniques

In the development, publication, and utilization of psychological assessment techniques, psychologists make every effort to promote the welfare and best interests of the client. They guard against the misuse of assessment results. They respect the client's right to know the results, the interpretations made, and the bases for their conclusions and recommendations. Psychologists make every effort to maintain the security of tests and other assessment techniques within limits of legal mandates. They strive to ensure the appropriate use of assessment techniques by others.

a. In using assessment techniques, psychologists respect the right of clients to have full explanations of the nature and purpose of the techniques in language the clients can understand, unless an explicit exception to this right has been agreed upon in advance. When the explanations are to be provided by others, psychologists establish procedures for ensuring the adequacy of these explanations.

b. Psychologists responsible for the development and standardization of psychological tests and other assessment techniques utilize established scientific procedures and observe the relevant APA standards.

c. In reporting assessment results, psychologists indicate any reservations that exist regarding validity or reliability because of the circumstances of the assessment or the inappropriateness of the norms for the person tested. Psychologists strive to ensure that the results of assessments and their interpretations are not misused by others.

d. Psychologists recognize that assessment results may become obsolete. They make every effort to avoid and prevent the misuse of obsolete measures.

e. Psychologists offering scoring and interpretation services are able to produce appropriate evidence for the validity of the programs and procedures used in arriving at interpretations. The public offering of an automated interpretation service is considered a professional-to-professional consultation. Psychologists make every effort to avoid misuse of assessment reports.

f. Psychologists do not encourage or promote the use of psychological assessment techniques by inappropriately trained or otherwise unqualified persons through teaching, sponsorship, or supervision.

Principle 9: Research with human participants

The decision to undertake research rests upon a considered judgment by the individual psychologist about how best to contribute to psychological science and human welfare. Having made the decision to conduct research, the psychologist considers alternative directions in which research energies and resources might be invested. On the basis of this consideration, the psychologist carries out the investigation with respect and concern for the dignity and welfare of the people who participate and with cognizance of federal and state regulations and professional standards governing the conduct of research with human participants.

a. In planning a study, the investigator has the responsibility to make a careful evaluation of its ethical acceptability. To the extent that the weighing of scientific and human values suggests a compromise of any principle, the investigator incurs a correspondingly serious obligation to seek ethical advice and to observe stringent safeguards to protect the rights of human participants.

b. Considering whether a participant in a planned study will be a "subject at risk" or a "subject at minimal risk," according to recognized standards, is of primary ethical concern to the investigator.

c. The investigator always retains the responsibility for ensuring ethical practice in research. The investigator is also responsible for the ethical treatment of research participants by collaborators, assistants, students, and employees, all of whom, however, incur similar obligations.

d. Except in minimal-risk research, the investigator establishes a clear and fair agreement with research participants, prior to their participation, that clarifies the obligations and responsibilities of each. The investigator has the obligation to honor all promises and commitments included in that agreement. The investigator informs the participants of all aspects of the research that might reasonably be expected to influence willingness to participate and explains all other aspects of the research about which the participants inquire. Failure to make full disclosure prior to obtaining informed consent requires additional safeguards to protect the welfare and dignity of the research participants. Research with children or with participants who have impairments that would limit understanding and/or communication requires special safeguarding procedures.

e. Methodological requirements of a study may make the use of concealment or deception necessary. Before conducting such a study, the investigator has a special responsibility to (i) determine whether the use of such techniques is justified by the study's prospective scientific, educational, or applied value; (ii) determine whether alternative procedures are available that do not use concealment or deception; and (iii) ensure that the participants are provided with sufficient explanation as soon as possible.

f. The investigator respects the individual's freedom to decline to participate in or to withdraw from the research at any time. The obligation to protect this freedom requires careful thought and consideration when the investigator is in a position of authority or influence over the participant. Such positions of authority include, but are not limited to, situations in which research participation is required as part of

employment or in which the participant is a student, client, or employee of the investigator.

g. The investigator protects the participant from physical and mental discomfort, harm, and danger that may arise from research procedures. If risks of such consequences exist, the investigator informs the participant of that fact. Research procedures likely to cause serious or lasting harm to a participant are not used unless the failure to use these procedures might expose the participant to risk of greater harm, or unless the research has great potential benefit and fully informed and voluntary consent is obtained from each participant. The participant should be informed of procedures for contacting the investigator within a reasonable time period following participation should stress, potential harm, or related questions or concerns arise.

h. After the data are collected, the investigator provides the participant with information about the nature of the study and attempts to remove any misconceptions that may have arisen. Where scientific or humane values justify delaying or withholding this information, the investigator incurs a special responsibility to monitor the research and to ensure that there are no damaging consequences for the participant.

i. Where research procedures result in undesirable consequences for the individual participant, the investigator has the responsibility to detect and remove or correct these consequences, including long-term effects.

j. Information obtained about a research participant during the course of an investigation is confidential unless otherwise agreed upon in advance. When the possibility exists that others may obtain access to such information, this possibility, together with the plans for protecting confidentiality, is explained to the participant as part of the procedure for obtaining informed consent.

Principle 10: Care and use of animals

An investigator of animal behavior strives to advance understanding of basic behavioral principles and/or to contribute to the improvement of human health and welfare. In seeking these ends, the investigator ensures the welfare of animals and treats them humanely. Laws and regulations notwithstanding, an animal's immediate protection depends upon the scientist's own conscience.

a. The acquisition, care, use, and disposal of all animals are in compliance with current federal, state or provincial, and local laws and regulations.

b. A psychologist trained in research methods and experienced in the care of laboratory animals closely supervises all procedures involving animals and is responsible for ensuring appropriate consideration of their comfort, health, and humane treatment.

c. Psychologists ensure that all individuals using animals under their supervision have received explicit instruction in experimental methods and in the care, maintenance, and handling of the species being used. Responsibilities and activities of individuals participating in a research project are consistent with their respective competencies.

d. Psychologists make every effort to minimize discomfort, illness, and pain of animals. A procedure subjecting animals to pain, stress, or privation is used only when an alternative procedure is unavailable and the goal is justified by its prospective scientific, educational, or applied value. Surgical procedures are performed under appropriate anesthesia; techniques to avoid infection and minimize pain are followed during and after surgery.

e. When it is appropriate that the animal's life be terminated, it is done rapidly and painlessly.

G. Specialty Guidelines for the Delivery of Services by Counseling Psychologists, *American Psychological Association*

The Specialty Guidelines that follow are based on the generic *Standards for Providers of Psychological Services* originally adopted by the American Psychological Association (APA) in September 1974 and revised in January 1977. Together with the generic *Standards*, these Specialty Guidelines state the official policy of the Association regarding delivery of services by counseling psychologists. Admission to the practice of psychology is regulated by state statute. It is the position of the Association that licensing be based on generic, and not on specialty, qualifications. Specialty guidelines serve the additional purpose of providing potential users and other interested groups with essential information about particular services available from the several specialties in professional psychology.

Professional psychology specialties have evolved from generic practice in psychology and are supported by university training programs. There are now at least four recognized professional specialties—clinical, counseling, school, and industrial/organizational psychology.

The knowledge base in each of these specialty areas has increased, refining the state of the art to the point that a set of uniform specialty guidelines is now possible and desirable. The present Guidelines are intended to educate the public, the profession, and other interested parties regarding specialty professional practices. They are also intended to facilitate the continued systematic development of the profession.

The content of each Specialty Guideline reflects a consensus of university faculty and public and private practitioners regarding the knowledge base, services provided, problems addressed, and clients served.

Traditionally, all learned disciplines have treated the designation of specialty practice as a reflection of preparation in greater depth in a particular subject matter, together with a voluntary limiting of focus to a more restricted area of practice by the professional. Lack of specialty designation does not preclude general providers of psychological services from using the methods or dealing with the populations of any specialty, except insofar as psychologists voluntarily refrain from providing services they are not trained to render. It is the intent of these guidelines, however, that after the grandparenting period, psychologists not put themselves forward as *specialists* in a given area of practice unless they meet the qualifications noted in the Guidelines (see Definitions). Therefore, these Guidelines are meant to apply only to those psychologists who voluntarily wish to be designated as *counseling psychologists*. They do not apply to other psychologists.

Specialty Guidelines for the Delivery of Services by Counseling Psychologists, by the American Psychological Association. Copyright 1981 by the American Psychological Association. Reprinted by permission of the publisher.

These *Specialty Guidelines* were prepared by the APA Committee on Standards for Providers of Psychological Services (COSPOPS), chaired by Durand F. Jacobs, with the advice of the officers and committee chairpersons of the Division of Counseling Psychology (Division 17). Barbara A. Kirk and Milton Schwebel served successively as the counseling psychology representative of COSPOPS, and Arthur Centor and Richard Kilburg were the Central Office liaisons to the committee. Norman Kagan, Samuel H. Osipow, Carl E. Thoresen, and Allen E. Ivey served successively as Division 17 presidents.

These Guidelines represent the profession's best judgment of the conditions, credentials, and experience that contribute to competent professional practice. The APA strongly encourages, and plans to participate in, efforts to identify professional practitioner behaviors and job functions and to validate the relation between these and desired client outcomes. Thus, future revisions of these Guidelines will increasingly reflect the results of such efforts.

These Guidelines follow the format and, wherever applicable, the wording of the generic *Standards*. The intent of these Guidelines is to improve the quality, effectiveness, and accessibility of psychological services. They are meant to provide guidance to providers, users, and sanctioners regarding the best judgment of the profession on these matters. Although the Specialty Guidelines have been derived from and are consistent with the generic *Standards*, they may be used as separate documents. However, *Standards for Providers of Psychological Services* shall remain the basic policy statement and shall take precedence where there are questions of interpretation.

Professional psychology in general and counseling psychology as a specialty have labored long and diligently to codify a uniform set of guidelines for the delivery of services by counseling psychologists that would serve the respective needs of users, providers, third-party purchasers, and sanctioners of psychological services.

The Committee on Professional Standards, established by the APA in January 1980, is charged with keeping the generic *Standards* and the Specialty Guidelines responsive to the needs of the public and the profession. It is also charged with continually reviewing, modifying, and extending them progressively as the profession and the science of psychology develop new knowledge, improved methods, and additional modes of psychological services.

The Specialty Guidelines for the Delivery of Services by Counseling Psychologists that follow have been established by the APA as a means of self-regulation to protect the public interest. They guide the specialty practice of counseling psychology by specifying important areas of quality assurance and performance that contribute to the goal of facilitating more effective human functioning.

Principles and implications of the Specialty Guidelines

These Specialty Guidelines emerged from and reaffirm the same basic principles that guided the development of the generic *Standards for Providers of Psychological Services:*

1. These Guidelines recognize that admission to the practice of psychology is regulated by state statute.

2. It is the intention of the APA that the generic *Standards* provide appropriate guidelines for statutory licensing of psychologists. In addition, although it is the position of the APA that licensing be generic and not in specialty areas, these Specialty Guidelines in counseling psychology provide an authoritative reference for use in credentialing specialty providers of counseling psychological services by such groups as divisions of the APA and state associations and by boards and agencies that find such criteria useful for quality assurance.

3. A uniform set of Specialty Guidelines governs the quality of services to all users of counseling psychological services in both the private and the public sectors. Those receiving counseling psychological services are protected by the same kinds of safeguards, irrespective of sector; these include constitutional guarantees, statutory regulation, peer review, consultation, record review, and supervision.

4. A uniform set of Specialty Guidelines governs counseling psychological service functions offered by counseling psychologists, regardless of setting or form of remuneration. All counseling psychologists in professional practice recognize and are responsive to a uniform set of Specialty Guidelines, just as they are guided by a common code of ethics.

5. Counseling psychology Guidelines establish clear, minimally acceptable levels of quality for covered counseling psychological service functions, regardless of the nature of the users, purchasers, or sanctioners of such covered services.

6. All persons providing counseling psychological services meet specified levels of training and experience that are consistent with, and appropriate to, the functions they perform. Counseling psychological services provided by persons who do not meet the APA qualifications for a professional counseling psychologist (see Definitions) are supervised by a professional counseling psychologist. Final responsibility and accountability for services provided rest with professional counseling psychologists.

7. When providing any of the covered counseling psychological service functions at any time and in any setting, whether public or private, profit or nonprofit, counseling psychologists observe these Guidelines in order to promote the best interests and wel-

fare of the users of such services. The extent to which counseling psychologists observe these Guidelines is judged by peers.

8. These Guidelines, while assuring the user of the counseling psychologist's accountability for the nature and quality of services specified in this document, do not preclude the counseling psychologist from using new methods or developing innovative procedures in the delivery of counseling services.

These Specialty Guidelines have broad implications both for users of counseling psychological services and for providers of such services:

1. Guidelines for counseling psychological services provide a foundation for mutual understanding between provider and user and facilitate more effective evaluation of services provided and outcomes achieved.

2. Guidelines for counseling psychologists are essential for uniformity in specialty credentialing of counseling psychologists.

3. Guidelines give specific content to the profession's concept of ethical practice as it applies to the functions of counseling psychologists.

4. Guidelines for counseling psychological services may have significant impact on tomorrow's education and training models for both professional and support personnel in counseling psychology.

5. Guidelines for the provision of counseling psychological services in human service facilities influence the determination of acceptable structure, budgeting, and staffing patterns in these facilities.

6. Guidelines for counseling psychological services require continual review and revision.

The Specialty Guidelines here presented are intended to improve the quality and delivery of counseling psychological services by specifying criteria for key aspects of the practice setting. Some settings may require additional and/or more stringent criteria for specific areas of service delivery.

Systematically applied, these Guidelines serve to establish a more effective and consistent basis for evaluating the performance of individual service providers as well as to guide the organization of counseling psychological service units in human service settings.

Definitions

Providers of counseling psychological services refers to two categories of persons who provide counseling psychological services:

A. *Professional counseling psychologists.* Professional counseling psychologists have a doctoral degree from a regionally accredited university or professional school providing an organized, sequential counseling psychology program in an appropriate academic department in a university or college, or in an appropriate department or unit of a professional school. Counseling psychology programs that are accredited by the American Psychological Association are recognized as meeting the definition of a counseling psychology program. Counseling psychology programs that are not accredited by the American Psychological Association meet the definition of a counseling psychology program if they satisfy the following criteria:

1. The program is primarily psychological in nature and stands as a recognizable, coherent organizational entity within the institution.

2. The program provides an integrated, organized sequence of study.

3. The program has an identifiable body of students who are matriculated in that program for a degree.

4. There is a clear authority with primary responsibility for the core and specialty areas, whether or not the program cuts across administrative lines.

5. There is an identifiable psychology faculty, and a psychologist is responsible for the program.

The professional counseling psychologist's doctoral education and training experience is defined by the institution offering the program. Only counseling psychologists, that is, those who meet the appropriate education and training requirements, have the minimum professional qualifications to provide unsupervised counseling psychological services. A professional counseling psychologist and others providing counseling psychological services under supervision (described below) form an integral part of a multilevel counseling psychological service delivery system.

B. All other persons who provide counseling psychological services under the supervision of a professional counseling psychologist. Although there may be variations in the titles of such persons, they are not referred to as counseling psychologists. Their functions may be indicated by use of the adjective *psychological* preceding the noun, for example, *psychological associate, psychological assistant, psychological technician,* or *psychological aide.*

Counseling psychological services refers to services provided by counseling psychologists that apply principles, methods, and procedures for facilitating effective functioning during the life-span developmental process. In providing such services, counseling psychologists approach practice with a significant emphasis on positive aspects of growth and adjustment and with a developmental orientation. These services are intended to help persons acquire or alter personal–social skills, improve adaptability to changing life demands, enhance environmental coping skills, and develop a variety of problem-solving and decision-making capabilities. Counseling psychological services are used by individuals, couples, and families of all age groups to cope with problems connected with education, career choice, work, sex, marriage, family, other social relations, health, aging, and handicaps of a social or physical nature. The services are offered in such organizations as educational, rehabilitation, and health institutions and in a variety of other public and private agencies committed to service in one or more of the problem areas cited above. Counseling psychological services include the following.

A. Assessment, evaluation, and diagnosis. Procedures may include, but are not limited to, behavioral observation, interviewing, and administering and interpreting instruments for the assessment of educational achievement, academic skills, aptitudes, interests, cognitive abilities, attitudes, emotions, motivations, psychoneurological status, personality characteristics, or any other aspect of human experience and behavior that may contribute to understanding and helping the user.

B. Interventions with individuals and groups. Procedures include individual and group psychological counseling (e.g., education, career, couples, and family counseling) and may use a therapeutic, group process, or social-learning approach, or any other deemed to be appropriate. Interventions are used for purposes of prevention, remediation, and rehabilitation; they may incorporate a variety of psychological modalities, such as psychotherapy, behavior therapy, marital and family therapy, biofeedback techniques, and environmental design.

C. Professional consultation relating to A and B above, for example, in connection with developing in-service training for staff or assisting an educational institution or organization to design a plan to cope with persistent problems of its students.

D. Program development services in the areas of A, B, and C above, such as assisting a rehabilitation center to design a career-counseling program.

E. Supervision of all counseling psychological services, such as the review of assessment and intervention activities of staff.

F. Evaluation of all services noted in A through E above and research for the purpose of their improvement.

A *counseling psychological service unit* is the functional unit through which counseling psychological services are provided; such a unit may be part of a larger psychological service organization comprising psychologists of more than one specialty and headed by a professional psychologist:

A. A counseling psychological service unit provides predominantly counseling psychological services and is composed of one or more professional counseling psychologists and supporting staff.

B. A counseling psychological service unit may operate as a functional or geographic component of a larger multipsychological service unit or of a governmental, educational, correctional, health, training, industrial, or commercial organizational unit, or it may operate as an independent professional service.

C. A counseling psychological service unit may take the form of one or more counseling psychologists providing professional services in a multidisciplinary setting.

D. A counseling psychological service unit may also take the form of a private practice, composed of one or more counseling psychologists serving individuals or groups, or the form of a psychological consulting firm serving organizations and institutions.

Users of counseling psychological services include:

A. Direct users or recipients of counseling psychological services.

B. Public and private institutions, facilities, or organizations receiving counseling psychological services.

C. Third-party purchasers—those who pay for the delivery of services but who are not the recipients of services.

D. Sanctioners—those who have a legitimate concern with the accessibility, timeliness, efficacy, and standards of quality attending the provision of counseling psychological services. Sanctioners may include members of the user's family, the court, the probation officer, the school administrator, the employer, the union representative, the facility director, and so on. Sanctioners may also include various governmental, peer review, and accreditation bodies concerned with the assurance of quality.

Guideline 1: Providers

1.1 *Each counseling psychological service unit offering psychological services has available at least one professional counseling psychologist and as many more professional counseling psychologists as are necessary to assure the adequacy and quality of services offered.*

INTERPRETATION: The intent of this Guideline is that one or more providers of psychological services in any counseling psychological service unit meet the levels of training and experience of the professional counseling psychologist as specified in the preceding definitions.

When a professional counseling psychologist is not available on a full-time basis, the facility retains the services of one or more professional counseling psychologists on a regular part-time basis. The counseling psychologist so retained directs the psychological services, including supervision of the support staff, has the authority and participates sufficiently to assess the need for services, reviews the content of services provided, and assumes professional responsibility and accountability for them.

The psychologist directing the service unit is responsible for determining and justifying appropriate ratios of psychologists to users and psychologists to support staff, in order to ensure proper scope, accessibility, and quality of services provided in that setting.

1.2 *Providers of counseling psychological services who do not meet the requirements for the professional counseling psychologist are supervised directly by a professional counseling psychologist who assumes professional responsibility and accountability for the services provided. The level and extent of supervision may vary from task to task so long as the supervising psychologist retains a sufficiently close supervisory relationship to meet this Guideline. Special proficiency training or supervision may be provided by a professional psychologist of another specialty or by a professional from another discipline whose competence in the given area has been demonstrated by previous training and experience.*

INTERPRETATION: In each counseling psychological service unit there may be varying levels of responsibility with respect to the nature and quality of services provided. Support personnel are considered to be responsible for their functions and behavior when assisting in the provision of counseling psychological services and are accountable to the professional counseling psychologist. Ultimate professional responsibility and accountability for the services provided require that the supervisor review reports and test protocols, and review and discuss intervention plans, strategies, and outcomes. Therefore, the supervision of all counseling psychological services is provided directly by a professional counseling psychologist in a face-to-face arrangement involving individual and/or group supervision. The extent of supervision is determined by the needs of the providers, but in no event is it less than 1 hour per week for each support staff member providing counseling psychological services.

To facilitate the effectiveness of the psychological service unit, the nature of the supervisory relationship is communicated to support personnel in writing. Such communications delineate the duties of the employees, describing the range and types of services to be provided. The limits of independent action and decision making are defined. The description of responsibility specifies the means by which the employee will contact the professional counseling psychologist in the event of emergency or crisis situations.

1.3 *Wherever a counseling psychological service unit exists, a professional counseling psychologist is responsible for planning, directing, and reviewing the provision of counseling psychological services. Whenever the counseling psychological service unit is part of a larger professional psychological service encompassing various psychological specialties, a professional psychologist shall be the administrative head of the service.*

INTERPRETATION: The counseling psychologist who directs or coordinates the unit is expected to maintain an ongoing or periodic review of the adequacy of services and to formulate plans in accordance with the results of such evaluation. He or she coordinates the activities of the counseling psychology unit with other professional, administrative, and technical groups, both within and outside the institution or agency. The counseling psychologist has related responsibilities including, but not limited to, directing the training and research activities of the service, maintaining a high level of professional and ethical practice, and ensuring that staff members function only within the areas of their competency.

To facilitate the effectiveness of counseling services by raising the level of staff sensitivity and professional skills, the counseling psychologist designated as director is responsible for participating in the selection of staff and support personnel whose qualifications and skills (e.g., language, cultural and experiential background, race, sex, and age) are relevant to the needs and characteristics of the users served.

1.4 *When functioning as part of an organizational setting, professional counseling psychologists bring their backgrounds and skills to bear on the goals of the organization, whenever appropriate, by participation in the planning and development of overall services.*

INTERPRETATION: Professional counseling psychologists participate in the maintenance of high professional standards by representation on committees concerned with service delivery.

As appropriate to the setting, their activities may include active participation, as voting and as office-holding members, on the facility's professional staff and on other executive, planning, and evaluation boards and committees.

1.5 *Counseling psychologists maintain current knowledge of scientific and professional developments to preserve and enhance their professional competence.*

INTERPRETATION: Methods through which knowledge of scientific and professional developments may be gained include, but are not limited to, reading scientific and professional publications, attendance at professional workshops and meetings, participation in staff development programs, and other forms of continuing education. The counseling psychologist has ready access to reference material related to the provision of psychological services. Counseling psychologists are prepared to show evidence periodically that they are staying abreast of current knowledge and practices in the field of counseling psychology through continuing education.

1.6 *Counseling psychologists limit their practice to their demonstrated areas of professional competence.*

INTERPRETATION: Counseling psychological services are offered in accordance with the providers' areas of competence as defined by verifiable training and experience. When extending services beyond the range of their usual practice, counseling psychologists obtain pertinent training or appropriate professional supervision. Such training or supervision is consistent with the extension of functions performed and services provided. An extension of services may involve a change in the theoretical orientation of the counseling psychologist, in the modality or techniques used, in the type of client, or in the kinds of problems or disorders for which services are to be provided.

1.7 *Professional psychologists who wish to qualify as counseling psychologists meet the same requirements with respect to subject matter and professional skills that apply to doctoral education and training in counseling psychology.*

INTERPRETATION: Education of doctoral-level psychologists to qualify them for specialty practice in counseling psychology is under the auspices of a department in a regionally accredited university or of a professional school that offers the doctoral degree in counseling psychology. Such education is individualized, with due credit being given for relevant course work and other requirements that have previously been satisfied. In addition, doctoral-level training supervised by a counseling psychologist is required. Merely taking an internship in counseling psychology or acquiring experience in a practicum setting is not adequate preparation for becoming a counseling psychologist when prior education has not been in that area. Fulfillment of such an individualized educational program is attested to by the awarding of a certificate by the supervising department or professional school that indicates the successful completion of preparation in counseling psychology.

1.8 *Professional counseling psychologists are encouraged to develop innovative theories and procedures and to provide appropriate theoretical and/or empirical support for their innovations.*

INTERPRETATION; A specialty of a profession rooted in a science intends continually to explore and experiment with a view to developing and verifying new and improved ways of serving the public and documents the innovations.

Guideline 2: Programs

2.1 *Composition and organization of a counseling psychological service unit:*

2.1.1 *The composition and programs of a counseling psychological service unit are responsive to the needs of the persons or settings served.*

INTERPRETATION: A counseling psychological service unit is structured so as to facilitate effective and economical delivery of services. For example, a counseling psychological service unit serving predominantly a low-income, ethnic, or racial minority group has a staffing pattern and service programs that are adapted to the linguistic, experiential, and attitudinal characteristics of the users.

2.1.2 *A description of the organization of the counseling psychological service unit and its lines of responsibility and accountability for the delivery of psychological services is available in written form to the staff of the unit and to users and sanctioners upon request.*

INTERPRETATION: The description includes lines of responsibility, supervisory relationships, and the level and extent of accountability for each person who provides psychological services.

2.1.3 *A counseling psychological service unit includes sufficient numbers of professional and support personnel to achieve its goals, objectives, and purposes.*

INTERPRETATION: The work load and diversity of psychological services required and the specific goals and objectives of the setting determine the numbers and qualifications of professional and support personnel in the counseling psychological service unit. Where shortages in personnel exist, so that psychological services cannot be rendered in a professional manner, the director of the counseling psychological service unit initiates action to remedy such shortages. When this fails, the director appropriately modifies the scope or work load of the unit to maintain the quality of the services rendered and, at the same time, makes continued efforts to devise alternative systems for delivery of services.

2.2 Policies:

2.2.1 *When the counseling psychological service unit is composed of more than one person or is a component of a larger organization, a written statement of its objectives and scope of services is developed, maintained, and reviewed.*

INTERPRETATION: The counseling psychological service unit reviews its objectives and scope of services annually and revises them as necessary to ensure that the psychological services offered are consistent with staff competencies and current psychological knowledge and practice. This statement is discussed with staff, reviewed with the appropriate administrator, and distributed to users and sanctioners upon request, whenever appropriate.

2.2.2 *All providers within a counseling psychological service unit support the legal and civil rights of the users.*

INTERPRETATION: Providers of counseling psychological services safeguard the interests of the users with regard to personal, legal, and civil rights. They are continually

sensitive to the issue of confidentiality of information, the short-term and long-term impacts of their decisions and recommendations, and other matters pertaining to individual, legal, and civil rights. Concerns regarding the safeguarding of individual rights of users include, but are not limited to, problems of access to professional records in educational institutions, self-incrimination in judicial proceedings, involuntary commitment to hospitals, protection of minors or legal incompetents, discriminatory practices in employment selection procedures, recommendation for special education provisions, information relative to adverse personnel actions in the armed services, and adjudication of domestic relations disputes in divorce and custodial proceedings. Providers of counseling psychological services take affirmative action by making themselves available to local committees, review boards, and similar advisory groups established to safeguard the human, civil, and legal rights of service users.

2.2.3 *All providers within a counseling psychological service unit are familiar with and adhere to the American Psychological Association's* Standards for Providers of Psychological Services, Ethical Principles of Psychologists, Standards for Educational and Psychological Tests, Ethical Principles in the Conduct of Research with Human Participants, *and other official policy statements relevant to standards for professional services issued by the Association.*

INTERPRETATION: Providers of counseling psychological services maintain current knowledge of relevant standards of the American Psychological Association.

2.2.4 *All providers within a counseling psychological service unit conform to relevant statutes established by federal, state, and local governments.*

INTERPRETATION: All providers of counseling psychological services are familiar with and conform to appropriate statutes regulating the practice of psychology. They also observe agency regulations that have the force of law and that relate to the delivery of psychological services (e.g., evaluation for disability retirement and special education placements). In addition, all providers are cognizant that federal agencies such as the Veterans Administration, the Department of Education, and the Department of Health and Human Services have policy statements regarding psychological services. Providers are familiar as well with other statutes and regulations, including those addressed to the civil and legal rights of users (e.g., those promulgated by the federal Equal

Employment Opportunity Commission), that are pertinent to their scope of practice.

It is the responsibility of the American Psychological Association to maintain current files of those federal policies, statutes, and regulations relating to this section and to assist its members in obtaining them. The state psychological associations and the state licensing boards periodically publish and distribute appropriate state statutes and regulations, and these are on file in the counseling psychological service unit or the larger multi-psychological service unit of which it is a part.

2.2.5 *All providers within a counseling psychological service unit inform themselves about and use the network of human services in their communities in order to link users with relevant services and resources.*

INTERPRETATION: Counseling psychologists and support staff are sensitive to the broader context of human needs. In recognizing the matrix of personal and social problems, providers make available to clients information regarding human services such as legal aid societies, social services, employment agencies, health resources, and educational and recreational facilities. Providers of counseling psychological services refer to such community resources and, when indicated, actively intervene on behalf of the users.

Community resources include the private as well as the public sectors. Consultation is sought or referral made within the public or private network of services whenever required in the best interest of the users. Counseling psychologists, in either the private or the public setting, utilize other resources in the community whenever indicated because of limitations within the psychological service unit providing the services. Professional counseling psychologists in private practice know the types of services offered through local community mental health clinics and centers, through family-service, career, and placement agencies, and through reading and other educational improvement centers and know the costs and the eligibility requirements for those services.

2.2.6 *In the delivery of counseling psychological services, the providers maintain a cooperative relationship with colleagues and co-workers in the best interest of the users.*

INTERPRETATION: Counseling psychologists recognize the areas of special competence of other professional psychologists and of professionals in other fields for either consultation or referral purposes. Providers of counseling psychological services make appropriate use of other professional, research, technical, and administrative resources to serve the best interests of users and establish and maintain cooperative arrangements with such other resources as required to meet the needs of users.

2.3 *Procedures:*

2.3.1 *Each counseling psychological service unit is guided by a set of procedural guidelines for the delivery of psychological services.*

INTERPRETATION: Providers are prepared to provide a statement of procedural guidelines, in either oral or written form, in terms that can be understood by users, including sanctioners and local administrators. This statement describes the current methods, forms, procedures, and techniques being used to achieve the objectives and goals for psychological services.

2.3.2 *Providers of counseling psychological services develop plans appropriate to the providers' professional practices and to the problems presented by the users.*

INTERPRETATION: A counseling psychologist, after initial assessment, develops a plan describing the objectives of the psychological services and the manner in which they will be provided. To illustrate, the agreement spells out the objective (e.g., a career decision), the method (e.g., short-term counseling), the roles (e.g., active participation by the user as well as the provider), and the cost. This plan is in written form. It serves as a basis for obtaining understanding and concurrence from the user and for establishing accountability and provides a mechanism for subsequent peer review. This plan is, of course, modified as changing needs dictate.

A counseling psychologist who provides services as one member of a collaborative effort participates in the development, modification (if needed), and implementation of the overall service plan and provides for its periodic review.

2.3.3 *Accurate, current, and pertinent documentation of essential counseling psychological services provided is maintained.*

INTERPRETATION: Records kept of counseling psychological services include, but are not limited to, identifying data, dates of services, types of services, significant actions taken, and outcome at termination. Providers of counseling psychological services ensure that essential information concerning services rendered is recorded within a reasonable time following their completion.

2.3.4 *Each counseling psychological service unit follows an established record retention and disposition policy.*

INTERPRETATION: The policy on record retention and disposition conforms to state statutes or federal regulations where such are applicable. In the absence of such regulations, the policy is (a) that the full record be maintained intact for at least 4 years after the completion of planned services or after the date of last contact with the user, whichever is later; (b) that if a full record is not retained, a summary of the record be maintained for an additional 3 years; and (c) that the record may be disposed of no sooner than 7 years after the completion of planned services or after the date of last contact, whichever is later.

In the event of the death or incapacity of a counseling psychologist in independent practice, special procedures are necessary to ensure the continuity of active service to users and the proper safeguarding of records in accordance with this Guideline. Following approval by the affected user, it is appropriate for another counseling psychologist, acting under the auspices of the professional standards review committee (PSRC) of the state, to review the record with the user and recommend a course of action for continuing professional service, if needed. Depending on local circumstances, appropriate arrangements for record retention and disposition may also be recommended by the reviewing psychologist.

This Guideline has been designed to meet a variety of circumstances that may arise, often years after a set of psychological services has been completed. Increasingly, psychological records are being used in forensic matters, for peer review, and in response to requests from users, other professionals, and other legitimate parties requiring accurate information about the exact dates, nature, course, and outcome of a set of psychological services. The 4-year period for retention of the full record covers the period of either undergraduate or graduate study of most students in postsecondary educational institutions, and the 7-year period for retention of at least a summary of the record covers the period during which a previous user is most likely to return for counseling psychological services in an educational institution or other organization or agency.

2.3.5 *Providers of counseling psychological services maintain a system to protect confidentiality of their records.*

INTERPRETATION: Counseling psychologists are responsible for maintaining the confidentiality of information about users of services, from whatever source derived. All persons supervised by counseling psychologists, including nonprofessional personnel and students, who have access to records of psychological services maintain this confidentiality as a condition of employment and/or supervision.

The counseling psychologist does not release confidential information, except with the written consent of the user directly involved or his or her legal representative. The only deviation from this rule is in the event of clear and imminent danger to, or involving, the user. Even after consent for release has been obtained, the counseling psychologist clearly identifies such information as confidential to the recipient of the information. If directed otherwise by statute or regulations with the force of law or by court order, the psychologist seeks a resolution to the conflict that is both ethically and legally feasible and appropriate.

Users are informed in advance of any limits in the setting for maintenance of confidentiality of psychological information. For instance, counseling psychologists in agency, clinic, or hospital settings inform their clients that psychological information in a client's record may be available without the client's written consent to other members of the professional staff associated with service to the client. Similar limitations on confidentiality of psychological information may be present in certain educational, industrial, military, or other institutional settings, or in instances in which the user has waived confidentiality for purposes of third-party payment.

Users have the right to obtain information from their psychological records. However, the records are the property of the psychologist or the facility in which the psychologist works and are, therefore, the responsibility of the psychologist and subject to his or her control.

When the user's intention to waive confidentiality is judged by the professional counseling psychologist to be contrary to the user's best interests or to be in conflict with the user's civil and legal rights, it is the responsibility of the counseling psychologist to discuss the implications of releasing psychological information and to assist the user in limiting disclosure only to information required by the present circumstance.

Raw psychological data (e.g., questionnaire returns or test protocols) in which a user is identified are released only with the written consent of the user or his or her legal representative and released only to a person recognized by the counseling psychologist as qualified and competent to use the data.

Any use made of psychological reports, records, or data for research or training purposes is consistent with this Guideline. Additionally, providers of counseling psychological services comply with statutory confidentiality requirements and those embodied in the American Psychological Association's *Ethical Principles of Psychologists*.

Providers of counseling psychological services who use information about individuals that is stored in large computerized data banks are aware of the possible misuse of such data as well as the benefits and take necessary measures to ensure that such information is used in a socially responsible manner.

Guideline 3: Accountability

3.1 *The promotion of human welfare is the primary principle guiding the professional activity of the counseling psychologist and the counseling psychological service unit.*

INTERPRETATION: Counseling psychologists provide services to users in a manner that is considerate, effective, economical, and humane. Counseling psychologists are responsible for making their services readily accessible to users in a manner that facilitates the users' freedom of choice.

Counseling psychologists are mindful of their accountability to the sanctioners of counseling psychological services and to the general public, provided that appropriate steps are taken to protect the confidentiality of the service relationship. In the pursuit of their professional activities, they aid in the conservation of human, material, and financial resources.

The counseling psychological service unit does not withhold services to a potential client on the basis of that user's race, color, religion, gender, sexual orientation, age, or national origin; nor does it provide services in a discriminatory or exploitative fashion. Counseling psychologists who find that psychological services are being provided in a manner that is discriminatory or exploitative to users and/or contrary to these Guidelines or to state or federal statutes take appropriate corrective action, which may include the refusal to provide services. When conflicts of interest arise, the counseling psychologist is guided in the resolution of differences by the principles set forth in the American Psychological Association's *Ethical Principles of Psychologists* and "Guidelines for Conditions of Employment of Psychologists."

Recognition is given to the following considerations in regard to the withholding of service: (a) the professional right of counseling psychologists to limit their practice to a specific category of users with whom they have achieved demonstrated competence (e.g., adolescents or families); (b) the right and responsibility of counseling psychologists to withhold an assessment procedure when not validly applicable; (c) the right and responsibility of counseling psychologists to withhold services in specific instances in which their own limitations or client characteristics might impair the quality of the services; (d) the obligation of counseling psychologists to seek to ameliorate through peer review, consultation, or other personal therapeutic procedures those factors that inhibit the provision of services to particular individuals; and (e) the obligation of counseling psychologists who withhold services to assist clients in obtaining services from other sources.

3.2 *Counseling psychologists pursue their activities as members of the independent, autonomous profession of psychology.*

INTERPRETATION: Counseling psychologists, as members of an independent profession, are responsible both to the public and to their peers through established review mechanisms. Counseling psychologists are aware of the implications of their activities for the profession as a whole. They seek to eliminate discriminatory practices instituted for self-serving purposes that are not in the interest of the users (e.g., arbitrary requirements for referral and supervision by another profession). They are cognizant of their responsibilities for the development of the profession, participate where possible in the training and career development of students and other providers, participate as appropriate in the training of paraprofessionals or other professionals, and integrate and supervise the implementation of their contributions within the structure established for delivering psychological services. Counseling psychologists facilitate the development of, and participate in, professional standards review mechanisms.

Counseling psychologists seek to work with other professionals in a cooperative manner for the good of the users and the benefit of the general public. Counseling psychologists associated with multidisciplinary settings support the principle that members of each participating profession have equal rights and opportunities to share all privileges and responsibilities of full membership in human service facilities and to administer service programs in their respective areas of competence.

3.3 *There are periodic, systematic, and effective evaluations of counseling psychological services.*

INTERPRETATION: When the counseling psychological service unit is a component of a larger organization, regular evaluation of progress in achieving goals is provided for in the service delivery plan, including consideration of the effectiveness of counseling psychological services relative to costs in terms of use of time and money and the availability of professional and support personnel.

Evaluation of the counseling psychological service delivery system is conducted internally and, when possible, under independent auspices as well. This evaluation includes an assessment of effectiveness (to determine what the service unit accomplished), efficiency (to determine the total costs of providing the services), continuity (to ensure that the services are appropriately linked to other human services), availability (to determine appropriate levels and distribution of services and personnel), accessibility (to ensure that the services are barrier free to users), and adequacy (to determine whether the services meet the identified needs for such services).

There is a periodic reexamination of review mechanisms to ensure that these attempts at public safeguards are effective and cost efficient and do not place unnecessary encumbrances on the providers or impose unnecessary additional expenses on users or sanctioners for services rendered.

3.4 *Counseling psychologists are accountable for all aspects of the services they provide and are responsive to those concerned with these services.*

INTERPRETATION: In recognizing their responsibilities to users, sanctioners, third-party purchasers, and other providers, and where appropriate and consistent with the users' legal rights and privileged communications, counseling psychologists make available information about, and provide opportunity to participate in, decisions concerning such issues as initiation, termination, continuation, modification, and evaluation of counseling psychological services.

Depending on the settings, accurate and full information is made available to prospective individual or organizational users regarding the qualifications of providers, the nature and extent of services offered, and where appropriate, financial and social costs.

Where appropriate, counseling psychologists inform users of their payment policies and their willingness to assist in obtaining reimbursement. To assist their users, those who accept reimbursement from a third party are acquainted with the appropriate statutes and regulations, the procedures for submitting claims, and the limits on confidentiality of claims information, in accordance with pertinent statutes.

Guideline 4: Environment

4.1 *Providers of counseling psychological services promote the development in the service setting of a physical, organizational, and social environment that facilitates optimal human functioning.*

INTERPRETATION: Federal, state, and local requirements for safety, health, and sanitation are observed.

As providers of services, counseling psychologists are concerned with the environment of their service unit, especially as it affects the quality of service, but also as it impinges on human functioning in the larger context. Physical arrangements and organizational policies and procedures are conducive to the human dignity, self-respect, and optimal functioning of users and to the effective delivery of service. Attention is given to the comfort and the privacy of providers and users. The atmosphere in which counseling psychological services are rendered is appropriate to the service and to the users, whether in an office, clinic, school, college, university, hospital, industrial organization, or other institutional setting.

H. Code of Ethics for
Certified Clinical Mental Health Counselors,
National Academy of
Certified Clinical Mental Health Counselors

(This code is an adaptation of the code of the Board of Licensed Professional Counselors in Virginia)

PREAMBLE

Certified Clinical Mental Health Counselors believe in the dignity and worth of the individual. They are committed to increasing knowledge of human behavior and understanding of themselves and others. While pursuing these endeavors, they make every reasonable effort to protect the welfare of those who seek their services or of any subject that may be the object of study. They use their skills only for purposes consistent with these values and do not knowingly permit their misuse by others. While demanding for themselves freedom of inquiry and communication, certified clinical mental health counselors accept the responsibility this freedom confers: competence, objectivity in the application of skills and concern for the best interests of clients, colleagues, and society in general. In the pursuit of these ideals, clinical mental health counselors subscribe to the following principles:

Principle 1: Responsibility

In their commitment to the understanding of human behavior, clinical mental health counselors value objectivity and integrity, and in providing services they maintain the highest standards. They accept responsibility for the consequences of their work and make every effort to insure that their services are used appropriately.

a. Clinical mental health counselors accept ultimate responsibility for selecting appropriate areas for investigation and the methods relevant to minimize the possibility that their finding will be misleading. They provide thorough discussion of the limitations of their data and alternative hypotheses, especially where their work touches on social policy or might be misconstrued to the detriment of specific age, sex, ethnic, socio-economic, or other social categories. In publishing reports of their work, they never discard observations that may modify the interpretation of results. Clinical mental health counselors take credit only for the work they have actually done. In pursuing research, clinical mental health counselors ascertain that their efforts will not lead to changes in individuals or organizations unless such changes are part of the agreement at the time of obtaining informed consent. Clinical mental health counselors clarify in advance the expectations for sharing and utilizing research data. They avoid dual relationships which may limit objectivity, whether theoretical, political, or monetary, so that interference with data, subjects, and milieu is kept to a minimum.

b. As employees of an institution or agency, clinical

Code of Ethics for Certified Clinical Mental Health Counselors, by the National Academy of Certified Clinical Mental Health Counselors. Reprinted by permission.

mental health counselors have the responsibility of remaining alert to institutional pressures which may distort reports of counseling findings or use them in ways counter to the promotion of human welfare.

c. When serving as members of governmental or other organizational bodies, clinical mental health counselors remain accountable as individuals to the Code of Ethics of the National Academy of Certified Mental Health Counselors.

d. As teachers, clinical mental health counselors recognize their primary obligation to help others acquire knowledge and skill. They maintain high standards of scholarship and objectivity by presenting counseling information fully and accurately, and by giving appropriate recognition to alternative viewpoints.

e. As practitioners, clinical mental health counselors know that they bear a heavy social responsibility because their recommendations and professional actions may alter the lives of others. They therefore remain fully cognizant of their impact and alert to personal, social, organizational, financial or political situations or pressures which might lead to misuse of their influence.

f. Clinical mental health counselors provide reasonable and timely feedback to employees, trainees, supervisors, students and others whose work they may evaluate.

Principle 2: Competence

The maintenance of high standards of professional competence is a responsibility shared by all clinical mental health counselors in the interest of the public and the profession as a whole. Clinical mental health counselors recognize the boundaries of their competence and the limitations of their techniques and only provide services, use techniques, or offer opinions as professionals that meet recognized standards. Throughout their careers, clinical mental health counselors maintain knowledge of professional information related to the services they render.

a. Clinical mental health counselors accurately represent their competence, education, training and experience.

b. As teachers, clinical mental health counselors perform their duties based on careful preparation so that their instruction is accurate, up-to-date and scholarly.

c. Clinical mental health counselors recognize the need for continuing training to prepare themselves to serve persons of all ages and cultural backgrounds. They are open to new procedures and sensitive to differences between groups of people and changes in expectations and values over time.

d. Clinical mental health counselors with the responsibility for decisions involving individuals or policies based on test results should know and understand literature relevant to the tests used and testing problems with which they deal.

e. Clinical mental health counselors/practitioners recognize that their effectiveness depends in part upon their ability to maintain sound interpersonal relations, that temporary or more enduring aberrations on their part may interfere with their abilities or distort their appraisals of others. Therefore, they refrain from undertaking any activity in which their personal problems are likely to lead to inadequate professional services or harm to a client, or, if they are already engaged in such activitiy when they become aware of their personal problems, they would seek competent professional assistance to determine whether they should suspend or terminate services to one or all of their clients.

Principle 3: Moral and legal standards

Clinical mental health counselors' moral, ethical and legal standards of behavior are a personal matter to the same degree as they are for any other citizen, except as these may compromise the fulfillment of their professional responsibilities, or reduce the trust in counseling or counselors held by the general public. Regarding their own behavior, clinical mental health counselors should be aware of the prevailing community standards and of the possible impact upon the quality of professional services provided by their conformance to or deviation from these standards. Clinical mental health counselors should also be aware of the possible impact of their public behavior upon the ability of colleagues to perform their professional duties.

a. To protect public confidence in the profession of counseling, clinical mental health counselors will avoid public behavior that is clearly in violation of accepted moral and legal standards.

b. To protect students, counselors/teachers will be aware of the diverse backgrounds of students and, when dealing with topics that may give offense, will see that the material is treated objectively, that it is clearly relevant to the course, and that it is treated in a manner for which the student is prepared.

c. Providers of counseling services conform to the statutes relating to such services as established by their state and its regulating professional board(s).

d. As employees, clinical mental health counselors refuse to participate in employer's practices which are inconsistent with the moral and legal standards established by federal or state legislation regarding the treatment of employees or of the public. In particular and for example, clinical mental health counselors will not condone practices which result in illegal or otherwise unjustifiable discrimination on the basis of race, sex, religion or national origin in hiring, promotion or training.

e. In providing counseling services to clients clinical mental health counselors avoid any action that will violate or diminish the legal and civil rights of clients or of others who may be affected by the action.

f. Sexual conduct, not limited to sexual intercourse, between clinical mental health counselors and clients is specifically in violation of this code of ethics. This does not, however, prohibit the use of explicit instructional aids including films and video tapes. Such use is within accepted practices of trained and competent sex therapists.

Principle 4: Public statements

Clinical mental health counselors in their professional roles may be expected or required to make public statements providing counseling information, professional opinions, or supply information about the availability of counseling products and services. In making such statements, clinical mental health counselors take full account of the limits and uncertainties of present counseling knowledge and techniques. They represent, as objectively as possible, their professional qualifications, affiliations, and functions, as well as those of the institutions or organizations with which the statements may be associated. All public statements, announcements of services, and promotional activities should serve the purpose of providing sufficient information to aid the consumer public in making informed judgments and choices on matters that concern it.

a. When announcing professional services, clinical mental health counselors limit the information to: name, highest relevant degree conferred, certification or licensure, address, telephone number, office hours, cost of services, and a brief explanation of the types of services offered but not evaluative as to their quality of uniqueness. They will not contain testimonials by implication. They will not claim uniqueness of skill or methods beyond those available to others in the profession unless determined by acceptable and public scientific evidence.

b. In announcing the availability of counseling services or products, clinical mental health counselors will not display their affiliations with organizations or agencies in a manner that implies the sponsorship or certification of the organization or agency. They will not name their employer or professional associations unless the services are in fact to be provided by or under the responsible, direct supervision and continuing control of such organizations or agencies.

c. Clinical mental health counselors associated with the development or promotion of counseling device, books, or other products offered for commercial sale will make every effort to insure that announcements and advertisement are presented in a professional and factually informative manner without unsupported claims of superiority; [all information] must be supported by scientifically acceptable evidence or by willingness to aid and encourage independent professional scrutiny or scientific test.

d. Clinical mental health counselors engaged in radio, television or other public media activities will not participate in commercial announcements recommending to the general public the purchase or use of any proprietary or single-source product or service.

e. Clinical mental health counselors who describe counseling or the services of professional counselors to the general public accept the obligation to present the material fairly and accurately, avoiding misrepresentation through sensationalism, exaggeration or superficiality. Clinical mental health counselors will be guided by the primary obligation to aid the public in forming their own informed judgements, opinions and choices.

f. As teachers, clinical mental health counselors ensure that statements in catalogs and course outlines are accurate, particularly in terms of subject matter to be covered, bases for grading, and nature of classroom experiences. As practitioners providing private services, CMH counselors avoid improper, direct solicitation of clients and the conflict of interest inherent therein.

g. Clinical mental health counselors accept the obligation to correct others who may represent their professional qualifications or associations with products or services in a manner incompatible with these guidelines.

Principle 5: Confidentiality

Clinical mental health counselors have a primary obligation to safeguard information about individuals obtained in the course of teaching, practice, or research. Personal information is communicated to others only with the person's written consent or in those circumstances where there is clear and imminent danger to the client, to other or to society. Disclosures of counseling information are restricted to what is necessary, relevant, and verifiable.

a. All materials in the official record shall be shared with the client who shall have the right to decide what information may be shared with anyone beyond the immediate provider of service and to be informed of the implications of the materials to be shared.
b. The anonymity of clients served in public and other agencies is preserved, if at all possible, by withholding names and personal identifying data. If external conditions require reporting such information, the client shall be so informed.
c. Information received in confidence by one agency or person shall not be forwarded to another person or agency without the client's written permission.
d. Service providers have a responsibility to insure the accuracy and to indicate the validity of data shared with their parties.
e. Case reports presented in classes, professional meetings, or in publications shall be so disguised that no identification is possible unless the client or responsible authority has read the report and agreed in writing to its presentation or publication.
f. Counseling reports and records are maintained under conditions of security and provisions are made for their destruction when they have outlived their usefulness. Clinical mental health counselors insure that privacy and confidentiality are maintained by all persons in the employ or volunteers, and community aides.
g. Clinical mental health counselors who ask that an individual reveal personal information in the course of interviewing, testing or evaluation, or who allow such information to be divulged, do so only after making certain that the person or authorized representative is fully aware of the purposes of the interview, testing or evaluation and of the ways in which the information will be used.
h. Sessions with clients are taped or otherwise recorded only with their written permission or the written permission of a responsible guardian. Even with guard-
ian written consent, one should not record a session against the expressed wishes of a client.
i. Where a child or adolescent is the primary client, the interests of the minor shall be paramount.
j. In work with families, the rights of each family member should be safeguarded. The provider of service also has the responsibility to discuss the contents of the record with the parent and/or child, as appropriate, and to keep separate those parts which should remain the property of each family member.

Principle 6: Welfare of the consumer

Clinical mental health counselors respect the integrity and protect the welfare of the people and groups with whom they work. When there is a conflict of interest between the client and the clinical mental health counselor employing institution, the clinical mental health counselors clarify the nature and direction of their loyalties and responsibilities and keep all parties informed of their commitments. Clinical mental health counselors fully inform consumers as to the purpose and nature of any evaluative, treatment, educational or training procedure, and they freely acknowledge that clients, students, or subjects have freedom of choice with regard to participation.

a. Clinical mental health counselors are continually cognizant both of their own needs and of their inherently powerful position "vis-à-vis" clients, in order to avoid exploiting the client's trust and dependency. Clinical mental health counselors make every effort to avoid dual relationships with clients and/or relationships which might impair their professional judgement or increase the risk of client exploitation. Examples of such dual relationships include treating an employee or superviser, treating a close friend or family relative and sexual relationships with clients.
b. Where clinical mental health counselors' work with members of an organization goes beyond reasonable conditions of employment, clinical mental health counselors recognize possible conflicts of interests that may arise. When such conflicts occur, clinical mental health counselors clarify the nature of the conflict and inform all parties of the nature and directions of the loyalties and responsibilities involved.
c. When acting as supervisors, trainers, or employers, clinical mental health counselors accord recipients informed choice, confidentiality, and protection from physical and mental harm.

d. Financial arrangements in professional practice are in accord with professional standards that safeguard the best interests of the client and that are clearly understood by the client in advance of billing. This may best be done by the use of a contract. Clinical mental health counselors are responsible for assisting clients in finding needed services in those instances where payment of the usual fee would be a hardship. No commission or rebate or other form of remuneration may be given or received for referral of clients for professional services, whether by an individual or by an agency.

e. Clinical mental health counselors are responsible for making their services readily accessible to clients in a manner that facilitates the client's ability to make an informed choice when selecting a service provider. This responsibility includes a clear written description of what the client may expect in the way of tests, reports, billing, therapeutic regime and schedules.

f. Clinical mental health counselors who find that their services are not beneficial to the client have the responsibility to make this known to the responsible persons.

g. Clinical mental health counselors are accountable to the parties who refer and support counseling services and to the general public and are cognizant of the indirect or long-range effects of their intervention.

h. The clinical mental health counselor attempts to terminate a private service or consulting relationship when it is reasonably clear to the clinical mental health counselor that the consumer is not benefitting from it. If a consumer is receiving services from another mental health professional, clinical mental health counselors do not offer their services directly to the consumer without informing the professional persons already involved in order to avoid confusion and conflict for the consumer.

Principle 7: Professional relationship

Clinical mental health counselors act with due regard to the needs and feelings of their colleagues in counseling and other professions. Clinical mental health counselors respect the prerogatives and obligations of the institutions or organizations with which they are associated.

a. Clinical mental health counselors understand the areas of competence of related professions and make full use of other professional, technical, and administrative resources which best serve the interests of consumers. The absence of formal relationships with other professional workers does not relieve clinical mental health counselors from the responsibility of securing for their clients the best possible professional service; indeed, this circumstance presents a challenge to the professional competence of clinical mental health counselors, requiring special sensitivity to problems outside their areas of training, and foresight, diligence, and tact in obtaining the professional assistance needed by clients.

b. Clinical mental health counselors know and take into account the traditions and practices of other professional groups with which they work and cooperate fully with members of such groups when research, services, and other functions are shared or in working for the benefit of public welfare.

c. Clinical mental health counselors strive to provide positive conditions for those they employ and that they spell out clearly the conditions of such employment. They encourage their employees to engage in activities that facilitate their further professional development.

d. Clinical mental health counselors respect the viability, reputation, and the proprietary right of organizations which they serve. Clinical mental health counselors show due regard for the interest of their present or prospective employers. In those instances where they are critical of policies, they attempt to effect change by constructive action within the organization.

e. In the pursuit of research, clinical mental health counselors give sponsoring agencies, host institutions, and publication channels the same respect and opportunity for giving informed consent that they accord to individual research participants. They are aware of their obligation to future research workers and insure that host institutions are given feedback information and proper acknowledgment.

f. Credit is assigned to those who have contributed to a publication, in proportion to their contribution.

g. When a clinical mental health counselor violates ethical standards, clinical mental health counselors who know first-hand of such activities should, if possible, attempt to rectify the situation. Failing an informal solution, clinical mental health counselors should bring such unethical activities to the National Academy of Certified Clinical Mental Health Counselors.

Principle 8: Utilization of assessment techniques

In the development, publication, and utilization of counseling assessment techniques, clinical mental health counselors follow relevant standards. Individuals examined, or their legal guardians, have the right to know the results, the interpretations made, and where appropriate, the particulars on which final judgment was based. Test users should take precautions to protect test security but not at the expense of an individual's right to understand the basis for decisions that adversely affect that individual or that individual's dependents.

a. The client has the right to have and the provider has the responsibility to give explanations of test results in language the client can understand.
b. When a test is published or otherwise made available for operational use, it should be accompanied by a manual (or other published or readily available information) that makes every reasonable effort to describe fully the development of the test, the rationale, specifications followed in writing items analysis or other research. The test, the manual, the record forms and other accompanying material should help users make correct interpretations of the test results and should warn against common misuses. The test manual should state explicitly the purposes and applications for which the test is recommended and identify any special qualifications required to administer the test and to interpret it properly. Evidence of validity and reliability, along with other relevant research data, should be presented in support of any claims made.
c. Norms presented in test manuals should refer to defined and clearly described populations. These populations should be the groups with whom users of the test will ordinarily wish to compare the persons tested. Test users should consider the possibility of bias in tests or in test items. When indicated, there should be an investigation of possible differences in validity for ethnic, sex, or other subsamples that can be identified when the test is given.
d. Clinical mental health counselors who have the responsibility for decisions about individuals or policies that are based on test results should have a thorough understanding of counseling or educational measurement and of validation and other test research.
e. Clinical mental health counselors should develop procedures for systematically eliminating from data files test score information that has, because of the lapse of time, become obsolete.

f. Any individual or organization offering test scoring and interpretation services must be able to demonstrate that their programs are based on appropriate research to establish the validity of the programs and procedures used in arriving at interpretations. The public offering of an automated test interpretation service will be considered as a professional-to-professional consultation. In this the formal responsibility of the consultant is to the consultee but his/her ultimate and overriding responsibility is to the client.
g. Counseling services for the purpose of diagnosis, treatment, or personalized advice are provided only in the context of a professional relationship, and are not given by means of public lectures or demonstrations, newspaper or magazine articles, radio or television programs, mail, or similar media. The preparation of personnel reports and recommendations based on test data secured solely by mail is unethical unless such appraisals are an integral part of a continuing client relationship with a company, as a result of which the consulting clinical mental health counselor has intimate knowledge of the client's personal situation and can be assured thereby that his written appraisals will be adequate to the purpose and will be properly interpreted by the client. These reports must not be embellished with such detailed analysis of the subject's personality traits as would be appropriate only for intensive interviews with the subjects.

Principle 9: Pursuit of research activities

The decision to undertake research should rest upon a considered judgment by the individual clinical mental health counselor about how best to contribute to counseling and to human welfare. Clinical mental health counselors carry out their investigations with respect for the people who participate and with concern for their dignity and welfare.

a. In planning a study the investigator has the personal responsibility to make a careful evaluation of its ethical acceptability, taking into account the following principles for research with human beings. To the extent that this appraisal, weighing scientific and humane values, suggests a deviation from any principle, the investigator incurs an increasingly serious obligation to seek ethical advice and to observe more stringent safeguards to protect the rights of the human research participants.

b. Clinical mental health counselors know and take into account the traditions and practices of other professional groups with members of such groups when research, services, and other functions are shared or in working for the benefit of public welfare.

c. Ethical practice requires the investigator to inform the participant of all features of the research that reasonably might be expected to influence willingness to participate, and to explain all other aspects of the research about which the participant inquires. Failure to make full disclosure gives added emphasis to the investigator's abiding responsibility to protect the welfare and dignity of the research participant.

d. Openness and honesty are essential characteristics of the relationship between investigator and research participant. When the methodological requirements of a study necessitate concealment or deception, the investigator is required to insure as soon as possible the participant's understanding of the reasons for this action and to restore the quality of the relationship with the investigator.

e. In the pursuit of research, clinical mental health counselors give sponsoring agencies, host institutions, and publication channels the same respect and opportunity for giving informed consent that they accord to individual research participants. They are aware of their obligation to future research workers and insure that host institutions are given feedback information and proper acknowledgment.

f. Credit is assigned to those who have contributed to a publication, in proportion to their contribution.

g. The ethical investigator protects participants from physical and mental discomfort, harm and danger. If the risk of such consequences exists, the investigator is required to inform the participant of that fact, secure consent before proceeding, and take all possible measures to minimize distress. A research procedure may not be used if it is likely to cause serious and lasting harm to participants.

h. After the data are collected, ethical practice requires the investigator to provide the participant with a full clarification of the nature of the study and to remove any misconceptions that may have arisen. Where scientific or humane values justify delaying or withholding information the investigator acquires a special responsibility to assure that there are no damaging consequences for the participants.

i. Where research procedures may result in undesirable consequences for the participant, the investigator has the responsibility to detect and remove or correct these consequences, including, where relevant, longterm after effects.

j. Information obtained about the research participants during the course of an investigation is confidential. When the possibility exists that others may obtain access to such information, ethical research practice requires that the possibility, together with the plans for protecting confidentiality be explained to the participants as a part of the procedure for obtaining informed consent.

Index

To the owner of this book:

Writing *Issues and Ethics in the Helping Professions* (2nd Edition) was both meaningful and challenging to us, and we hope that, as you read it, you found yourself challenged to clarify your positions on the issues we've raised. Only through your comments and the comments of others can we assess the impact of this book and be in a position to improve it in the future.

School: _____ Instructor's name: _____

1. In what class did you use this book? _____

2. What did you like <u>most</u> about this book? _____

   _____

   _____

3. What did you like <u>least</u> about this book? _____

   _____

   _____

4. How useful were the pre-chapter inventories and the other inventories within the chapters? _____

   _____

   _____

5. How useful were the cases and examples in helping you formulate and clarify your thoughts on the issues?

   _____

   _____

6. How valuable were the end-of-chapter activities and exercises? _____

   _____

   _____

7. What issues that we explored were most relevant and most important to you? _____

   _____

   _____

8. What topics do you think should be expanded or added to this book in future editions? _____

   _____

   _____

9. In the space below or in a separate letter, please let us know what other comments about the book you'd like to make. We welcome your suggestions! Thank you for taking the time to write to us.

Optional:

Your name: _____ Date: _____

May Brooks/Cole quote you, either in promotion for *Issues and Ethics in the Helping Professions* or in future publishing ventures?

Yes _____ No _____

Sincerely,

Gerald Corey
Marianne Schneider Corey
Patrick Callanan

FOLD HERE